20

TWENTIETH PUBLICATION DESIGN ANNUAL

20

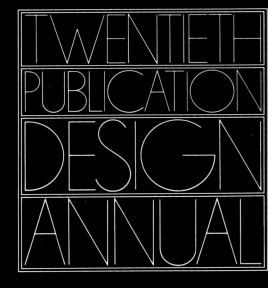

ACKNOWLEDGEMENTS

DESIGNER:	*B. Martin Pedersen* *Jonson Pedersen Hinrichs Shakery Inc.*
ART DIRECTOR/ PRODUCTION MANAGER:	*Randell Pearson* *Jonson Pedersen Hinrichs Shakery Inc.*
TYPOGRAPHY:	*U.S. Lithograph Inc.*
PUBLICATION DESIGN COMPETITION CHAIRMAN:	*Michael Valenti*
COMMITTEE:	*Diana LaGuardia* *Thomas P. Ruis* *Amy Bogert*
EXHIBITION CHAIRMAN:	*Virginia Smith* *Jean Chambers* *Vera Steiner*
	Herlin Press–West Haven, Connecticut
	RIS Paper Co.–New York, New York
DESIGNER OF CALL FOR ENTRIES AND EXHIBITION POSTER:	*Louise Fili*
COVER PHOTO:	*Richard Levy* *New York, New York*

OFFICERS AND MEMBERS OF THE BOARD OF DIRECTORS

PRESIDENT:	*Melissa Tardiff*
VICE PRESIDENTS:	*Thomas P. Ruis* *Alice Cooke*
SECRETARY:	*Amy Bogert*
TREASURER:	*Nancy Cutler*
BOARD MEMBERS:	*Lee Ann Jaffee* *Vera Steiner* *Michael Grossman* *Steven Heller* *Carla Barr* *Robert Altemus* *Diana LaGuardia* *Jerry Demoney* *David Armario* *Jack Golden* *Donald Mulligan*
MADISON SQUARE PRESS:	*Gerald McConnell–President*
SOCIETY OF PUBLICATION DESIGNERS:	*Bride Whelan–Director* *Carol McCranie–Production Assistant*
MASTER EAGLE GALLERY NEW YORK, NEW YORK:	*Clarence Bayliss*

Printed in Japan

Distributors to the trade in the United States:
Robert Silver Associates
307 East 37th Street, New York, NY 10036

Distributors to the trade in Canada:
General Publishing Co. Ltd., 30 Lesmill Road
Don Mills, Ontario, Canada M3B 2T6

Distributed throughout the rest of the world by:
RotoVision SA, 10 Rue de l'Arquebuse, Casa Postale 434
CH-1211 Genève 11 Suisse

Publisher:
Madison Square Press, Inc.
10 East 23rd Street, New York, NY 10010

ISBN 0-942604-10-5
Library of Congress Catalog Card Number:
0885-6370

CONTENTS

TWENTIETH PUBLICATION DESIGN ANNUAL

PRESIDENT'S LETTER

Imagine yourself in the very near future. You step out of your BMW and it yells at you to lock the door. You put a small metallic card into your apartment door and it springs open. Your kids are fighting over who will get the computer first and you're still wondering how to use it. Your bull terrier is standing transfixed in front of the VCR, and what do you have for consolation in this shower of electronic images? Your old magazines. Those issues still on paper, not on floppy discs.

To Benjamin Franklin this would all be wild and wonderful. After all, he got us started with all this electronic blitz by holding a kite and key up to the sky. Ever the innovator, he also had the very first idea for a magazine in 1741. It was called the "General Magazine and Historical Chronicle for all the British Plantations in America," and had a planned circulation of 1000.

It was a good idea but he underestimated one truth we all know in publishing: a good idea is quickly stolen. His idea was so good in fact that a rival printer in Philadelphia, Andrew Bradford, decided to publish one also, and called it, "The American Magazine." He also managed to get it on the newsstands three days before Mr. Franklin's. Hence was established the cutthroat competition and rivalry that exists to this very day in publishing. The Franklin Legacy.

Today's magazines, ephemeral as they might be, are hot commodities. Recall if you will the late sixties and Marshall McCluhan. There were intimations that print would be relegated to the dusty shelves of the Smithsonian. Television, the media, was hot. Now, 20 years later, magazines are even hotter; the darlings of the business community. They are big business, started, sold, and traded at a rapid fire pace for dazzling sums. While being cash flow machines, a magazine's real assets rest in its talented staff: the creators and thinkers behind the printed page.

What will become of our publications in the 21st century? It's obvious that new technologies have already affected our physical methods of production and design. In this decade alone we will likely see more technological advances than in the entire machine age.

Television technology drastically reduced the time frame between when an event occurred and when it became news on a screen. Using similar technology, satellite transmissions, electronic imaging, laser scanners and high speed typesetting, that time frame has been significantly reduced for print as well. Newspaper, T.V. and magazines all are borrowing from each other's format. At what point will they converge or overlap?

Imagine if you will the day when acid rain has decimated all of our forests. Perhaps then magazines will become electronic transmissions stored on floppy discs.

This may well be the age of the personalized magazine. The single magazine audience as we know it today will not exist. In its place will be magazines fragmented into very particular subject areas, coded to your interests and sorted in huge data banks, awaiting a call to your computer screen.

In a recent visit to a printing plant in Milwaukee I saw the history of printing in this century under one roof. They still had a hot metal composing room on the premises. It was presided over by Fred Carsky who had been there for 60 years. Upstairs were the laser scanners. I couldn't help but think that Fred seemed much closer in spirit to Benjamin Franklin than to today's technology which has long ago passed him by.

As Art Directors we need to be concerned about how our own jobs will be affected by the new technology. Fundamentally, our tasks won't change that much; an idea is an idea, whether it is expressed in print or electronically. There will be a learning curve until we adapt.

However, we should keep in mind that behind all this burgeoning technology is talent. Creative expression and communication are the language of an art director's soul. And that is one thing, just about the only thing, that will not be computerized, digitized or laser scanned.

Melissa Tardiff

HERB LUBALIN AWARD

1984 Herb Lubalin Award Winner,
Cipe Pineles Burtin (at right)
with award presenter,
SPD President Melissa Tardiff.

This year's Herb Lubalin award for continuing excellence in graphic design was presented to Cipe Pineles Burtin.

This award was established three years ago to honor a person who has been outstanding and influential in the field of publication design throughout their career.

Cipe Pineles Burtin has been a moving force in the field of publications design for many years. She is exuberant, a bundle of energy and enthusiasm, and full of Viennese charm. She is a role model for women in particular, and all good art directors in general. She was the first woman to be admitted to the New York Art Director's Club and the only female member of their Hall of Fame.

She began her career 50 odd years ago as a protegé of Dr. Aga of Conde Nast. Her initiation as an Art Director was at Seventeen Magazine. She made her mark on publication design when she began to assign fine artists as illustrators for the magazine's fiction pieces. The artists were challenged by the freedom she offered them, without the usual editors' and art directors' constraints.

She continues to influence future talent through her teaching at Parsons School of Design. There are many who have passed thru her classroom during her 24 years of teaching. Teaching magazine design is a difficult task at best, but Cipe has distilled her philosophy to the essence of this business.

In addition, she is herself an extremely gifted artist. She is as adept at her painting and illustrations as she is at designing a page. Her wit and humor are apparent in the work she continues to do at Parsons as Director of Publications.

SPD

The art of publication design is a specialized area in the graphic arts. Editorial designers and Art Directors are specialists whose unique skills blend the diverse elements of a publication into a unified visual concept that has recognizable continuity from issue to issue.

The Society of Publication Designers was created to offer a professional meeting ground for designers and Art Directors, and provides a means of continuing communication and exchanges of ideas with others in the field.

One way of continuing this dialogue is to assemble, judge, and show the best work done each year by designers and art directors in a national juried competition. This competition seeks to encourage experimentation and to serve as a source of new ideas in graphic design, as well as to recognize the consistently excellent work being done by new as well as proven designers in the publication field.

The Society has been incorporated as a non-profit, educationally oriented professional association since 1964. Its functions and activities are governed by a chartered Constitution. The variety of activities offered by the Society include a monthly Speaker's Evening, which brings together an individual or panel of distinguished professionals to share with the membership unique contributions to publication design. The membership receives a bi-monthly newsletter called GRIDS which highlights activities and general information of the Society, and the various goings-on amidst the publications community. The SPD Awards Gala, honoring the recipients of the Gold, Silver and Merit Awards of the yearly Competition is a highlight of the Spring season, and is attended by some of the country's most illustrious designers. The Awards Exhibition of the Society, held yearly at the Master Eagle Gallery, gives the members an opportunity to meet and greet the designers and directors as well as view and enjoy the individual winning pieces of publication work. The SPD Annual, a full color book, is available free to the membership, which catalogues the annual winning entries for reference and artistic and editorial concepts. The Society is also implementing a JOB MART service to the membership which will keep a list of possible positions available, to match with those individuals looking for employment in the professional arena of the publication designer.

The Society of Publication Designers is a constant influence in maintaining the standards of excellence and quality in publication design. By recognizing and promoting current achievements and innovative graphic practices, the members are constantly associated with the best and most up-to-date works available.

The Society hopes to share the enthusiasm that is part of the profession, and continue to grow and become more exciting with new and innovative programs and a growing and active membership.

JUDGES

LOUISE FILI
Art Director–Pantheon Books
Designer of 1984 Call For Entries Poster

MICHAEL VALENTI
Art Director–Science Digest
Chairman–1984 Publication Design Competition 20

STEVEN HELLER
Art Director–New York Times Book Review
Judge–1984 Publication Design Competition 20

WILL HOPKINS
Art Director–American Photographer
Principal–Will Hopkins Group
Judge–1984 Publication Design Competition 20

MARGERY PETERS
Art Director–Fortune Magazine
Judge–1984 Publication Design Competition 20

PAULA SCHER
Principal–Koppel & Scher
Judge–1984 Publication Design Competition 20

MELISSA TARDIFF
Art Director–Town and Country Magazine
President–Society of Publication Designers, 1984–85
Judge–1984 Publication Design Competition 20

VINCENT WINTER
Principal–Vincent Winter Studio
Judge–1984 Publication Design Competition 20

COVERS

TWENTIETH
PUBLICATION
DESIGN
ANNUAL

1

PUBLICATION: *The Boston Globe Magazine*
ART DIRECTOR: *Ronn Campisi*
DESIGNER: *Ronn Campisi*
ILLUSTRATOR: *Gene Grief*
PUBLISHER: *Globe Newspaper Co.*
CATEGORY: *Tabloid/Cover*
AWARD: *Gold*

2

PUBLICATION: *Fortune Magazine*
ART DIRECTOR: *Margery Peters*
ILLUSTRATOR: *Gary Hallgren*
PUBLISHER: *Fortune Magazine*
CATEGORY: *Illustration-Cover*
AWARD: *Gold*

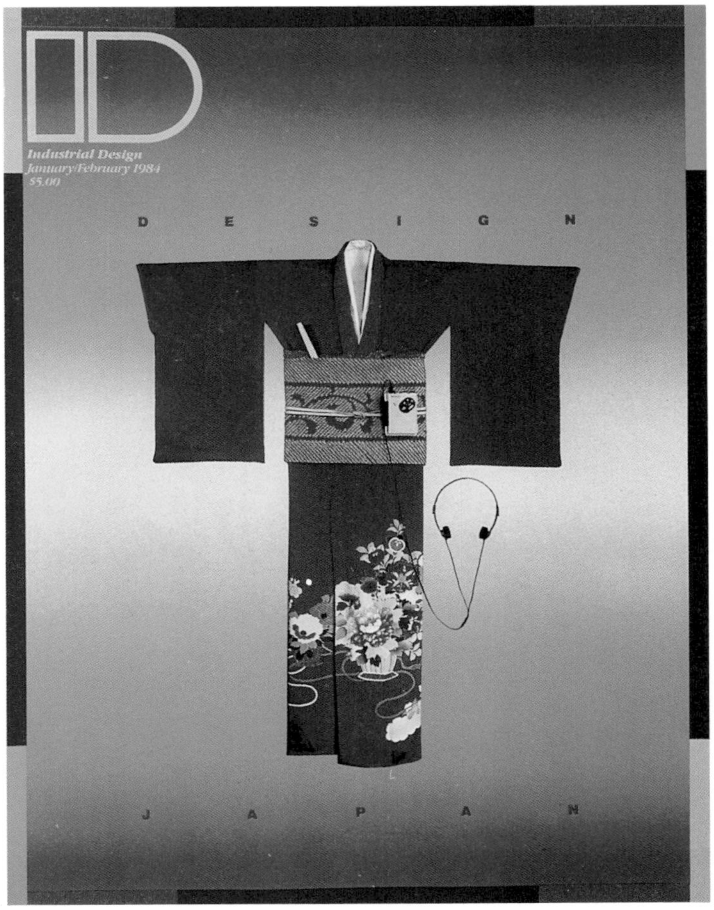

3

PUBLICATION: *Industrial Design Magazine*
ART DIRECTOR: *Karen Krieger*
DESIGNER: *Annlee Polus*
PHOTOGRAPHER: *Steve Cooper*
PUBLISHER: *Design Publications, Inc.*
CATEGORY: *Design-Cover*
AWARD: *Gold*

4

PUBLICATION: *The New York Times Magazine*
ART DIRECTOR: *Ken Kendrick*
DESIGNER: *Ken Kendrick*
ILLUSTRATOR: *Matt Mahurin*
PUBLISHER: *The New York Times*
CATEGORY: *Illustration-Cover*
AWARD: *Gold*

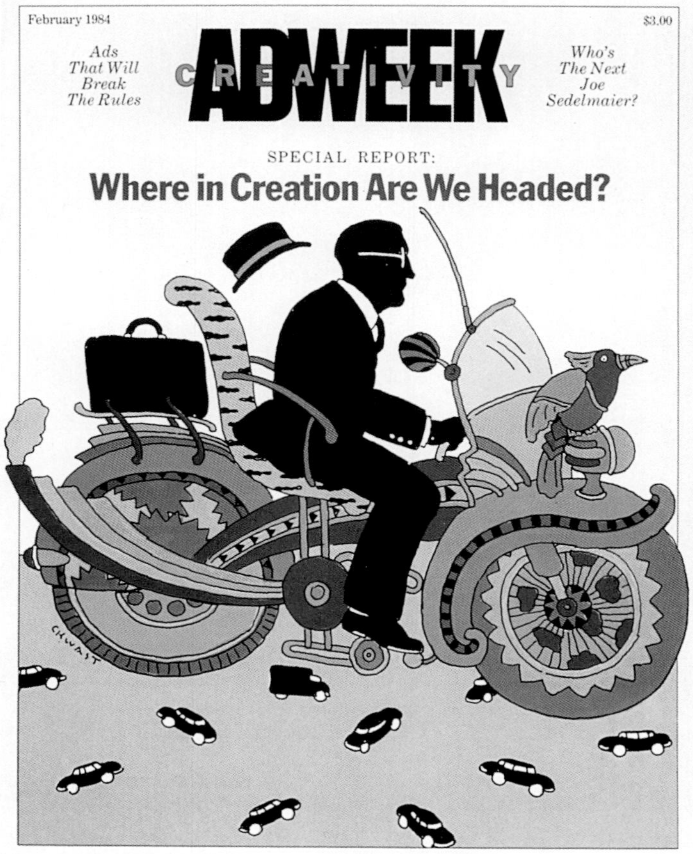

5

PUBLICATION: *Adweek Special Report*
ART DIRECTOR: *Walter Bernard*
Giona Maiarelli
DESIGNER: *Arlene Lappen*
ILLUSTRATOR: *Seymour Chwast*
PUBLISHER: *Wenda, Harris & Malaird*
CATEGORY: *Illustration-Cover*
AWARD: *Silver*

6

PUBLICATION: *Adweek Special Report*
ART DIRECTOR: *Walter Bernard*
Giona Maiarelli
DESIGNER: *Giona Maiarelli*
ILLUSTRATOR: *Seymour Chwast*
PUBLISHER: *Wenda, Harris & Malaird*
CATEGORY: *Illustration-Cover*
AWARD: *Silver*

7

PUBLICATION: *Adweek Special Report*
ART DIRECTOR: *Walter Bernard*
Giona Maiarelli
DESIGNER: *Giona Maiarelli*
ILLUSTRATOR: *Andrzej Dudzinski*
PUBLISHER: *Wenda, Harris, Malaird*
CATEGORY: *Illustration-Cover*
AWARD: *Silver*

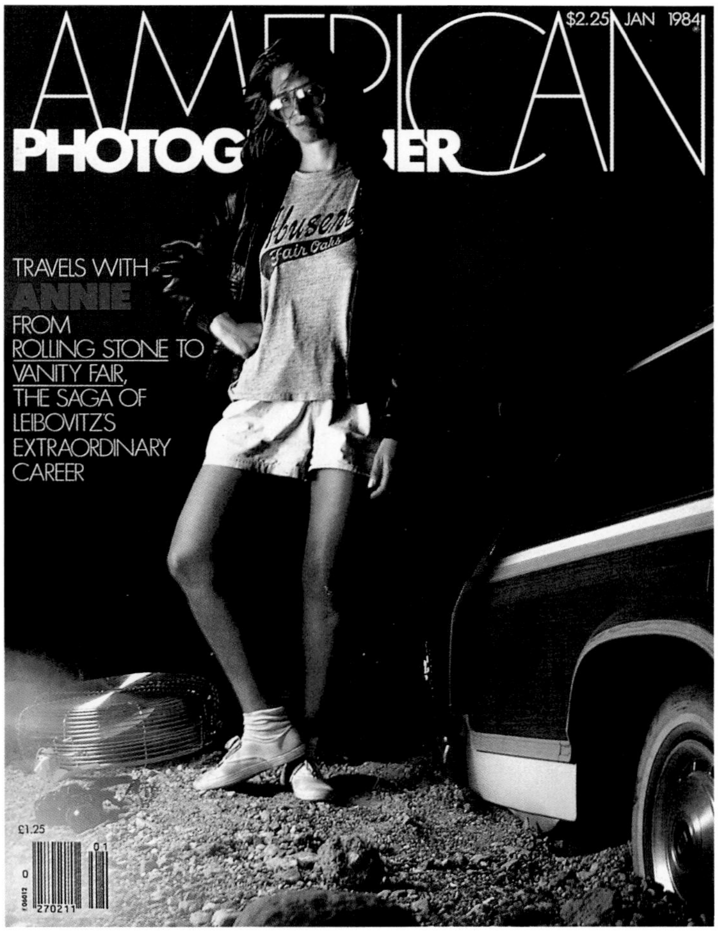

8

PUBLICATION: *American Photographer*
ART DIRECTOR: *Will Hopkins*
Ronna Gilbert
DESIGNER: *Will Hopkins*
PHOTOGRAPHER: *Michael Fuller*
PUBLISHER: *CBS Magazine*
CATEGORY: *Design-Cover*
AWARD: *Silver*

9

PUBLICATION: *American Photographer*
ART DIRECTOR: *Will Hopkins*
DESIGNER: *Will Hopkins*
PHOTOGRAPHER: *Richard Avedon*
PUBLISHER: *CBS Magazine*
CATEGORY: *Cover-Design*
AWARD: *Silver*

10

PUBLICATION: *Architectural Record*
ART DIRECTOR: *Alex Stillano*
DESIGNER: *Alberto Bucchianeri*
PHOTOGRAPHER: *Ezra Stoller*
PUBLISHER: *McGraw-Hill*
CATEGORY: *Cover-Design*
AWARD: *Silver*

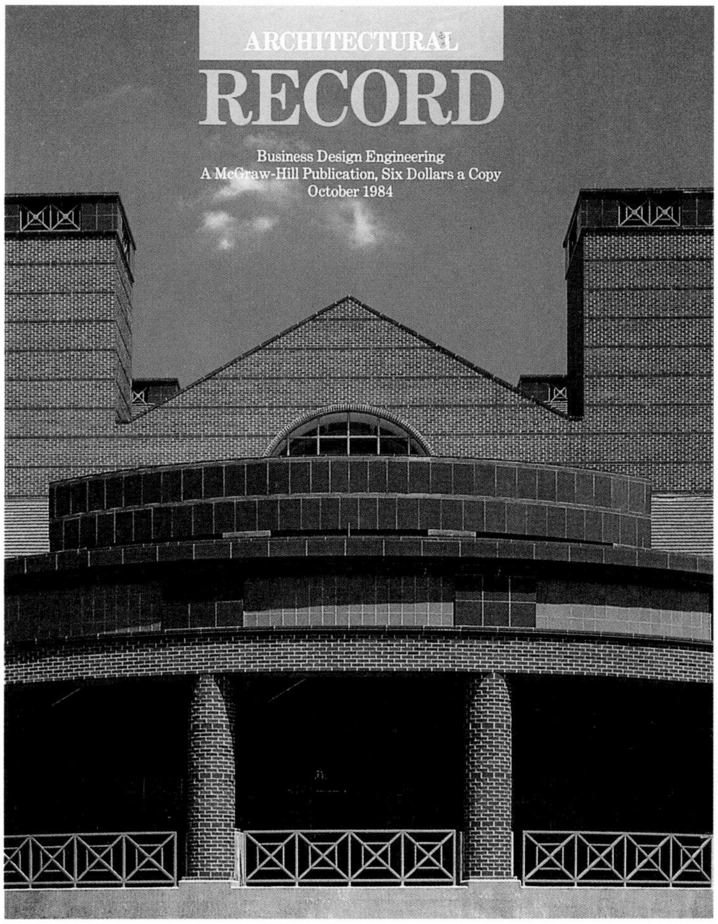

11

PUBLICATION: *Architectural Record*
ART DIRECTOR: *Alex Stillano*
DESIGNER: *Alberto Bucchianeri*
PHOTOGRAPHER: *Paul Warchol*
PUBLISHER: *McGraw-Hill*
CATEGORY: *Design-Cover*
AWARD: *Silver*

12

PUBLICATION: *Architectural Record*
ART DIRECTOR: *Alex Stillano*
DESIGNER: *Anna-Egger Schlesinger*
PHOTOGRAPHER: *Timothy Hursley*
PUBLISHER: *McGraw-Hill*
CATEGORY: *Design-Cover*
AWARD: *Silver*

13

PUBLICATION: *Architectural Record*
ART DIRECTOR: *Alex Stillano*
DESIGNER: *Anna-Egger Schlesinger*
ILLUSTRATOR: *James Wines*
PUBLISHER: *McGraw-Hill*
CATEGORY: *Design-Cover*
AWARD: *Silver*

14

PUBLICATION: *Architectural Record*
ART DIRECTOR: *Alex Stillano*
DESIGNER: *Anna-Egger Schlesinger*
PUBLISHER: *McGraw-Hill*
CATEGORY: *Design-Cover*
AWARD: *Silver*

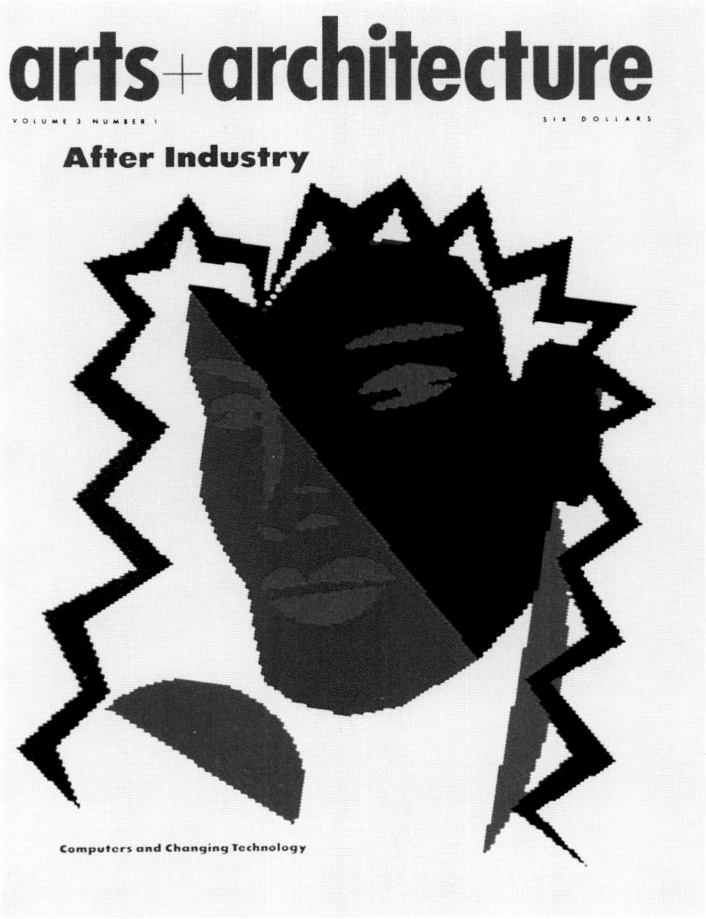

15

PUBLICATION: *Arts & Architecture*
ART DIRECTOR: *Rip Georges*
ILLUSTRATOR: *Barbara Nessim*
PUBLISHER: *Arts & Architecture, Inc.*
CATEGORY: *Design-Cover*
AWARD: *Silver*

16

PUBLICATION: *Arts & Architecture*
ART DIRECTOR: *Rip Georges*
DESIGNER: *Jayme Odgers*
PUBLISHER: *Arts & Architecture, Inc.*
CATEGORY: *Design-Cover*
AWARD: *Silver*

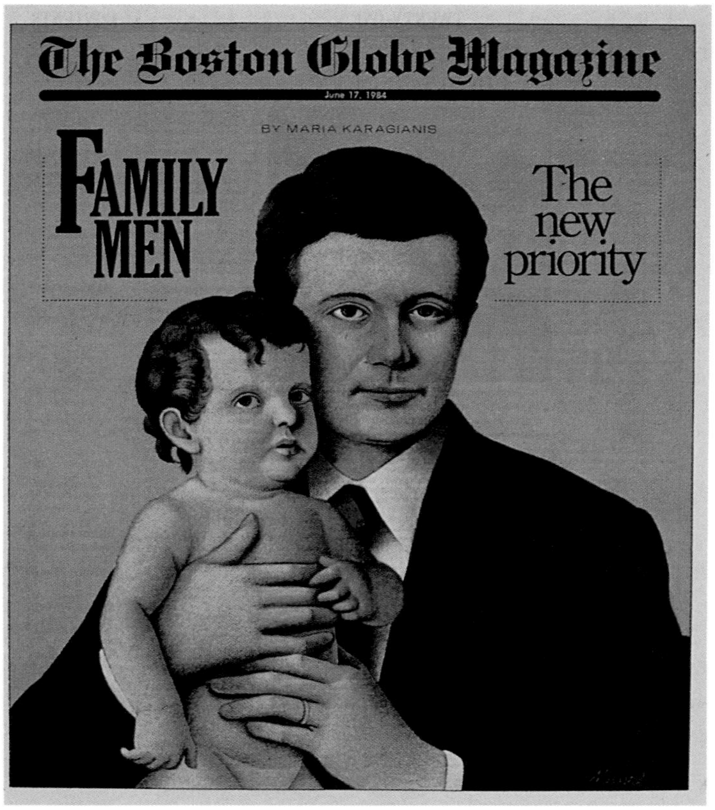

18

PUBLICATION: *The Boston Globe Magazine*
ART DIRECTOR: *Ronn Campisi*
DESIGNER: *Ronn Campisi*
ILLUSTRATOR: *Richard Mantel*
PUBLISHER: *Globe Newspaper Co.*
CATEGORY: *Tabloid/Design-Cover*
AWARD: *Silver*

19

PUBLICATION: *The Boston Globe Magazine*
ART DIRECTOR: *Ronn Campisi*
DESIGNER: *Ronn Campisi*
PHOTOGRAPHER: *Jerry Berndt*
PUBLISHER: *Globe Newspaper Co.*
CATEGORY: *Tabloid/Design-Cover*
AWARD: *Silver*

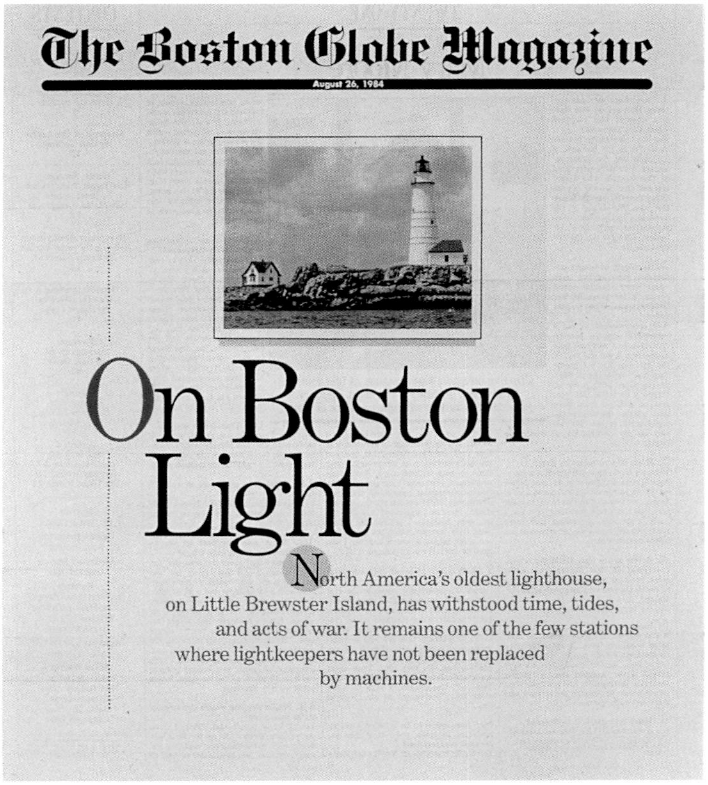

20

PUBLICATION: *The Boston Globe Magazine*
ART DIRECTOR: *Ronn Campisi*
DESIGNER: *Ronn Campisi*
PHOTOGRAPHER: *Ted Dully*
PUBLISHER: *Globe Newspaper Co.*
CATEGORY: *Tabloid/Design-Cover*
AWARD: *Silver*

21

PUBLICATION: *The Boston Globe*
ART DIRECTOR: *Holly Nixholm*
DESIGNER: *Holly Nixholm*
ILLUSTRATOR: *Dave Calver*
PUBLISHER: *Globe Newspaper Co.*
CATEGORY: *Tabloid/*
Cover Illustration
AWARD: *Silver*

22

PUBLICATION: *The Plain Dealer Magazine*
ART DIRECTOR: *Sam Capuano*
DESIGNER: *Sam Capuano*
ILLUSTRATOR: *Scott Reynolds*
PUBLISHER: *The Plain Dealer Publishing Co.*
CATEGORY: *Tabloid/Cover-Illustration*
AWARD: *Silver*

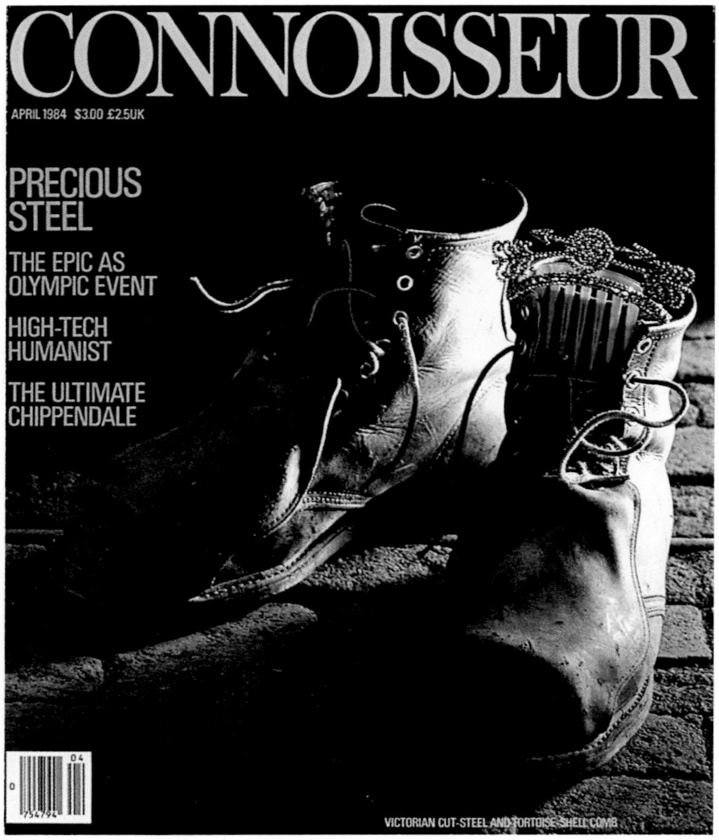

23

PUBLICATION: *Connoisseur*
ART DIRECTOR: *Carla Barr*
DESIGNER: *Carla Barr*
PHOTOGRAPHER: *Alen MacWeeney*
PUBLISHER: *Hearst Corporation*
CATEGORY: *Design-Cover*
AWARD: *Silver*

24

PUBLICATION: *Connoisseur*
ART DIRECTOR: *Carla Barr*
DESIGNER: *Carla Barr*
PHOTOGRAPHER: *Michael O'Neill*
PUBLISHER: *Hearst Corporation*
CATEGORY: *Design-Cover*
AWARD: *Silver*

25

PUBLICATION: *Games*
ART DIRECTOR: *Barry Simon*
DESIGNER: *Barry Simon*
PHOTOGRAPHER: *Hughes Colson*
PUBLISHER: *Playboy Enterprises, Inc.*
CATEGORY: *Design-Cover*
AWARD: *Silver*

26

PUBLICATION: *Geo Magazine*
ART DIRECTOR: *Mary K. Baumann*
PHOTOGRAPHER: *Chris Callis*
PUBLISHER: *Knapp Communications Corp.*
CATEGORY: *Design-Cover*
AWARD: *Silver*

27

PUBLICATION: *Industrial Design Magazine*
ART DIRECTOR: *Karen Krieger*
DESIGNER: *Annlee Polus*
PHOTOGRAPHER: *Tom Wedell*
PUBLISHER: *Design Publications, Inc.*
CATEGORY: *Design-Cover*
AWARD: *Silver*

28

PUBLICATION: *Mother Jones Magazine*
ART DIRECTOR: *Louise Kollenbaum*
DESIGNER: *Dian-Aziza Ooka*
ILLUSTRATOR: *Matt Mahurin*
PUBLISHER: *Foundation for National Progress*
CATEGORY: *Illustration-Cover*
AWARD: *Silver*

29

PUBLICATION: *New York Magazine*
ART DIRECTOR: *Robert Best*
ILLUSTRATOR: *Dennis Ziemieski*
PUBLISHER: *Murdoch Magazines*
CATEGORY: *Design Cover*
AWARD: *Silver*

30

PUBLICATION: *New York Daily News*
ART DIRECTOR: *Janet Froelich, Tom Ruis*
ILLUSTRATOR: *Seth Jaben*
PUBLISHER: *New York News, Inc.*
CATEGORY: *Illustration-Cover*
AWARD: *Silver*

31

PUBLICATION: *New York News*
ART DIRECTOR: *Vasken Kalayjian*
DESIGNER: *Vasken Kalayjian*
ILLUSTRATOR: *Guy Billout*
PUBLISHER: *YPO*
CATEGORY: *Design-Cover*
AWARD: *Silver*

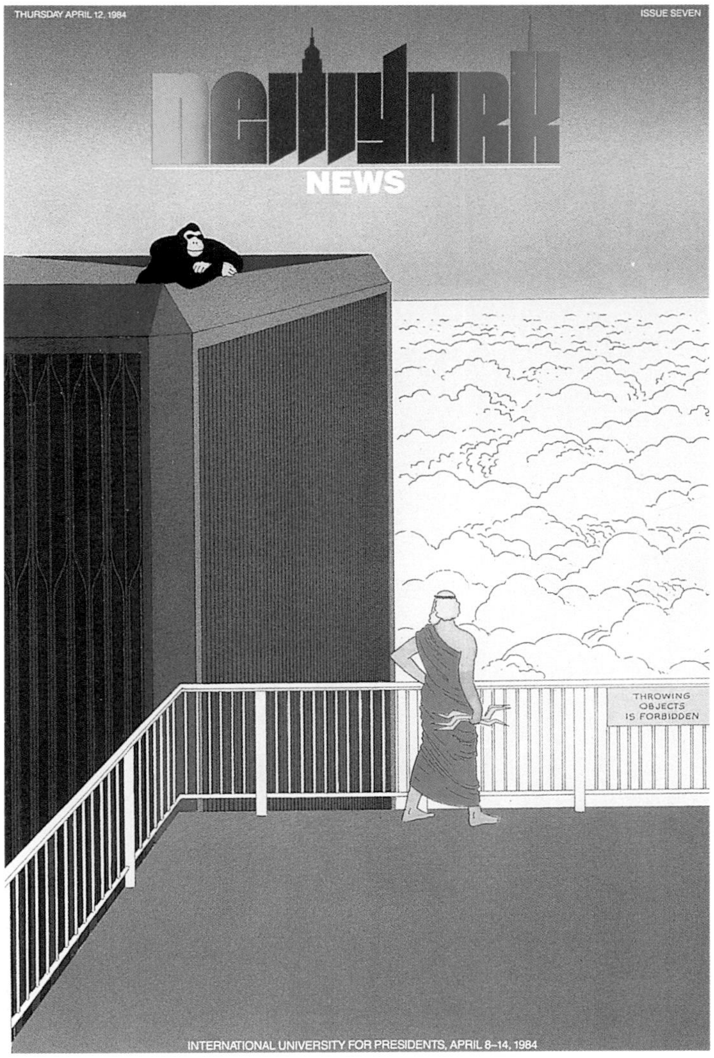

32

PUBLICATION: *New York News*
ART DIRECTOR: *Vasken Kalayjian*
DESIGNER: *Vasken Kalayjian*
ILLUSTRATOR: *Guy Billout*
PUBLISHER: *YPO*
CATEGORY: *Design-Cover*
AWARD: *Silver*

33

PUBLICATION: *New York News*
ART DIRECTOR: *Vasken Kalayjian*
DESIGNER: *Vasken Kalayjian*
ILLUSTRATOR: *Guy Billout*
PUBLISHER: *YPO*
CATEGORY: *Design-Cover*
AWARD: *Silver*

34

PUBLICATION: *New York News*
ART DIRECTOR: *Vasken Kalayjian*
DESIGNER: *Vasken Kalayjian*
ILLUSTRATOR: *Guy Billout*
PUBLISHER: *YPO*
CATEGORY: *Design-Cover*
AWARD: *Silver*

35

PUBLICATION: *New York News*
ART DIRECTOR: *Vasken Kalayjian*
DESIGNER: *Vasken Kalayjian*
ILLUSTRATOR: *Guy Billout*
PUBLISHER: *YPO*
CATEGORY: *Design-Cover*
AWARD: *Silver*

36

PUBLICATION: *The New York Times Magazine*
ART DIRECTOR: *Ken Kendrick*
DESIGNER: *Howard Klein*
ILLUSTRATOR: *Brad Holland*
PUBLISHER: *The New York Times*
CATEGORY: *Illustration-Cover*
AWARD: *Silver*

37

PUBLICATION: *The New York Times Magazine*
ART DIRECTOR: *Ken Kendrick*
DESIGNER: *Ken Kendrick*
PHOTOGRAPHER: *James Nachtwey*
PUBLISHER: *The New York Times*
CATEGORY: *Cover-Design*
AWARD: *Silver*

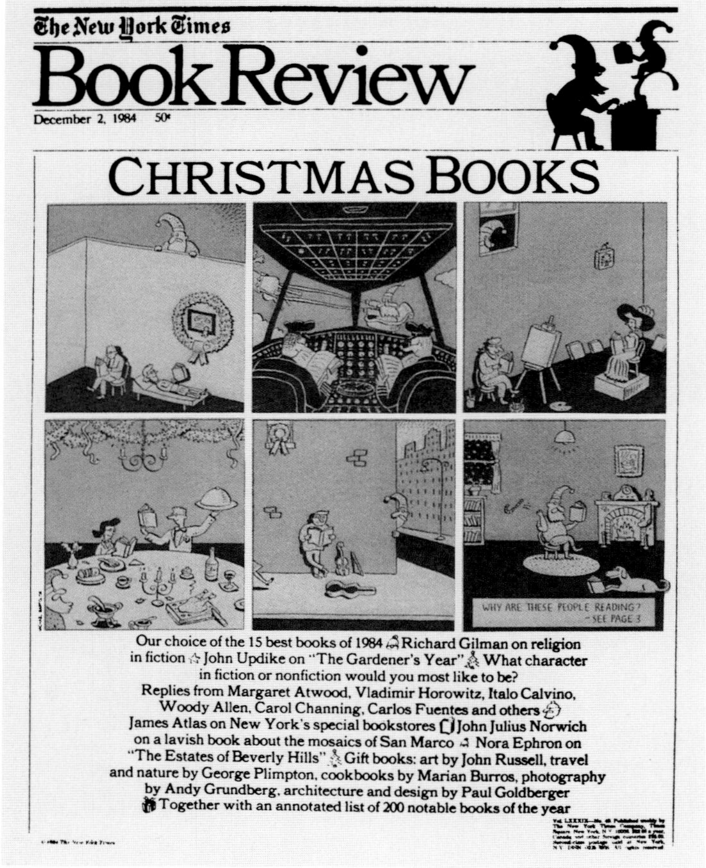

38

PUBLICATION: *New York Times Book Review*
ART DIRECTOR: *Steve Heller*
DESIGNER: *Steve Heller*
ILLUSTRATOR: *Michael Bartalos*
PUBLISHER: *The New York Times*
CATEGORY: *Design-Cover*
AWARD: *Silver*

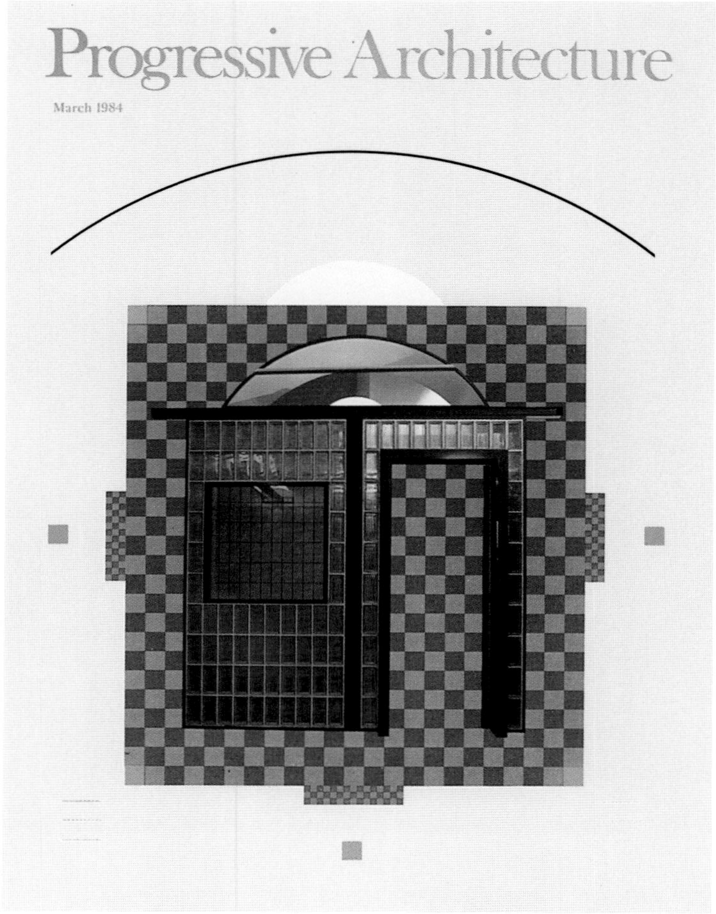

39

PUBLICATION: *Progressive Architecture*
ART DIRECTOR: *Kenneth Windsor*
DESIGNER: *Kenneth Windsor*
ILLUSTRATOR: *Kenneth Windsor*
PHOTOGRAPHER: *Elenore Littasy*
PUBLISHER: *Reinhold Publishing*
CATEGORY: *Design-Cover*
AWARD: *Silver*

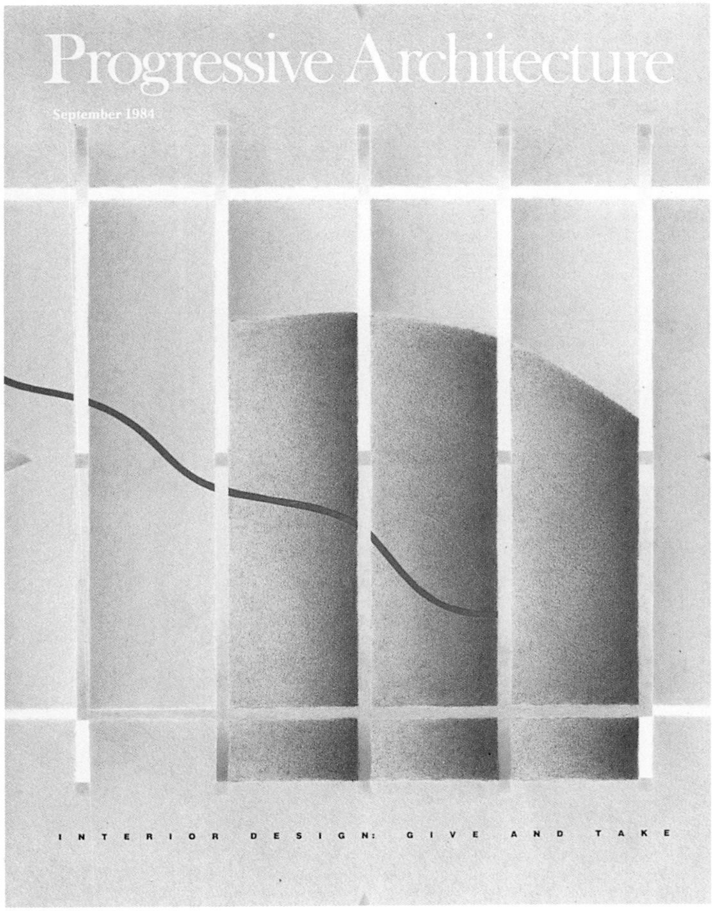

40

PUBLICATION: *Progressive Architecture*
ART DIRECTOR: *Kenneth Windsor*
DESIGNER: *Kenneth Windsor*
ILLUSTRATOR: *Kenneth Windsor*
PUBLISHER: *Reinhold Publishing*
CATEGORY: *Design-Cover*
AWARD: *Silver*

41

PUBLICATION: *Progressive Architecture*
ART DIRECTOR: *Kenneth Windsor*
DESIGNER: *Kenneth Windsor*
PHOTOGRAPHER: *Norman McGrath*
PUBLISHER: *Reinhold Publishing*
CATEGORY: *Design-Cover*
AWARD: *Silver*

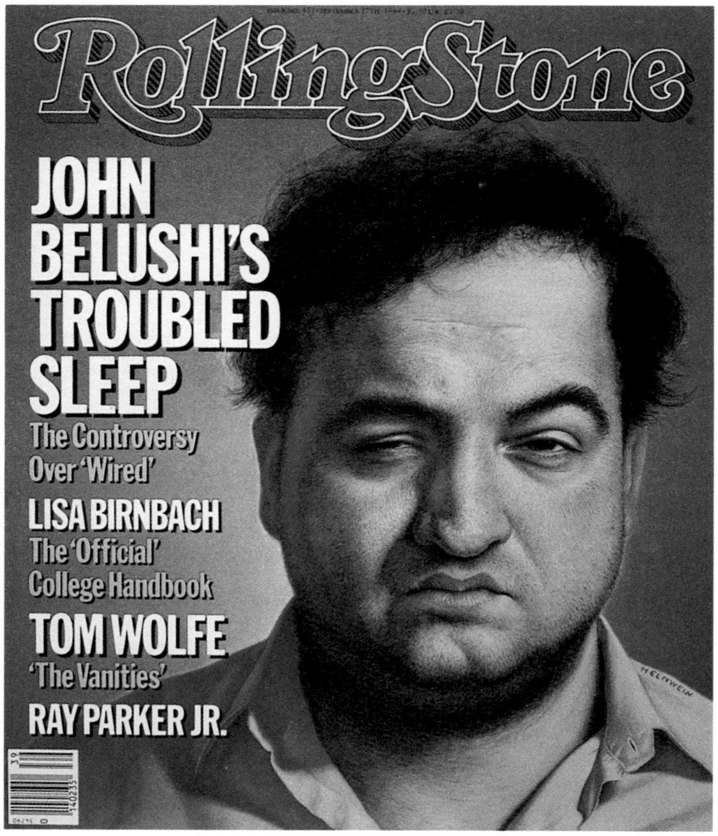

42

PUBLICATION: *Rolling Stone*
ART DIRECTOR: *Derek Ungless*
DESIGNER: *Derek Ungless*
ILLUSTRATOR: *Helnwein*
PUBLISHER: *Straight Arrow Publishers, Inc.*
CATEGORY: *Illustration-Cover*
AWARD: *Silver*

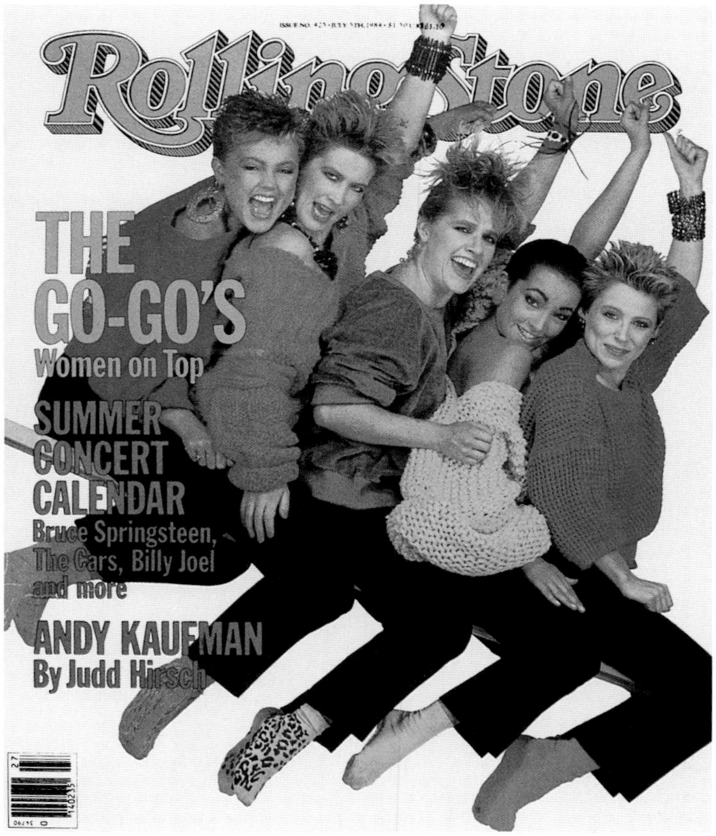

43

PUBLICATION: *Rolling Stone*
ART DIRECTOR: *Derek Ungless*
DESIGNER: *Derek Ungless*
PHOTOGRAPHER: *Albert Watson*
Photo Ed.: Laurie Kratochvil
PUBLISHER: *Straight Arrow Publishers, Inc.*
CATEGORY: *Photography-Cover*
AWARD: *Silver*

44

PUBLICATION: *Rolling Stone*
ART DIRECTOR: *Derek Ungless*
DESIGNER: *Derek Ungless*
PHOTOGRAPHER: *Steven Meisel*
Photo Ed.: Laurie Kratochvil
PUBLISHER: *Straight Arrow Publishers, Inc.*
CATEGORY: *Design-Cover*
AWARD: *Silver*

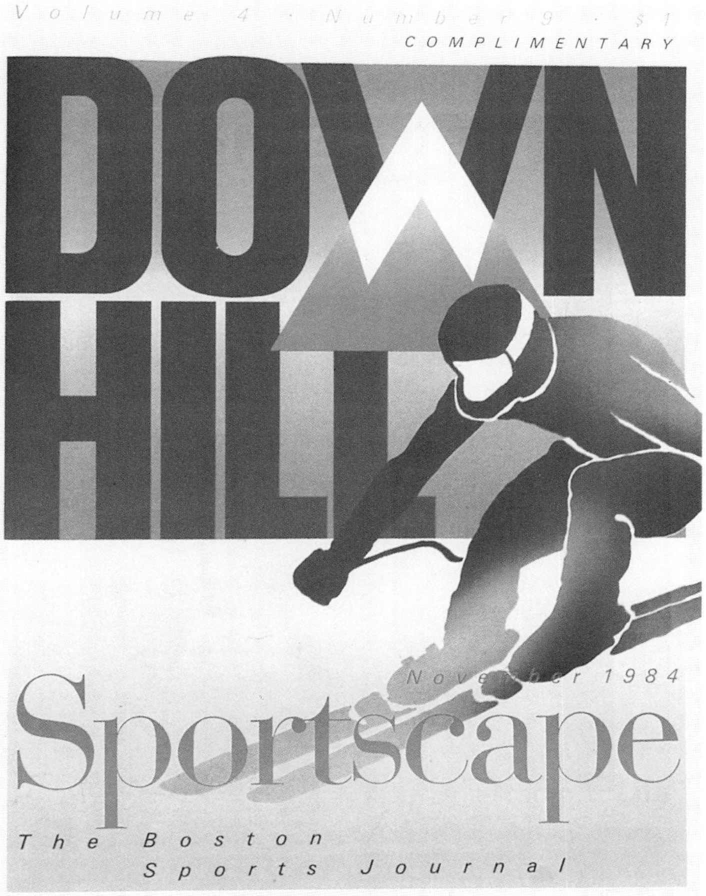

45

PUBLICATION: *Sportscape*
ART DIRECTOR: *Gerald Millet*
DESIGNER: *Lark Carrier*
ILLUSTRATOR: *Lark Carrier*
PUBLISHER: *Lehman Millet Inc.*
CATEGORY: *Tabloid/News Design-Cover*
AWARD: *Silver*

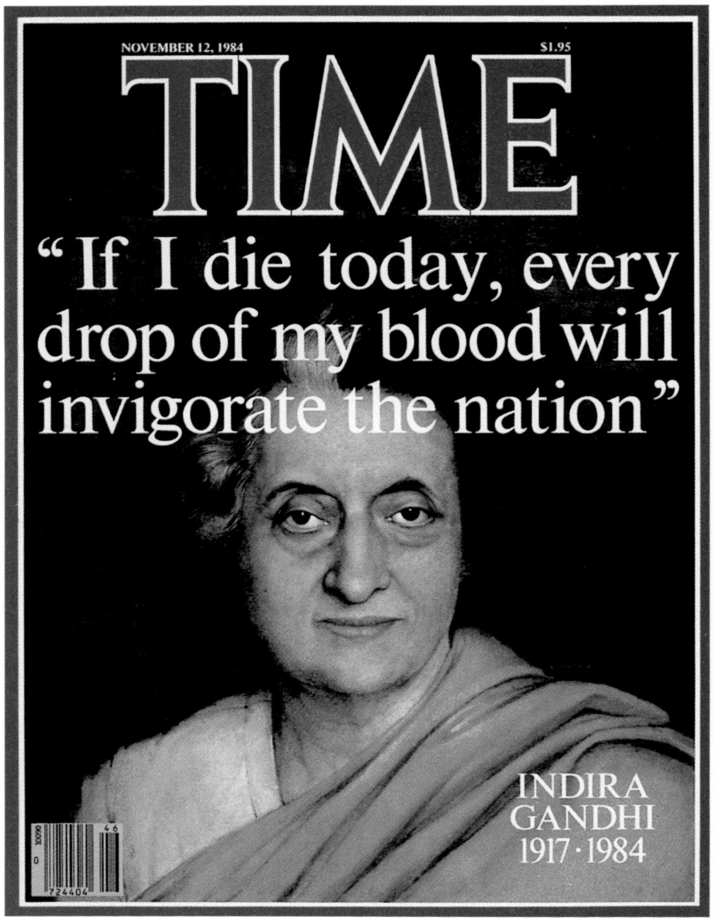

46

PUBLICATION: *Time Magazine*
ART DIRECTOR: *Rudy Hoglund*
ILLUSTRATOR: *Mario Donizetti*
PUBLISHER: *Time Incorporated*
CATEGORY: *Illustration-Cover*
AWARD: *Silver*

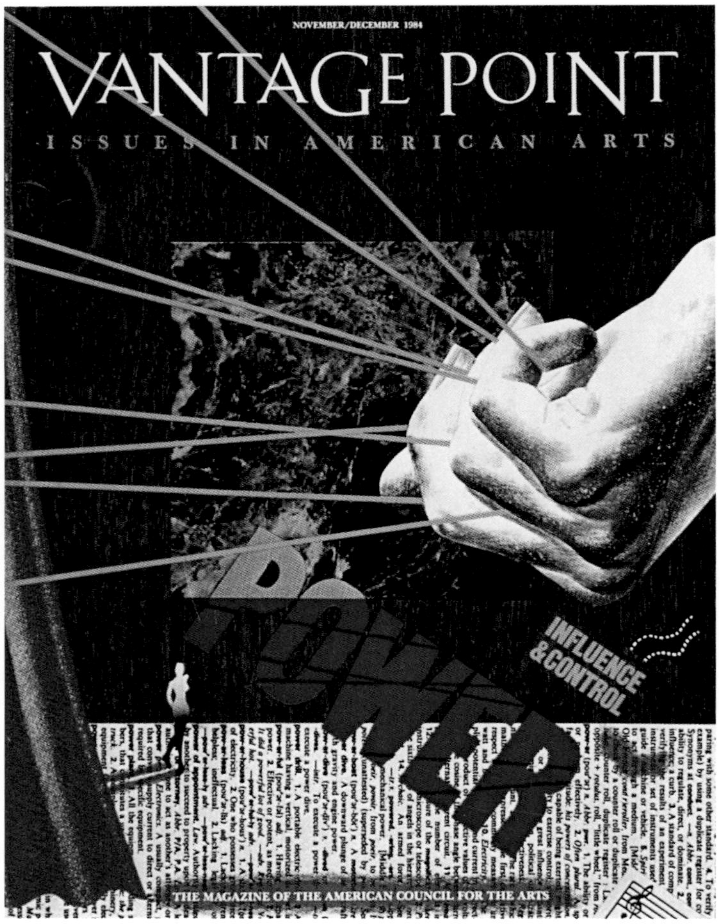

47

PUBLICATION: *Vantage Point*
ART DIRECTOR: *Steven Hoffman*
DESIGNER: *Steven Hoffman*
ILLUSTRATOR: *Gene Grief*
PUBLISHER: *American Council for the Arts*
CATEGORY: *Design-Cover*
AWARD: *Silver*

48

PUBLICATION: *Vantage Point*
ART DIRECTOR: *Steven Hoffman*
DESIGNER: *Steven Hoffman*
ILLUSTRATOR: *Wendy Burden*
PUBLISHER: *American Council for the Arts*
CATEGORY: *Design-Cover*
AWARD: *Silver*

49

PUBLICATION: *Vision*
ART DIRECTOR: *Terry Koppel*
DESIGNER: *Drew Hodges*
PHOTOGRAPHER: *Phillipe Halsman*
PUBLISHER: *Alexis, Parks Publishing*
CATEGORY: *Design-Cover*
AWARD: *Silver*

50

PUBLICATION: *American Bookseller*
ART DIRECTOR: *Amy Bogert*
DESIGNER: *Amy Bogert*
PHOTOGRAPHER: *Joan Adelson*
PUBLISHER: *Booksellers Publishing, Inc.*
CATEGORY: *Design-Cover*
AWARD: *Merit*

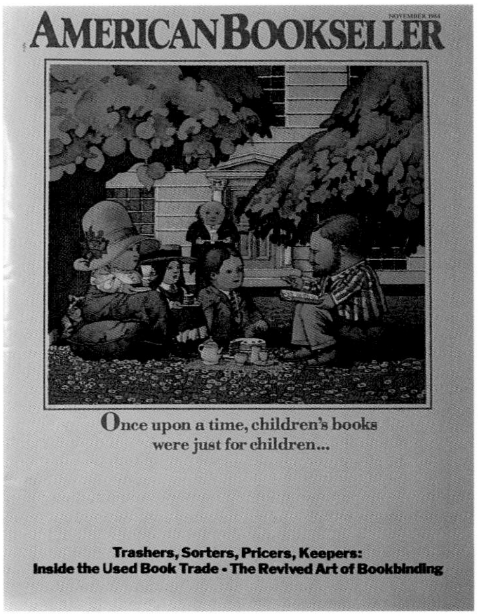

51

PUBLICATION: *American Bookseller*
ART DIRECTOR: *Amy Bogert*
ILLUSTRATOR: *Roy Gerrard*
PUBLISHER: *Booksellers Publishing, Inc.*
CATEGORY: *Illustration-Cover*
AWARD: *Merit*

52

PUBLICATION: *American Bookseller*
ART DIRECTOR: *Amy Bogert*
ILLUSTRATOR: *Steven Guarnaccia*
PUBLISHER: *Booksellers Publishing, Inc.*
CATEGORY: *Illustration-Cover*
AWARD: *Merit*

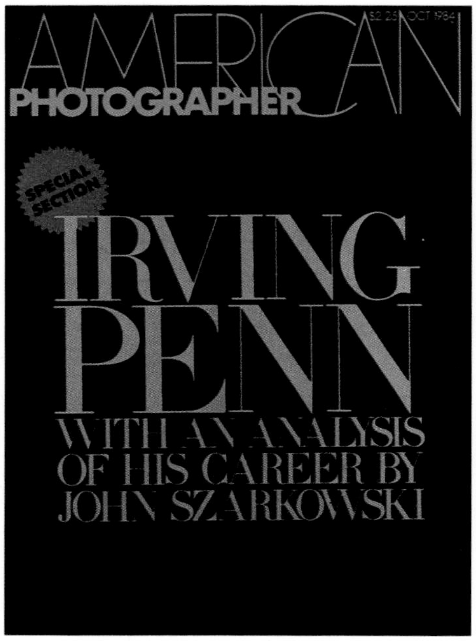

54

PUBLICATION: *American Photographer*
ART DIRECTOR: *Will Hopkins*
DESIGNER: *Will Hopkins*
PHOTOGRAPHER: *Irving Penn*
PUBLISHER: *CBS Publications*
CATEGORY: *Design-Cover*
AWARD: *Merit*

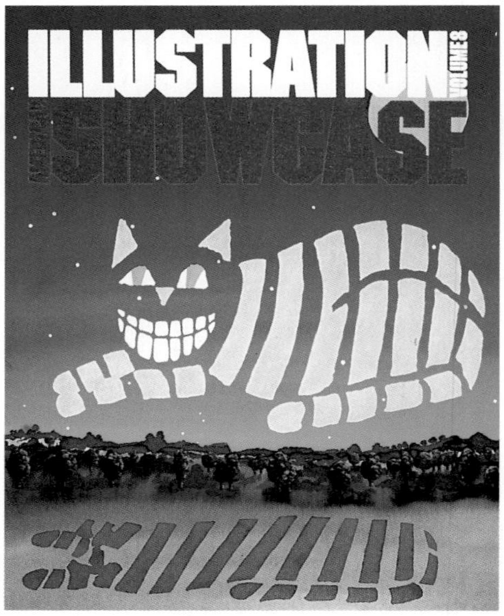

53

PUBLICATION: *American Illustration Showcase 8*
ART DIRECTOR: *Bob Conge*
Michael Toomey
DESIGNER: *Michael Toomey*
ILLUSTRATOR: *Bob Conge*
PUBLISHER: *American Showcase*
CATEGORY: *Illustration-Cover*
AWARD: *Merit*

56

PUBLICATION: *Architectural Record*
ART DIRECTOR: *Alex Stillano*
DESIGNER: *Alberto Bucchianeri*
PHOTOGRAPHER: *Timothy Hursley*
PUBLISHER: *McGraw-Hill*
CATEGORY: *Cover-Design*
AWARD: *Merit*

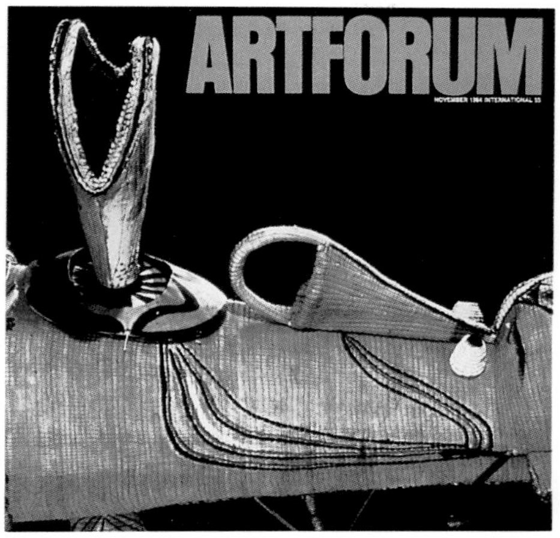

57

PUBLICATION: *Architectural Record*
ART DIRECTOR: *Alex Stillano*
DESIGNER: *Anna Schlesinger*
PHOTOGRAPHER: *Michael George*
PUBLISHER: *McGraw-Hill*
CATEGORY: *Design-Cover*
AWARD: *Merit*

58

PUBLICATION: *Artforum*
ART DIRECTOR: *Roger Gorman*
DESIGNER: *Frances Reinfeld*
PUBLISHER: *Reiner Design Consultants, Inc.*
CATEGORY: *Design-Cover*
AWARD: *Merit*

59

PUBLICATION: *Artforum*
ART DIRECTOR: *Frances Reinfeld*
DESIGNER: *Roger Gorman*
PHOTOGRAPHER: *Rebecca Horn*
PUBLISHER: *Reiner Design Consultants, Inc.*
CATEGORY: *Design-Cover*
AWARD: *Merit*

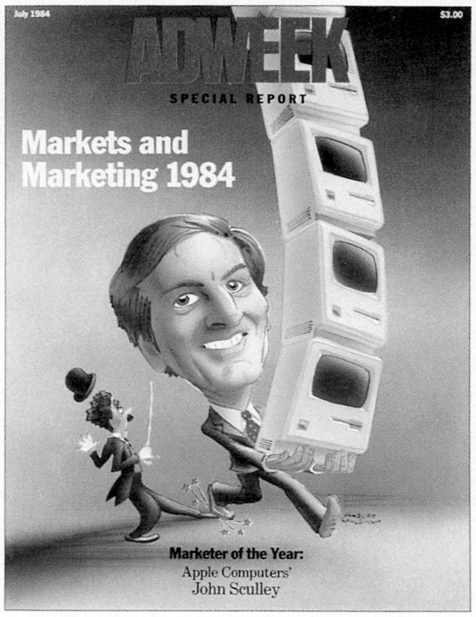

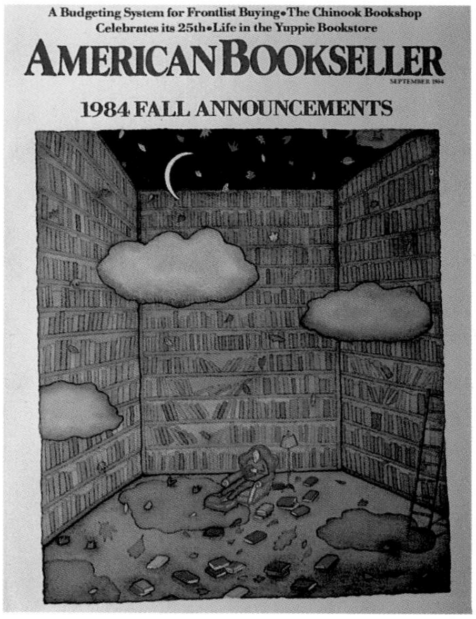

60

PUBLICATION: *Adweek Special Report*
ART DIRECTOR: *Giona Mairelli*
Walter Bernard
DESIGNER: *Giona Maiarelli*
ILLUSTRATOR: *John Alcorn*
PUBLISHER: *Wenda, Harris, & Malaird*
CATEGORY: *Illustration-Cover*
AWARD: *Merit*

61

PUBLICATION: *Adweek Special Report*
ART DIRECTOR: *Arlene Lappen*
Walter Bernard
DESIGNER: *Arlene Lappen*
ILLUSTRATOR: *Robert Grossmann*
PUBLISHER: *Wenda, Harris & Malaird*
CATEGORY: *Illustration-Cover*
AWARD: *Merit*

62

PUBLICATION: *American Bookseller*
ART DIRECTOR: *Amy Bogert*
DESIGNER: *Amy Bogert*
ILLUSTRATOR: *Lonni Sue Johnson*
PUBLISHER: *Booksellers Publishing Inc.*
CATEGORY: *Illustration-Cover*
AWARD: *Merit*

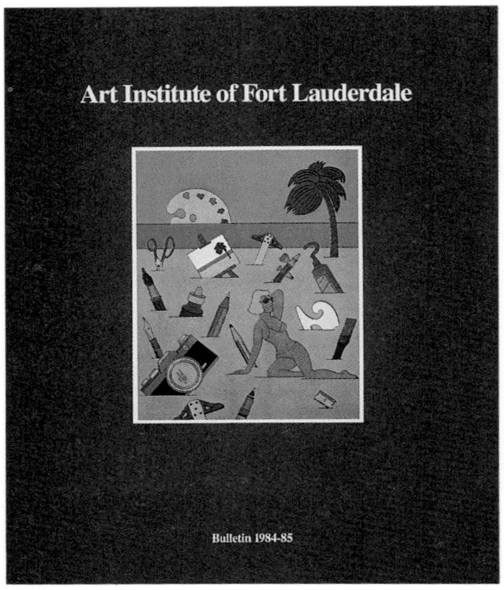

63

PUBLICATION: *Art Institute of Fort Lauderdale (The Design Schools)*
ART DIRECTOR: *Edward A. Hamilton*
DESIGNER: *Leslie Osher*
ILLUSTRATOR: *Seymour Chwast*
PUBLISHER: *The Design Schools*
CATEGORY: *Illustration-Cover*
AWARD: *Merit*

64

PUBLICATION: *Art Direction Magazine*
ART DIRECTOR: *Amy Sussman Heit*
DESIGNER: *Mike Quon*
ILLUSTRATOR: *Mike Quon*
PUBLISHER: *Advertising Trade Publications, Inc.*
CATEGORY: *Cover-Illustration*
AWARD: *Merit*

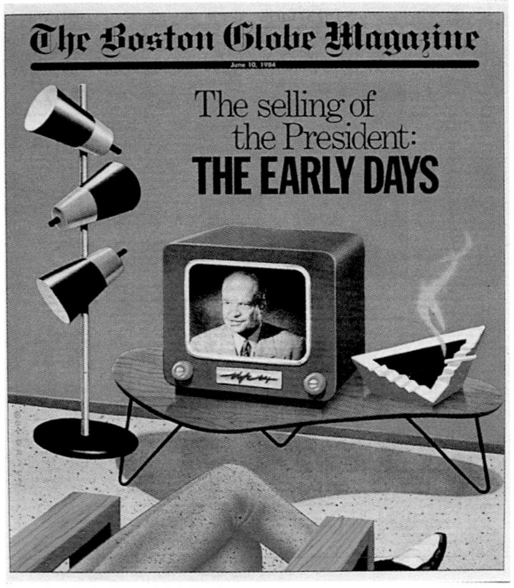

66

PUBLICATION: *The Boston Globe Mag.*
ART DIRECTOR: *Ronn Campisi*
DESIGNER: *Ronn Campisi*
ILLUSTRATOR: *Marty Braun*
PUBLISHER: *Globe Newspaper Co.*
CATEGORY: *Design-Cover*
AWARD: *Merit*

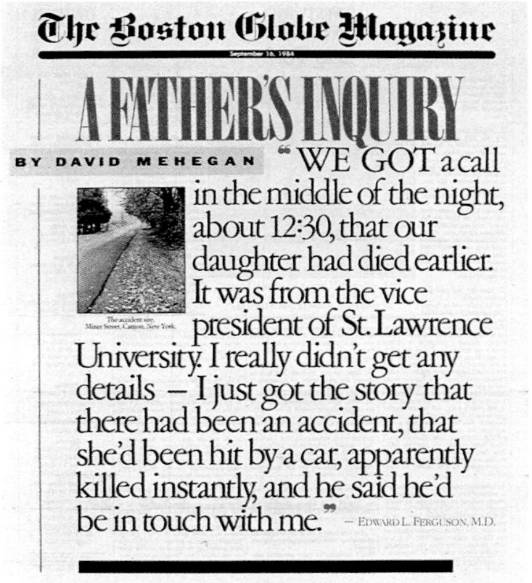

The Boston Globe Magazine

A FATHER'S INQUIRY

BY DAVID MEHEGAN

"WE GOT a call in the middle of the night, about 12:30, that our daughter had died earlier. It was from the vice president of St. Lawrence University. I really didn't get any details — I just got the story that there had been an accident, that she'd been hit by a car, apparently killed instantly, and he said he'd be in touch with me." — EDWARD L. FERGUSON, M.D.

67

PUBLICATION: *The Boston Globe Mag.*
ART DIRECTOR: *Ronn Campisi*
DESIGNER: *Ronn Campisi*
PUBLISHER: *Globe Newspaper Co.*
CATEGORY: *Cover Design*
AWARD: *Merit*

68

PUBLICATION: *Consumer Electronics Monthly*
ART DIRECTOR: *David Armario*
DESIGNER: *David Armario*
ILLUSTRATOR: *Akio Matsuyoshi*
PUBLISHER: *CES Publishing*
CATEGORY: *Cover Design*
AWARD: *Merit*

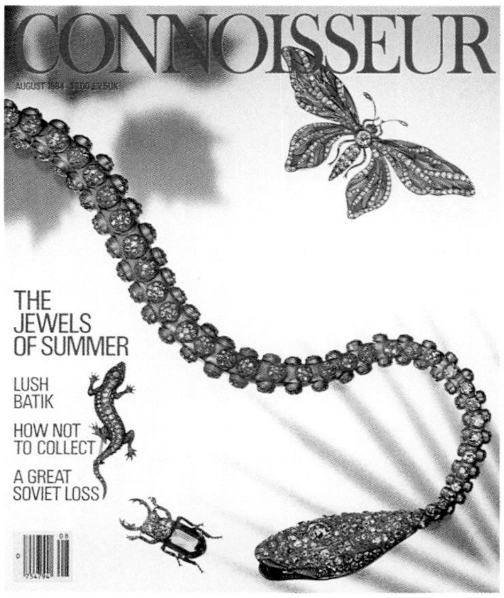

69

PUBLICATION: *Connoisseur Magazine*
ART DIRECTOR: *Carla Barr*
DESIGNER: *Carla Barr*
PHOTOGRAPHER: *Kenro Izu*
PUBLISHER: *Hearst Corporation*
CATEGORY: *Design-Cover*
AWARD: *Merit*

70

PUBLICATION: *Connoisseur Magazine*
ART DIRECTOR: *Carla Barr*
DESIGNER: *Carla Barr*
PHOTOGRAPHER: *Jay Maisel*
PUBLISHER: *Hearst Corporation*
CATEGORY: *Design-Cover*
AWARD: *Merit*

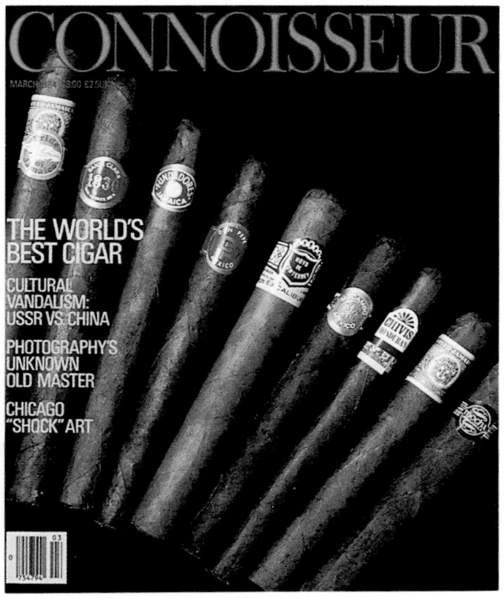

71

PUBLICATION: *Connoisseur Magazine*
ART DIRECTOR: *Carla Barr*
DESIGNER: *Carla Barr*
PHOTOGRAPHER: *Tomas Sennett*
PUBLISHER: *Hearst Corporation*
CATEGORY: *Design-Cover*
AWARD: *Merit*

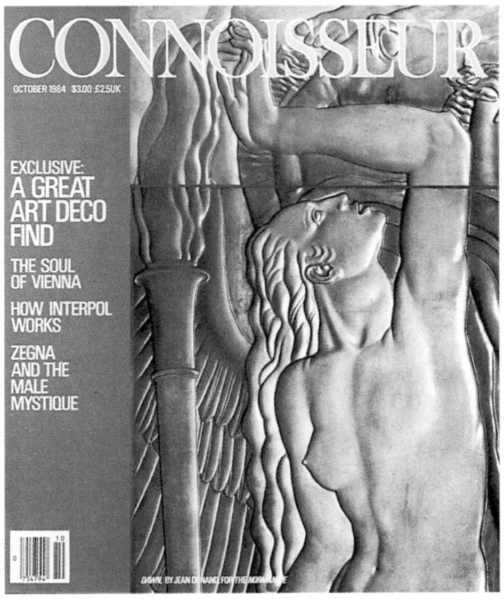

72

PUBLICATION: *Connoisseur Magazine*
ART DIRECTOR: *Carla Barr*
DESIGNER: *Carla Barr*
PHOTOGRAPHER: *Olaf Wahlund*
PUBLISHER: *Hearst Corporation*
CATEGORY: *Design-Cover*
AWARD: *Merit*

73

PUBLICATION: *Connoisseur Magazine*
ART DIRECTOR: *Carla Barr*
DESIGNER: *Carla Barr*
PHOTOGRAPHER: *Alan Macweeney*
PUBLISHER: *Hearst Publications*
CATEGORY: *Design-Cover*
AWARD: *Merit*

74

PUBLICATION: *Connoisseur Magazine*
ART DIRECTOR: *Carla Barr*
DESIGNER: *Carla Barr*
PHOTOGRAPHER: *Chris Callis*
PUBLISHER: *Hearst Publications*
CATEGORY: *Design-Cover*
AWARD: *Merit*

DIALOGUE
AGENDA & DIRECTORY OF SUPPLIERS · DALLAS · FEBRUARY 9, 1984
AN INDUSTRY SERVICE OF MEETINGS & CONVENTIONS MAGAZINE

75

PUBLICATION: *Dialogue*
ART DIRECTOR: *Lee Ann Jaffee*
ILLUSTRATOR: *Nicholas Gaetano*
PUBLISHER: *Lee Ann Jaffee Design*
CATEGORY: *Cover-Illustration*
AWARD: *Merit*

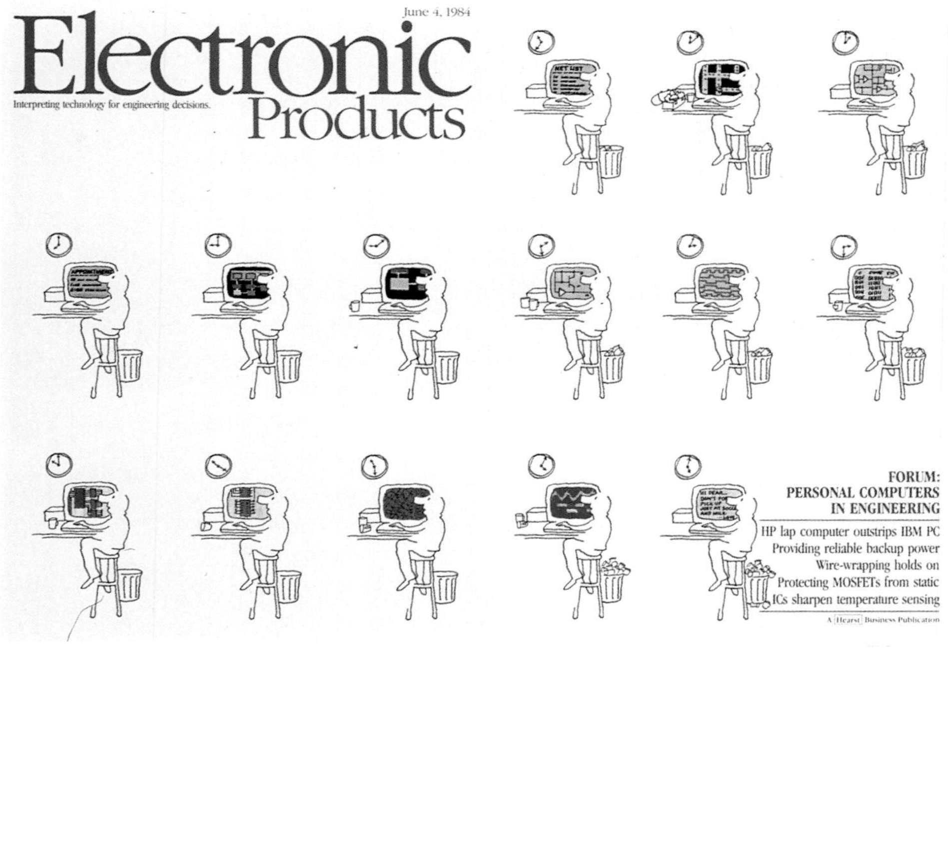
June 4, 1984
Electronic Products
Interpreting technology for engineering decisions.
FORUM:
PERSONAL COMPUTERS
IN ENGINEERING
HP lap computer outstrips IBM PC
Providing reliable backup power
Wire-wrapping holds on
Protecting MOSFETs from static
ICs sharpen temperature sensing
A Hearst Business Publication

76

PUBLICATION: *Electronic Products Magazine*
ART DIRECTOR: *Virginia Murphy-Hamill*
DESIGNER: *Virginia Murphy-Hamill*
ILLUSTRATOR: *Virginia Murphy-Hamill*
PUBLISHER: *Hearst Business Communications, Inc.*
CATEGORY: *Design-Cover*
AWARD: *Merit*

77

PUBLICATION: *Family Weekly*
ART DIRECTOR: *Altemus/Rick Stark*
DESIGNER: *Altemus*
PHOTOGRAPHER: *Walter Loss Jr.*
CATEGORY: *Photo-Cover*
AWARD: *Merit*

78

PUBLICATION: *Family Weekly*
ART DIRECTOR: *Altemus/Rick Stark*
DESIGNER: *Altemus/Rick Stark*
ILLUSTRATOR: *William Low*
CATEGORY: *Illustration-Cover*
AWARD: *Merit*

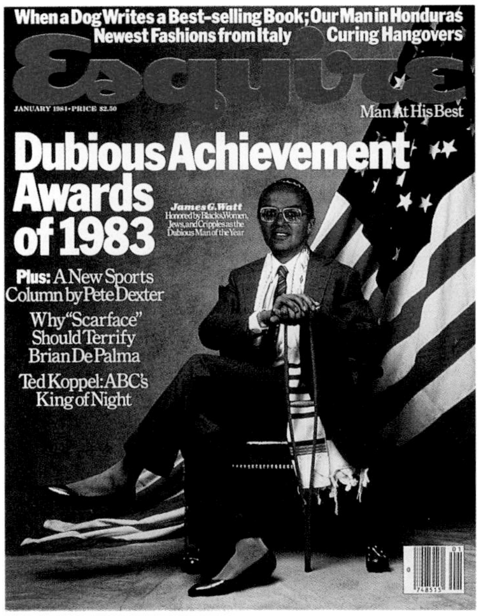

79

PUBLICATION: *Esquire*
ART DIRECTOR: *April Silver*
PHOTOGRAPHY: *Jean Moss*
PUBLISHER: *Esquire Associates*
CATEGORY: *Cover-Design*
AWARD: *Merit*

80

PUBLICATION: *Fortune Magazine*
ART DIRECTOR: *Margery Peters*
DESIGNER: *Margery Peters*
ILLUSTRATOR: *Edward Sorel*
PUBLISHER: *Fortune Magazine*
CATEGORY: *Illustration-Cover*
AWARD: *Merit*

81

PUBLICATION: *Fortune Magazine*
ART DIRECTOR: *Margery Peters*
DESIGNER: *Margery Peters*
ILLUSTRATOR: *Guy Billout*
PUBLISHER: *Fortune Magazine*
CATEGORY: *Illustration-Cover*
AWARD: *Merit*

82

PUBLICATION: *Fortune Magazine*
ART DIRECTOR: *Margery Peters*
DESIGNER: *Margery Peters*
ILLUSTRATOR: *Bob Gale*
PUBLISHER: *Fortune Magazine*
CATEGORY: *Illustration-Cover*
AWARD: *Merit*

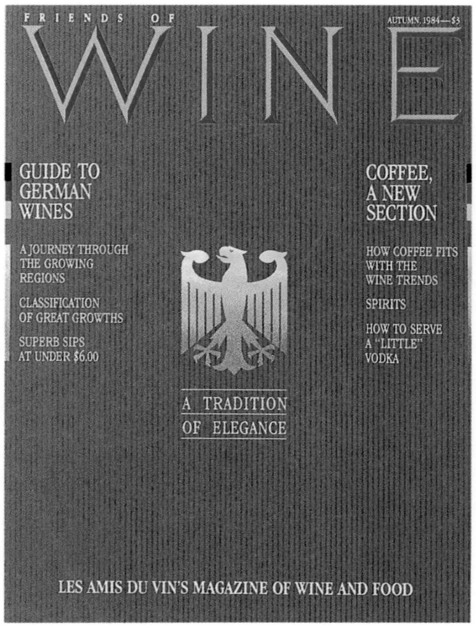

83

PUBLICATION: *Friends of Wine Magazine*
ART DIRECTOR: *Duk Engelhardt*
DESIGNER: *Duk Engelhardt*
ILLUSTRATOR: *Duk Engelhardt*
PUBLISHER: *Fortune Magazine*
CATEGORY: *Design-Cover*
AWARD: *Merit*

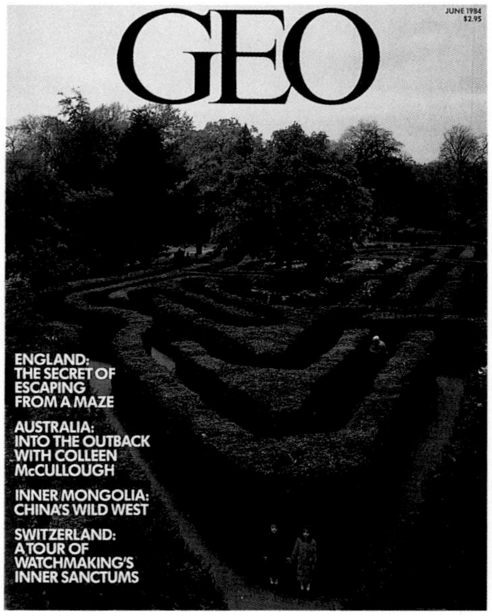

84

PUBLICATION: *Geo Magazine*
ART DIRECTOR: *John Tom Cohoe*
DESIGNER: *John Tom Cohoe*
PHOTOGRAPHER: *Kenneth Griffiths*
PUBLISHER: *Knapp Communications*
CATEGORY: *Design-Cover*
AWARD: *Merit*

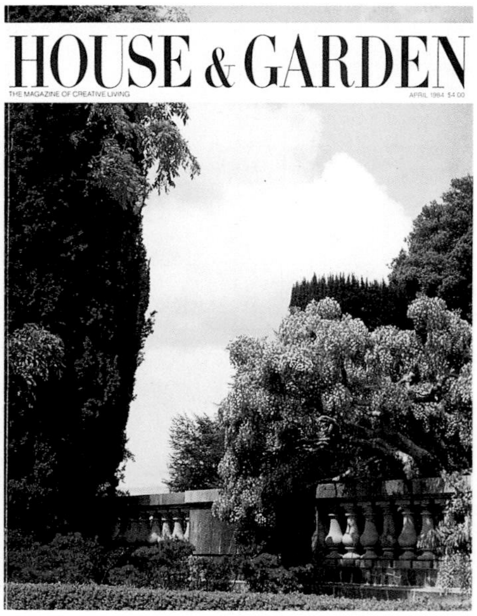

85

PUBLICATION: *House & Garden*
ART DIRECTOR: *Lloyd Ziff*
DESIGNER: *Ken Lee Grant*
PHOTOGRAPHER: *Russell MacMasters*
PUBLISHER: *Conde Nast Publications*
CATEGORY: *Photo-Cover*
AWARD: *Merit*

87

PUBLICATION: *HNG Magazine*
ART DIRECTOR: *R. Wayne Ford*
DESIGNER: *R. Wayne Ford*
PUBLISHER: *Houston Natural Gas Corp.*
CATEGORY: *Design-Cover*
AWARD: *Merit*

88

PUBLICATION: *Industrial Launderer*
ART DIRECTOR: *Jack Lefkowitz*
DESIGNER: *Jack Lefkowitz*
ILLUSTRATOR: *M. V. Strnad*
PUBLISHER: *Jack Lefkowitz, Inc.*
CATEGORY: *Design Cover*
AWARD: *Merit*

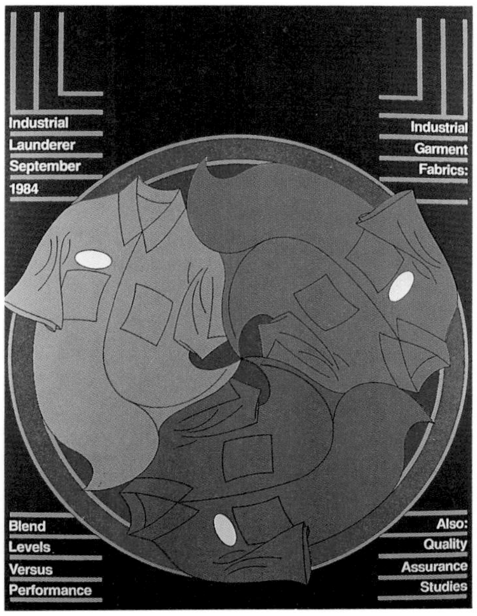

89

PUBLICATION: *Industrial Launderer*
ART DIRECTOR: *Jack Lefkowitz*
DESIGNER: *Jack Lefkowitz*
ILLUSTRATOR: *M. V. Strnad*
PUBLISHER: *Jack Lefkowitz, Inc.*
CATEGORY: *Design-Cover*
AWARD: *Merit*

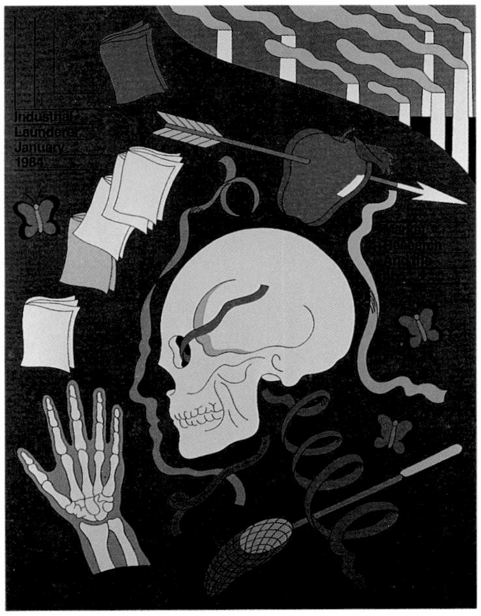

90

PUBLICATION: *Industrial Launderer*
ART DIRECTOR: *Jack Lefkowitz*
DESIGNER: *Jack Lefkowitz*
ILLUSTRATOR: *M. V. Strnad*
PUBLISHER: *Jack Lefkowitz, Inc.*
CATEGORY: *Design-Cover*
AWARD: *Merit*

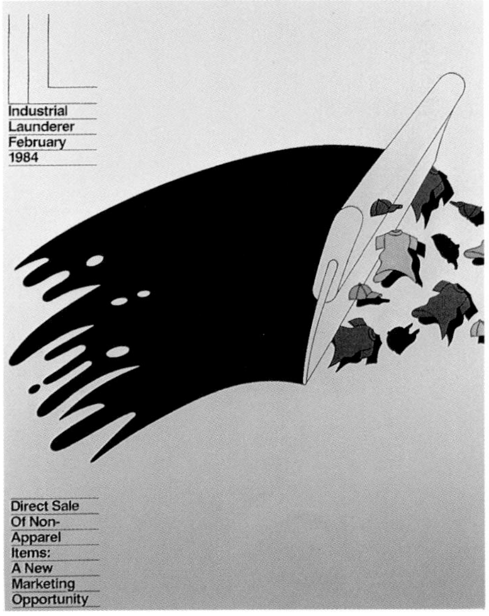

91

PUBLICATION: *Industrial Launderer*
ART DIRECTOR: *Jack Lefkowitz*
DESIGNER: *Jack Lefkowitz*
ILLUSTRATOR: *M. V. Strnad*
PUBLISHER: *Jack Lefkowitz, Inc.*
CATEGORY: *Design-Cover*
AWARD: *Merit*

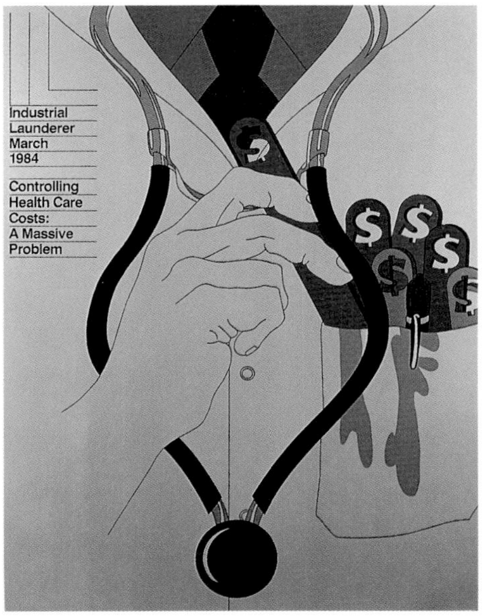

92

PUBLICATION: *Industrial Launderer*
ART DIRECTOR: *Jack Lefkowitz*
DESIGNER: *Jack Lefkowitz*
ILLUSTRATOR: *M. V. Strnad*
PUBLISHER: *Jack Lefkowitz, Inc.*
CATEGORY: *Design-Cover*
AWARD: *Merit*

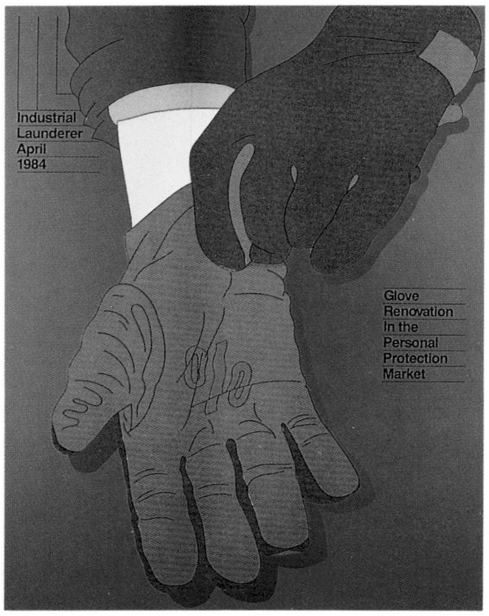

93

PUBLICATION: *Industrial Launderer*
ART DIRECTOR: *Jack Lefkowitz*
DESIGNER: *Jack Lefkowitz*
ILLUSTRATOR: *M. V. Strnad*
PUBLISHER: *Jack Lefkowitz, Inc.*
CATEGORY: *Design-Cover*
AWARD: *Merit*

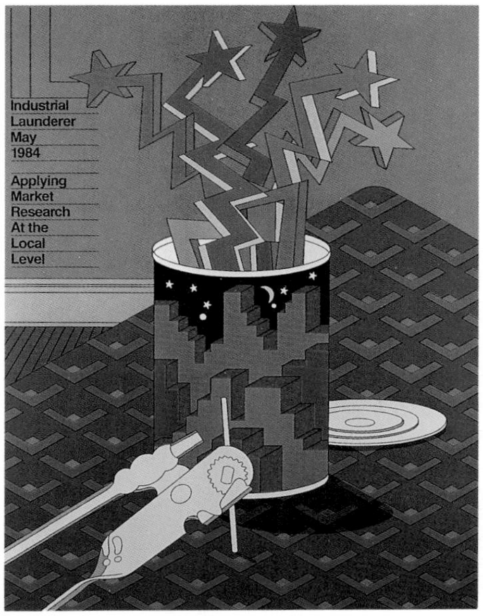

94

PUBLICATION: *Industrial Launderer*
ART DIRECTOR: *Jack Lefkowitz*
DESIGNER: *Jack Lefkowitz*
ILLUSTRATOR: *M. V. Strnad*
PUBLISHER: *Jack Lefkowitz, Inc.*
CATEGORY: *Cover-Design*
AWARD: *Merit*

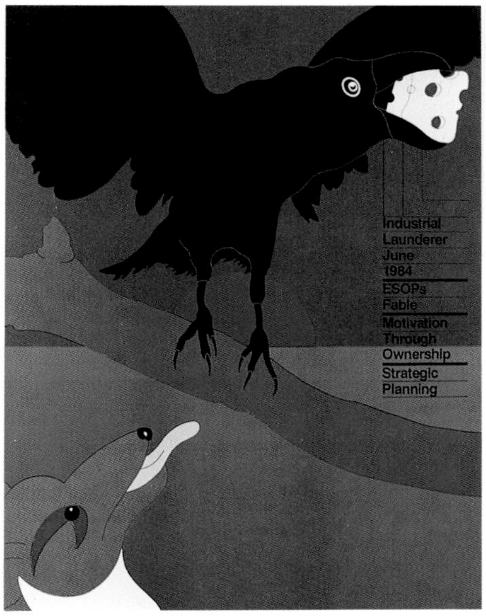

95

PUBLICATION: *Industrial Launderer*
ART DIRECTOR: *Jack Lefkowitz*
DESIGNER: *Jack Lefkowitz*
ILLUSTRATOR: *M. V. Strnad*
PUBLISHER: *Jack Lefkowitz, Inc.*
CATEGORY: *Cover-Design*
AWARD: *Merit*

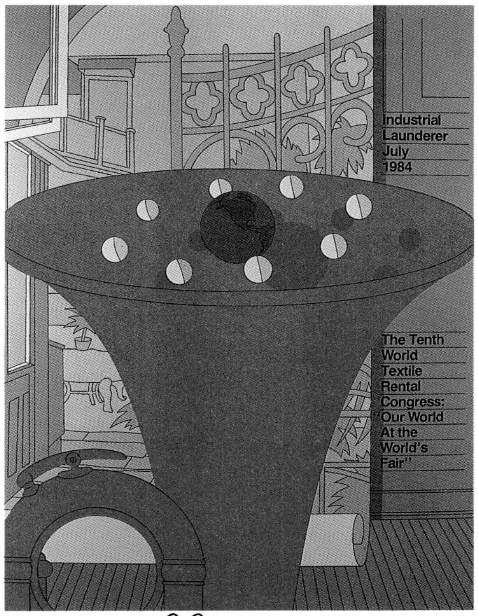

96

PUBLICATION: *Industrial Launderer*
ART DIRECTOR: *Jack Lefkowitz*
DESIGNER: *Jack Lefkowitz*
ILLUSTRATOR: *M. V. Strnad*
PUBLISHER: *Jack Lefkowitz, Inc.*
AWARD: *Cover-Design*
AWARD: *Merit*

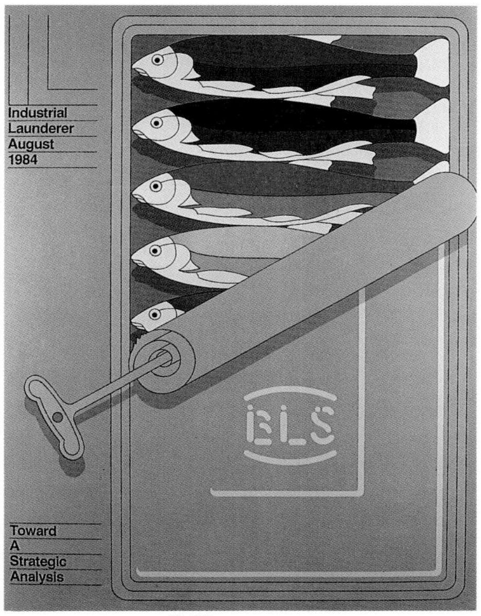

97

PUBLICATION: *Industrial Launderer*
ART DIRECTOR: *Jack Lefkowitz*
DESIGNER: *Jack Lefkowitz*
ILLUSTRATOR: *M. V. Strnad*
PUBLISHER: *Jack Lefkowitz, Inc.*
CATEGORY: *Design-Cover*
AWARD: *Merit*

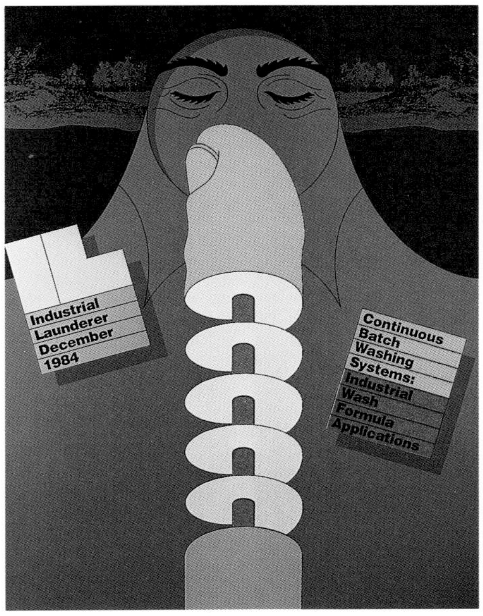

99

PUBLICATION: *Industrial Launderer*
ART DIRECTOR: *Jack Lefkowitz*
DESIGNER: *Jack Lefkowitz*
ILLUSTRATOR: *M. V. Strnad*
PUBLISHER: *Jack Lefkowitz, Inc.*
CATEGORY: *Design-Cover*
AWARD: *Merit*

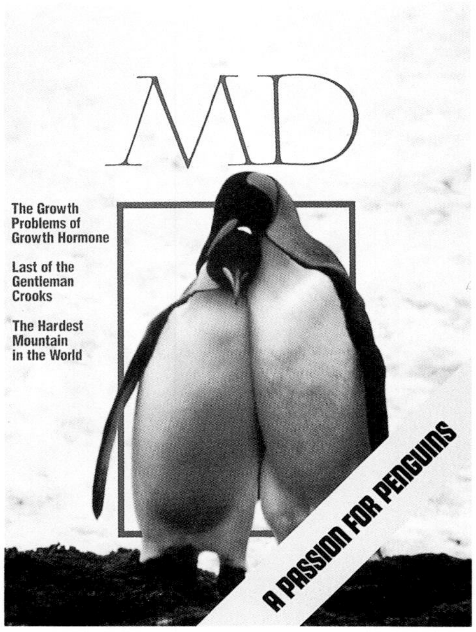

100

PUBLICATION: *MD Magazine*
ART DIRECTOR: *Merrill Cason, Al Foti*
DESIGNER: *Al Foti*
PHOTOGRAPHER: *Bruno Zehnder*
PUBLISHER: *MD Publications, Inc.*
CATEGORY: *Cover-Design*
AWARD: *Merit*

101

PUBLICATION: *Maxwell House Messenger*
ART DIRECTOR: *Graig Bernhardt*
DESIGNER: *Graig Bernhardt*
ILLUSTRATOR: *Nancy Stahl*
PUBLISHER: *Bernhardt Design Group*
CATEGORY: *Cover-Design*
AWARD: *Merit*

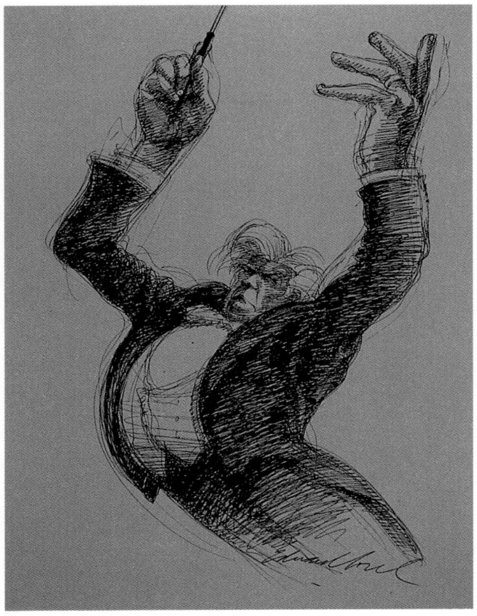

102

PUBLICATION: *Mead Black & White*
ART DIRECTOR: *Bennett Robinson*
DESIGNER: *Bennett Robinson*
ILLUSTRATOR: *Edward Sorel*
PUBLISHER: *Corporate Graphics, Inc.*
CATEGORY: *Cover-Design*
AWARD: *Merit*

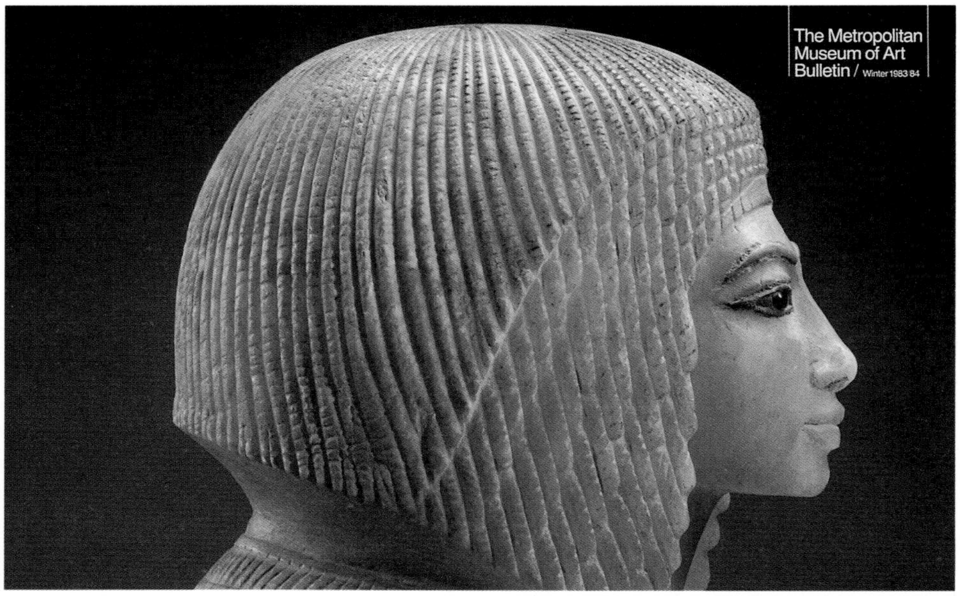

103

PUBLICATION: *Metropolitan Museum of Art Bulletin*
ART DIRECTOR: *Joan Holt*
DESIGNER: *Antony Drobinski*
PHOTOGRAPHER: *Lynton Gardiner*
CATEGORY: *Cover-Design*
AWARD: *Merit*

105

PUBLICATION: *National Lampoon*
ART DIRECTOR: *Michael Grossman*
DESIGNER: *Michael Grossman*
PHOTOGRAPHER: *Michael Watson*
PUBLISHER: *Mid-America Web Press*
CATEGORY: *Design-Cover*
AWARD: *Merit*

106

PUBLICATION: *Daily News Magazine*
ART DIRECTOR: *Janet Froelich*
Thomas P. Ruis
ILLUSTRATOR: *Terry Allen*
PUBLISHER: *New York News, Inc.*
CATEGORY: *Illustration-Cover*
AWARD: *Merit*

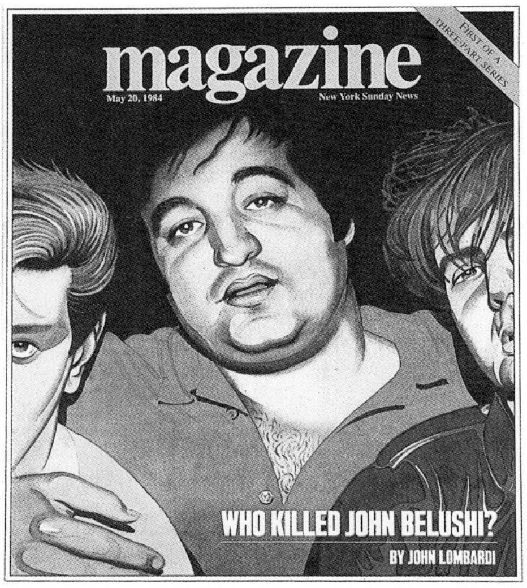

107

PUBLICATION: *Daily News Magazine*
ART DIRECTOR: *Janet Froelich*
Thomas P. Ruis
ILLUSTRATOR: *Jeffrey Smith*
PUBLISHER: *New York News, Inc.*
CATEGORY: *Illustration-Cover*
AWARD: *Merit*

108

PUBLICATION: *Newsweek*
ART DIRECTOR: *Ron Meyerson*
Bob Engle
ILLUSTRATOR: *Brad Holland*
PUBLISHER: *Newsweek, Inc.*
CATEGORY: *Illustration-Cover*
AWARD: *Silver*

109

PUBLICATION: *Daily News Magazine*
ART DIRECTOR: *Janet Froelich*
Thomas P. Ruis
ILLUSTRATOR: *Robert Risco*
PUBLISHER: *New York News, Inc.*
CATEGORY: *Illustration-Cover*
AWARD: *Merit*

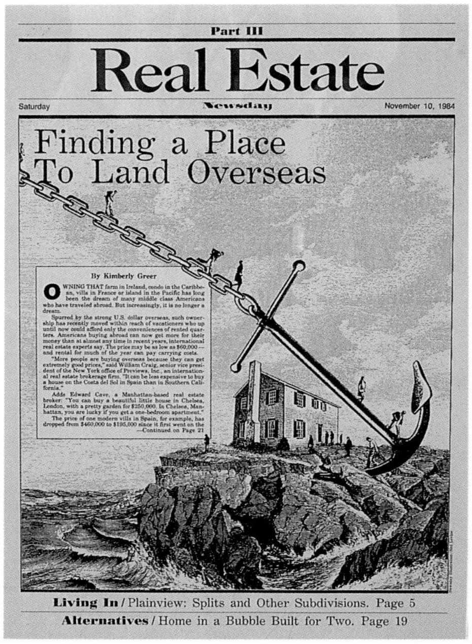

111

PUBLICATION: *Newsday*
ART DIRECTOR: *Bob Eisner*
DESIGNER: *Jeff Massaro*
ILLUSTRATOR: *Ned Levine*
PUBLISHER: *Newsday*
CATEGORY: *Design-Cover*
AWARD: *Merit*

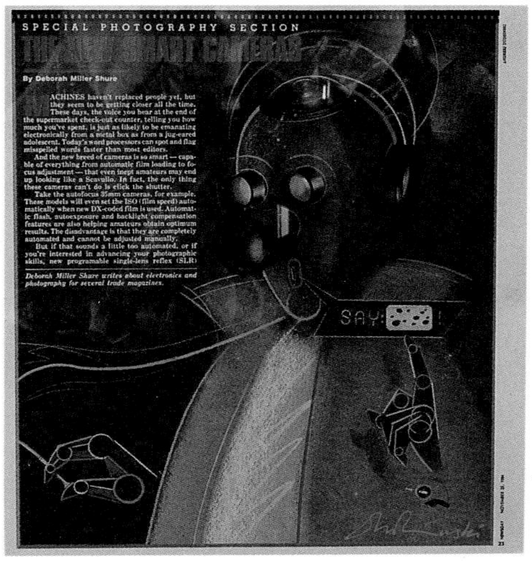

112

PUBLICATION: *Newsday*
ART DIRECTOR: *Miriam Smith*
DESIGNER: *Miriam Smith*
ILLUSTRATOR: *Andrew Dudzinski*
PUBLISHER: *Newsday*
CATEGORY: *Illustration-Cover*
AWARD: *Merit*

113

PUBLICATION: *New York Magazine*
ART DIRECTOR: *Robert Best*
DESIGNER: *Patricia Von Brachel*
ILLUSTRATOR: *Alan Reingold*
PUBLISHER: *Murdoch Magazines*
CATEGORY: *Design-Cover*
AWARD: *Merit*

114

PUBLICATION: *New York Magazine*
ART DIRECTOR: *Robert Best*
DESIGNER: *Jordan Schaps*
PHOTOGRAPHER: *Tony McGee*
PUBLISHER: *Murdoch Magazines*
CATEGORY: *Photography-Cover*
AWARD: *Merit*

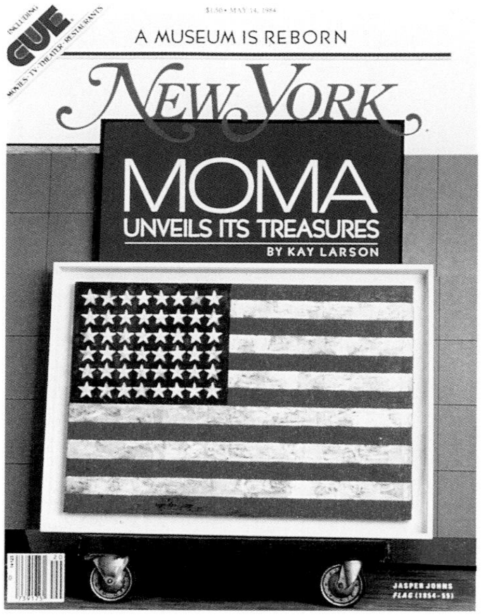

115

PUBLICATION: *New York Magazine*
ART DIRECTOR: *Robert Best*
DESIGNER: *Karen Mullarkey*
PHOTOGRAPHER: *Adam Bartos*
PUBLISHER: *Murdoch Magazines*
CATEGORY: *Design-Cover*
AWARD: *Merit*

116

PUBLICATION: *New York Magazine*
ART DIRECTOR: *Robert Best*
DESIGNER: *Jordan Schaps*
PHOTOGRAPHER: *Langdon Clay*
PUBLISHER: *Murdoch Magazines*
CATEGORY: *Photography-Cover*
AWARD: *Merit*

117

PUBLICATION: *New York Magazine*
ART DIRECTOR: *Robert Best*
DESIGNER: *Patricia Von Brachel*
ILLUSTRATOR: *Laurie Rosenwald*
PUBLISHER: *Murdoch Magazines*
CATEGORY: *Design-Cover*
AWARD: *Merit*

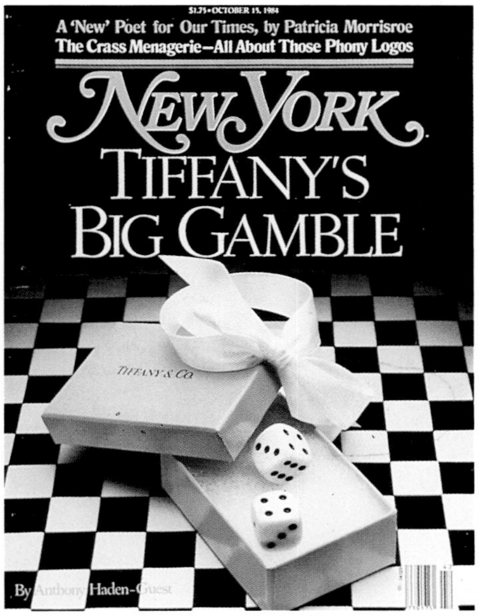

118

PUBLICATION: *New York Magazine*
ART DIRECTOR: *Robert Best*
DESIGNER: *Jordan Schaps*
PHOTOGRAPHER: *Frank Spinelli*
PUBLISHER: *Murdoch Magazines*
CATEGORY: *Photography-Cover*
AWARD: *Merit*

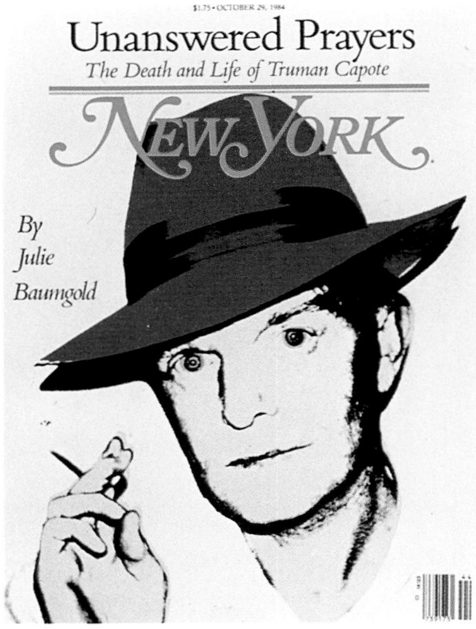

119

PUBLICATION: *New York Magazine*
ART DIRECTOR: *Robert Best*
DESIGNER: *Patricia Von Brachel, Karen Mullarkey*
ILLUSTRATOR: *Andy Warhol*
PUBLISHER: *Murdoch Magazines*
CATEGORY: *Design-Cover*
AWARD: *Merit*

120

PUBLICATION: *New York Times Magazine*
ART DIRECTOR: *Ken Kendrick*
DESIGNER: *Ken Kendrick*
PUBLISHER: *The New York Times*
CATEGORY: *Photography-Cover*
AWARD: *Merit*

121

PUBLICATION:	*New York Times Magazine*
ART DIRECTOR:	*Ken Kendrick*
DESIGNER:	*Ken Kendrick*
PUBLISHER:	*The New York Times*
CATEGORY:	*Design-Cover*
AWARD:	*Merit*

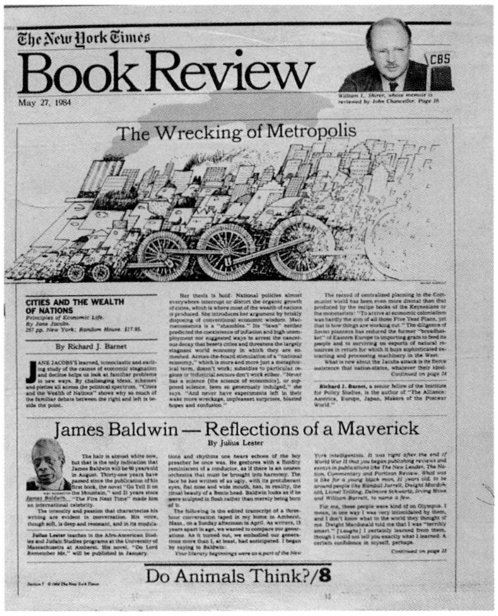
The New York Times
Book Review
May 27, 1984
The Wrecking of Metropolis
CITIES AND THE WEALTH OF NATIONS
By Richard J. Barnet
James Baldwin — Reflections of a Maverick
By Julius Lester
Do Animals Think?/8

122

PUBLICATION: *New York Times-Book Review*
ART DIRECTOR: *Steve Heller*
DESIGNER: *Steve Heller*
ILLUSTRATOR: *Maciek Albrecht*
PUBLISHER: *The New York Times*
CATEGORY: *Tabloid/Newsprint Cover-Design*
AWARD: *Merit*

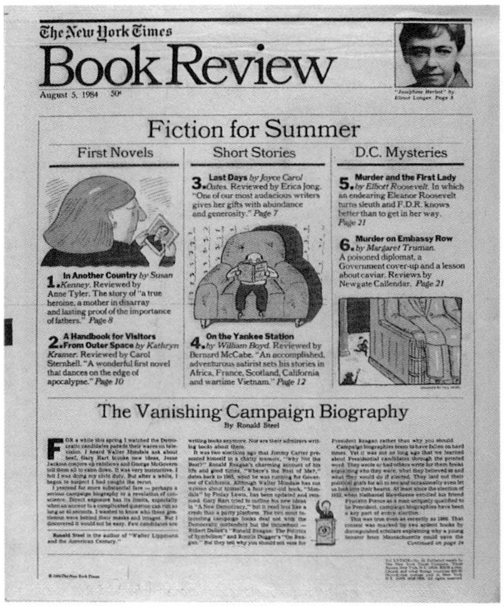
The New York Times
Book Review
August 5, 1984
Fiction for Summer
First Novels
Short Stories
D.C. Mysteries
1. In Another Country by Susan Kenney. Reviewed by Anne Tyler. The story of "a true heroine, a mother in disarray and lasting proof of the importance of fathers." Page 8
2. A Handbook for Visitors From Outer Space by Kathryn Kramer. Reviewed by Carol Sternhell. "A wonderful first novel that dances on the edge of apocalypse." Page 10
3. Last Days by Joyce Carol Oates. Reviewed by Erica Jong. "One of our most audacious writers gives her gifts with abundance and generosity." Page 7
4. On the Yankee Station by William Boyd. Reviewed by Bernard McCabe. "An accomplished, adventurous satirist sets his stories in Africa, France, Scotland, California and wartime Vietnam." Page 12
5. Murder and the First Lady by Elliott Roosevelt. In which an endearing Eleanor Roosevelt turns sleuth and F.D.R. knows better than to get in her way. Page 21
6. Murder on Embassy Row by Margaret Truman. A poisoned diplomat, a Government cover-up and a lesson about caviar. Reviews by Newgate Callendar. Page 21
The Vanishing Campaign Biography
By Ronald Steel

123

PUBLICATION: *New York Times-Book Review*
ART DIRECTOR: *Steve Heller*
DESIGNER: *Steve Heller*
ILLUSTRATOR: *Paul Meisel*
PUBLISHER: *The New York Times*
CATEGORY: *Tabloid/Newsprint Cover-Design*
AWARD: *Merit*

The New York Times
Book Review
November 25, 1984
An Artist Who Shook the Earth
MATISSE
By John Russell
The Death of the Jewish Novel
By Alan Lelchuk
A Jesuit in Cathay/11

124

PUBLICATION: *New York-Times Book Review*
ART DIRECTOR: *Steve Heller*
DESIGNER: *Steve Heller*
PUBLISHER: *The New York Times*
CATEGORY: *Tabloid/Newsprint Cover-Design*
AWARD: *Merit*

The solid, self-assured presence of Manhattan's newest row houses 10

ARTS/ENTERTAINMENT

Now Peter Brook presents an English version of 'La Tragédie de Carmen' 17

Books: 'Life and Death on 10 West,' Eric Lax's drama of clinical research 21

The New York Times

THE Home SECTION

Silencing the Sounds of the Noisy City

The Household Employee And the Benefits Dilemma

Living on Steichen's Pond — C6

125

PUBLICATION: *New York Times Home Section*
ART DIRECTOR: *Nicki Kalish*
DESIGNER: *Nicki Kalish*
ILLUSTRATOR: *Diana Bryan*
PUBLISHER: *The New York Times*
CATEGORY: *Tabloid/Newsprint Cover-Design*
AWARD: *Merit*

The New York Times

Travel

Sunday, March 25, 1984

Section 10

AROUND THE CARIBBEAN

Island to Island In Off Season

Surveying a tide of off-peak benefits. By Barbara Crossette/ Ports of call: What to do when the cruise ship comes in. By Stanley Carr/ Coping with luxury at Caneel Bay. By Charlotte Curtis. Pages 16 to 24.

15 Favorite Paris Bistros

Where home cooking and old-fashioned quality thrive. By R. W. Apple Jr. Page 9.

Java Treasure 6

The Sloane Rangers 12

A Country Retreat 14

Land of Aphrodite

In Cyprus, mosaics depict stories of gods and goddesses, and tombs recall aristocracy under the Ptolemies. By Sarah Caudwell. Page 27.

126

PUBLICATION: *New York Times Travel Section*
ART DIRECTOR: *Tom Bodkin*
DESIGNER: *Tom Bodkin*
ILLUSTRATOR: *Gary Hallgren*
PUBLISHER: *The New York Times*
CATEGORY: *Tabloid/Newsprint Cover-Design*
AWARD: *Merit*

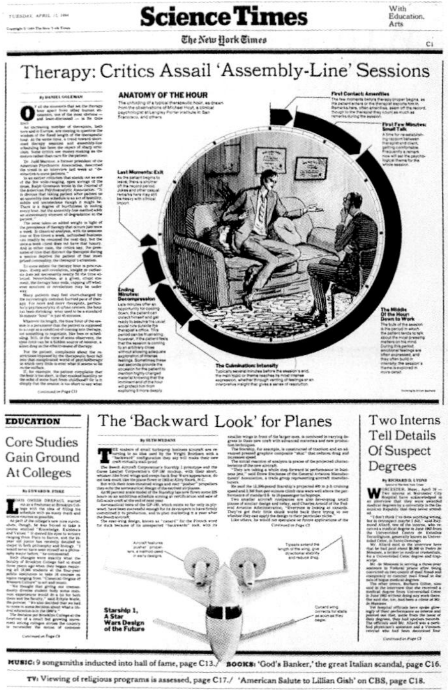
Science Times

The New York Times

Therapy: Critics Assail 'Assembly-Line' Sessions

ANATOMY OF THE HOUR

EDUCATION

Core Studies Gain Ground At Colleges

The 'Backward Look' for Planes

Two Interns Tell Details Of Suspect Degrees

MUSIC: 9 songsmiths inducted into hall of fame, page C13./ BOOKS: 'God's Banker,' the great Italian scandal, page C16.

TV: Viewing of religious programs is assessed, page C17./ 'American Salute to Lillian Gish' on CBS, page C18.

127

PUBLICATION: *New York Times Science Times*
ART DIRECTOR: *Gary Cosimini*
DESIGNER: *Gary Cosimini*
ILLUSTRATOR: *Elliot Banfield*
PUBLISHER: *The New York Times*
CATEGORY: *Tabloid/Newsprint Design-Cover*
AWARD: *Merit*

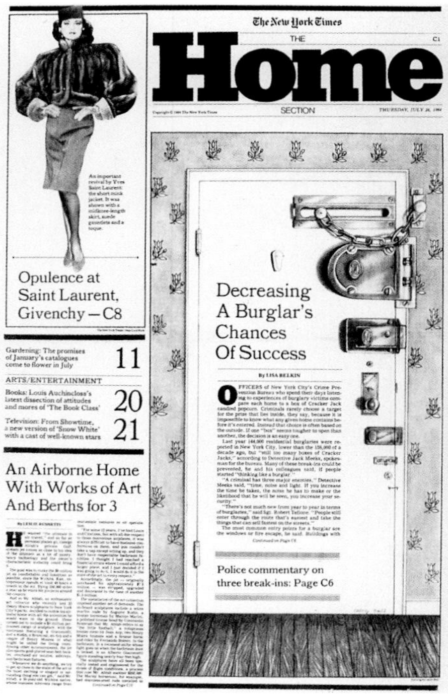
The New York Times

THE Home SECTION

Opulence at Saint Laurent, Givenchy — C8

Gardening: The promises of January's catalogues come to flower in July 11

ARTS/ENTERTAINMENT

Books: Louis Auchincloss's latest dissection of attitudes and mores of "The Book Class" 20

Television: From Showtime, a new version of 'Snow White' with a cast of well-known stars 21

An Airborne Home With Works of Art And Berths for 3

Decreasing A Burglar's Chances Of Success

Police commentary on three break-ins: Page C6

128

PUBLICATION: *New York Times Home Section*
ART DIRECTOR: *Nicki Kalish*
DESIGNER: *Nicki Kalish*
ILLUSTRATOR: *Cathy Hull*
PUBLISHER: *The New York Times*
CATEGORY: *Tabloid/Newsprint Design-Cover*
AWARD: *Merit*

Conference

Music

Movies

Books

The Living Section

FOOD/STYLE/ENTERTAINMENT

The New York Times

A Coffee Drinker's Guide to Decaffeinated Brands

In Divorced Families, Paying for College

Culinary Touch That's All-American

Tuition costs rarely figure in settlements.

129

PUBLICATION: *New York Times Living Section*
ART DIRECTOR: *Nancy Sterngold*
DESIGNER: *Nancy Sterngold*
ILLUSTRATOR: *Elliot Banfield*
PUBLISHER: *The New York Times*
CATEGORY: *Tabloid/Newsprint Design-Cover*
AWARD: *Merit*

The New York Times

Travel

Sunday, September 16, 1984

Section 10

Westward Across the Pacific

Islands In Time

Atoll-hopping. By Robert Trumbull. Page 15.

Xian: Where a sculptured army, 22 centuries old, comes vividly to life. By Michael Specter. Page 16.

Echoes Of China

Returning to Taiwan. By Fox Butterfield. Page 9.

Pastoral And Cozy

New Zealand journey. By Fletcher Knebel. Page 21.

Kyoto: When a great Zen temple opens its doors. Page 12.

Korea's Buffer

At Panmunjom, on the frontier of tension. By Clyde Haberman. Page 22.

What's Doing... 10

Historic Yokohama 24

130

PUBLICATION: *New York Times Travel Section*
DESIGNER: *Linda Brewer*
PUBLISHER: *The New York Times*
CATEGORY: *Tabloid/Newsprint Design-Cover*
AWARD: *Merit*

The New York Times

Travel

Sunday, October 28, 1984

Section 10

SOUTH TO THE SUN

Finding the Special Caribbean

Updates from 34 islands. By Stanley Carr/ Expert advice on choice tables. By Bryan Miller/ Tranquil little Anguilla. By Barbaralee Diamonstein/ Shedding inhibitions. By Jane O'Reilly/ Discovering Belize. By Donald E. Westlake and Abby Adams/ What's Doing . . . San Juan. By Manuel Suarez. Pages 14 to 32.

London Legends

A nostalgic stroll through the city's theater district. By Benedict Nightingale Page 9.

Getting Cash on the Road 3

Practical Traveler: A growing number of automatic-teller networks make it increasingly easy to get money even when you're far from home. By Eric N. Berg

View From the Cyclist's Seat 10

A monthlong trip across the United States by bike delights the eye, challenges the muscles and nourishes the spirit. By Gwyn Ballard

A True-Life Adventure Tale 45

Five urban males, with lots of gear and even more gumption, take on the "uncanoeable" rapids of Canada's Moisie River. By Bruce Porter

131

PUBLICATION:	*New York Times Travel Section*
ART DIRECTOR:	*Linda Brewer*
DESIGNER:	*Linda Brewer*
PUBLISHER:	*The New York Times*
CATEGORY:	*Cover-Design Tabloid/Newsprint*
AWARD:	*Merit*

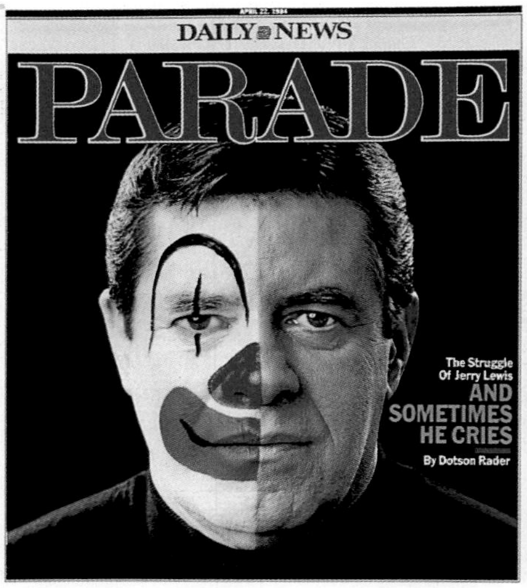

132

PUBLICATION: *Parade Magazine*
ART DIRECTOR: *Ira Yoffee*
Christopher Austopchuk
DESIGNER: *Ira Yoffee*
Christopher Austopchuk
PHOTOGRAPHER: *Eddie Adams*
PUBLISHER: *Parade Publications, Inc.*
CATEGORY: *Tabloid/Newsprint*
Cover-Design
AWARD: *Merit*

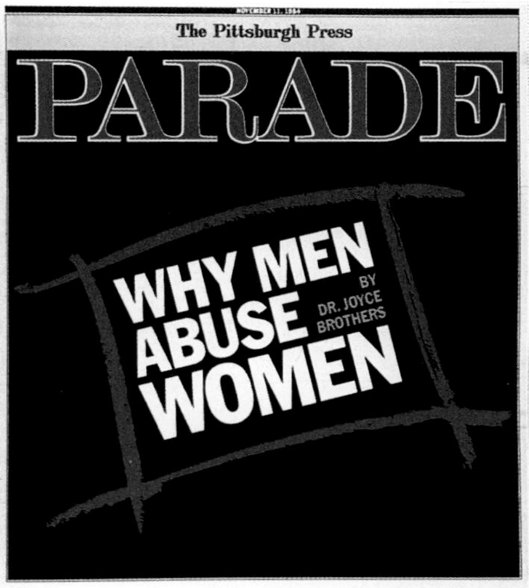

133

PUBLICATION: *Parade Magazine*
ART DIRECTOR: *Ira Yoffee*
Christopher Austopchuk
DESIGNER: *Ira Yoffee*
Christopher Austopchuk
PUBLISHER: *Parade Publications, Inc.*
CATEGORY: *Tabloid/Newsprint*
Cover- Design
AWARD: *Merit*

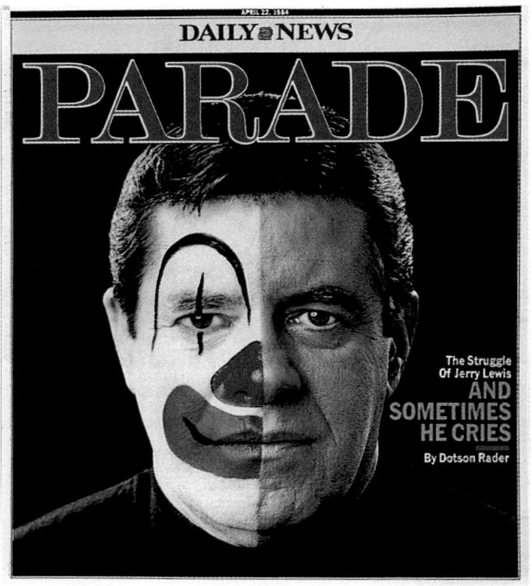

135

PUBLICATION: *Parade Magazine*
ART DIRECTOR: *Ira Yoffee*
Christopher Austopchuk
DESIGNER: *Ira Yoffee*
Christopher Austopchuk
PHOTOGRAPHER: *Eddie Adams*
PUBLISHER: *Parade Publications, Inc.*
CATEGORY: *Tabloid/Newsprint*
Cover-Photography
AWARD: *Merit*

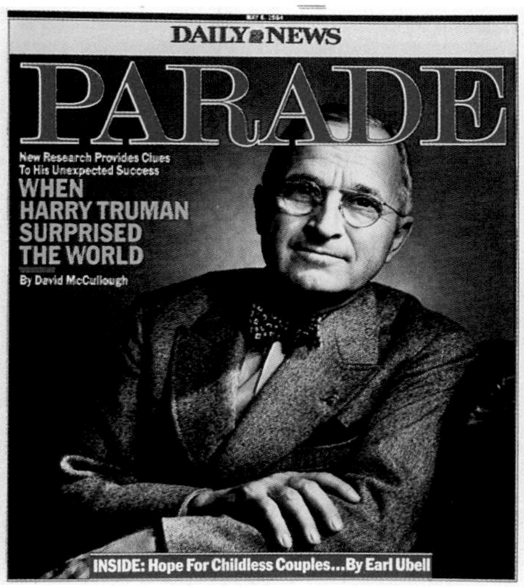

136

PUBLICATION: *Parade Magazine*
ART DIRECTOR: *Ira Yoffee*
Christopher Austopchuk
DESIGNER: *Ira Yoffee*
Christopher Austopchuk
PHOTOGRAPHER: *Yosuf Karsh*
PUBLISHER: *Parade Publications, Inc.*
CATEGORY: *Tabloid/Newsprint*
Cover-Design
AWARD: *Merit*

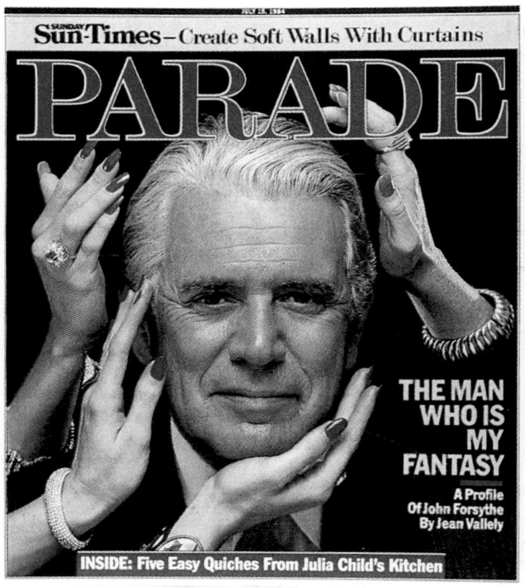

137

PUBLICATION: *Parade Magazine*
ART DIRECTOR: *Ira Yoffee*
Christopher Austopchuk
DESIGNER: *Ira Yoffee*
Christopher Austopchuk
PHOTOGRAPHER: *Eddie Adams*
PUBLISHER: *Parade Publications, Inc.*
CATEGORY: *Tabloid/Newsprint*
Cover-Design
AWARD: *Merit*

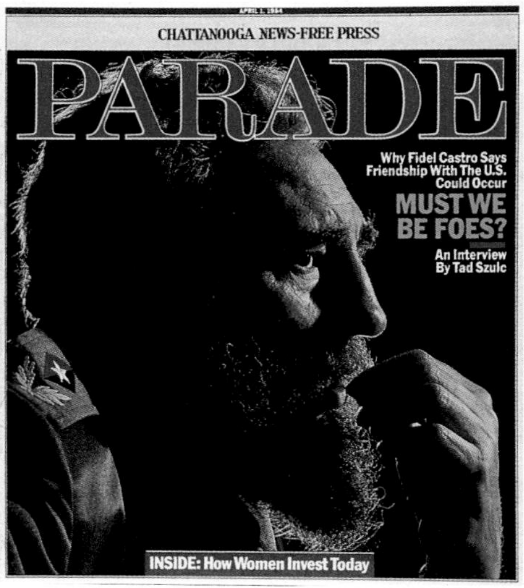

138

PUBLICATION: *Parade Magazine*
ART DIRECTOR: *Ira Yoffee*
Christopher Austopchuk
DESIGNER: *Ira Yoffee*
Christopher Austopchuk
PHOTOGRAPHER: *Eddie Adams*
PUBLISHER: *Parade Publications, Inc.*
CATEGORY: *Tabloid/Newsprint*
Cover-Design
AWARD: *Merit*

139

PUBLICATION: *Pfizer 1983 Annual Report*
Corporate Graphics, Inc.
ART DIRECTOR: *Bennett Robinson*
DESIGNER: *Jim Hatch*
PHOTOGRAPHER: *Mark Godfrey*
PUBLISHER: *Corporate Graphics, Inc.*
CATEGORY: *Annual Report*
Cover-Design
AWARD: *Merit*

140

PUBLICATION: *The Plain Dealer Magazine*
ART DIRECTOR: *Gerard A. Sealy*
DESIGNER: *Gerard A. Sealy*
ILLUSTRATOR: *Mark Anderson*
PUBLISHER: *The Plain Dealer Publishing Co.*
CATEGORY: *Cover-Design*
AWARD: *Merit*

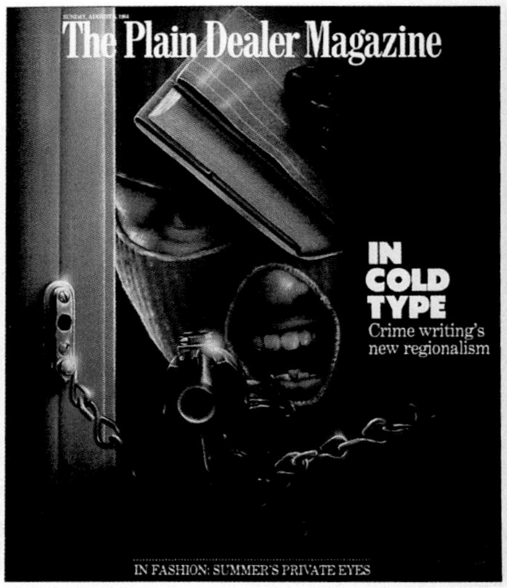

141

PUBLICATION: *The Plain Dealer Magazine*
ART DIRECTOR: *Gerard A. Sealy*
DESIGNER: *Gerard A. Sealy*
ILLUSTRATOR: *Bob Novak*
PUBLISHER: *The Plain Dealer Publishing Co.*
CATEGORY: *Cover Design*
AWARD: *Merit*

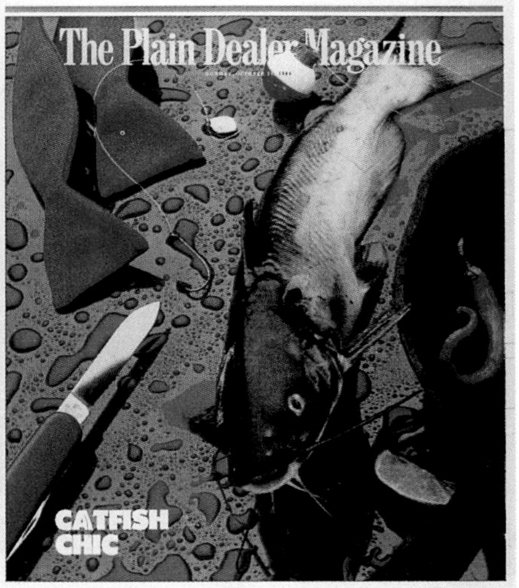

142

PUBLICATION: *The Plain Dealer Magazine*
ART DIRECTOR: *Gerard A. Sealy*
DESIGNER: *Gerard A. Sealy*
PHOTOGRAPHER: *Beth Segal*
PUBLISHER: *The Plain Dealer Publishing Co.*
CATEGORY: *Cover Design/Tabloid*
AWARD: *Merit*

143

PUBLICATION: *The Plain Dealer Magazine*
ART DIRECTOR: *Gerard A. Sealy*
DESIGNER: *Gerard A. Sealy*
ILLUSTRATOR: *Greg Spalenka*
PUBLISHER: *The Plain Dealer Publishing, Co.*
CATEGORY: *Cover Design/Tabloid*
AWARD: *Merit*

144

PUBLICATION: *The Plain Dealer Magazine*
ART DIRECTOR: *Gerard A. Sealy*
DESIGNER: *Gerard A. Sealy*
PHOTOGRAPHER: *Roman Sapecki*
PUBLISHER: *The Plain Dealer Publishing, Co.*
CATEGORY: *Tabloid/Newsprint Cover-Design*
AWARD: *Merit*

145

PUBLICATION: *The Plain Dealer Magazine*
ART DIRECTOR: *Sam Capuano*
DESIGNER: *Sam Capuano*
ILLUSTRATOR: *Richard McNeel*
PUBLISHER: *The Plain Dealer Publishing, Co.*
CATEGORY: *Cover-Design*
AWARD: *Merit*

146

PUBLICATION: *The Plain Dealer Magazine*
ART DIRECTOR: *Gerard A. Sealy*
DESIGNER: *Gerard A. Sealy*
ILLUSTRATOR: *Merle Nacht*
PUBLISHER: *The Plain Dealer Publishing, Co.*
CATEGORY: *Cover-Design*
AWARD: *Merit*

147

PUBLICATION: *Playboy Magazine*
ART DIRECTOR: *Tom Staebler*
DESIGNER: *Kerig Pope*
ILLUSTRATOR: *Wilson McLean*
PUBLISHER: *Playboy Enterprises, Inc.*
CATEGORY: *Illustration/Cover*
AWARD: *Merit*

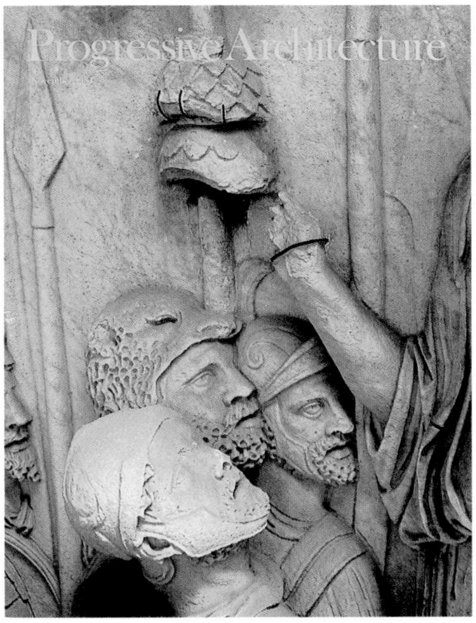

148

PUBLICATION: *Progressive Architecture*
ART DIRECTOR: *Kenneth Windsor*
DESIGNER: *Kenneth Windsor*
PHOTOGRAPHER: *Barbara Bini*
PUBLISHER: *Reinhold Publishing*
CATEGORY: *Cover-Design*
AWARD: *Merit*

148

PUBLICATION: *Progressive Architecture*
ART DIRECTOR: *Kenneth Windsor*
DESIGNER: *Kenneth Windsor*
PHOTOGRAPHER: *Masao Arai*
Shinkenchiku
PUBLISHER: *Reinhold Publishing*
CATEGORY: *Cover-Design*
AWARD: *Merit*

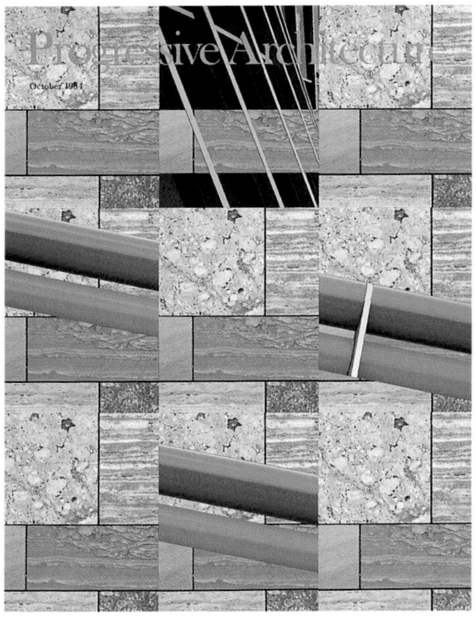

149

PUBLICATION: *Progressive Architecture*
ART DIRECTOR: *Kenneth Windsor*
DESIGNER: *Kenneth Windsor*
PHOTOGRAPHER: *Richard Bryant*
PUBLISHER: *Reinhold Publishing*
CATEGORY: *Cover-Design*
AWARD: *Merit*

150

PUBLICATION: *Progressive Architecture*
ART DIRECTOR: *Kenneth Windsor*
DESIGNER: *Kenneth Windsor*
ILLUSTRATOR: *David Scott*
PHOTOGRAPHER: *Wolfgang Hoyt @ESTO*
PUBLISHER: *Reinhold Publishing*
CATEGORY: *Cover-Design*
AWARD: *Merit*

151

PUBLICATION: *Progressive Architecture*
ART DIRECTOR: *Kenneth Windsor*
DESIGNER: *Kenneth Windsor*
PHOTOGRAPHER: *Robert Schezen*
PUBLISHER: *Reinhold Publishing*
CATEGORY: *Design-Cover*
AWARD: *Merit*

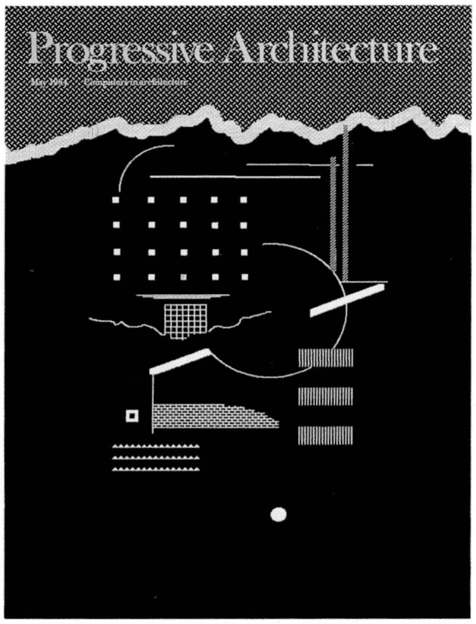

152

PUBLICATION: *Progressive Architecture*
ART DIRECTOR: *Kenneth Windsor*
DESIGNER: *Kenneth Windsor*
ILLUSTRATOR: *Kenneth Windsor*
PUBLISHER: *Reinhold Publishing*
CATEGORY: *Design-Cover*
AWARD: *Merit*

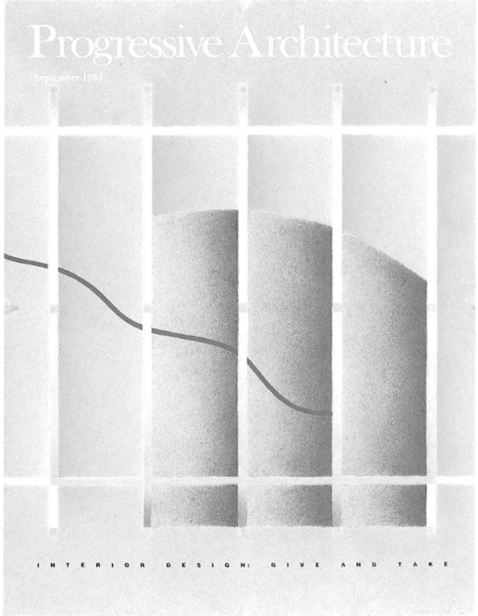

153

PUBLICATION: *Progressive Architecture*
ART DIRECTOR: *Kenneth Windsor*
DESIGNER: *Kenneth Windsor*
ILLUSTRATOR: *Kenneth Windsor*
PUBLISHER: *Reinhold Publishing*
CATEGORY: *Illustration-Cover*
AWARD: *Merit*

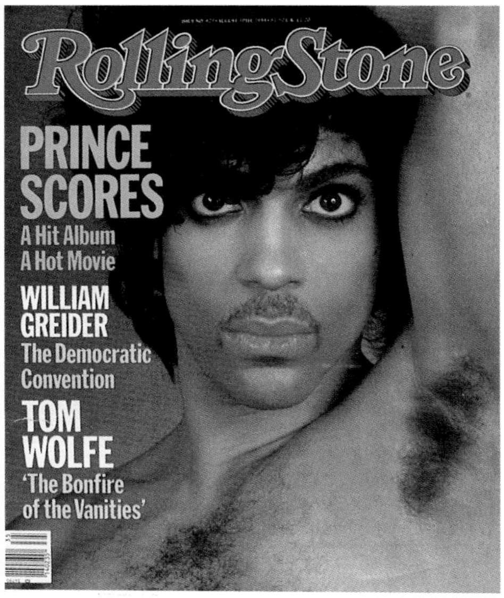

154

PUBLICATION: *Rolling Stone*
ART DIRECTOR: *Derek Ungless*
DESIGNER: *Derek Ungless*
PHOTOGRAPHER: *Laurie Kratochvil*
PUBLISHER: *Straight Arrow Publishers, Inc.*
CATEGORY: *Photography-Cover*
AWARD: *Merit*

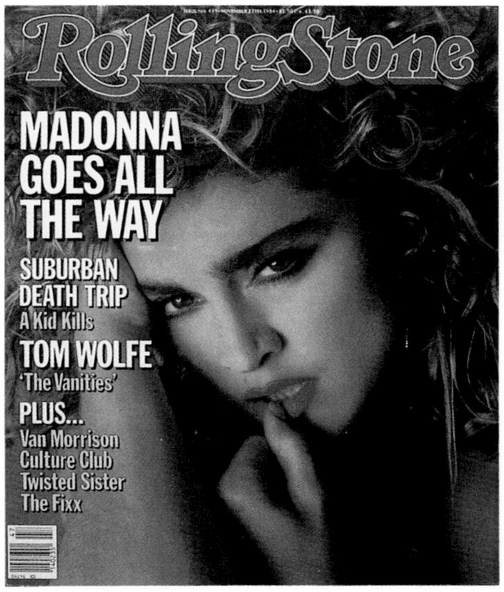

155

PUBLICATION: *Rolling Stone*
ART DIRECTOR: *Derek Ungless*
DESIGNER: *Derek Ungless*
ILLUSTRATOR: *Steven Meisel*
PHOTOGRAPHER: *Laurie Kratochvil*
PUBLISHER: *Straight Arrow Publishers, Inc.*
CATEGORY: *Photography-Cover*
AWARD: *Merit*

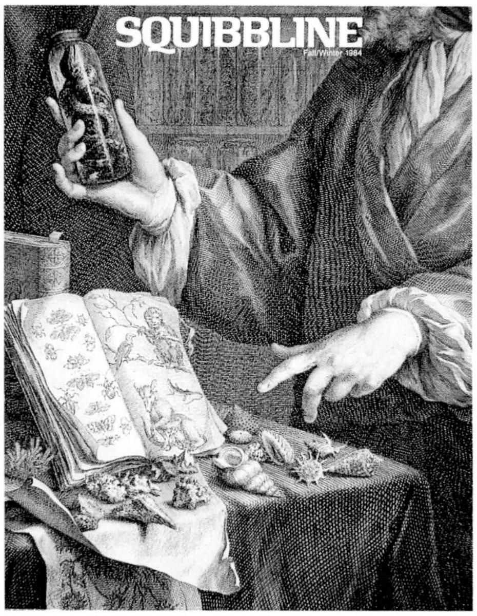

157

PUBLICATION: *Squibbline*
ART DIRECTOR: *Anthony Russell*
DESIGNER: *Mark Ulrich*
ILLUSTRATOR: *Albert Seba*
PUBLISHER: *Anthony Russell, Inc.*
CATEGORY: *Design-Cover*
AWARD: *Merit*

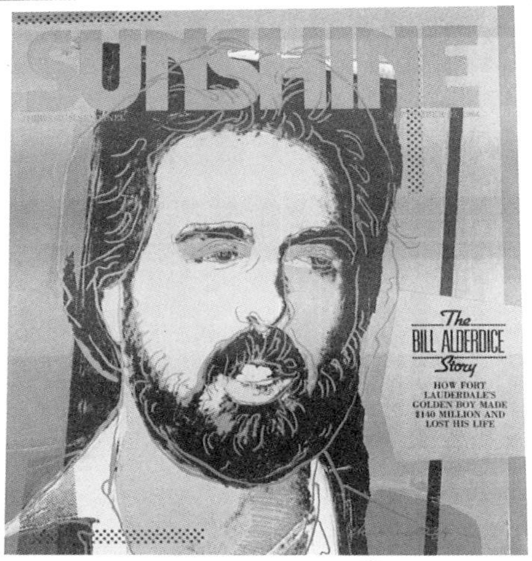

158

PUBLICATION: *Sunshine Magazine*
ART DIRECTOR: *Greg Paul*
DESIGNER: *Greg Paul*
ILLUSTRATOR: *Mark Chickinelli*
PUBLISHER: *Fort Lauderdale News & Sun-Sentinel-*
CATEGORY: *Design-Cover*
AWARD: *Merit*

159

PUBLICATION: *Small Press Magazine*
ART DIRECTOR: *Traci Churchill*
DESIGNER: *Traci Churchill*
ILLUSTRATOR: *James Grashow*
PUBLISHER: *Hansen Publishing*
CATEGORY: *Design-Cover*
AWARD: *Merit*

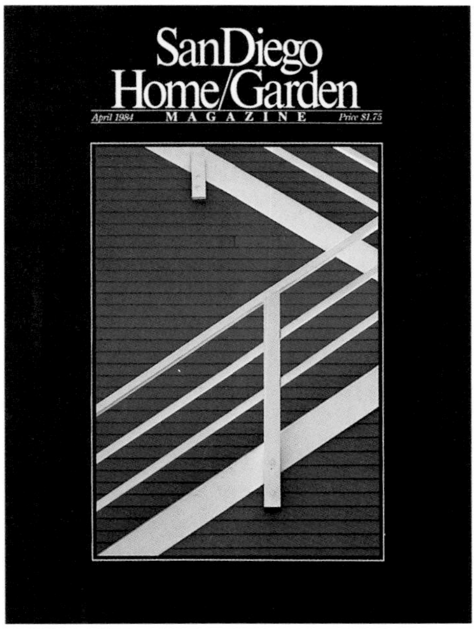

160

PUBLICATION: *San Diego Home/Garden*
ART DIRECTOR: *Fernando Manual Martinez*
DESIGNER: *Fernando Manual Martinez*
ILLUSTRATOR: *Russ Widstrand*
PUBLISHER: *San Diego Home/Garden Ltd.*
CATEGORY: *Design-Cover*
AWARD: *Merit*

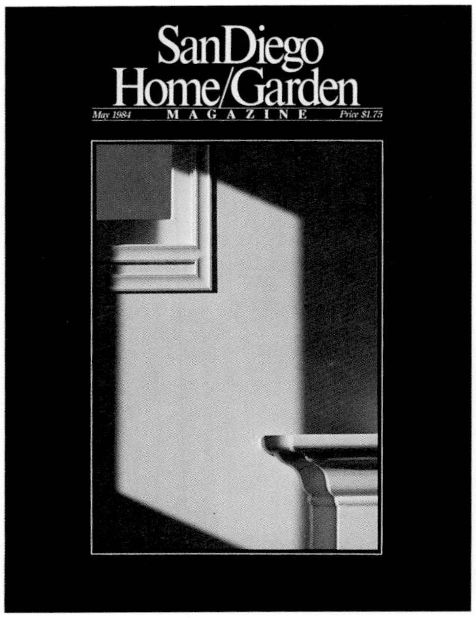

161

PUBLICATION: *San Diego Home/Garden*
ART DIRECTOR: *Fernando Manual Martinez*
DESIGNER: *Fernando Manual Martinez*
PHOTOGRAPHER: *Kimball/Nanessence*
PUBLISHER: *San Diego Home/Garden Ltd.*
CATEGORY: *Design-Cover*
AWARD: *Merit*

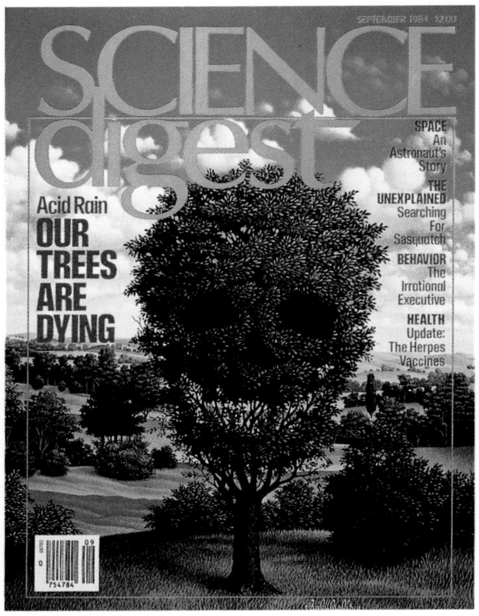

162

PUBLICATION: *Science Digest*
ART DIRECTOR: *Michael Valenti*
DESIGNER: *Michael Valenti*
ILLUSTRATOR: *Braldt Bralds*
PUBLISHER: *Hearst Corp.*
CATEGORY: *Illustration-Cover*
AWARD: *Merit*

163

PUBLICATION: *Sierra*
ART DIRECTOR: *Bill Prochnow*
DESIGNER: *Dugald Stermer*
Bill Prochnow
ILLUSTRATOR: *Dugald Stermer*
PUBLISHER: *The Sierra Club*
CATEGORY: *Illustration-Cover*
AWARD: *Merit*

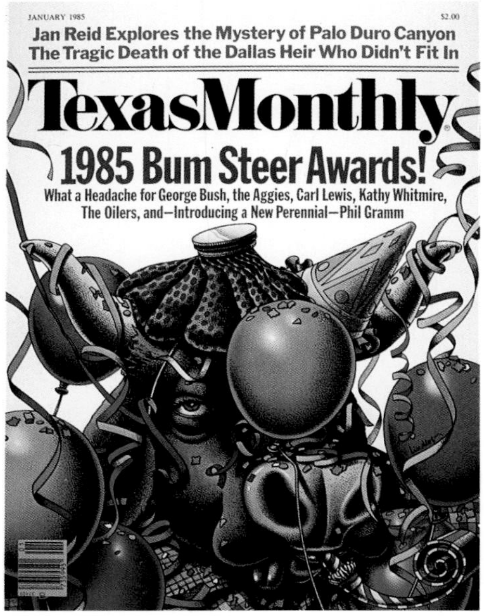

164

PUBLICATION: *Texas Monthly Magazine*
ART DIRECTOR: *Fred Woodward*
DESIGNER: *Fred Woodward*
ILLUSTRATOR: *Tom Curry*
PUBLISHER: *Texas Monthly, Inc.*
CATEGORY: *Illustration-Cover*
AWARD: *Merit*

165

PUBLICATION: *Texas Monthly Magazine*
ART DIRECTOR: *Fred Woodward*
DESIGNER: *Fred Woodward*
ILLUSTRATOR: *Dave Calver*
PUBLISHER: *Texas Monthly, Inc.*
CATEGORY: *Illustration-Cover*
AWARD: *Merit*

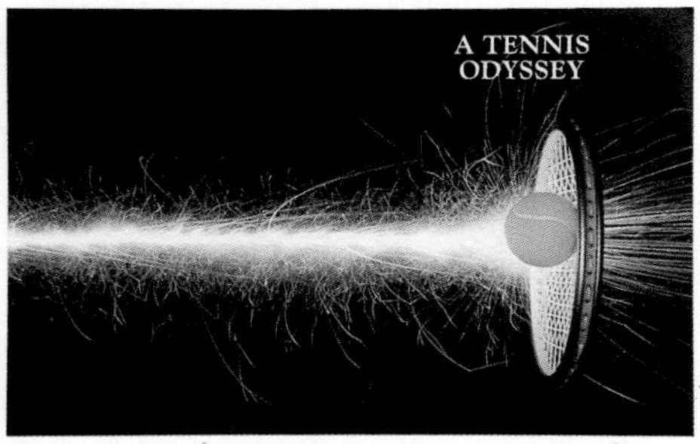

166

PUBLICATION: *A Tennis Odyssey*
ART DIRECTOR: *Jeff Babitz*
DESIGNER: *Jeff Babitz*
PHOTOGRAPHER: *Bruce Casetiss*
PUBLISHER: *Volvo/Pro Serve*
CATEGORY: *Photography-Cover*
AWARD: *Merit*

167

PUBLICATION: *Time Magazine*
ART DIRECTOR: *Rudy Hoglund*
PHOTOGRAPHER: *Gordon Munro*
PUBLISHER: *Time, Inc.*
CATEGORY: *Photography-Cover*
AWARD: *Merit*

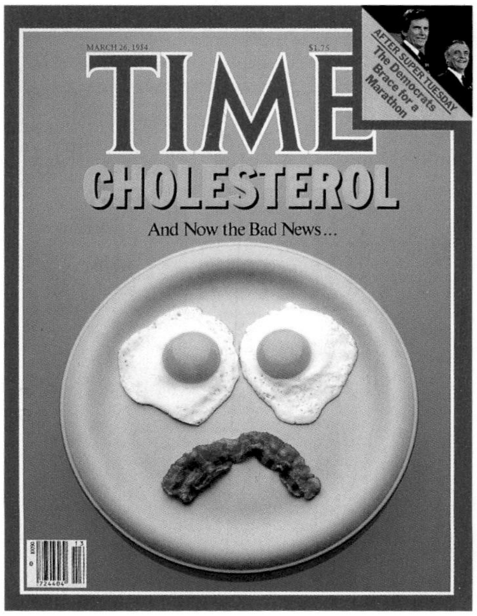

168

PUBLICATION: *Time Magazine*
ART DIRECTOR: *Rudy Hoglund*
DESIGNER: *Tom Bentkowski*
PHOTOGRAPHER: *Andrew Vnangst*
PUBLISHER: *Time, Inc.*
CATEGORY: *Design-Cover*
AWARD: *Merit*

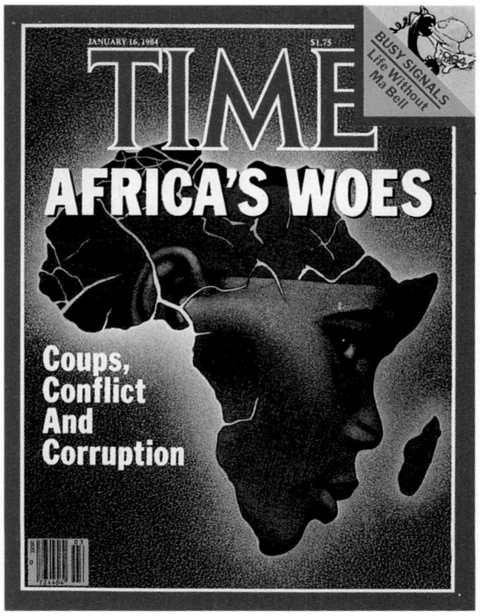

169

PUBLICATION: *Time Magazine*
ART DIRECTOR: *Rudy Hoglund*
ILLUSTRATOR: *Alex Gnidziejko*
PUBLISHER: *Time, Inc.*
CATEGORY: *Illustration-Cover*
AWARD: *Merit*

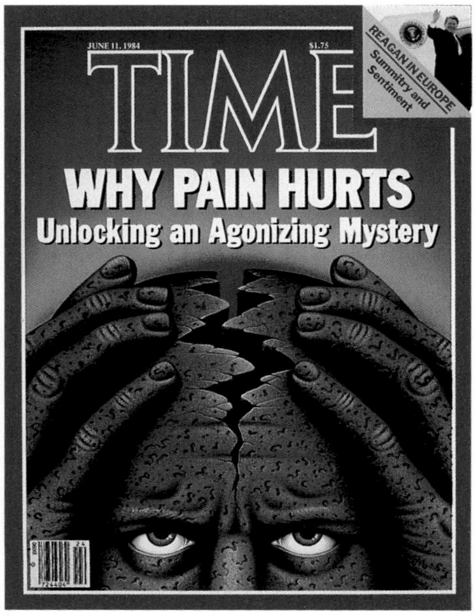

170

PUBLICATION: *Time Magazine*
ART DIRECTOR: *Rudy Hoglund*
Irene Ramp
ILLUSTRATOR: *James Marsh*
PUBLISHER: *Time, Inc.*
CATEGORY: *Illustration-Cover*
AWARD: *Merit*

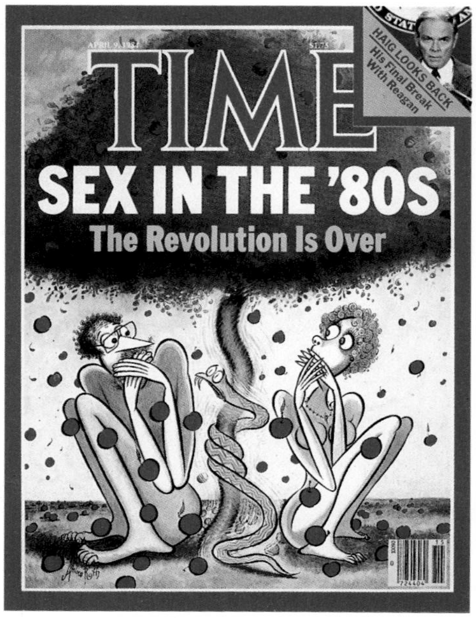

171

PUBLICATION: *Time Magazine*
ART DIRECTOR: *Rudy Hoglund*
ILLUSTRATOR: *Arnold Roth*
PUBLISHER: *Time, Inc.*
CATEGORY: *Illustration-Cover*
AWARD: *Merit*

172

PUBLICATION: *Time Magazine*
ART DIRECTOR: *Rudy Hoglund*
ILLUSTRATOR: *Gottfreid Helnwein*
PUBLISHER: *Time, Inc.*
CATEGORY: *Illustration-Cover*
AWARD: *Merit*

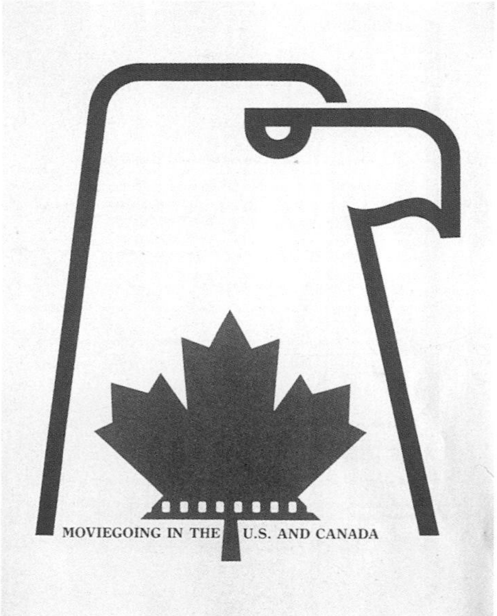

174

PUBLICATION: *Members Of The Newspaper Advertising Bureau*
ART DIRECTOR: *Tom Clemente, Lynn Anderson*
DESIGNER: *Lynn Anderson*
PUBLISHER: *Newspaper Advertising Bureau*
CATEGORY: *Design-Cover*
AWARD: *Merit*

TWENTIETH PUBLICATION DESIGN ANNUAL

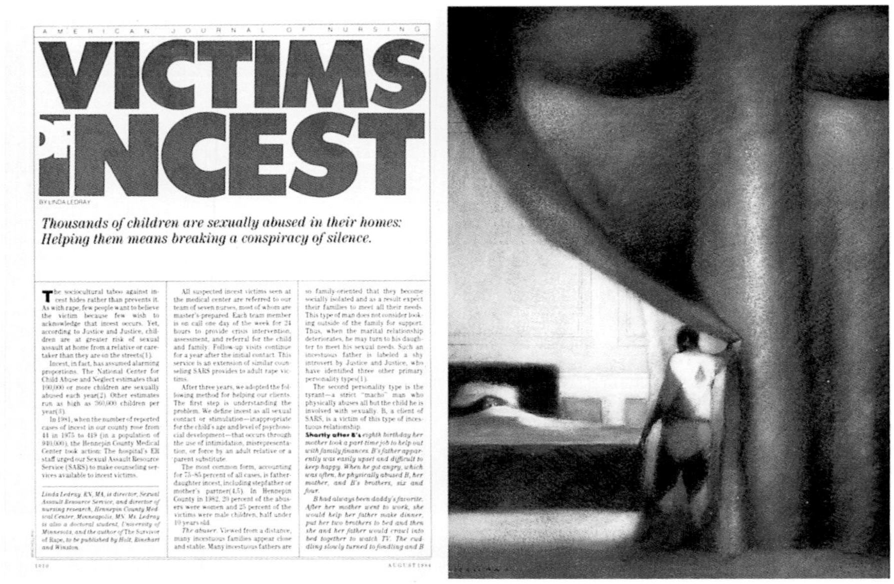

175

PUBLICATION: *American Journal of Nursing*
ART DIRECTOR: *Forbes Linkhorn*
DESIGNER: *James Ramage*
ILLUSTRATOR: *Brad Holland*
PUBLISHER: *American Journal of Nursing Co.*
CATEGORY: *Illustration-Spread*
AWARD: *Silver*

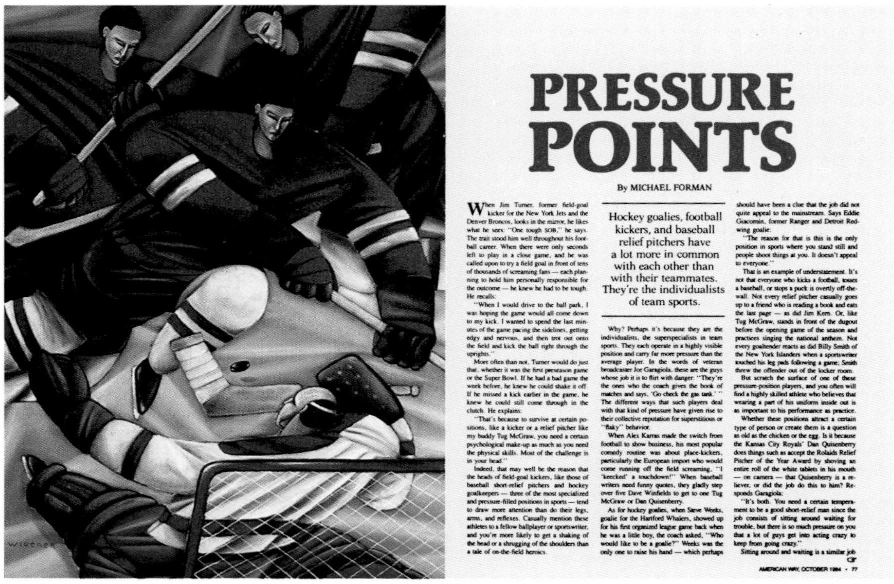

176

PUBLICATION: *American Way Magazine*
ART DIRECTOR: *Diane Marince*
Michael Fuld
ILLUSTRATOR: *Terry Widener*
PUBLISHER: *American Airlines*
CATEGORY: *Illustration-Single Page*
AWARD: *Silver*

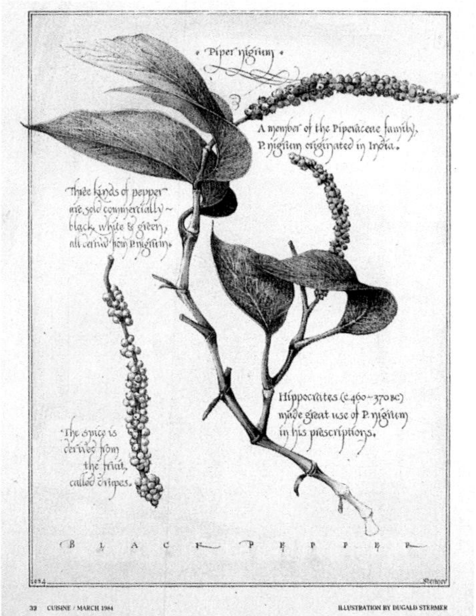

177

PUBLICATION: *Cuisine*
ART DIRECTOR: *Doug May*
DESIGNER: *Dugald Stermer*
ILLUSTRATOR: *Dugald Stermer*
PUBLISHER: *CBS Publications*
CATEGORY: *Illustration-Single Page*
AWARD: *Silver*

178

PUBLICATION: *Games Magazine*
ART DIRECTOR: *David Herbick*
DESIGNER: *David Herbick*
ILLUSTRATOR: *Alex Muranski*
PUBLISHER: *Playboy Enterprises, Inc.*
CATEGORY: *Illustration-Single Page*
AWARD: *Silver*

179

PUBLICATION: *Mademoiselle*
ART DIRECTOR: *Kati Korpijaakko*
DESIGNER: *Lynn Robb*
PHOTOGRAPHER: *Deborah Turbeville*
PUBLISHER: *Conde Nast Publications*
CATEGORY: *Photo-Single Page Spread*
AWARD: *Silver*

180

PUBLICATION: *Mother Jones Magazine*
ART DIRECTOR: *Louise Kollenbaum*
DESIGNER: *Dian-Aziza Ooka*
ILLUSTRATOR: *Brad Holland & Calligraphy by Mark Twain Behrens*
PUBLISHER: *Foundation for National Progress*
CATEGORY: *Illustration-Single Page Spread*
AWARD: *Silver*

A L L E L U I A !

UPON THE OCCASION OF THIS YEAR'S VERNAL EQUINOX, WHEN WE COMMEMorate the Mystery of the Resurrection, the most basic tenet of what is (if the word of the president of the United States is anything to go by) our state religion, it behooves each of us, Fundamentalist and un-American alike, to doff our Easter bonnets and contemplate that age-old question: Are you washed in the blood of the Lamb? the Rabbit? the Baby Chick? a Druse? a Nicaraguan? a Grenadian? What this nation, under God, needs is a good old-fashioned Christian bloodbath! Say Amen, somebody!

ILLUSTRATION BY KINUKO CRAFT

182

PUBLICATION: *National Lampoon*
ART DIRECTOR: *Michael Grossman*
DESIGNER: *Michael Grossman*
ILLUSTRATOR: *Kinuko Craft*
PUBLISHER: *Mid-America Web Press*
CATEGORY: *Illustration-Single Page Spread*
AWARD: *Silver*

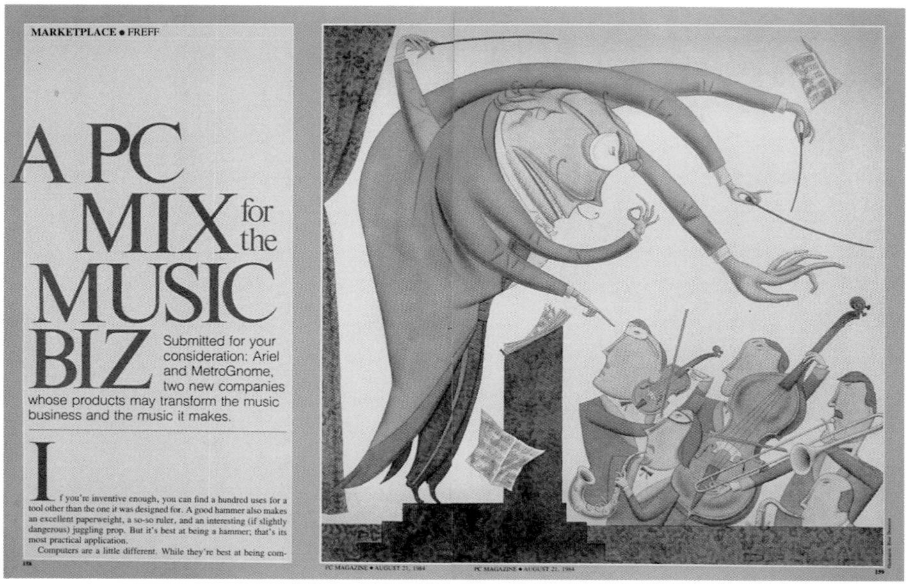

183

PUBLICATION: *PC Magazine*
ART DIRECTOR: *Mitch Shostak, Mary Zisk*
DESIGNER: *Roz Migdal*
ILLUSTRATOR: *Blair Drawson*
DIRECTOR: *Peter Blank*
PUBLISHER: *Ziff/Davis*
CATEGORY: *Illustration-Single Page Spread*
AWARD: *Silver*

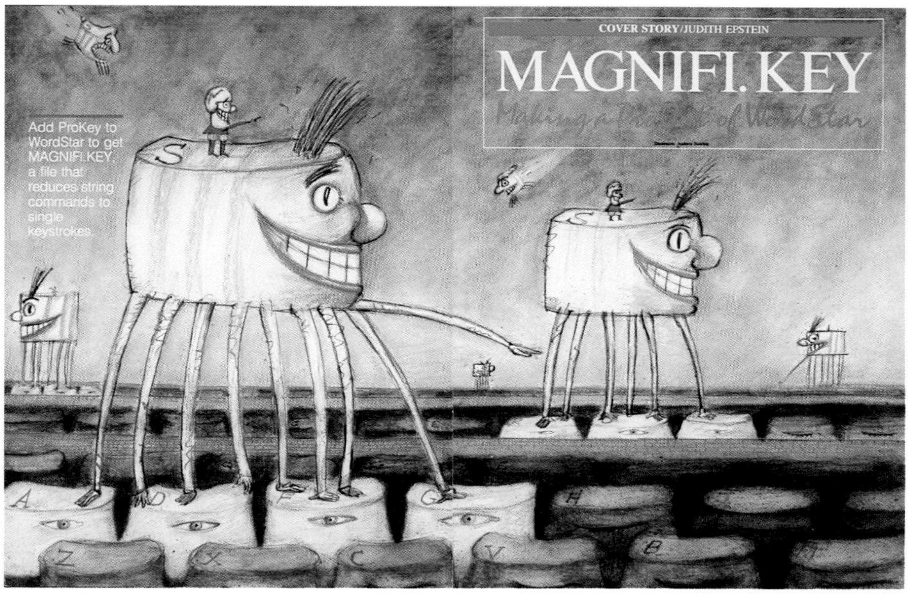

184

PUBLICATION: *PC Magazine*
ART DIRECTOR: *Mary Zisk*
DESIGNER: *Mitch Shostak*
Louise White
ILLUSTRATOR: *Andrew Shachat*
PUBLISHER: *Ziff-Davis*
CATEGORY: *Illustration-Single Page Spread*
AWARD: *Silver*

185

PUBLICATION: *Playboy Magazine*
ART DIRECTOR: *Tom Staebler*
DESIGNER: *Kerig Pope*
ILLUSTRATOR: *Blair Drawson*
PUBLISHER: *Playboy Enterprises, Inc.*
CATEGORY: *Illustration-Single Page Spread*
AWARD: *Silver*

fiction
by gabriel
garcia marquez
author of *One Hundred Years of Solitude*

THE TRAIL OF YOUR BLOOD ON THE SNOW

the roses were as radiant and fresh as the woman sleeping by his side

AT DUSK, when they reached the border, Nena Daconte realized that the finger where she wore her wedding ring was still bleeding. The *guardia civil*, a woolen blanket thrown over his patent-leather tricornered hat, examined the passports by the light of a carbide lantern while making a great effort to keep from being knocked down by the force of the wind blowing out of the Pyrenees. Although both were diplomatic passports and in order, the *guardia* lifted his lantern to make sure that the photographs matched the faces.

Nena Daconte was practically a child, with the eyes of a happy bird and molasses-colored skin that radiated Caribbean sunshine in the gloomy January dusk, and she was bundled up to her neck in a coat of ermine pelts that couldn't have been bought with the combined annual salaries of that whole border garrison. Billy Sanchez de Avila, her husband and the driver of the car, was one year younger than she and almost as beautiful and was wearing a tartan sports coat and a baseball cap. Unlike his wife, he was tall and athletic, and he had the jutting jaw of a cowardly bully. But what most obviously revealed their status was the platinum-plated car whose engine breathed like a living beast and that was like no other ever seen on that frontier of poor people. The back seat was piled high with excessively new luggage and a mound of still-unopened gifts. There was also the tenor saxophone that had been the dominant passion in Nena Daconte's life before she succumbed to the contradictory charms of her loving, tough-guy beach boy.

When the *guardia* returned their stamped passports, Billy Sanchez asked him where they could find a pharmacy to tend to his wife's finger, and the *guardia* shouted into the wind that they should ask over in Hendaye, on the French side. But the guards in Hendaye were sitting around a table in their shirt sleeves, playing cards and *(continued on page 94)*

ILLUSTRATION BY MEL ODOM

186

PUBLICATION: *Playboy Magazine*
ART DIRECTOR: *Tom Staebler*
DESIGNER: *Kerig Pope*
ILLUSTRATOR: *Mel Odom*
PUBLISHER: *Playboy Enterprises, Inc.*
CATEGORY: *Illustration Single Page Spread*
AWARD: *Silver*

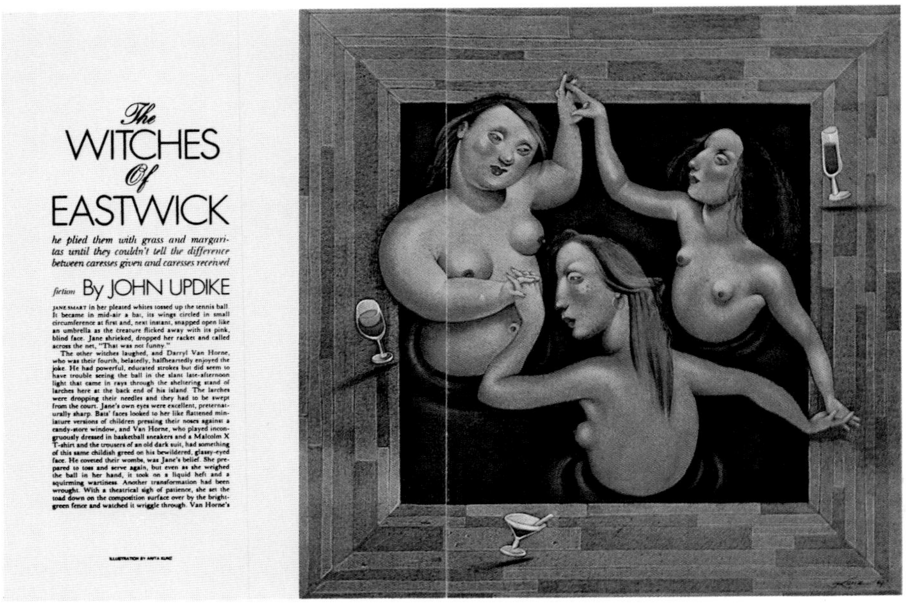

The WITCHES Of EASTWICK

he plied them with grass and margaritas until they couldn't tell the difference between caresses given and caresses received

fiction By JOHN UPDIKE

JANE SMART in her pleated whites tossed up the tennis ball. It became in mid-air a bat, its wings circled in small circumference at first and, next instant, snapped open like an umbrella as the creature flicked away with its pink, blind face. Jane shrieked, dropped her racket and called across the net, "That was not funny."

The other witches laughed, and Darryl Van Horne, who was their fourth, belatedly, halfheartedly enjoyed the joke. He had powerful, educated strokes but did seem to have trouble seeing the ball in the slant late-afternoon light that came in rays through the sheltering stand of larches here at the back end of his island. The larches were dropping their needles and they had to be swept from the court. Jane's own eyes were excellent, preternaturally sharp. Bats' faces looked to her like flattened miniature versions of children pressing their noses against a candy-store window, and Van Horne, who played incongruously dressed in basketball sneakers and a Malcolm X T-shirt and the trousers of an old dark suit, had something of this same childish greed on his bewildered, glassy-eyed face. He coveted their wombs, was Jane's belief. She prepared to toss and serve again, but even as she weighed the ball in her hand, it took on a liquid heft and a squirming wartiness. Another transformation had been wrought. With a theatrical sigh of patience, she set the toad down on the composition surface over by the bright-green fence and watched it wriggle through. Van Horne's

187

PUBLICATION: *Playboy Magazine*
ART DIRECTOR: *Tom Staebler*
DESIGNER: *Kerig Pope*
ILLUSTRATOR: *Anita Kunz*
PUBLISHER: *Playboy Enterprises, Inc.*
CATEGORY: *Illustration-Single Page Spread*
AWARD: *Silver*

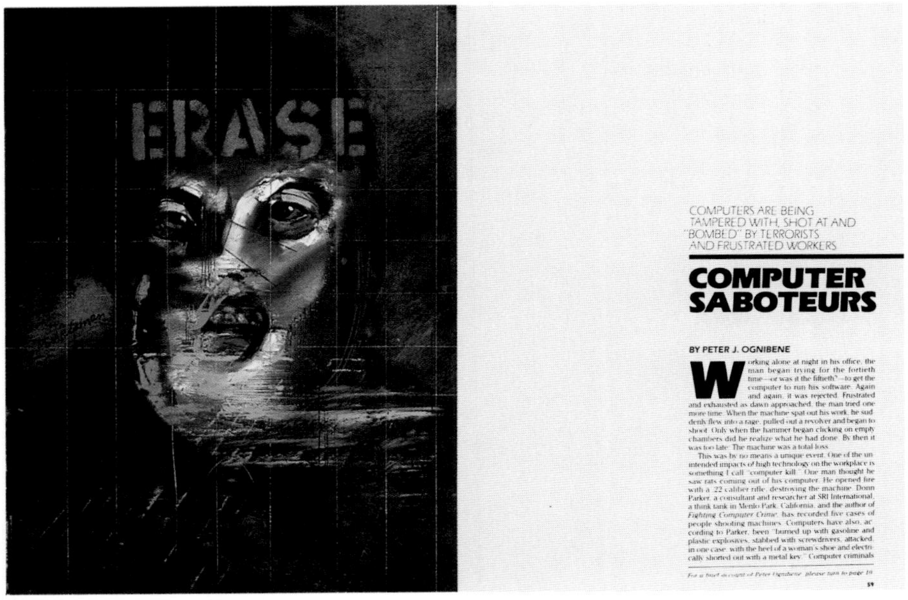

COMPUTERS ARE BEING TAMPERED WITH, SHOT AT AND "BOMBED" BY TERRORISTS AND FRUSTRATED WORKERS

COMPUTER SABOTEURS

BY PETER J. OGNIBENE

Working alone at night in his office, the man began trying for the fortieth time—or was it the fiftieth?—to get the computer to run his software. Again and again, it was rejected. Frustrated and exhausted as dawn approached, the man tried one more time. When the machine spat out his work, he suddenly flew into a rage, pulled out a revolver and began to shoot. Only when the hammer began clicking on empty chambers did he realize what he had done. By then it was too late. The machine was a total loss.

This was by no means a unique event. One of the unintended impacts of high technology on the workplace is something I call "computer kill." One man thought he saw rats coming out of his computer. He opened fire with a .22 caliber rifle, destroying the machine. Donn Parker, a consultant and researcher at SRI International, a think tank in Menlo Park, California, and the author of *Fighting Computer Crime*, has recorded five cases of people shooting machines. Computers have also, according to Parker, been "burned up with gasoline and plastic explosives, stabbed with screwdrivers, attacked, in one case, with the heel of a woman's shoe and electrically shorted out with a metal key." Computer criminals

For a brief account of Peter Ognibene, please turn to page 10

59

188

PUBLICATION: *Science Digest*
ART DIRECTOR: *Michael Valenti*
DESIGNER: *David Bayer*
ILLUSTRATOR: *Marshall Arisman*
PUBLISHER: *Hearst Corporation*
CATEGORY: *Illustration-Single Page Spread*
AWARD: *Silver*

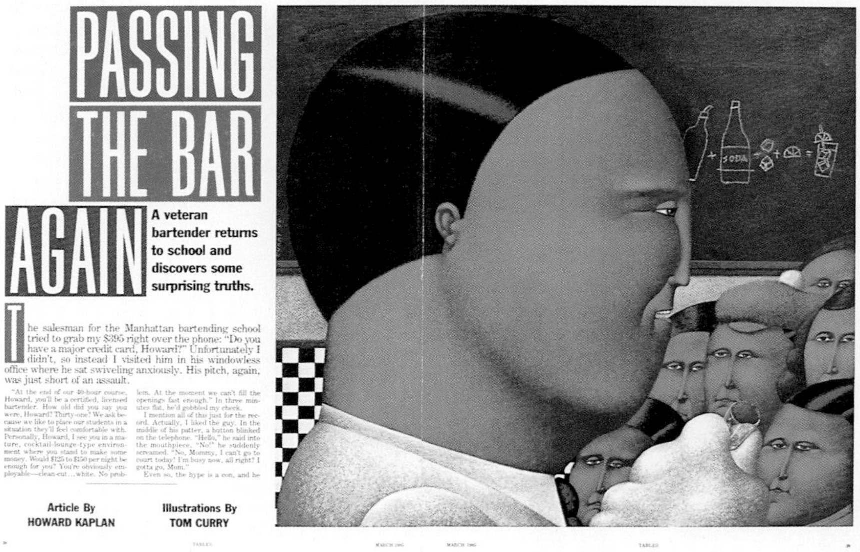

189

PUBLICATION: *Tables*
ART DIRECTOR: *Shelley Williams*
DESIGNER: *Shelley Williams*
ILLUSTRATOR: *Tom Curry*
PUBLISHER: *13•30 Corporation*
CATEGORY: *Illustration-Single Page Spread*
AWARD: *Silver*

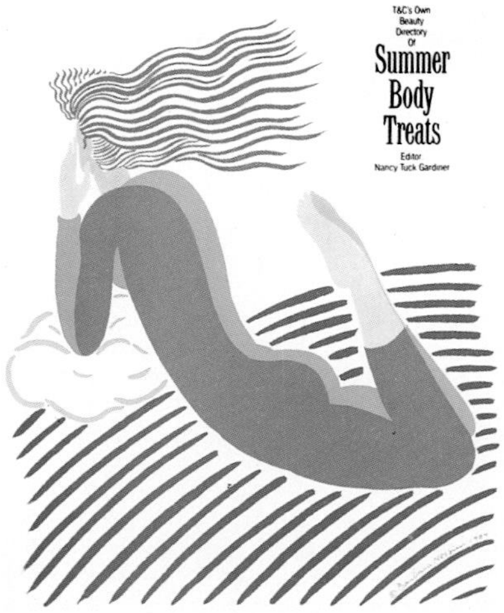

190

PUBLICATION: *Town & Country*
ART DIRECTOR: *Melissa Tardiff*
DESIGNER: *Richard Turtletaub*
ILLUSTRATOR: *Barbara Nessim*
PUBLISHER: *Hearst Corp.*
CATEGORY: *Illustration-Single Page Spread*
AWARD: *Silver*

JESSE'S HELMSMAN
Raleigh lawyer Thomas Ellis planned the strategy that established Jesse Helms as the New Right's most powerful spokesman. Now Ellis's skills are being put to the test as Helms faces his toughest reelection fight.
BY JILL ABRAMSON
47

191

PUBLICATION: *American Lawyer*
ART DIRECTOR: *John Belknap*
DESIGNER: *Zoltan Scheffer*
PUBLISHER: *Am. Law Publishing Co.*
CATEGORY: *Design-Single Page Spread*
AWARD: *Merit*

192

PUBLICATION: *Architectural Record*
ART DIRECTOR: *Alex Stillano*
DESIGNER: *Alberto Bucchianeri*
PHOTOGRAPHER: *Tomio Ohashi*
PUBLISHER: *McGraw-Hill*
CATEGORY: *Photo-Single Page Spread*
AWARD: *Merit*

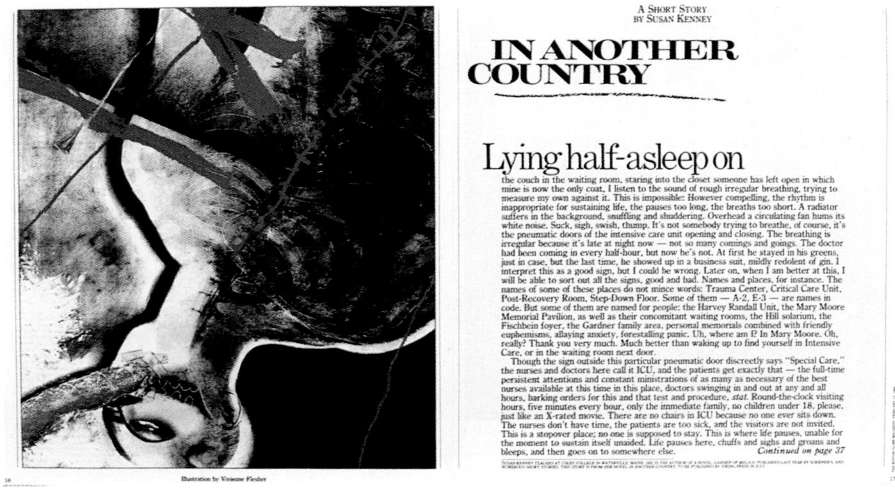

A SHORT STORY
BY SUSAN KENNEY

IN ANOTHER COUNTRY

Lying half-asleep on the couch in the waiting room, staring into the closet someone has left open in which mine is now the only coat, I listen to the sound of rough irregular breathing, trying to measure my own against it. This is impossible: However compelling, the rhythm is inappropriate for sustaining life, the pauses too long, the breaths too short. A radiator suffers in the background, snuffling and shuddering. Overhead a circulating fan hums its white noise. Suck, sigh, swish, thump. It's not somebody trying to breathe, of course, it's the pneumatic doors of the intensive care unit opening and closing. The breathing is irregular because it's late at night now — not so many comings and goings. The doctor had been coming in every half-hour, but now he's not. At first he stayed in his greens, just in case, but the last time, he showed up in a business suit, mildly redolent of gin. I interpret this as a good sign, but I could be wrong. Later on, when I am better at this, I will be able to sort out all the signs, good and bad. Names and places, for instance. The names of some of these places do not mince words: Trauma Center, Critical Care Unit, Post-Recovery Room, Step-Down Floor. Some of them — A-2, E-3 — are names in code. But some of them are named for people: the Harvey Randall Unit, the Mary Moore Memorial Pavilion, as well as their concomitant waiting rooms, the Hill solarium, the Fischbein foyer, the Gardner family area, personal memorials combined with friendly euphemisms, allaying anxiety, forestalling panic. Uh, where am I? In Mary Moore. Oh, really? Thank you very much. Much better than waking up to find yourself in Intensive Care, or in the waiting room next door.

Though the sign outside this particular pneumatic door discreetly says "Special Care," the nurses and doctors here call it ICU, and the patients get exactly that — the full-time persistent attentions and constant ministrations of as many as necessary of the best nurses available at this time in this place, doctors swinging in and out at any and all hours, barking orders for this and that test and procedure, *stat.* Round-the-clock visiting hours, five minutes every hour, only the immediate family, no children under 18, please, just like an X-rated movie. There are no chairs in ICU because no one ever sits down. The nurses don't have time, the patients are too sick, and the visitors are not invited. This is a stopover place; no one is supposed to stay. This is where life pauses, unable for the moment to sustain itself unaided. Life pauses here, chuffs and sighs and groans and bleeps, and then goes on to somewhere else. *Continued on page 37*

Illustration by Vivienne Flesher

195

PUBLICATION: *The Boston Globe Mag.*
ART DIRECTOR: *Ronn Campisi*
DESIGNER: *Ronn Campisi*
ILLUSTRATOR: *Vivienne Flesher*
PUBLISHER: *Globe Newspaper Co.*
CATEGORY: *Design-Spread*
AWARD: *Merit*

QUIRK OF FATE

A SHORT
STORY BY
CONALL RYAN

HOPELESSLY in love with me, Maddy Sullivan, the famous Maddy Sullivan, seemed on the brink of confessing it when Johnny Ray Quirk strode into the Cafe Vittoria and shot Mario "Disco" Banzetti dead under the mural of Naples.

"I'm sorry," Maddy said, "but this ruins everything."

After firing three rounds into Disco Banzetti's chest, Johnny Ray Quirk turned and surveyed the crowd for interference, eyes flat and dull as beer mug rings. Cappuccino spouts hissed. Ceiling fans hummed. For a moment, he pointed the gun at me, then ran back out across the loose ribbon of traffic on Hanover Street.

"I know that guy," I said.

"Oh, great," Maddy said.

Johnny Ray Quirk spent most nights wrapped around a pint of Guinness at the Tamo'Shanty in Dorchester, a dusty pub with plastic mugs and steel-barred windows where the consumption of liquor is augmented by a keen interest in the ponies, a passing fancy with the dogs, and a thriving market for televisions, stereo equipment, and foreign cars with low mileage and new paint jobs. The kind of place where you can shoot a game of pool and arrange to have your apartment building burned down. Our acquaintance resulted from Quirk's infatuation with a Wellesley College student who got sick of finding him on the fire escape outside her dorm room at odd hours in the morning. My boss, Joe Venice, who conducts *Continued on page 22*

Illustration by Anthony Russo

196

PUBLICATION: *The Boston Globe Mag.*
ART DIRECTOR: *Ronn Campisi*
DESIGNER: *Ronn Campisi*
ILLUSTRATOR: *Anthony Russo*
PUBLISHER: *Globe Newspaper Co.*
CATEGORY: *Design-Spread*
AWARD: *Merit*

By Don Snyder · In 1944, a Maine woman blew the whistle on two strangers. Four decades later, the story continued.
The spies who came in from the coast
On a rainy afternoon
Illustration by Doug Smith

197

PUBLICATION: *The Boston Globe Mag.*
ART DIRECTOR: *Ronn Campisi*
DESIGNER: *Ronn Campisi*
ILLUSTRATOR: *Doug Smith*
PUBLISHER: *Globe Newspaper Co.*
CATEGORY: *Design-Spread*
AWARD: *Merit*

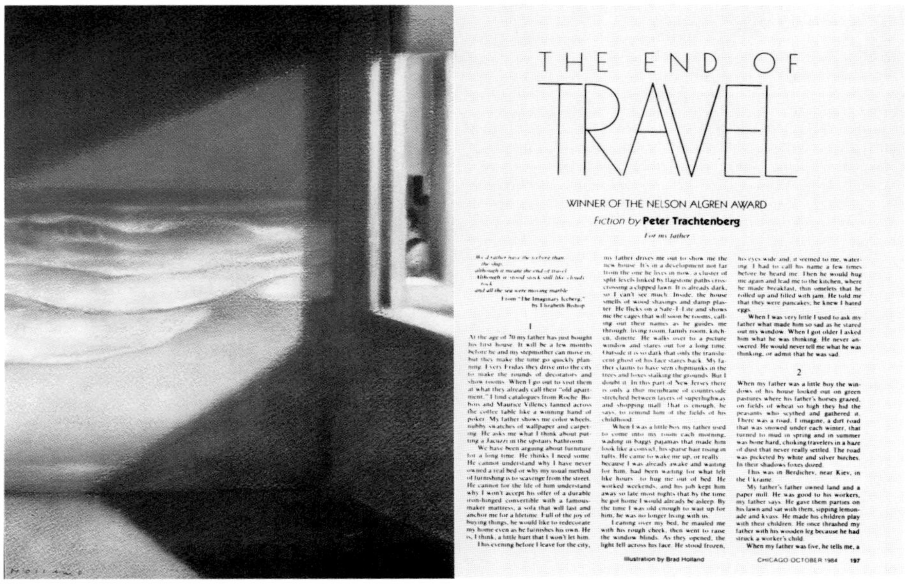
THE END OF TRAVEL
WINNER OF THE NELSON ALGREN AWARD
Fiction by Peter Trachtenberg
Illustration by Brad Holland
CHICAGO OCTOBER 1984 197

199

PUBLICATION: *Chicago*
ART DIRECTOR: *Robert J. Post*
DESIGNER: *Robert J. Post*
ILLUSTRATOR: *Brad Holland*
PUBLISHER: *WFMT, Inc.*
CATEGORY: *Illustration Spread*
AWARD: *Merit*

GALLERY
BODY PARTS AS SCULPTURE
With startling ingenuity and wondrous new materials, technologists have turned replacement surgery into a high art

200

PUBLICATION: *Discover*
ART DIRECTOR: *Eric Seidman*
DESIGNER: *Robert M. Daniels*
PHOTOGRAPHER: *Mark Godfrey*
PUBLISHER: *Time, Inc.*
CATEGORY: *Design-Single Page Spread*
AWARD: *Merit*

201

PUBLICATION: *Discover*
ART DIRECTOR: *Eric Seidman*
DESIGNER: *Robert M. Daniels*
ILLUSTRATOR: *Seymour Chwast*
PUBLISHER: *Time, Inc.*
CATEGORY: *Illustration-Single Page Spread*
AWARD: *Merit*

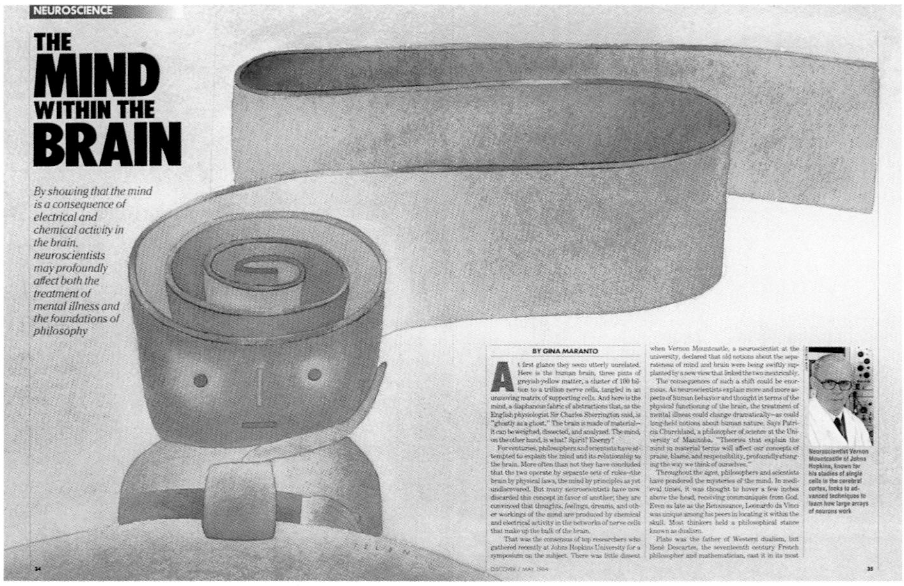

203

PUBLICATION: *Discover*
ART DIRECTOR: *Eric Seidman*
DESIGNER: *Theodore Kalomitakis*
ILLUSTRATOR: *Folon*
PUBLISHER: *Time, Inc.*
CATEGORY: *Illustration-Spread*
AWARD: *Merit*

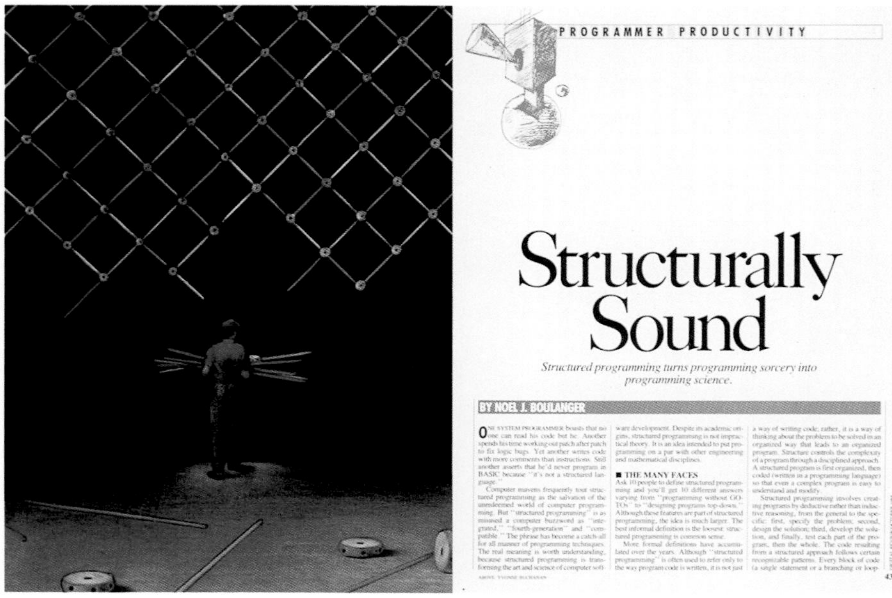

204

PUBLICATION: *Digital Review*
ART DIRECTOR: *Bill Jensen*
DESIGNER: *Bill Jensen*
ILLUSTRATOR: *Greg Spalenka*
PUBLISHER: *Ziff-Davis*
CATEGORY: *Illustration-Spread*
AWARD: *Merit*

PROGRAMMER PRODUCTIVITY
Managing the most precious computer commodity
IN THE COMPUTER BUSINESS, programmers are a hotter commodity than 256Kbit memory chips. In the end-user world, a BS in computer science is worth more than most MBAs. Proven UNIX and database gurus command salary plus equity compensation packages that would make NBA free agents proud. Companies that depend on programmers are learning to manage these special professionals and are learning that happy programmers are more productive programmers.
This month, Digital Review takes a look at three approaches to programmer productivity. First, California computerphile Shirley Brooks reports on how Silicon Valley companies find and keep good programmers. Next, Noel Boulanger searches for the significance behind the sound and fury of "structured programming." Our last article investigates the most radical, and hence most controversial, approach to working in the computer age—staying home. "Telecommuting" will change corporate, city and social structures. Now is the time to see where you fit in.
Illustrations by Greg Spalenka
34
35

205

PUBLICATION: *Digital Review*
ART DIRECTOR: *Bill Jensen*
DESIGNER: *Bill Jensen*
ILLUSTRATOR: *Greg Spalenka*
PUBLISHER: *Ziff-Davis*
CATEGORY: *Illustration-Spread*
AWARD: *Merit*

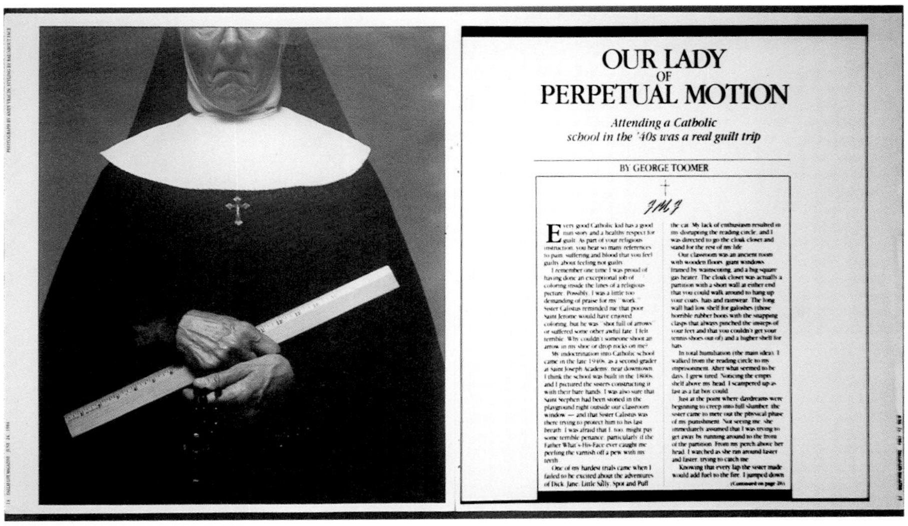

206

PUBLICATION: *Dallas Life Magazine*
ART DIRECTOR: *Ginny Pitre*
DESIGNER: *Tom Zielinski*
PHOTOGRAPHER: *Andy Vracin*
PUBLISHER: *The Dallas Morning News*
CATEGORY: *Design-Spread*
AWARD: *Merit*

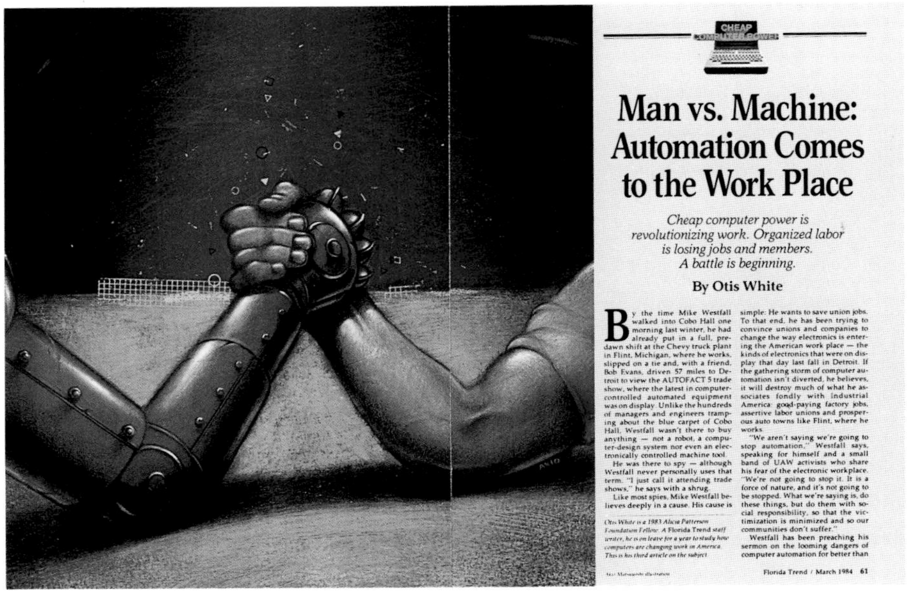

CHEAP COMPUTER POWER
Man vs. Machine: Automation Comes to the Work Place
Cheap computer power is revolutionizing work. Organized labor is losing jobs and members. A battle is beginning.
By Otis White
By the time Mike Westfall walked into Cobo Hall one morning last winter, he had already put in a full, pre-dawn shift at the Chevy truck plant in Flint, Michigan, where he works, slipped on a tie and, with a friend, Bob Evans, driven 57 miles to Detroit to view the AUTOFACT 5 trade show, where the latest in computer-controlled automated equipment was on display. Unlike the hundreds of managers and engineers tramping about the blue carpet of Cobo Hall, Westfall wasn't there to buy anything — not a robot, a computer-design system nor even an electronically controlled machine tool.
He was there to spy — although Westfall never personally uses that term. "I just call it attending trade shows," he says with a shrug.
Like most spies, Mike Westfall believes deeply in a cause. His cause is simple: He wants to save union jobs. To that end, he has been trying to convince unions and companies to change the way electronics is entering the American work place — the kinds of electronics that were on display that day last fall in Detroit. If the gathering storm of computer automation isn't diverted, he believes, it will destroy much of what he associates fondly with industrial America: good-paying factory jobs, assertive labor unions and prosperous auto towns like Flint, where he works.
"We aren't saying we're going to stop automation," Westfall says, speaking for himself and a small band of UAW activists who share his fear of the electronic workplace. "We're not going to stop it. It is a force of nature, and it's not going to be stopped. What we're saying is, do these things, but do them with social responsibility, so that the victimization is minimized and so our communities don't suffer."
Westfall has been preaching his sermon on the looming dangers of computer automation for better than
Otis White is a 1983 Alicia Patterson Foundation Fellow. A Florida Trend staff writer, he is on leave for a year to study how computers are changing work in America. This is his third article on the subject.
Florida Trend / March 1984 61

207

PUBLICATION: *Florida Trend*
ART DIRECTOR: *Steve Duckett*
DESIGNER: *Steve Duckett*
ILLUSTRATOR: *Akio Matsuyoshi*
PUBLISHER: *Florida Trend, Inc.*
CATEGORY: *Illustration-Cover*
AWARD: *Merit*

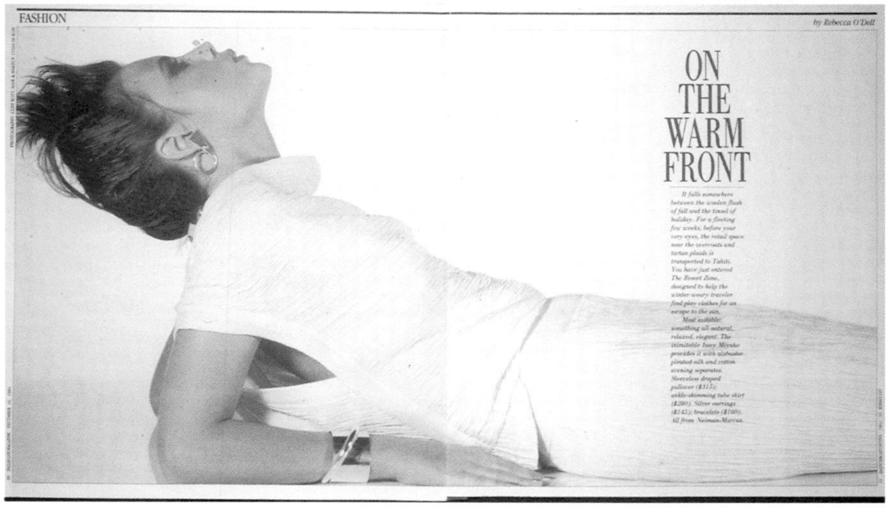

208

PUBLICATION: *Dallas Life Magazine*
ART DIRECTOR: *Ginny Pitre*
DESIGNER: *Ginny Pitre*
PHOTOGRAPHER: *Cliff Bott*
PUBLISHER: *The Dallas Morning News*
CATEGORY: *Design-Spread*
AWARD: *Merit*

209

PUBLICATION: *Esquire Magazine*
ART DIRECTOR: *April Silver*
DESIGNER: *John Miller*
ILLUSTRATOR: *Wolf Erlbruch*
PUBLISHER: *Esquire Associates*
CATEGORY: *Illustration-Spread*
AWARD: *Merit*

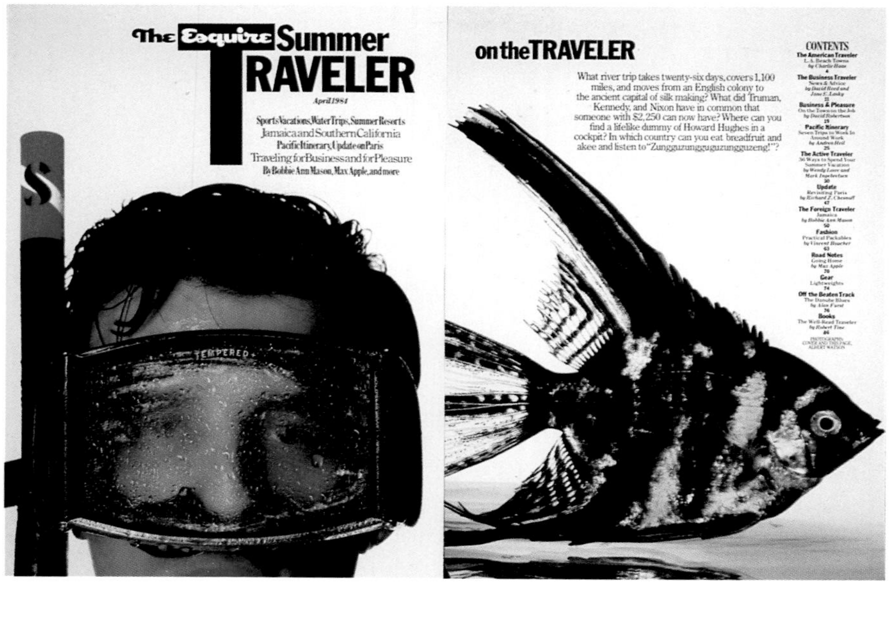

210

PUBLICATION: *Esquire Magazine*
ART DIRECTOR: *April Silver*
DESIGNER: *April Silver*
PHOTOGRAPHER: *Albert Watson*
PUBLISHER: *Esquire Associates*
CATEGORY: *Photography-Spread*
AWARD: *Merit*

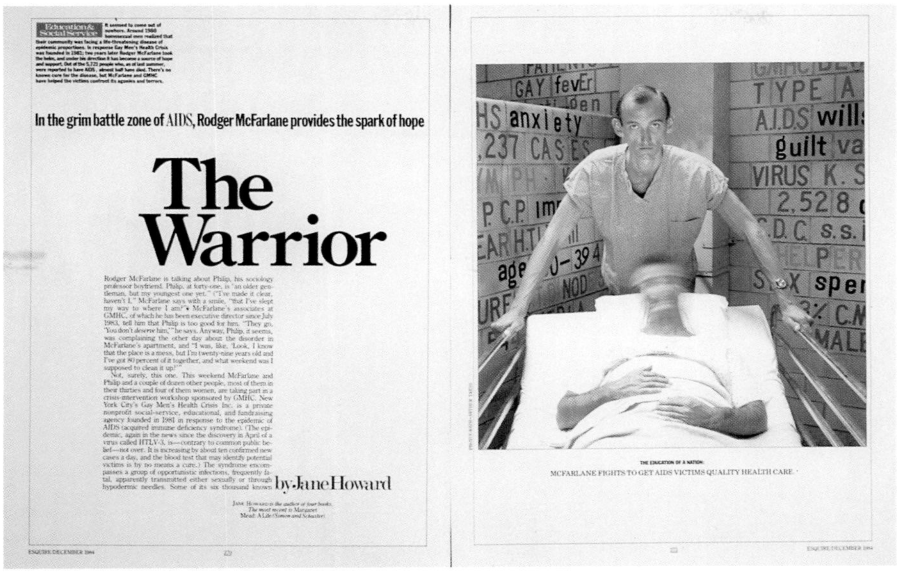

211

PUBLICATION: *Esquire Magazine*
ART DIRECTOR: *April Silver*
DESIGNER: *Bruce Ramsay*
PHOTOGRAPHER: *Arthur Tress*
PUBLISHER: *Esquire Associates*
CATEGORY: *Photography-Spread*
AWARD: *Merit*

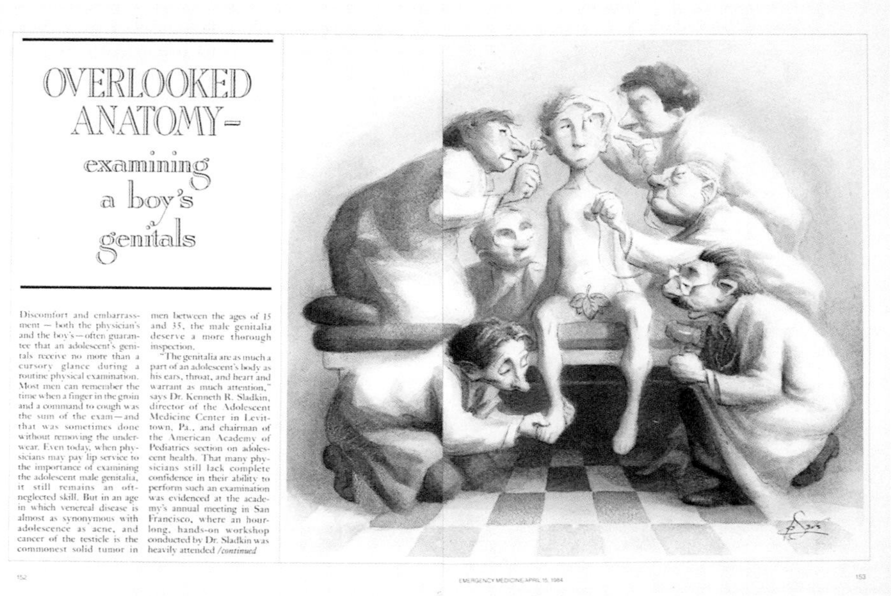

212

PUBLICATION: *Emergency Medicine*
ART DIRECTOR: *James T. Walsh*
DESIGNER: *James T. Walsh*
ILLUSTRATOR: *Peter de Séve*
PUBLISHER: *Cahners Publishing Co.*
CATEGORY: *Illustration-Spread*
AWARD: *Merit*

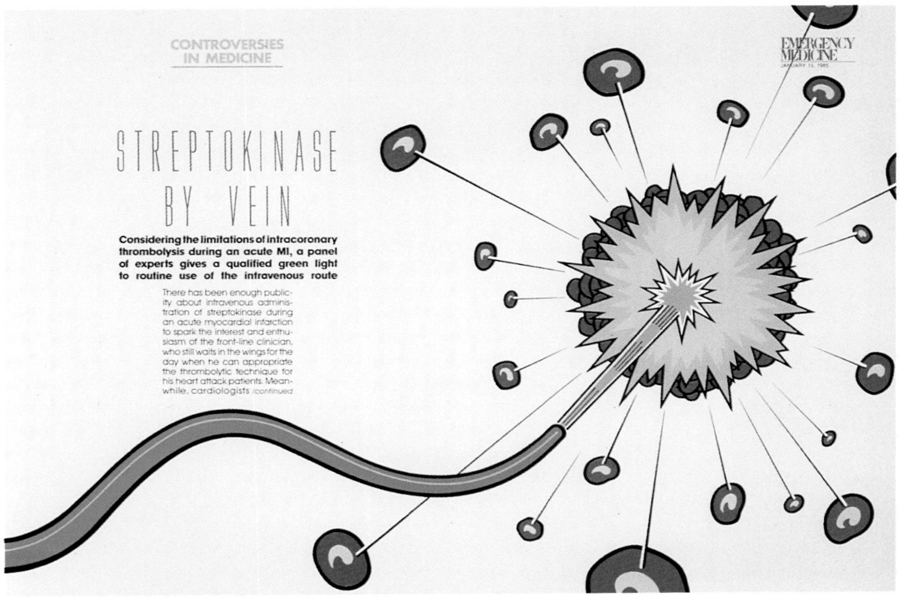

213

PUBLICATION: *Emergency Medicine*
ART DIRECTOR: *James T. Walsh*
DESIGNER: *Kerin Quigley*
ILLUSTRATOR: *David Coulson*
PUBLISHER: *Cahners Publishing Co.*
CATEGORY: *Design-Spread*
AWARD: *Merit*

On managing the febrile child

By Michael Levi, M.D.

A soaring temperature as the sole complaint is hardly uncommon and usually not much cause for concern—except in three specific illnesses

Probably the most common problem seen in the emergency room and the pediatrician's office is the child with high fever as the sole complaint. High fever in children is a very important problem and it's certainly not a new one; it's been around as long as children have. Recent reports notwithstanding, the vast majority of these children have benign illnesses, either viral or focal bacterial infections. There are a few children with high fever, however, who have life-threatening illnesses, including meningitis, sepsis, and pneumonia.

Body temperature is the result of an equilibrium between heat production, which is largely the by-product of metabolic activity in striated muscle in the awake child, and heat loss, much of which occurs at the body's surface. This equilibrium is monitored in the anterior hypothalamus by a "thermostat" that controls several physiologic mechanisms. To raise body temperature, the thermostat can increase metabolic activity by causing shivering—which is really just a marked increase in muscle contraction—or it can conserve heat by promoting peripheral vasoconstriction. To lower body temperature the thermostat can cause peripheral vasodilation, which increases the blood supply to the periphery and thereby increases heat loss. In addition, it can cause sweating and panting, both of which dissipate heat.

In general, the thermostat keeps the body temperature under tight control—though it doesn't, of course, keep it fixed at 98.6 °F. Body temperature normally shows a diurnal variation: the low point generally occurs sometime in the early morning and the high point in the late afternoon. The swing is much wider in children than in adults—generally between 98 and 100.4 °F. When you see a feverish child, it's important to warn parents about this temperature variation, especially if you see the child in the morning, because whatever fever he has then is likely to go higher in the afternoon, even with an-

continued

166

EMERGENCY MEDICINE / FEBRUARY 15, 1984 167

214

PUBLICATION: *Emergency Medicine*
ART DIRECTOR: *Jim Walsh*
DESIGNER: *Jim Walsh/Kerin Quigley*
ILLUSTRATOR: *Paul Yalowitz*
PUBLISHER: *Cahners Publishing Co.*
CATEGORY: *Illustration-Spread*
AWARD: *Merit*

When It Comes to Buying a Bank, Anyone Goes

First, Colombian wheeler-dealer Alberto Duque bought City National. Then, regulators stood by as two of his associates made a move to take over Florida's biggest bank.

By Penny Lernoux

Much research and money have gone into the science of bank security, yet some of the biggest robberies are committed by men armed only with a smile.

They get away with the money because slack management, greed for profits and corner-cutting encourage bank executives to deal with questionable customers. The bankers at first receive small, then increasingly larger gifts in thinly disguised kickbacks; the kickbacks lead to questionable loans and eventually to bank fraud.

That is the story of the Outrigger scandal in Miami in which Citibank and Chase Manhattan were stung for $20.3 million by con men connected to organized crime. Chase was robbed because it was so eager to drum up business that it failed to enforce internal regulations for loans, as in the Drysdale and Penn Square cases. For its part, Citibank did not inquire into the ethics or professional background of the people it employed — and paid through the nose for that omission.

Outrigger is the name of a luxurious condominium in North Miami begun in 1971 but never finished. One of its promoters had excellent contacts with Citibank, which suggested he seek financing for the Outrigger project from Miami National Bank in which Citibank owned stock. Miami National had previously been controlled by a henchman of Meyer Lansky, for many years the financial genius of organized crime, and thanks to these Mob connections the bank remained in excellent financial health. However, the bank's then-holding company, Data Lease Financial Corp., ran into difficulties and had to forfeit Miami National to Citibank in 1975 as collateral for an unpaid loan.

During Miami National's association with Outrigger, the Citibank subsidiary was stung for $2.8 million. A Justice Department Organized Crime Strike Force found that the bank had exceeded its legal lending limits by at least $600,000 in loans to Outrigger and its shareholders. Bank officials were charged with doctoring Miami National's annual report by under-reporting losses, "thus grossly misstating the true financial condition" of the bank.

Among those involved in the Outrigger project was Florida real estate promoter Robert Marlin. His now defunct L&C Construction Co. was the general contractor for Outrigger, and when an insurance company turned it down for a performance bond, Marlin went to Miami National Bank. According to the Justice Department, Miami National agreed to underwrite a $2.3 million guarantee for L&C, thereby further exposing the bank to demands by Outrigger promoters who could have filed claims from Miami National had L&C failed to perform. (Because of the risk involved, banks normally do not provide such guarantees for construction companies.) At the time Marlin was a member of the bank's board of directors and its loan committee. Although the Comptroller of the Currency ruled that Miami National did not have the authority to sign the underwriting agreement, Truman Skinner, the bank's lawyer, who was later indicted, ordered a vice president to authorize it. Skinner did not disclose his potential conflict of interest as director of Viking General, L&C's parent company, nor did anyone at the bank think to question why it was signing an

From the book In Banks We Trust, *by Penny Lernoux. Copyright 1984 by Penny Lernoux. Published by Doubleday & Co. Inc. Lernoux is an award-winning reporter whose work has appeared in* The Atlantic, Newsweek *and* Business Week.

Gary Kelley Illustrations

Florida Trend / April 1984 159

215

PUBLICATION: *Florida Trend*
ART DIRECTOR: *Steve Duckett*
DESIGNER: *Gary Bernloihr*
ILLUSTRATOR: *Gary Kelley*
PUBLISHER: *Florida Trend, Inc.*
CATEGORY: *Illustration-Spread*
AWARD: *Merit*

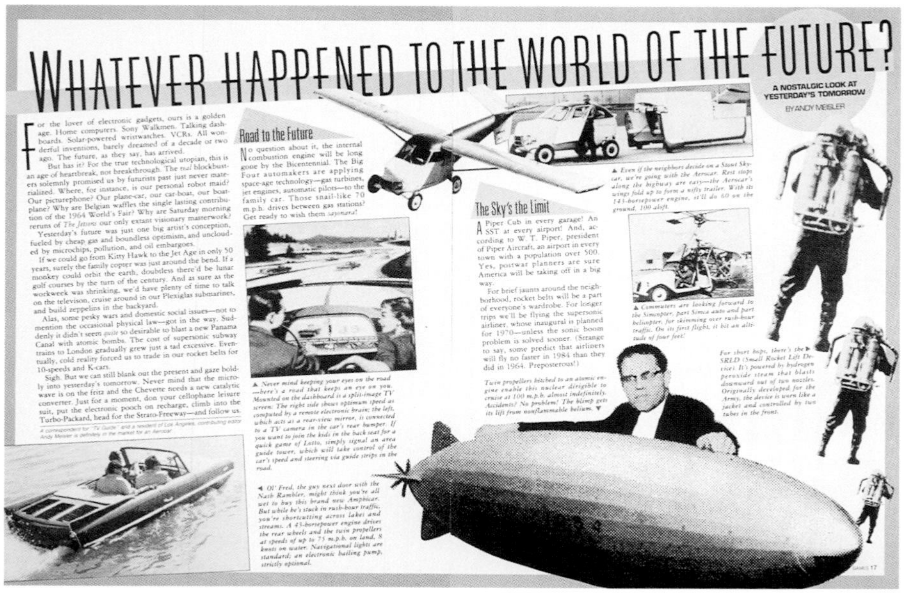

WHATEVER HAPPENED TO THE WORLD OF THE FUTURE?

A NOSTALGIC LOOK AT YESTERDAY'S TOMORROW

BY ANDY MEISLER

For the lover of electronic gadgets, ours is a golden age. Home computers. Sony Walkmen. Talking dashboards. Solar-powered wristwatches. VCRs. All wonderful inventions, barely dreamed of a decade or two ago. The future, as they say, has arrived.

But has it? For the true technological utopian, this is an age of heartbreak, not breakthrough. The *real* blockbusters solemnly promised us by futurists past just never materialized. Where, for instance, is our personal robot maid? Our picturephone? Our plane-car, our car-boat, our boat-plane? Why are Belgian waffles the single lasting contribution of the 1964 World's Fair? Why are Saturday morning reruns of *The Jetsons* our only extant visionary masterwork?

Yesterday's future was just one big artist's conception, fueled by cheap gas and boundless optimism, and unclouded by microchips, pollution, and oil embargoes.

If we could go from Kitty Hawk to the Jet Age in only 50 years, surely the family copter was just around the bend. If a monkey could orbit the earth, doubtless there'd be lunar golf courses by the turn of the century. And as sure as the workweek was shrinking, we'd have plenty of time to talk on the televison, cruise around in our Plexiglas submarines, and build zeppelins in the backyard.

Alas, some pesky wars and domestic social issues—not to mention the occasional physical law—got in the way. Suddenly it didn't seem *quite* so desirable to blast a new Panama Canal with atomic bombs. The cost of supersonic subway trains to London gradually grew just a tad excessive. Eventually, cold reality forced us to trade in our rocket belts for 10-speeds and K-cars.

Sigh. But we can still blank out the present and gaze boldly into yesterday's tomorrow. Never mind that the microwave is on the fritz and the Chevette needs a new catalytic converter. Just for a moment, don your cellophane leisure suit, put the electronic pooch on recharge, climb into the Turbo-Packard, head for the Strato-Freeway—and follow us.

A correspondent for "TV Guide" and a resident of Los Angeles, contributing editor Andy Meisler is definitely in the market for an Aerocar.

Road to the Future

No question about it, the internal combustion engine will be long gone by the Bicentennial. The Big Four automakers are applying space-age technology—gas turbines, jet engines, automatic pilots—to the family car. Those snail-like 70 m.p.h. drives between gas stations? Get ready to wish them *sayonara!*

▲ *Never mind keeping your eyes on the road—here's a road that keeps an eye on you. Mounted on the dashboard is a split-image TV screen: The right side shows optimum speed as computed by a remote electronic brain; the left, which acts as a rear-view mirror, is connected to a TV camera in the car's rear bumper. If you want to join the kids in the back seat for a quick game of Lotto, simply signal an area guide tower, which will take control of the car's speed and steering via guide strips in the road.*

◀ *Ol' Fred, the guy next door with the Nash Rambler, might think you're all wet to buy this brand new Amphicar. But while he's stuck in rush-hour traffic, you're shortcutting across lakes and streams. A 43-horsepower engine drives the rear wheels and the twin propellers at speeds of up to 75 m.p.h. on land, 8 knots on water. Navigational lights are standard; an electronic bailing pump, strictly optional.*

The Sky's the Limit

A Piper Cub in every garage! An SST at every airport! And, according to W. T. Piper, president of Piper Aircraft, an airport in every town with a population over 500. Yes, postwar planners are sure America will be taking off in a big way.

For brief jaunts around the neighborhood, rocket belts will be a part of everyone's wardrobe. For longer trips we'll be flying the supersonic airliner, whose inaugural is planned for 1970—unless the sonic boom problem is solved sooner. (Strange to say, some predict that airliners will fly no faster in 1984 than they did in 1964. Preposterous!)

Twin propellers hitched to an atomic engine enable this nuclear dirigible to cruise at 100 m.p.h. almost indefinitely. Accidents? No problem! The blimp gets its lift from nonflammable helium. ▼

▲ *Even if the neighbors decide on a Stout Skycar, we're going with the Aerocar. Rest stops along the highway are easy—the Aerocar's wings fold up to form a nifty trailer. With its 143-horsepower engine, it'll do 60 on the ground, 100 aloft.*

▲ *Commuters are looking forward to the Simcopter, part Simca auto and part helicopter, for skimming over rush-hour traffic. On its first flight, it hit an altitude of four feet!*

For short hops, there's the ▶ *SRLD (Small Rocket Lift Device). It's powered by hydrogen peroxide steam that blasts downward out of two nozzles. Originally developed for the Army, the device is worn like a jacket and controlled by two tubes in the front.*

216

PUBLICATION: *Games Magazine*
ART DIRECTOR: *Barry Simon*
DESIGNER: *Barry Simon*
PUBLISHER: *Playboy Enterprises, Inc.*
CATEGORY: *Design-Spread*
AWARD: *Merit*

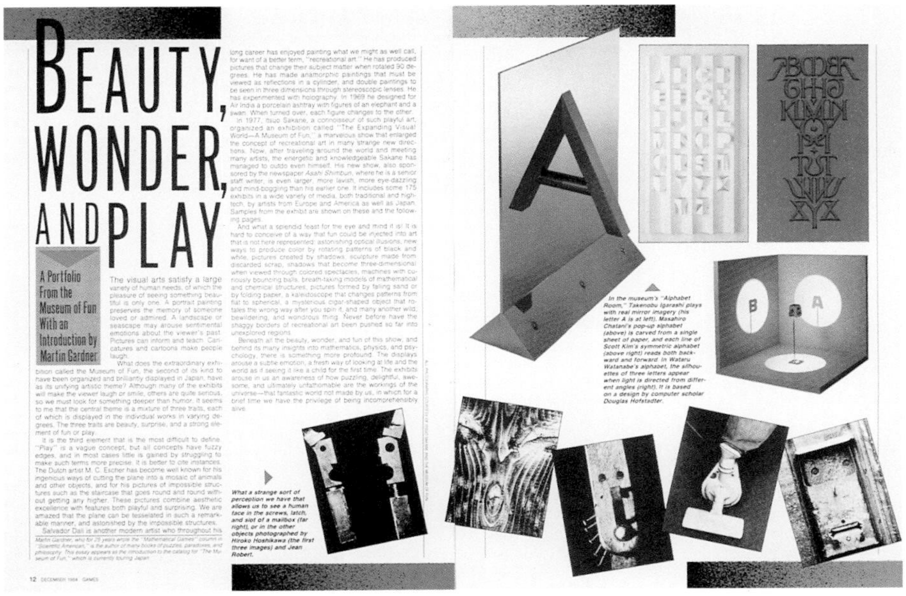

217

PUBLICATION: *Games Magazine*
ART DIRECTOR: *David Herbick*
DESIGNER: *David Herbick*
PUBLISHER: *Playboy Enterprises, Inc.*
CATEGORY: *Design-Spread*
AWARD: *Merit*

A FATHER'S FIRST WORDS
BY BOB GREENE
When you're drawing up your list of life's miracles, you might place near the top the first moment your baby smiles at you.

218

PUBLICATION: *Daily News Magazine*
ART DIRECTOR: *Janet Froelich*
Thomas P. Ruis
ILLUSTRATOR: *Ivan Chermayeff*
PUBLISHER: *New York News, Inc.*
CATEGORY: *Illustration-Story Pres.*
AWARD: *Merit*

219

PUBLICATION: *House & Garden*
ART DIRECTOR: *Lloyd Ziff*
DESIGNER: *Lloyd Ziff*
PHOTOGRAPHER: *Kenneth McGowan*
PUBLISHER: *Conde Nast Publications*
CATEGORY: *Design-Spread*
AWARD: *Merit*

AT THE TABLE

STOLEN TIME

A treacherous tale of sharks and watches

By Steven M. L. Aronson

In our days at Yale we'd been whales for pleasure, we two. And now some sober years later we were back in New Haven—back at the very tables down at Mory's—not eating barracuda, eating swordfish, when we encountered a shark of a sharper tooth.

To undergraduates Mory's was a kind of collegial teething ring. To graduates all through the years it was hallowed ground. There every Monday evening of the college year the Whiffenpoofs still sing "To the tables down at Mory's," sending a nostalgic thrill along the marrow.

My dinner companion was Jay Mellon—heir—not hostage, to fortune, one of the world's mammoth ones. Directly after graduation he had moved to Kenya, the country of his heart's desire. A far cry then from the tourist-trampled game park it is today, Nairobi for five intrepid years had served as Jay's headquarters for the hunting and scientific expeditions he made all over Africa. Now, with his comprehensive collection of African trophies, more than a hundred of them records, Jay could truly be said to have embroidered his own real-life unicorn tapestry.

Confrontations with Africa's most dangerous game animals—elephant, rhino, buffalo, lion, leopard—in some of the wildest regions left on earth were meat and drink to him. Nobody else of my acquaintance—indeed, of the acquaintance of any of my acquaintances, living as we all do in the postwar twentieth century—had hunted sitatunga on the Sese Islands in Lake Victoria or white-tailed gnu in South Africa, let alone stalked Abyssinian ibex, Somali Soemmering's gazelle, Hunter's hartebeest, Mrs. Gray's lechwe, Lord Derby's eland, vaal rehbok, bontebok, blesbok, and dibatag. It was good to see Jay again.

"Yale was hell spelled backwards, and you can say *that* again!" he expostulated good-naturedly as we were shown to our table. "Remember 'The History of Ancient Rome'? I signed up for that course because I'd heard the Romans knew how to enjoy themselves better than anybody else and I wanted to find out how they did it. But the guy who taught it was the greatest Rembrandt-genius of boredom I ever met. If he couldn't put you to sleep in twenty minutes, you were an insomniac!" So it was to be an evening of easy reminiscing.

As Jay went on, I noticed he was wearing two watches, one on each wrist—stainless steel on the right, gold on the left. "This one tells the time in Nairobi," he explained, tapping the gold.

The last time I had seen Jay was in the British Virgin Islands. A group of us had gathered there to explore the wreck of the *Rhône*, the great propeller-driven steamship that had sunk off Tortola in 1867. We were about to dive in when a barracuda, about six menacing feet long, was sighted lurking by our boat. We all stared over the edge, intimidated. Suddenly Jay dove into that sea of danger, and the barracuda shot away at the splash. As far as I was concerned, if Jay never did another thing in all his life, there would always be a touch of Spartacus to him.

I reminded him now of his moment of glory. "Hell," he dismissed it, "with a shark I wouldn't have done that. But a barracuda would never bite anybody. I don't know how they got their bloodthirsty reputation. Maybe because they *look* nasty. They've got all these big teeth and they're constantly opening and closing their yaps underwater. So people *think* they're going to bite them. It's ridiculous. You can float right past a *(Continued on page 88)*

86 HOUSE & GARDEN

220

PUBLICATION: *House & Garden*
ART DIRECTOR: *Lloyd Ziff*
DESIGNER: *Cathy Hall*
PHOTOGRAPHER: *Stephen Kelemen*
PUBLISHER: *Conde Nast Publications*
CATEGORY: *Illustration-Spread*
AWARD: *Merit*

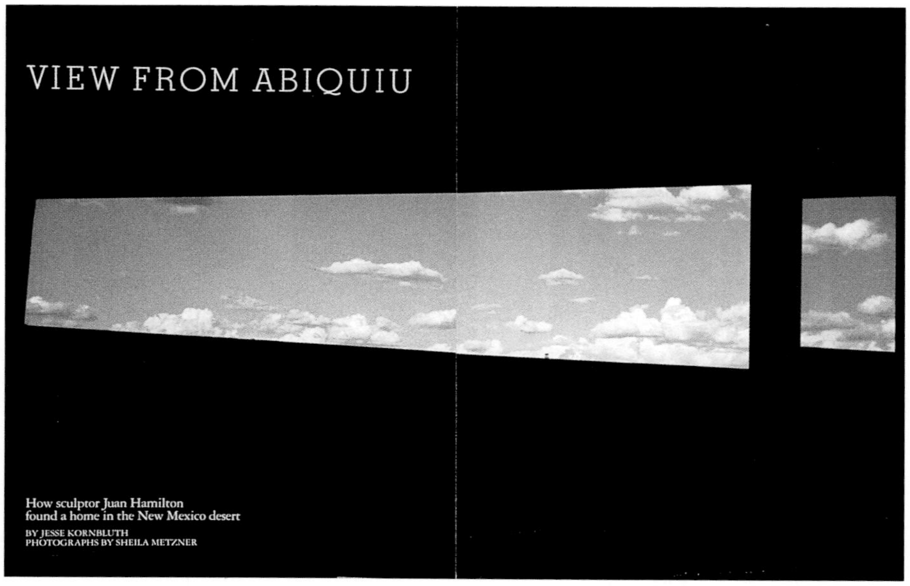
VIEW FROM ABIQUIU
How sculptor Juan Hamilton found a home in the New Mexico desert
BY JESSE KORNBLUTH
PHOTOGRAPHS BY SHEILA METZNER

221

PUBLICATION: *House & Garden*
ART DIRECTOR: *Loyd Ziff*
DESIGNER: *Lloyd Ziff*
PHOTOGRAPHER: *Sheila Metzner*
PUBLISHER: *Conde Nast Publications*
CATEGORY: *Design-Spread*
AWARD: *Merit*

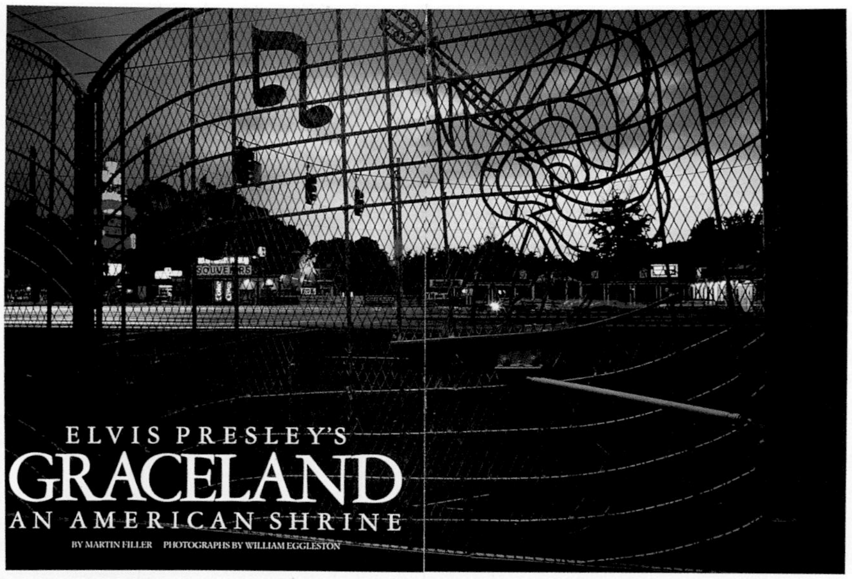
ELVIS PRESLEY'S
GRACELAND
AN AMERICAN SHRINE
BY MARTIN FILLER PHOTOGRAPHS BY WILLIAM EGGLESTON

222

PUBLICATION: *House & Garden*
ART DIRECTOR: *Lloyd Ziff*
DESIGNER: *Lloyd Ziff*
PHOTOGRAPHER: *William Eggleston*
PUBLISHER: *Conde Nast Publications*
CATEGORY: *Photography-Spread*
AWARD: *Merit*

VIEW FROM ABIQUIU
How sculptor Juan Hamilton
found a home in the New Mexico desert
BY JESSE KORNBLUTH
PHOTOGRAPHS BY SHEILA METZNER

223

PUBLICATION: *House & Garden*
ART DIRECTOR: *Lloyd Ziff*
DESIGNER: *Lloyd Ziff*
PHOTOGRAPHER: *Sheila Metzner*
PUBLISHER: *Conde Nast Publications*
CATEGORY: *Photography-Spread*
AWARD: *Merit*

The Singular Success of Glenn Close

BY ANN FERRAR

It's about 15 minutes into the first act of *The Real Thing*, Tom Stoppard's Pirandellian Broadway play about infidelity, when Glenn Close makes her entrance. At the sight of her the audience bursts into applause, bringing the action to a halt. For an instant, the actress is frozen by amazement. As her character falls away from her, it seems she can barely restrain the urge to look back over her shoulder—it's as if the audience had slipped her a gushy note, which she was certain she'd received by mistake.

"I love it!" beams the 36-year-old Close, who is perhaps best known for her work in films such as *The Big Chill* and *The World According to Garp*. "The other night I overheard two women

Close is at a crossroads. She broke off a relationship, moved into an apartment on her own and is wondering whether to have a child before the proverbial biological clock winds down.

225

PUBLICATION: *Living Anew*
ART DIRECTOR: *Terry Koppel*
DESIGNER: *Terry Koppel*
PHOTOGRAPHER: *Nancy Ellison*
PUBLISHER: *Mantel, Koppel & Scher*
CATEGORY: *Design-Spread*
AWARD: *Merit*

WORLD CLASS
clothes to celebrate an olympic season

226

PUBLICATION: *Mademoiselle*
ART DIRECTOR: *Paula Greif*
DESIGNER: *Paula Greif*
PHOTOGRAPHER: *Stephen Meisel*
PUBLISHER: *Conde Nast Publications*
CATEGORY: *Photography-Spread*
AWARD: *Merit*

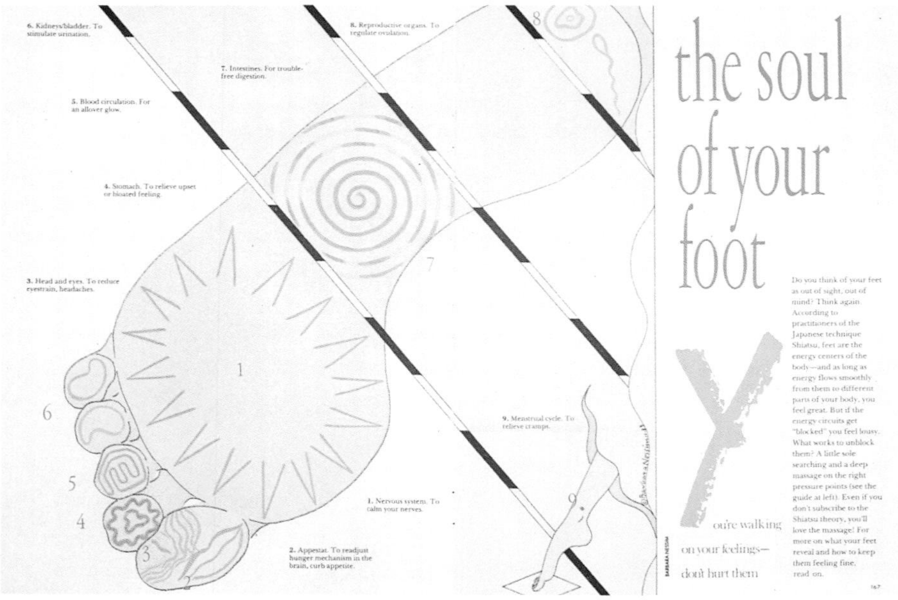

227

PUBLICATION: *Mademoiselle*
ART DIRECTOR: *Paula Greif*
DESIGNER: *Wynn Dan*
ILLUSTRATOR: *Barbara Nessim*
PUBLISHER: *Conde Nast Publications*
CATEGORY: *Illustration-Spread*
AWARD: *Merit*

228

PUBLICATION: *Mademoiselle*
ART DIRECTOR: *Kati Korpijakko*
ILLUSTRATOR: *Wendy Burden*
PUBLISHER: *Conde Nast Publications*
CATEGORY: *Illustration-Spread*
AWARD: *Merit*

229

PUBLICATION: *Mademoiselle*
ART DIRECTOR: *Kati Korpijaako*
DESIGNER: *Marilu Lopez*
PHOTOGRAPHER: *Michel Compte*
PUBLISHER: *Conde Nast Publications*
CATEGORY: *Design-Spread*
AWARD: *Merit*

Investment

Ten Debt-Free Stocks That Could Sprint

These fast-growing firms aren't hampered by high interest rates.

by Jordan E. Goodman

231

PUBLICATION: *Money Magazine*
ART DIRECTOR: *Margaret Ottosen*
ILLUSTRATOR: *Lane Smith*
PUBLISHER: *Time, Inc.*
CATEGORY: *Single Page Spread/Illustration*
AWARD: *Merit*

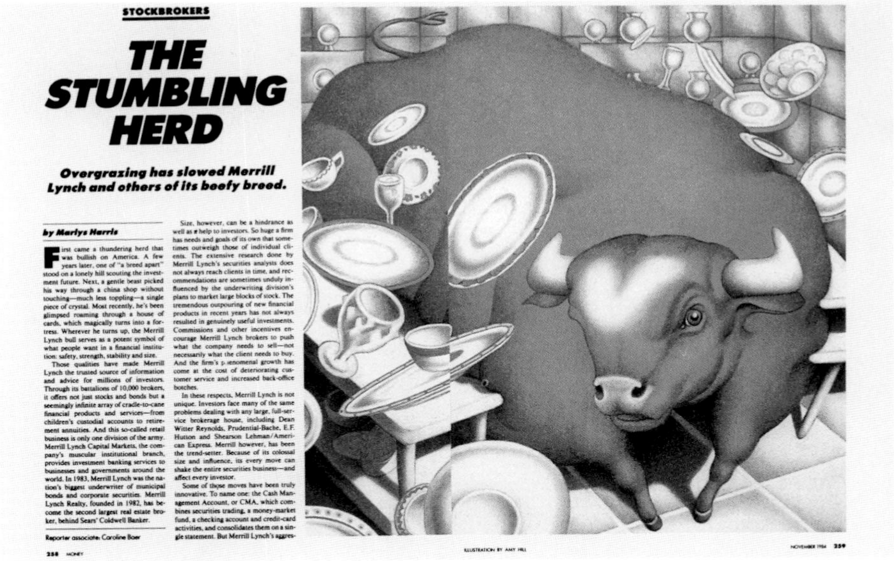

STOCKBROKERS

THE STUMBLING HERD

Overgrazing has slowed Merrill Lynch and others of its beefy breed.

by Marlys Harris

232

PUBLICATION: *Money Magazine*
ART DIRECTOR: *Ellen Blissman*
ILLUSTRATOR: *Amy Hill*
PUBLISHER: *Time, Inc.*
CATEGORY: *Illustration-Spread*
AWARD: *Merit*

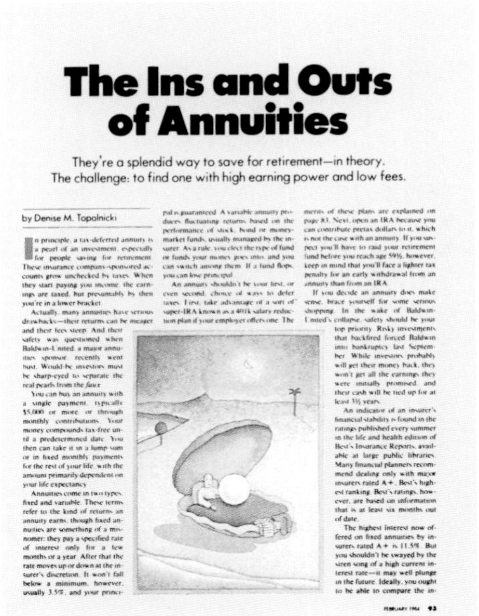

The Ins and Outs of Annuities

They're a splendid way to save for retirement—in theory. The challenge: to find one with high earning power and low fees.

by Denise M. Topolnicki

233

PUBLICATION: *Money Magazine*
ART DIRECTOR: *Ellen Blissman*
ILLUSTRATOR: *John Alfred Dorn, III*
PUBLISHER: *Time, Inc.*
CATEGORY: *Illustration-Spread*
AWARD: *Merit*

234

PUBLICATION: *Money Magazine*
ART DIRECTOR: *Margaret Ottosen*
ILLUSTRATOR: *Rudy Laslo*
PUBLISHER: *Time, Inc.*
CATEGORY: *Illustration-Spread*
AWARD: *Merit*

235

PUBLICATION: *Meetings & Conventions*
ART DIRECTOR: *Lee Ann Jaffee*
ILLUSTRATOR: *Nicholas Gaetano*
PUBLISHER: *Lee Ann Jaffee Design*
CATEGORY: *Design-Spread*
AWARD: *Merit*

236

PUBLICATION: *Meetings & Conventions Magazine*
ART DIRECTOR: *Lee Ann Jaffee*
ILLUSTRATOR: *Nicholas Gaetano*
PUBLISHER: *Lee Ann Jaffee Design*
CATEGORY: *Illustration-Spread*
AWARD: *Merit*

239

PUBLICATION: *Mother Jones Magazine*
ART DIRECTOR: *Louise Kollenbaum*
DESIGNER: *Martha Geering*
PHOTOGRAPHER: *Penny Wolin*
PUBLISHER: *Foundation For National Progress*
CATEGORY: *Photography-Spread*
AWARD: *Merit*

JOHN LYDON'S

PIL

I remember when the first pictures started showing up in the American papers. They looked pretty bad. All those drastically zoned-out kids with their hair up in spikes and safety pins stuck through their cheeks, bondage gear, swastikas, black leather, rags, chains, noserings, purple hair, creative scars, public nausea, nipple cutouts, the whole gleeful array, and I thought that it was likely the most pointless dramatization of mass disaffection I had seen, adequate perhaps to show the onlooking world (and parents, I thought, parents) how immedicably wounded and distorted a declining civilization had managed to make them feel so young, so butchered out of the body of common humanity. Aliens.

I wasn't on the rock scene, but I did read the articles and thought, well, we're gonna see weirder things than this.

THE LATE GREAT JOHNNY ROTTEN BLOWS UP THE WORLD AND MAKES A HOME IN THE AFTERSHOCK.

Rafi Zabor

240

PUBLICATION: *Musician Magazine*
ART DIRECTOR: *Gary Koepke*
DESIGNER: *Gary Koepke*
PHOTOGRAPHER: *Deborah Feingold*
PUBLISHER: *Billboard Publications*
CATEGORY: *Design-Spread*
AWARD: *Merit*

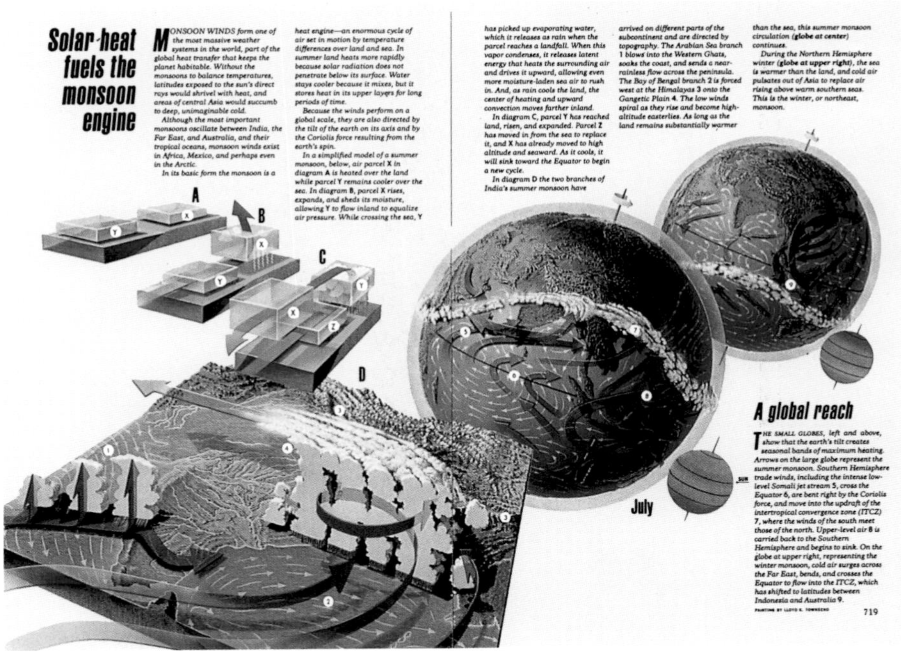

Solar-heat fuels the monsoon engine

MONSOON WINDS form one of the most massive weather systems in the world, part of the global heat transfer that keeps the planet habitable. Without the monsoons to balance temperatures, latitudes exposed to the sun's direct rays would shrivel with heat, and areas of central Asia would succumb to deep, unimaginable cold.

Although the most important monsoons oscillate between India, the Far East, and Australia, and their tropical oceans, monsoon winds exist in Africa, Mexico, and perhaps even in the Arctic.

In its basic form the monsoon is a heat engine—an enormous cycle of air set in motion by temperature differences over land and sea. In summer land heats more rapidly because solar radiation does not penetrate below its surface. Water stays cooler because it mixes, but it stores heat in its upper layers for long periods of time.

Because the winds perform on a global scale, they are also directed by the tilt of the earth on its axis and by the Coriolis force resulting from the earth's spin.

In a simplified model of a summer monsoon, below, air parcel X *in diagram* A *is heated over the land while parcel* Y *remains cooler over the sea. In diagram* B*, parcel* X *rises, expands, and sheds its moisture, allowing* Y *to flow inland to equalize air pressure. While crossing the sea,* Y *has picked up evaporating water, which it releases as rain when the parcel reaches a landfall. When this vapor condenses, it releases latent energy that heats the surrounding air and drives it upward, allowing even more moisture-laden sea air to rush in. And, as rain cools the land, the center of heating and upward convection moves farther inland.*

In diagram C*, parcel* Y *has reached land, risen, and expanded. Parcel* Z *has moved in from the sea to replace it, and* X *has already moved to high altitude and seaward. As it cools, it will sink toward the Equator to begin a new cycle.*

In diagram D *the two branches of India's summer monsoon have arrived on different parts of the subcontinent and are directed by topography. The Arabian Sea branch* 1 *blows into the Western Ghats, soaks the coast, and sends a near-rainless flow across the peninsula. The Bay of Bengal branch* 2 *is forced west at the Himalayas* 3 *onto the Gangetic Plain* 4*. The low winds spiral as they rise and become high-altitude easterlies. As long as the land remains substantially warmer than the sea, this summer monsoon circulation* (**globe at center**) *continues.*

During the Northern Hemisphere winter (**globe at upper right**)*, the sea is warmer than the land, and cold air pulsates out of Asia to replace air rising above warm southern seas. This is the winter, or northeast, monsoon.*

A global reach

THE SMALL GLOBES, left and above, show that the earth's tilt creates seasonal bands of maximum heating. Arrows on the large globe represent the summer monsoon. Southern Hemisphere trade winds, including the intense low-level Somali jet stream 5*, cross the Equator* 6*, are bent right by the Coriolis force, and move into the updraft of the intertropical convergence zone (ITCZ)* 7*, where the winds of the south meet those of the north. Upper-level air* 8 *is carried back to the Southern Hemisphere and begins to sink. On the globe at upper right, representing the winter monsoon, cold air surges across the Far East, bends, and crosses the Equator to flow into the ITCZ, which has shifted to latitudes between Indonesia and Australia* 9*.*

PAINTING BY LLOYD K. TOWNSEND 719

242

PUBLICATION: *National Geographic*
ART DIRECTOR: *Allen Carroll*
DESIGNER: *Allen Carroll*
ILLUSTRATOR: *Lloyd Townsend*
PUBLISHER: *National Geographic Society*
CATEGORY: *Illustration-Spread*
AWARD: *Merit*

AS TOLD TO MIMI POND

Every Boy's Guide to His Own Rat Pack

IT ALL STARTED WHEN my stupid little brother stepped on my Walkman and crushed it. I was so pissed. Mom said he'd have to pay for it out of his allowance, but he only gets twenty-five cents a week, so it'd be two years before I could even listen to my Def Leppard tape again. All there was left to do was watch TV.

One night, about 3:00 A.M., the only thing on was "Mary Tyler Moore," which is totally pukey, or this movie with Frank Sinatra. We're the only people on the block who don't have cable, which is really a bummer, and I know why. Mom says it'd just give me a chance to watch the dirty stuff, and she doesn't want me "exposed" to it. Like I don't already know that stuff anyway. Anyway I go over to Jason's house and watch it over there while his mom's at work. This is how weird Jason is: he'd rather play Space Invaders.

Anyway, so this Frank Sinatra movie comes on, and it's real strange. It's called *Ocean's 11*, or something. Like all these guys in suits and stuff. But they were kind of cool—kind of new wave, like my older brother would like to look, but he doesn't, 'cause he's such a pizza face. Okay, so there's these eleven guys, who used to be in the same Army battalion together, and they all decide

50 NATIONAL LAMPOON · MARCH 1984

MARCH 1984 · NATIONAL LAMPOON 51

244

PUBLICATION: *National Lampoon*
ART DIRECTOR: *Michael Grossman*
DESIGNER: *Marianne Gaffney*
ILLUSTRATOR: *Stephen Kroninger*
PUBLISHER: *Mid-America Web Press*
CATEGORY: *Illustration Spread*
AWARD: *Merit*

THE ALTAR BOYS' PICNIC

BY FRED GRAVER

THERE were days when Leonard Zagreb felt that he alone carried on the tradition of the Zagreb twins. Days when he felt he couldn't count on his brother, Stephen, to do his part in keeping the Zagreb twins on the

245

PUBLICATION: *National Lampoon*
ART DIRECTOR: *Michael Grossman*
Michael Delevante
ILLUSTRATOR: *Paul Yallowitz*
PUBLISHER: *Mid-America Web Press*
CATEGORY: *Illustration-Spread*
AWARD: *Merit*

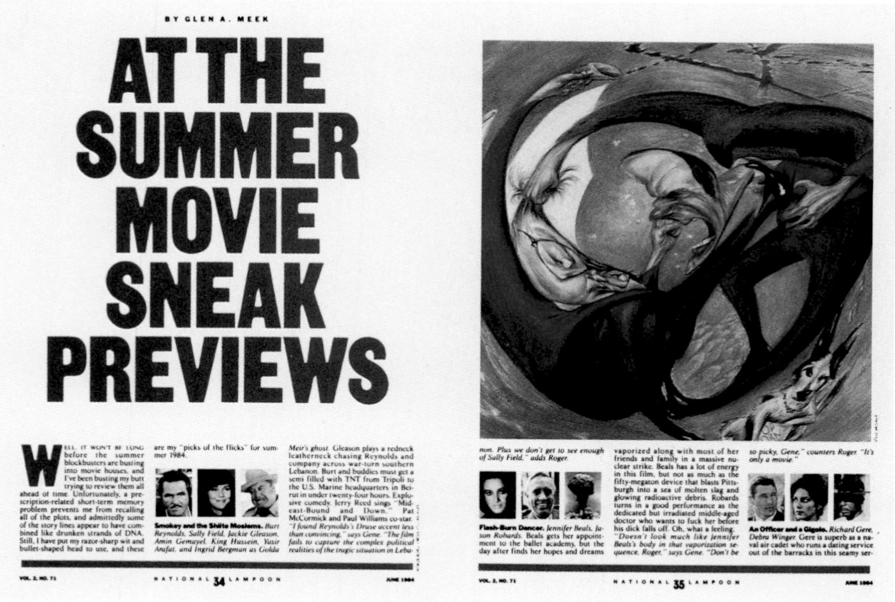

BY GLEN A. MEEK

AT THE SUMMER MOVIE SNEAK PREVIEWS

NATIONAL 34 LAMPOON

NATIONAL 35 LAMPOON

246

PUBLICATION: *National Lampoon*
ART DIRECTOR: *Michael Grossman*
DESIGNER: *Timothy McCarthy*
ILLUSTRATOR: *Steve Brodner*
PUBLISHER: *Mid-America Web Press*
CATEGORY: *Illustration-Single Page*
AWARD: *Merit*

247

PUBLICATION: *Daily News Magazine*
ART DIRECTOR: *Janet Froelich*
Thomas P. Ruis
PHOTOGRAPHER: *Tom Arma*
PUBLISHER: *New York News, Inc.*
CATEGORY: *Design-Spread*
AWARD: *Merit*

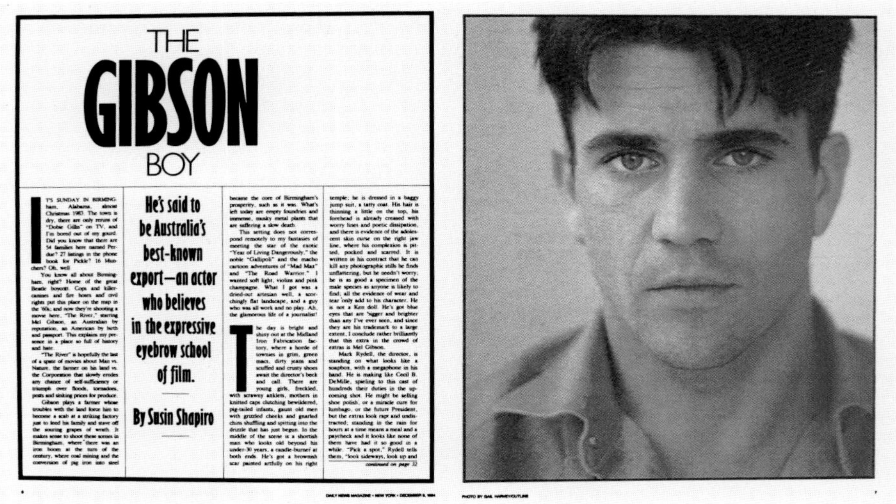

248

PUBLICATION: *Daily News Magazine*
ART DIRECTOR: *Janet Froelich*
Thomas P. Ruis
PHOTOGRAPHER: *Gail Harvey/Outline*
PUBLISHER: *New York News, Inc.*
CATEGORY: *Design-Single Page*
AWARD: *Merit*

249

PUBLICATION: *Daily News Magazine*
ART DIRECTOR: *Janet Froelich*
Thomas P. Ruis
ILLUSTRATOR: *Laurie Rosenwald*
PUBLISHER: *New York News, Inc.*
CATEGORY: *Illustration-Spread*
AWARD: *Merit*

CAN THIS MARRIAGE BE SAVED?
The plight of the computer widow.
BY EILEEN HAAS

250

PUBLICATION: *Daily News Magazine*
ART DIRECTOR: *Janet Froelich*
Thomas P. Ruis
ILLUSTRATOR: *Seth Jaben*
PUBLISHER: *New York News, Inc.*
CATEGORY: *Illustration-Spread*
AWARD: *Merit*

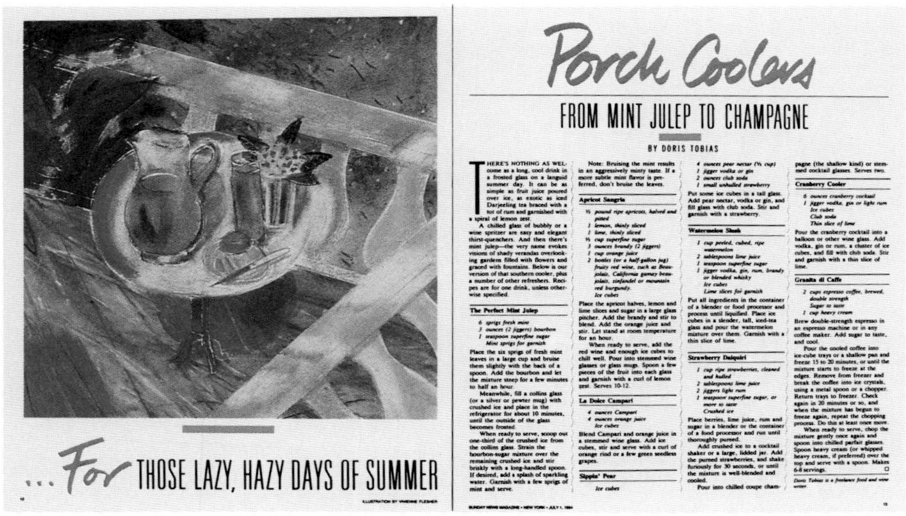

251

PUBLICATION: *Daily News Magazine*
ART DIRECTOR: *Janet Froelich*
Thomas P. Ruis
ILLUSTRATOR: *Vivienne Flesher*
PUBLISHER: *New York News, Inc.*
CATEGORY: *Illustration-Spread*
AWARD: *Merit*

252

PUBLICATION: *Newsweek*
ART DIRECTOR: *Robert Priest*
Margaret Joskow
ILLUSTRATOR: *Lane Smith*
PUBLISHER: *Newsweek, Inc.*
CATEGORY: *Illustration-Spread*
AWARD: *Merit*

GREAT PLACES TO HAVE A PARTY

New Yorkers are always looking for new places to hold really memorable parties. They dine, dance, drink, marry, and toast the night in high-pillared turn-of-the-century rooms with ornate ceilings. They rent venerable dining rooms designed for bishops' gatherings; spartan and spacious (and beautiful) rooms that once were warehouses; the mansions of the vanished rich.

Are you finally ready to give a sophisticated dance? Do you want your party space dramatic? Formal? Romantic? Rustic? Are you looking for a dignified room where you can honor a distinguished guest or a wonderful older person you love?

In the three years since my article "Forty Fabulous Places to Have a Party" appeared (November 23, 1981), the demand for party spaces has increased, and so has the number of private rooms available for renting. So, after hundreds of requests for reprints, here's an update. This time I've chosen rooms for as few as 20 and as many as 2,000.

I visited 150 places and settled on about 60. (Thirty of them—including yachts expensive enough and spaces ornate enough for the grandest occasion—will appear in next week's issue.) If I liked the look of a restaurant's private room, I ate two meals there. If I chose a loft, I sampled the food of the caterer who handles parties there. Sometimes, a room was totally bare—a glorious, freshly restored old space just begging for a crowd. Since rooms like these can intimidate people who cannot visualize them alive with flowers, candles, balloons, and potted palms, I asked Stephen Gallagher, a party planner, how he would make these spaces festive. When I wanted to know the history of a building, I called on the architectural historian Christopher Gray.

Now follow your mood. There's a range of prices here—low, medium, affordable, astronomical. Corporations can find spaces for the large groups they entertain, and you'll be able to choose a cozy back room for the 45 people in your office. In the end, it's the people who make a party—but the room helps.

BY BARBARA COSTIKYAN

PHOTOGRAPHED BY LANGDON CLAY

PARTY GUIDE
THE BALLROOM

No Wedding Guest Could Possibly Be Bored at a Tapas Reception at Rojas-Lombardi's.

JUNE 4, 1984/NEW YORK 41

253

PUBLICATION: *New York Magazine*
ART DIRECTOR: *Robert Best*
DESIGNER: *Patricia Von Brachel*
Don Morris
PHOTOGRAPHER: *Langdon Clay*
PUBLISHER: *Murdoch Magazines*
CATEGORY: *Design-Spread*
AWARD: *Merit*

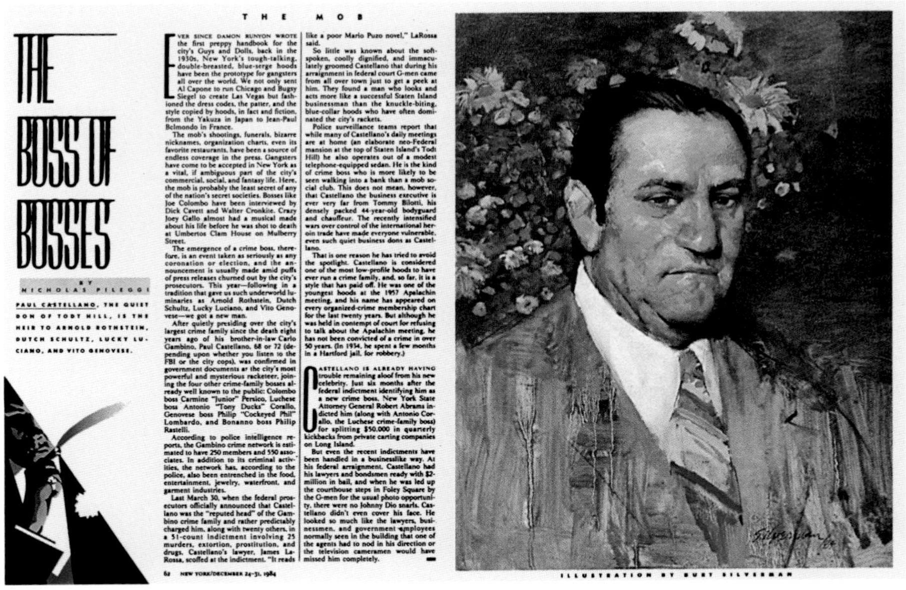

THE MOB

THE BOSS OF BOSSES

BY NICHOLAS PILEGGI

PAUL CASTELLANO, THE QUIET DON OF TODT HILL, IS THE HEIR TO ARNOLD ROTHSTEIN, DUTCH SCHULTZ, LUCKY LUCIANO, AND VITO GENOVESE.

Ever since Damon Runyon wrote the first preppy handbook for the city's Guys and Dolls, back in the 1930s, New York's tough-talking, double-breasted, blue-serge hoods have been the prototype for gangsters all over the world. We not only sent Al Capone to run Chicago and Bugsy Siegel to create Las Vegas but fashioned the dress codes, the patter, and the style copied by hoods, in fact and fiction, from the Yakuza in Japan to Jean-Paul Belmondo in France.

The mob's shootings, funerals, bizarre nicknames, organization charts, even its favorite restaurants, have been a source of endless coverage in the press. Gangsters have come to be accepted in New York as a vital, if ambiguous part of the city's commercial, social, and fantasy life. Here, the mob is probably the least secret of any of the nation's secret societies. Bosses like Joe Colombo have been interviewed by Dick Cavett and Walter Cronkite. Crazy Joey Gallo almost had a musical made about his life before he was shot to death at Umbertos Clam House on Mulberry Street.

The emergence of a crime boss, therefore, is an event taken as seriously as any coronation or election, and the announcement is usually made amid puffs of press releases churned out by the city's prosecutors. This year—following in a tradition that gave us such underworld luminaries as Arnold Rothstein, Dutch Schultz, Lucky Luciano, and Vito Genovese—we got a new man.

After quietly presiding over the city's largest crime family since the death eight years ago of his brother-in-law Carlo Gambino, Paul Castellano, 68 or 72 (depending upon whether you listen to the FBI or the city cops), was confirmed in government documents as the city's most powerful and mysterious racketeer, joining the four other crime-family bosses already well known to the public: Colombo boss Carmine "Junior" Persico, Luchese boss Antonio "Tony Ducks" Corallo, Genovese boss Philip "Cockeyed Phil" Lombardo, and Bonanno boss Philip Rastelli.

According to police intelligence reports, the Gambino crime network is estimated to have 250 members and 550 associates. In addition to its criminal activities, the network has, according to the police, also been entrenched in the food, entertainment, jewelry, waterfront, and garment industries.

Last March 30, when the federal prosecutors officially announced that Castellano was the "reputed head" of the Gambino crime family and rather predictably charged him, along with twenty others, in a 51-count indictment involving 25 murders, extortion, prostitution, and drugs, Castellano's lawyer, James LaRossa, scoffed at the indictment. "It reads like a poor Mario Puzo novel," LaRossa said.

So little was known about the soft-spoken, coolly dignified, and immaculately groomed Castellano that during his arraignment in federal court G-men came from all over town just to get a peek at him. They found a man who looks and acts more like a successful Staten Island businessman than the knuckle-biting, blue-collar hoods who have often dominated the city's rackets.

Police surveillance teams report that while many of Castellano's daily meetings are at home (an elaborate neo-Federal mansion at the top of Staten Island's Todt Hill) he also operates out of a modest telephone-equipped sedan. He is the kind of crime boss who is more likely to be seen walking into a bank than a mob social club. This does not mean, however, that Castellano the business executive is ever very far from Tommy Bilotti, his densely packed 44-year-old bodyguard and chauffeur. The recently intensified wars over control of the international heroin trade have made everyone vulnerable, even such quiet business dons as Castellano.

That is one reason he has tried to avoid the spotlight. Castellano is considered one of the most low-profile hoods to have ever run a crime family, and, so far, it is a style that has paid off. He was one of the youngest hoods at the 1957 Apalachin meeting, and his name has appeared on every organized-crime membership chart for the last twenty years. But although he was held in contempt of court for refusing to talk about the Apalachin meeting, he has not been convicted of a crime in over 50 years. (In 1934, he spent a few months in a Hartford jail, for robbery.)

Castellano is already having trouble remaining aloof from his new celebrity. Just six months after the federal indictment identifying him as a new crime boss, New York State Attorney General Robert Abrams indicted him (along with Antonio Corallo, the Luchese crime-family boss) for splitting $50,000 in quarterly kickbacks from private carting companies on Long Island.

But even the recent indictments have been handled in a businesslike way. At his federal arraignment, Castellano had his lawyers and bondsmen ready with $2-million in bail, and when he was led up the courthouse steps in Foley Square by the G-men for the usual photo opportunity, there were no Johnny Dio snarls. Castellano didn't even cover his face. He looked so much like the lawyers, businessmen, and government employees normally seen in the building that one of the agents had to nod in his direction or the television cameramen would have missed him completely.

62 NEW YORK/DECEMBER 24-31, 1984

ILLUSTRATION BY BURT SILVERMAN

254

PUBLICATION: *New York Magazine*
ART DIRECTOR: *Robert Best*
ILLUSTRATOR: *Burt Silverman*
PUBLISHER: *Murdoch Magazines*
CATEGORY: *Illustration-Spread*
AWARD: *Merit*

MARTHA GRAHAM
GOING ON 90, MODERN DANCE'S DOYENNE MAY AGAIN CONFOUND FOLLOWERS WITH A CHANGE OF DIRECTION.
By Anna Kisselgoff

255

PUBLICATION: *New York Times*
ART DIRECTOR: *Ken Kendrick*
DESIGNER: *Martine Winter*
PHOTOGRAPHER: *Hiro*
PUBLISHER: *The New York Times*
CATEGORY: *Design-Spread*
AWARD: *Merit*

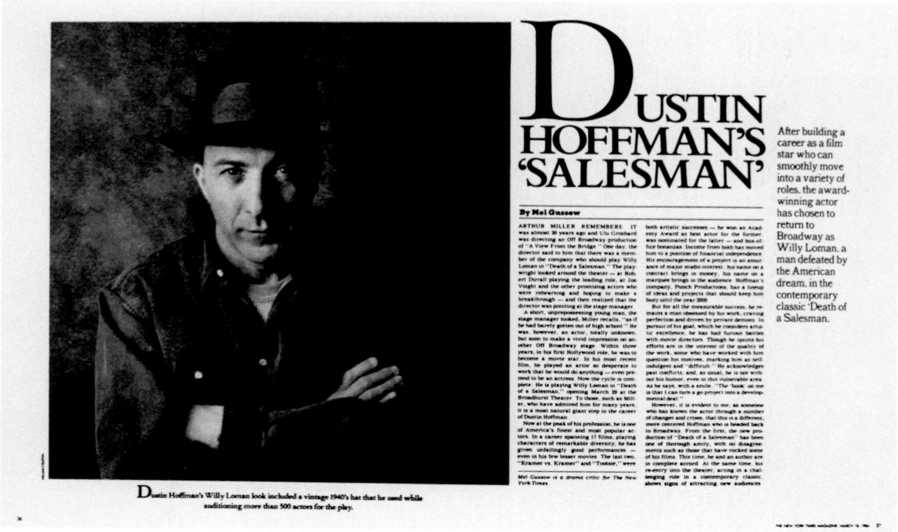
DUSTIN HOFFMAN'S 'SALESMAN'
After building a career as a film star who can smoothly move into a variety of roles, the award-winning actor has chosen to return to Broadway as Willy Loman, a man defeated by the American dream, in the contemporary classic 'Death of a Salesman.'
By Mel Gussow
Dustin Hoffman's Willy Loman look included a vintage 1940's hat that he used while auditioning more than 500 actors for the play.

256

PUBLICATION: *New York Times*
ART DIRECTOR: *Roger Black*
DESIGNER: *Martine Winter*
PHOTOGRAPHER: *William Coupon*
PUBLISHER: *The New York Times*
CATEGORY: *Design-Spread*
AWARD: *Merit*

MARTHA GRAHAM
GOING ON 90, MODERN DANCE'S DOYENNE MAY AGAIN CONFOUND FOLLOWERS WITH A CHANGE OF DIRECTION.
By Anna Kisselgoff

257

PUBLICATION: *New York Times*
ART DIRECTOR: *Ken Kendrick*
DESIGNER: *Martine Winter*
PHOTOGRAPHER: *Hiro*
PUBLISHER: *The New York Times*
CATEGORY: *Photography-Spread*
AWARD: *Merit*

Dustin Hoffman's Willy Loman look included a vintage 1940's hat that he used while auditioning more than 500 actors for the play.

DUSTIN HOFFMAN'S 'SALESMAN'

After building a career as a film star who can smoothly move into a variety of roles, the award-winning actor has chosen to return to Broadway as Willy Loman, a man defeated by the American dream, in the contemporary classic 'Death of a Salesman.'

By Mel Gussow

ARTHUR MILLER REMEMBERS IT was almost 20 years ago and Ulu Grosbard was directing an Off Broadway production of "A View From the Bridge." One day, the director said to him that there was a member of the company who should play Willy Loman in "Death of a Salesman." The playwright looked around the theater — at Robert Duvall playing the leading role, at Jon Voight and the other promising actors who were rehearsing and hoping to make a breakthrough — and then realized that the director was pointing at the stage manager.

A short, unprepossessing young man, the stage manager looked, Miller recalls, "as if he had barely gotten out of high school." He was, however, an actor, totally unknown, but soon to make a vivid impression on another Off Broadway stage. Within three years, in his first Hollywood role, he was to become a movie star. In his most recent film, he played an actor so desperate to work that he would do anything — even pretend to be an actress. Now the cycle is complete: He is playing Willy Loman in "Death of a Salesman," opening March 29 at the Broadhurst Theater. To those, such as Miller, who have admired him for many years, it is a most natural giant step in the career of Dustin Hoffman.

Now at the peak of his profession, he is one of America's finest and most popular actors. In a career spanning 17 films, playing characters of remarkable diversity, he has given unfailingly good performances — even in his few lesser movies. The last two, "Kramer vs. Kramer" and "Tootsie," were both artistic successes — he won an Academy Award as best actor for the former, was nominated for the latter — and box-office bonanzas. Income from both has moved him to a position of financial independence. His encouragement of a project is an assurance of major studio interest; his name on a contract brings in money; his name on a marquee brings in the audience. Hoffman's company, Punch Productions, has a lineup of ideas and projects that should keep him busy until the year 2000.

But for all the measurable success, he remains a man obsessed by his work, craving perfection and driven by private demons. In pursuit of his goal, which he considers artistic excellence, he has had furious battles with movie directors. Though he insists his efforts are in the interest of the quality of the work, some who have worked with him question his motives, marking him as self-indulgent and "difficult." He acknowledges past conflicts, and, as usual, he is not without his humor, even in this vulnerable area. As he says, with a smile, "The 'book' on me is that I can turn a go project into a developmental deal."

However, it is evident to me, as someone who has known the actor through a number of changes and crises, that this is a different, more centered Hoffman who is headed back to Broadway. From the first, the new production of "Death of a Salesman" has been one of thorough amity, with no disagreements such as those that have rocked some of his films. This time, he and an author are in complete accord. At the same time, his re-entry into the theater, acting in a challenging role in a contemporary classic, shows signs of attracting new audiences.

Mel Gussow is a drama critic for The New York Times.

258

PUBLICATION: *New York Times*
ART DIRECTOR: *Roger Black*
DESIGNER: *Martine Winter*
PHOTOGRAPHER: *William Coupon*
PUBLISHER: *The New York Times*
CATEGORY: *Photography-Spread*
AWARD: *Merit*

You're Fired, So You Buy a Ferret

BRIGHT LIGHTS, BIG CITY
By Jay McInerney.
182 pp. New York:
Vintage Books. Paper, $5.95.

By William Kotzwinkle

A YOUNG man works for a New York magazine in the Department of Factual Verification, where facts are tracked "through dusty volumes, along skeins of microfilm, across transcontinental telephone cables, till they prove good or are exposed as error." Factual error cannot appear in this magazine, and it sure sounds like The New Yorker, though it is never named in Jay McInerney's first novel, "Brights Lights, Big City." In any event, our hero does not fit in. "Should you call up the president of the Polar Explorers and ask if it's true that someone was wearing a headdress made out of walrus skin?" asks the narrator, who uses present-tense verbs and second-person pronouns, presumably apostrophizing himself. "Does it matter?"

It matters a great deal to the magazine, but our young man has had many long nights at New York clubs, utilizing a substance he refers to as "Bolivian Marching Powder." He is an amusing fellow, and he meets strange people — a baldheaded girl, for instance, with a scar tattooed on her scalp. "Her voice . . . is like the New Jersey State Anthem played through an electric shaver."

But none of this prepares him for labor in the Department of Factual Verification, run by a woman called the Clinger, who has a "mind like a steel mousetrap and a heart like a twelve-minute egg." Above her is a man called the Druid, who has "run the show for twenty years. . . . It pains him that he requires a staff to assist him. . . . There is officially no second-in-command, because that would imply an eventual changing of the guard, and the Druid cannot imagine the magazine without himself. The Kremlin must be a lot like this."

have built a reputation for scrupulous accuracy with regard to matters of fact. Our readers depend on us for the truth." The young man observes that the Clinger confuses fact with truth, but she fires him anyway. He buys the ferret. He returns at night to put the ferret in the Clinger's desk. The ferret bites him badly, and he has to flee. He ends up collapsing in a friend's bathtub after rummaging in her medicine cabinet and swallowing what he believes are her Valium. A daring fellow, this

fication is concerned, ficti
masquerade as flesh witho
he's safe there.
Jobless now, running
winds up in Friday's bar on
illegal age who speaks to
Powder. He reflects: "You
You still have some self-r
with her in her parents' a
taneous fellow, a most flu
His wife, Amanda, is a
left him. He appears at a
Astoria. Drunk, he tries to
is thrown out. A friend ask
all.
"Weren't you suspicio
her forehead?"
"Which sign was that
"The one that said, *Sp*
Term Leasing."
"We met in a bar. It
Mr. McInerney's stron
lots of it in "Bright Light
book that also introduces
Ghost, a recluse in the ma
working on a single article
an inventor responsible fo
cleaning revolution, who ha
rotary nose-hair clipper.

TO all this zaniness
strong sense for bi
another limo: "You
by the passage of
dows. Some of the lights ha
crystalline shards into the
that.
Mr. McInerney has w
shadows taking shape in h
know the lounges and the li
into dreams and hallucinat
sortment of street purveyo
watches and other objects

259

PUBLICATION: *New York Times-Book Review*
ART DIRECTOR: *Steve Heller*
DESIGNER: *Steve Heller*
ILLUSTRATOR: *Henrik Drescher*
PUBLISHER: *The New York Times*
CATEGORY: *Tabloid/Newsprint*
Single Page Design
AWARD: *Merit*

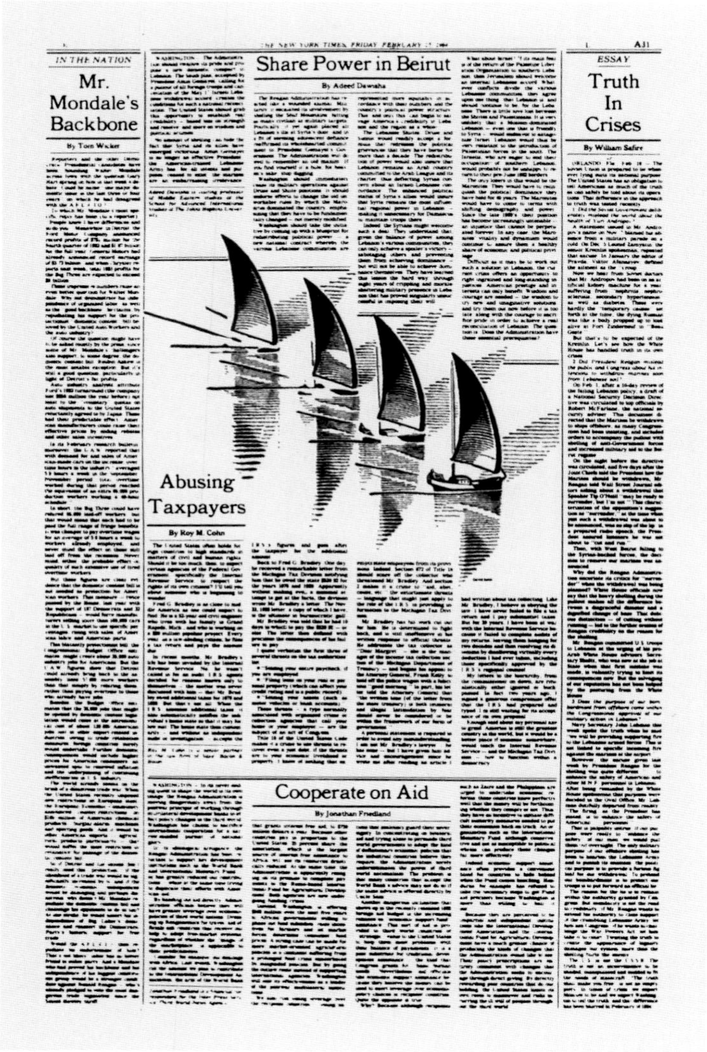

IN THE NATION

Mr. Mondale's Backbone

By Tom Wicker

Share Power in Beirut

By Adeed Dawisha

ESSAY

Truth In Crises

By William Safire

Abusing Taxpayers

By Roy M. Cohn

Cooperate on Aid

By Jonathan Friedland

IN THE NATION

Properly Blindsided

By Tom Wicker

To Kissinger Commission: History Warns Against Threats to Invade Nicaragua

By McGeorge Bundy

Lesson for Democrats: Don't Be Conservative

By Jeff Faux

FOREIGN AFFAIRS

Lemmings in Space

By Flora Lewis

260

PUBLICATION: *New York Times-Op-Ed Page*
ART DIRECTOR: *Jerelle Kraus*
DESIGNER: *Jerelle Kraus*
ILLUSTRATOR: *David Suter*
PUBLISHER: *The New York Times*
CATEGORY: *Tabloid/Newsprint Single Page*
AWARD: *Merit*

261

PUBLICATION: *New York Times-Op-Ed Page*
ART DIRECTOR: *Jerelle Kraus*
DESIGNER: *Jerelle Kraus*
ILLUSTRATOR: *R. O. Blechman*
PUBLISHER: *The New York Times*
CATEGORY: *Tabloid/Newsprint Single Page*
AWARD: *Merit*

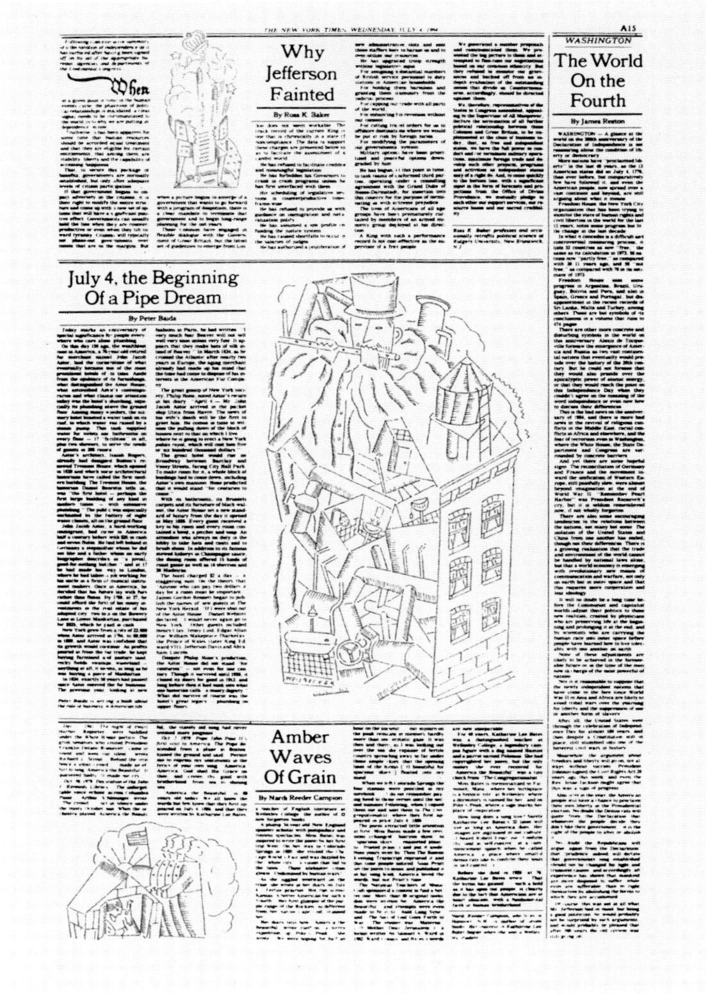

THE NEW YORK TIMES, WEDNESDAY, JULY 4, 1984 A15

Why Jefferson Fainted

By Ross K. Baker

WASHINGTON

The World On the Fourth

By James Reston

July 4, the Beginning Of a Pipe Dream

By Peter Bada

Amber Waves Of Grain

By Marsh Reeder Campion

Famine in Ethiopia: Days and Nights of Suffering

Famine in Ethiopia: Barren Hills, Exhausted People

A Land of Want

263

PUBLICATION: *New York Times*
ART DIRECTOR: *Roger Black*
DESIGNER: *Roger Black*
PHOTOGRAPHER: *Magnum/Sebastiao Salgado Jr.*
PUBLISHER: *The New York Times*
CATEGORY: *Tabloid-Newsprint*
Design Spread
AWARD: *Merit*

262

PUBLICATION: *New York Times-Op-Ed Page*
ART DIRECTOR: *Jerelle Kraus*
DESIGNER: *Jerelle Kraus*
ILLUSTRATOR: *Phillipe Weisbecker*
PUBLISHER: *The New York Times*
CATEGORY: *Tabloid/Newsprint*
Illustration-Single Page
AWARD: *Merit*

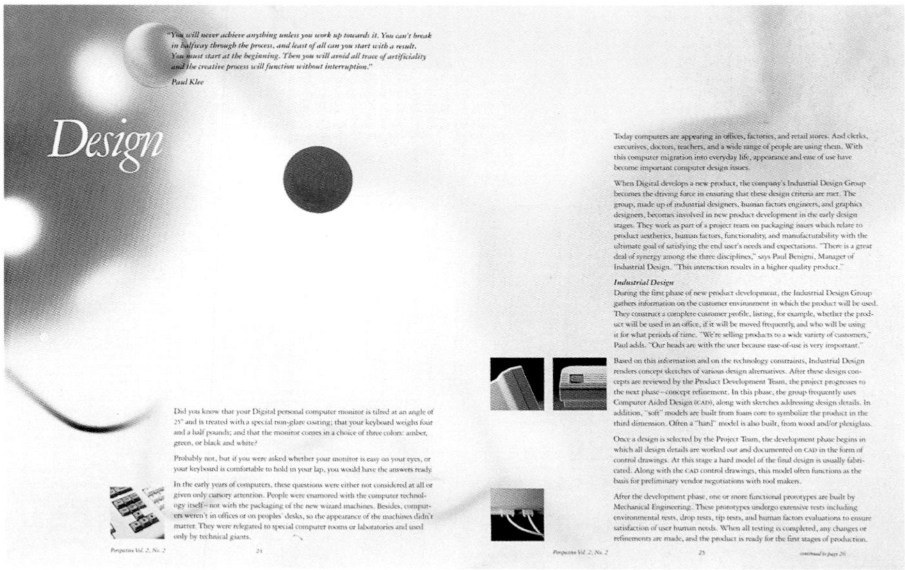

264

PUBLICATION: *Perspective*
ART DIRECTOR: *Gunta Abermanis*
DESIGNER: *John Costello*
PHOTOGRAPHER: *Tom Wedell*
Ken Raynor
PUBLISHER: *Digital Equipment Corp.*
CATEGORY: *Design-Spread*
AWARD: *Merit*

265

PUBLICATION: *Perspective*
ART DIRECTOR: *Gunta Abermanis*
DESIGNER: *Deborah Falck*
ILLUSTRATOR: *Jamie Hogan*
PUBLISHER: *Digital Equipment Corp.*
CATEGORY: *Illustration-Single Page*
AWARD: *Merit*

266

PUBLICATION: *The Plain Dealer Magazine*
ART DIRECTOR: *Gerard A. Sealy*
DESIGNER: *Gerard A. Sealy*
ILLUSTRATOR: *Merle Nacht*
PUBLISHER: *The Plain Dealer Publishing Co.*
CATEGORY: *Design-Spread/Tabloid*
AWARD: *Merit*

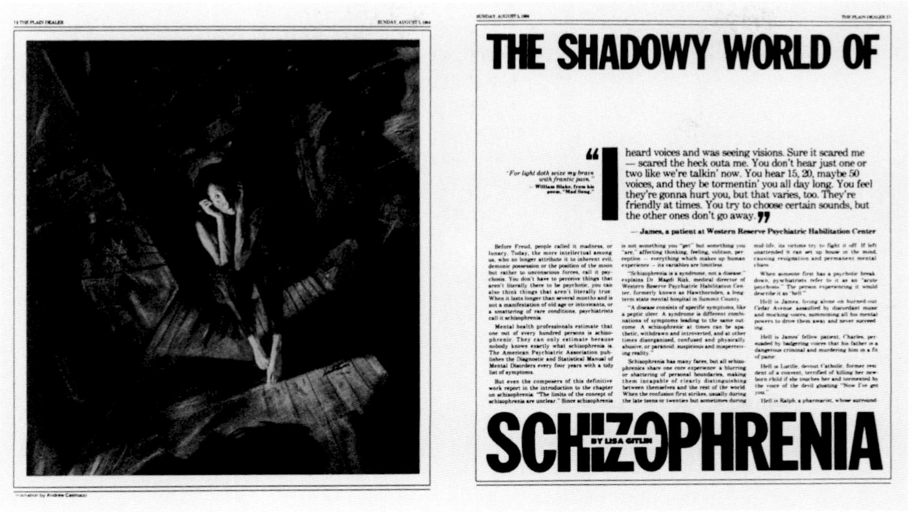

THE SHADOWY WORLD OF

"For light doth seize my brain with frantic pain." — William Blake, from his poem, "Mad Song."

"I heard voices and was seeing visions. Sure it scared me — scared the heck outa me. You don't hear just one or two like we're talkin' now. You hear 15, 20, maybe 50 voices, and they be tormentin' you all day long. You feel they're gonna hurt you, but that varies, too. They're friendly at times. You try to choose certain sounds, but the other ones don't go away."

— James, a patient at Western Reserve Psychiatric Habilitation Center

SCHIZOPHRENIA

BY LISA GITLIN

267

PUBLICATION: *The Plain Dealer Magazine*
ART DIRECTOR: *Gerard A. Sealy*
DESIGNER: *Gerard A. Sealy*
ILLUSTRATOR: *Andrew Castrucci*
PUBLISHER: *The Plain Dealer Publishing Co.*
CATEGORY: *Design Spread/Tabloid*
AWARD: *Merit*

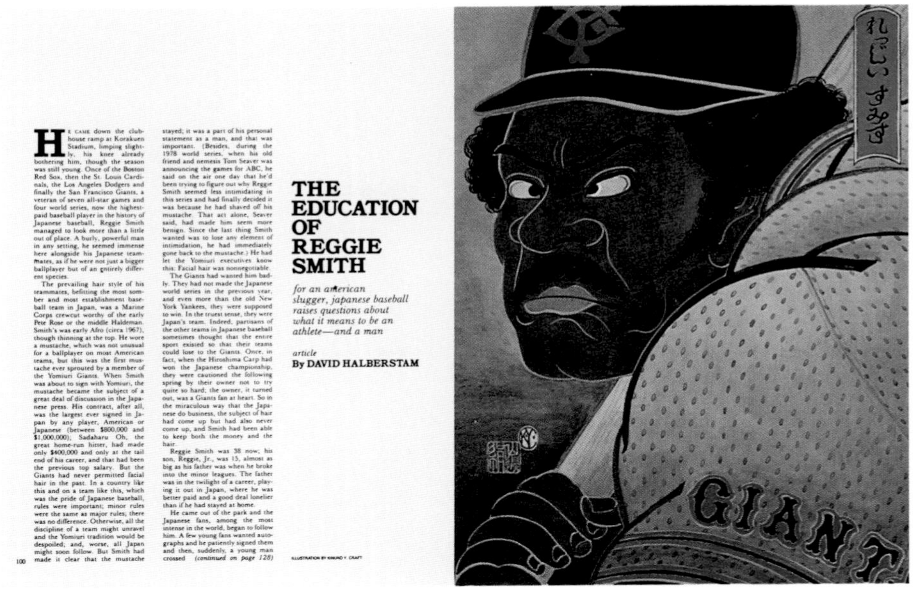

THE EDUCATION OF REGGIE SMITH

for an american slugger, japanese baseball raises questions about what it means to be an athlete—and a man

article By DAVID HALBERSTAM

(continued on page 128)

268

PUBLICATION: *Playboy Magazine*
ART DIRECTOR: *Tom Staebler*
DESIGNER: *Bruce Hansen*
ILLUSTRATOR: *Kinuko Y. Craft*
PUBLISHER: *Playboy Enterprises, Inc.*
CATEGORY: *Illustration Spread*
AWARD: *Merit*

mr. october looks at his yankee years the way he looks at hanging curves—he measures them patiently, then takes a vicious rip

MY LIFE IN PINSTRIPES

memoir By REGGIE JACKSON with MIKE LUPICA

269

PUBLICATION: *Playboy Magazine*
ART DIRECTOR: *Tom Staebler*
DESIGNER: *Theo Kouvatsos*
ILLUSTRATOR: *Robert Risko*
PUBLISHER: *Playboy Enterprises, Inc.*
CATEGORY: *Illustration Spread*
AWARD: *Merit*

AND ALL THROUGH THE HOUSE

an 87th precinct story

BY ED McBAIN

it was christmas eve, and crime was taking a strange kind of holiday

DETECTIVE STEVE CARELLA was alone in the squad room. It was very quiet for a Christmas Eve.

Normally, all hell broke loose the moment the stores closed. But tonight the squad room and the entire station house seemed unusually still. No phones ringing. No typewriters clacking away. No patrolmen popping upstairs to ask if any coffee was brewing in the clerical office down the hall. Just Carella, sitting at his desk and rereading the D.D. report he'd just typed, checking it for errors. He'd misspelled the "armed" in "armed robbery." It had come out "aimed robbery." He overscored the I with a ballpoint pen, giving the felony its true title. Armed robbery. Little liquor store on Culver Avenue. Guy walked in with a .357 Magnum and an empty potato sack. The owner hit a silent alarm and the two uniforms riding Boy One apprehended the thief as he was leaving the store.

Carella separated the carbons and the triplicate pages—white one in the uppermost basket, pink one in the basket marked for Miscolo in clerical, yellow one for the lieutenant. He looked up at the clock. Ten-thirty. The graveyard shift would be relieving at a quarter to 12, maybe a bit earlier, since it was Christmas Eve.

God, it was quiet around here.

He got up from his desk and walked around the bank of high cabinets that partitioned the rest of the squad room from a small sink in the corner opposite the detention cage. Quiet night like this one, you could fall asleep on the job. He opened the

270

PUBLICATION: *Playboy Magazine*
ART DIRECTOR: *Tom Staebler*
DESIGNER: *Kerig Pope*
ILLUSTRATOR: *Chris Van Allsburg*
PUBLISHER: *Playboy Enterprises, Inc.*
CATEGORY: *Illustration-Spread*
AWARD: *Merit*

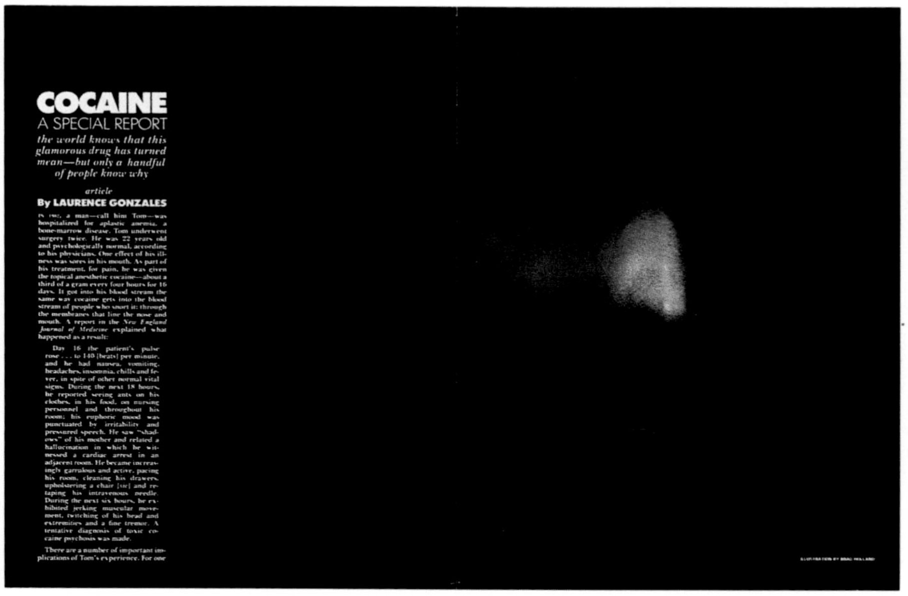

COCAINE

A SPECIAL REPORT

the world knows that this glamorous drug has turned mean—but only a handful of people know why

article

By LAURENCE GONZALES

[illegible], a man—call him Tom—was hospitalized for aplastic anemia, a bone-marrow disease. Tom underwent surgery twice. He was 22 years old and psychologically normal, according to his physicians. One effect of his illness was sores in his mouth. As part of his treatment, for pain, he was given the topical anesthetic cocaine—about a third of a gram every four hours for 16 days. It got into his blood stream the same way cocaine gets into the blood stream of people who snort it: through the membranes that line the nose and mouth. A report in the *New England Journal of Medicine* explained what happened as a result:

> Day 16 the patient's pulse rose . . . to 140 [beats] per minute, and he had nausea, vomiting, headaches, insomnia, chills and fever, in spite of other normal vital signs. During the next 18 hours, he reported seeing ants on his clothes, in his food, on nursing personnel and throughout his room; his euphoric mood was punctuated by irritability and pressured speech. He saw "shadows" of his mother and related a hallucination in which he witnessed a cardiac arrest in an adjacent room. He became increasingly garrulous and active, pacing his room, cleaning his drawers, upholstering a chair [sic] and retaping his intravenous needle. During the next six hours, he exhibited jerking muscular movement, twitching of his head and extremities and a fine tremor. A tentative diagnosis of toxic cocaine psychosis was made.

There are a number of important implications of Tom's experience. For one

271

PUBLICATION: *Playboy Magazine*
ART DIRECTOR: *Tom Staebler*
DESIGNER: *Kerig Pope*
ILLUSTRATOR: *Brad Holland*
PUBLISHER: *Playboy Enterprises, Inc.*
CATEGORY: *Illustration-Spread*
AWARD: *Merit*

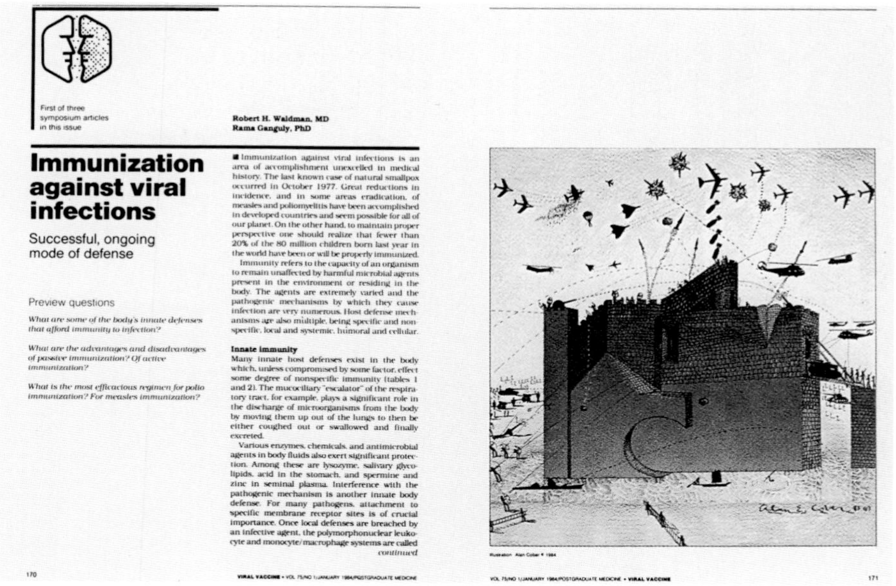

First of three symposium articles in this issue

Robert H. Waldman, MD
Rama Ganguly, PhD

Immunization against viral infections

Successful, ongoing mode of defense

Preview questions

What are some of the body's innate defenses that afford immunity to infection?

What are the advantages and disadvantages of passive immunization? Of active immunization?

What is the most efficacious regimen for polio immunization? For measles immunization?

■ Immunization against viral infections is an area of accomplishment unexcelled in medical history. The last known case of natural smallpox occurred in October 1977. Great reductions in incidence, and in some areas eradication, of measles and poliomyelitis have been accomplished in developed countries and seem possible for all of our planet. On the other hand, to maintain proper perspective one should realize that fewer than 20% of the 80 million children born last year in the world have been or will be properly immunized.

Immunity refers to the capacity of an organism to remain unaffected by harmful microbial agents present in the environment or residing in the body. The agents are extremely varied and the pathogenic mechanisms by which they cause infection are very numerous. Host defense mechanisms are also multiple, being specific and nonspecific, local and systemic, humoral and cellular.

Innate immunity

Many innate host defenses exist in the body which, unless compromised by some factor, effect some degree of nonspecific immunity (tables 1 and 2). The mucociliary "escalator" of the respiratory tract, for example, plays a significant role in the discharge of microorganisms from the body by moving them up out of the lungs to then be either coughed out or swallowed and finally excreted.

Various enzymes, chemicals, and antimicrobial agents in body fluids also exert significant protection. Among these are lysozyme, salivary glycolipids, acid in the stomach, and spermine and zinc in seminal plasma. Interference with the pathogenic mechanism is another innate body defense. For many pathogens, attachment to specific membrane receptor sites is of crucial importance. Once local defenses are breached by an infective agent, the polymorphonuclear leukocyte and monocyte/macrophage systems are called

continued

170 VIRAL VACCINE • VOL 75/NO 1/JANUARY 1984/POSTGRADUATE MEDICINE

Illustration: Alan Cober © 1984

VOL 75/NO 1/JANUARY 1984/POSTGRADUATE MEDICINE • VIRAL VACCINE 171

272

PUBLICATION: *Postgraduate Medicine*
ART DIRECTOR: *Tina Adamek*
ILLUSTRATOR: *Alan E. Cober*
PUBLISHER: *McGraw-Hill Publishing*
CATEGORY: *Illustration-Spread*
AWARD: *Merit*

Anxiety treatment
A commonsense approach

Marc A. Schuckit, MD

Preview
Anxiety must be considered a symptom, not a diagnosis. Although it can be a key symptom in the primary anxiety disorders, it also can occur with medical disorders and other psychiatric disorders. According to Dr Schuckit, the use of some commonsense guidelines can simplify recognition and treatment of anxiety in the general medical practice setting. In this article, he emphasizes differential diagnosis and the need for short-term use of pharmacotherapy.

Two of three patients seen by primary care physicians may have a medical or emotional disorder accompanied by a psychiatric complaint, most often anxiety.[1] The feeling of being sick or fearful without a clear cause may manifest itself through behavior, such as fidgeting or a look of distress, or through an actual complaint, such as nervousness. To treat such patients, the physician must accurately distinguish between medical [1] and psychiatric causes of the symptom of anxiety.

As is true of physical symptoms, emotional or psychiatric symptoms can be approached pragmatically. In other words, a particular symptom—in this case, anxiety—should suggest a number of possible diagnoses (table 1), each having its own prognosis and treatment.[2] The correct diagnostic label can then be determined by careful evaluation of all ancillary symptoms and the developmental course of the disorder.

In a general medical practice setting, medical disorders in which anxiety is inherent should be considered first in differential diagnosis, followed by chronic illness, chemical abuse, and primary psychiatric disorders. This leaves situational anxiety as the diagnosis by exclusion.

Medical disorders in which anxiety is inherent
Anxiety can occur as a psychologic reaction to a medical disorder. However, in 10% to 40% of the patients who seek medical attention because of anxiety or depression, a medical disorder per se is a major contributor. Anxiety is inherent in hyperthyroidism; most forms of cardiac disease, including angina and arrhythmias; respiratory diseases such as chronic obstructive lung disease and pulmonary embolism; endocrine disorders such as hypoglycemia; and rarer problems such as

pernicious anemia, porphyria, and if panic attacks are present, pheochromocytoma.[3,4]

Another medical disorder that has only recently received attention as a cause of anxiety is mitral valve prolapse. A nonejection midsystolic click occurs as the mitral valve prolapses and is often followed by a late systolic high-pitched murmur of mitral regurgitation, which is best heard over the apex.[5] Although 5% to 10% of the US population have mitral valve prolapse, most remain asymptomatic and never seek medical care because of it.[6] However, between 10% and 30% of patients identified as having mitral valve prolapse also have a panic disorder, and up to one third of patients affected by a panic disorder also have recognized mitral valve prolapse.[6] While the reason for the close association between these two distinct disorders has not yet been established, a genetic relationship is probable.[7]

For patients with a medical disorder in which anxiety is inherent, the physician's strategy should be not only to make the correct diagnosis and to aggressively treat the primary disorder but also, until the disorder is brought under control, to address the patient's state of psychologic distress. Patients can be trained to use relaxation

continued

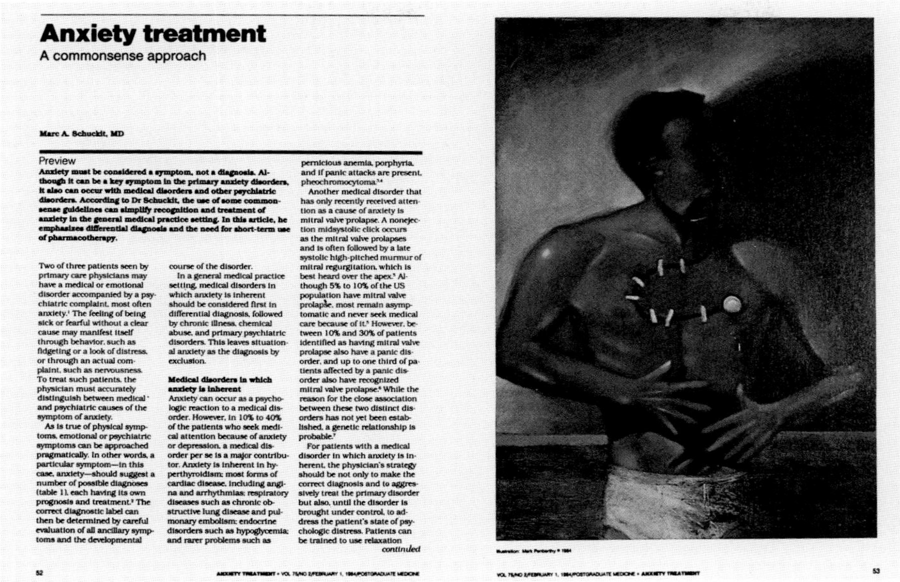

273
PUBLICATION: *Postgraduate Medicine*
ART DIRECTOR: *Tina Adamek*
ILLUSTRATOR: *Mark Penberthy*
PUBLISHER: *McGraw-Hill Publishing*
CATEGORY: *Illustration-Spread*
AWARD: *Merit*

First of four symposium articles in this issue

Neil C. Barnes, MD
John F. Costello, MD

Mast-cell-derived mediators in asthma
Arachidonic acid metabolites

Preview questions

How can the substances contained in the lipoxygenase pathway be characterized?

What is the most abundant cyclooxygenase product in mast cells?

What theory has been proposed to explain the mechanism of aspirin-induced asthma?

▪ The origin of the airway hyperreactivity seen in patients with bronchial asthma is probably multifactorial. Proposed mechanisms include vagal reflexes,[1] autonomic dysfunction,[2] inflammatory damage to the "tight" junction between bronchial epithelial cells,[3] and the complex effects of and interactions between a multitude of chemical mediators.[4]

Considerable interest has focused recently on the role of mediators derived from mast cells (figure 1). (Some mediators may also be released by basophils and neutrophils.) Release of chemical mediators from mast cells found in the bronchial wall is stimulated by antigen/IgE cross-linking on the mast cell surface and by other stimuli, such as exercise; it is also possible that asthmatics have "leakier" bronchial mast cells than normal subjects.[5]

Mediators released from mast cells can be divided into two groups (figure 1): the preformed mediators found within granules and those that are newly formed from metabolism of arachidonic acid in the cell membrane. Although preformed mediators almost certainly play an important role in asthma, further discussion here will be confined to the arachidonic acid metabolites, since they have been the subject of much recent interest and speculation.

Pathways of arachidonic acid metabolism
Arachidonic acid is formed in and released from the mast cell membrane (figure 2). When the membrane is stimulated (eg, by antigen/IgE union), methyl transferases act on phosphatidylethanolamine to form phosphatidylcholine. There is then an influx of calcium ions across the cell membrane; this, in turn, activates phospholipase A_2, and arachidonic acid is formed.

Arachidonic acid is metabolized by two distinct pathways: (1) the lipoxygenase pathway, whose products are the 5-hydroxyeicosatetraenoic acids (5-HETE) and leukotrienes (so named because they

continued

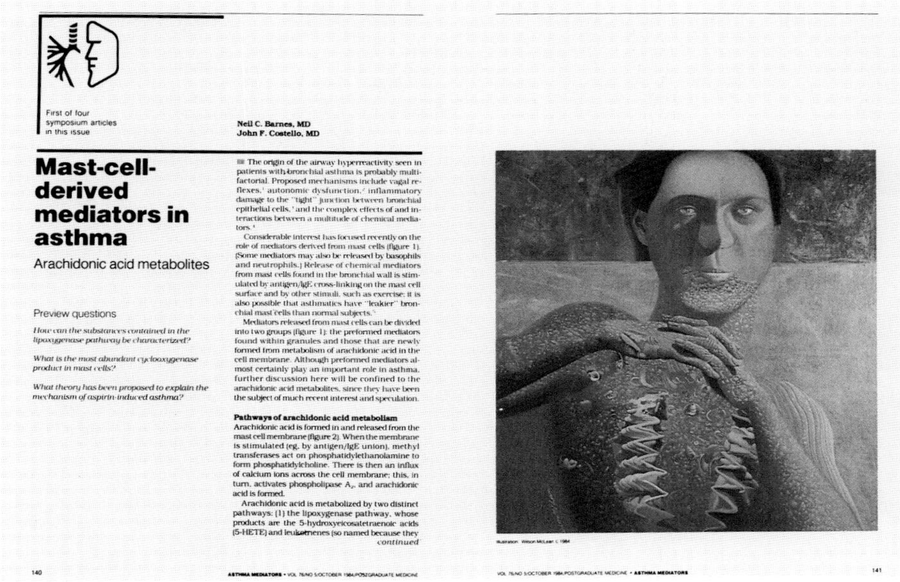

274
PUBLICATION: *Postgraduate Medicine*
ART DIRECTOR: *Tina Adamek*
ILLUSTRATOR: *Wilson McLean*
PUBLISHER: *McGraw-Hill Publishing*
CATEGORY: *Illustration-Spread*
AWARD: *Merit*

First of three symposium articles in this issue

Kevin J. Kiwak, MD

Establishing an etiology for torticollis

Preview questions

What are the most important elements in evaluation of torticollis?

With what conditions might torticollis be confused?

Into what categories can the causes of torticollis be divided?

▪ Torticollis is a contraction, often spasmodic, of the muscles of the neck, causing the head to be drawn to one side and usually to be rotated so that the chin points to the opposite side. The condition is not a diagnosis but rather a sign of an underlying disorder. As such, it should prompt an aggressive search for the cause. In this article I will briefly review the causes of torticollis—over 80 of which have been reported—and provide guidelines for a clinical approach to the patient with this problem.

Evaluation
Three basic questions must be considered by the physician in evaluating the patient with an abnormal neck posture.

1. Is this *actually* torticollis? The literature is replete with descriptions of various abnormal neck postures, many of which do not fit the classic definition of torticollis but are, nevertheless, labeled as such. The confusion, which is more than purely semantic, becomes important insofar as it affects the evaluation and treatment of the patient.

I have seen, for example, reports of "torticollis" in patients with myasthenia gravis[1] who in actuality have simple weakness of the neck muscles and resulting flexion of the neck. Also, incorrect associations of torticollis have been made with Meniere's disease, with benign paroxysmal vertigo, and with basilar artery migraine.[2] Can head tilt compensating for ocular strabismus be correctly considered as a cause of torticollis if the neck muscles are normal? And what about paroxysmal tonic neck deviation resulting from a dyskinetic syndrome? Each of these entities is clearly distinct from the problem being addressed here. To stretch the definition of torticollis to include these disorders only compounds the confusion in evaluation.

It is perhaps more important to adequately describe the findings in each patient than to try labeling all similar findings with a single name. In this article I will consider any abnormal neck

continued

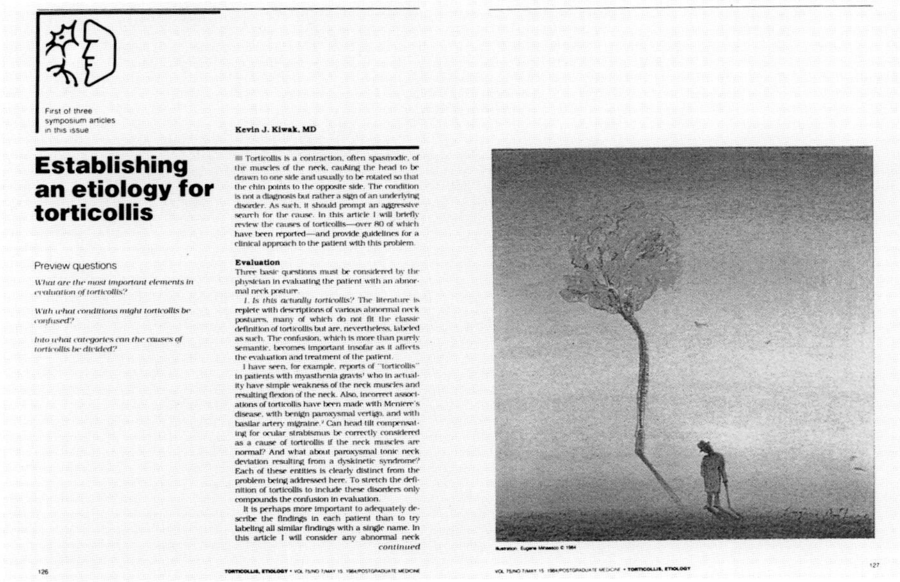

275
PUBLICATION: *Postgraduate Medicine*
ART DIRECTOR: *Tina Adamek*
ILLUSTRATOR: *Eugene Mihaesco*
PUBLISHER: *McGraw-Hill Publishing*
CATEGORY: *Illustration-Spread*
AWARD: *Merit*

The acutely swollen joint
First impressions may mislead

Ed Berg, MD

Preview
The cause of acute joint swelling may, at least in some cases, seem fairly obvious. However, the condition is often a manifestation of two or more concurrent, and possibly occult, pathologic problems. Dr Berg discusses differential diagnosis and stresses the importance of accurate history and workup.

The acutely swollen joint is a common diagnostic and therapeutic problem in primary care. The swelling can result from a variety of causes; in some cases determining the true culprit from among several potential causes can be a challenge. Accurate and quick diagnosis is of great importance, since some causal conditions (in particular sepsis) can become quite serious without prompt attention.

In cases where acute trauma is involved, the cause of acute joint swelling may seem obvious. However, the trauma may be superimposed on an underlying disease that is the true cause of the swelling and should thus not be accepted as the cause without a full evaluation.

X-ray films are mandatory in differential diagnosis, and examination of joint fluid is useful. Rafinsson and colleagues[1] have noted the significance of elevated ESR (>30 mm/hr [Westergren]) in the diagnosis of inflammation. The single most important diagnostic tool, however, is the history.

History should be taken with care and any clues fully explored, as they can be misleading. I am reminded of the case of a 15-year-old boy who presented to me with a history of recent trauma to the knee. On examination, the knee was noted to be swollen and mildly tender. An x-ray film showed a periosteal reaction with a lesion in the proximal tibia (figure 1a). Bone scan (figure 1b) showed marked uptake in the lesion, and at biopsy the diagnosis of osteogenic sarcoma was made. If the trauma had been accepted as the cause of the swelling, a grave error would have been made. In another case, a 19-year-old woman presented with an acutely swollen knee but no trauma. She had a history of endometrial carcinoma. An x-ray film showed a lytic lesion of the distal femur, which had a pathologic fracture into the joint. Again, reliance on just one part of the history would have resulted in serious misdiagnosis. These are unusual cases, certainly, but they illustrate the need for thorough history taking.

Once the clinician has uncovered the likely cause of swelling, he or she can proceed to specific treatment with confidence. Too often, treatment with corticosteroid injection is rushed into. This can be fruitless and indeed can be extremely dangerous, as steroids may suppress inflammation and actually enhance the infection. Thus, under no circumstances should the physician administer steroids until all possibility of infection has been erased.

The possible causes
In evaluation of the acutely swollen joint, two broad categories of causes should be kept in mind. inflammatory and noninflammatory conditions (table 1). I will comment on some of the specific conditions here, mainly the inflammatory ones, as these are the most ominous.

In every case of an acutely swollen joint, sepsis should be suspected and looked for (tables 2 and 3). Freed and colleagues,[2] in discussing a diagnostic approach to the potentially septic joint, have said that history, physical examination, joint x-ray films, synovial fluid cultures, Gram stain (figure 2), and/or examination for crystals yielded a diagnosis in 74% of the cases immediately or within two or three days. Other tests were not helpful acutely. These research-

continued

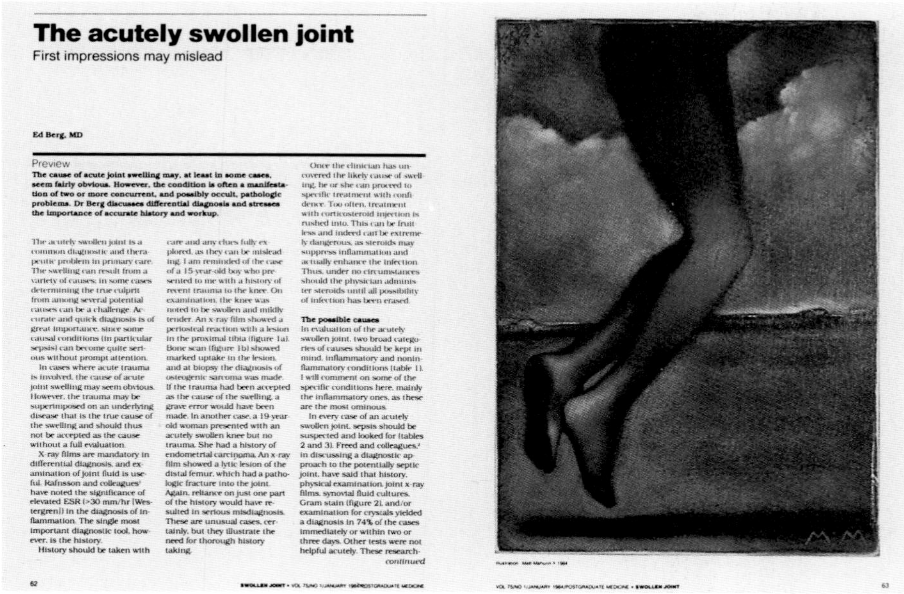

276
PUBLICATION: *Postgraduate Medicine*
ART DIRECTOR: *Tina Adamek*
ILLUSTRATOR: *Matt Mahurin*
PUBLISHER: *McGraw-Hill Publishing*
CATEGORY: *Illustration-Spread*
AWARD: *Merit*

Mayo Clinic

Angina pectoris
Clinical strategies in diagnosis

Clarence Shub, MD

Preview
Chest pain is one of the most common—and potentially serious—complaints the physician is called upon to evaluate. When angina pectoris is the suspected cause, diagnosis can often be based on the clinical examination and ECG. At times, however, additional cardiovascular testing is necessary and the physician must decide which tests will be most useful and practical. In this article, Dr Shub discusses diagnostic strategies that will help the physician who treats patients with chest pain.

Angina pectoris is a clinical diagnosis based on features of the history, physical examination, and ECG that suggest symptomatic myocardial ischemia. The various forms of the anginal syndrome include classic (Heberden's) angina, atypical angina, rest angina, unstable angina, postinfarction angina, and Prinzmetal's (variant) angina. Some of these forms are interrelated and may coexist.

Hierarchy of clinical strategies
The clinical examination, which includes a carefully obtained cardiac history, remains the first and foremost clinical strategy in the diagnosis of angina pectoris.[1] The diagnosis of pain due to myocardial ischemia (ie, angina) is made by characterizing the symptoms according to their quality, precipitating factors, location (figure 1), duration, and relief patterns. A history carefully taken should

© 1984 Mayo Foundation

elucidate whether or not the chest pain is anginal. For example, pain described as a "pressure" sensation, provoked by exertion, substernal in location, radiating to the left arm, of short duration, and relieved by rest or nitroglycerin is more likely to be anginal than pain described as "sharp," occurring at rest, spreading to other anatomic locations, of long duration (eg, hours), and affected by deep breathing or motion of the torso. In this manner, angina can usually be differentiated[2] from other types of chest pain, such as pain due to symptomatic diaphragmatic hernia, gallbladder disease, pericarditis, or musculoskeletal disorders of the chest or shoulders.

Analysis of the ECG is the second clinical strategy, since evidence of prior infarction or resting repolarization abnormalities may provide further diagnostic insights.[3] In some cases, however, the history is equivocal and physical examination and ECG results are normal or nonspecific.

Under these circumstances, additional cardiovascular testing becomes necessary as the next clinical strategy in this sequence. Proper use of this diagnostic strategy requires careful planning and a thorough knowledge of the performance characteristics of the tests involved.

Additional cardiovascular testing, as defined here, includes various noninvasive procedures that supplement the results of standard clinical examination, ECG, and chest roentgenogram. These procedures may include any combination of treadmill exercise testing, echocardiography (with or without Doppler studies), cardiac fluoroscopy, radionuclide angiography, cardiokymography, and thallium perfusion scintigraphy. Most of these tests are expensive and, to be cost-effective, should be ordered judiciously. Indiscriminate or automatic cardiovascular testing is not cost-effective, may lead to further testing and incorrect, confusing diagnoses, and wastes medical resources.

The last strategy to be considered is coronary angiography.

Noninvasive tests
Before ordering a cardiovascular test, the clinician should have in mind a specific question that the test can be expected to answer. The clinician also should know the test's sensitivity and

continued

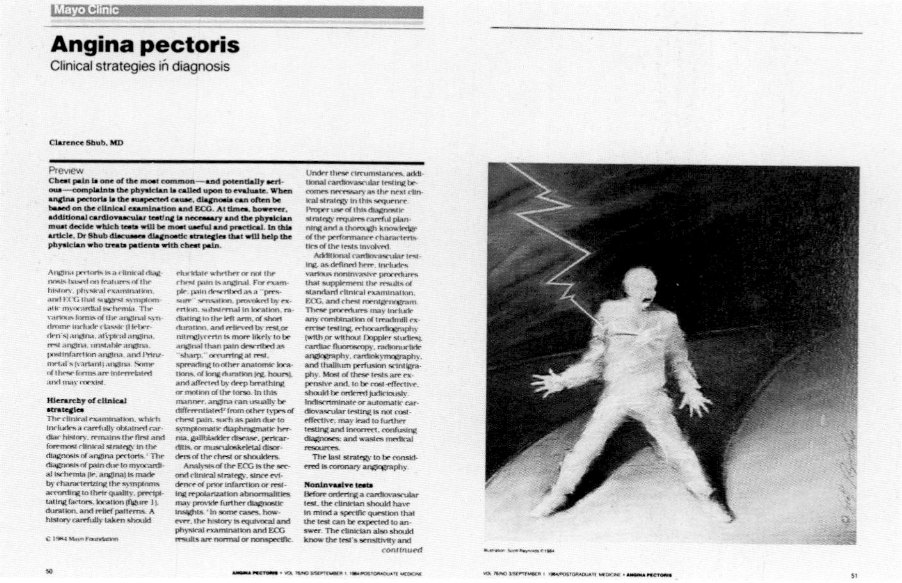

277
PUBLICATION: *Postgraduate Medicine*
ART DIRECTOR: *Tina Adamek*
ILLUSTRATOR: *Scott Reynolds*
PUBLISHER: *McGraw-Hill Publishing*
CATEGORY: *Illustration-Spread*
AWARD: *Merit*

First of five symposium articles in this issue

David A. Yngve, MD

Gait problems in children
A matter of rotation

Preview questions

Which rotational and gait problems require treatment? Which usually resolve spontaneously?

How is the specific location of a rotational problem identified?

Which conditions necessitate referral to a specialist?

■ Rotational and gait problems are a common cause of concern to physicians seeing young children. Many children with such problems are physiologically normal, and the condition will correct with growth. It is often difficult to convince parents that the apparent deformity will correct itself, however. Frequently, parents have received a barrage of opinions from grandparents, neighbors, and shoe salesmen, any of whom may be alarmists about benign conditions. Furthermore, some gait problems in young children do not spontaneously correct, so concern is valid. To separate the benign from the serious cases requires an understanding of the nature of each potential abnormality as well as of the pathogenesis and natural history.

Examination
The gait problems that frequently are caused by rotational abnormalities (figure 1). If the child is ambulatory, identification of the specific location of the rotational problem is made by first watching the child walk and then examining the patient prone on an examining table.[1,2]

Ask the child to walk in a large space such as a long hallway. First concentrate on the feet, observing if they turn in or out and estimating in degrees the amount of any turning. The deviation of the foot from the line of the child's progression is called the gait angle (figure 2). After observing the rotational alignment of the feet, observe the rotational alignment of the knees, ie, whether the patellae point inward, outward, or straight ahead.

If the feet and knees both turn in, the cause lies above the knees in the femurs. To examine for femoral torsion, have the child lie prone on the examining table, with the knees bent at right angles and the feet falling out to the side (figure 3a). This rotates the patellae inward and the femurs internally. Then externally rotate the femurs by crossing the lower legs (figure 3b). While performing these tests, make

continued

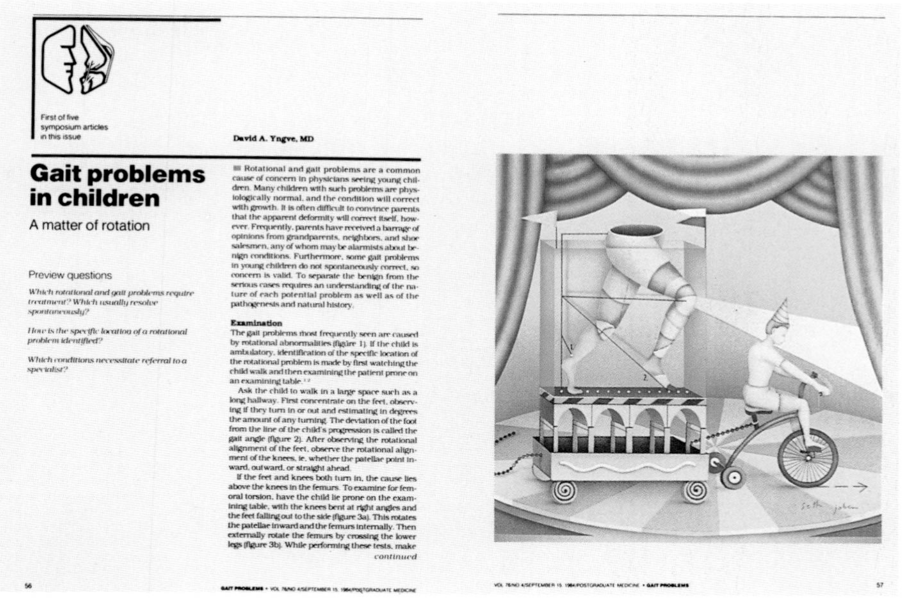

278
PUBLICATION: *Postgraduate Medicine*
ART DIRECTOR: *Tina Adamek*
ILLUSTRATOR: *Seth Jaben*
PUBLISHER: *McGraw-Hill Publishing*
CATEGORY: *Illustration-Spread*
AWARD: *Merit*

279

PUBLICATION: *Progressive Architecture*
ART DIRECTOR: *Kenneth Windsor*
DESIGNER: *Kenneth Windsor*
PHOTOGRAPHER: *Karant & Associates, Inc.*
PUBLISHER: *Reinhold Publishing*
CATEGORY: *Photography-Spread*
AWARD: *Merit*

280

PUBLICATION: *Progressive Architecture*
ART DIRECTOR: *Kenneth Windsor*
DESIGNER: *Kenneth Windsor*
PHOTOGRAPHER: *Wolfgant Hoyt @ESTO*
PUBLISHER: *Reinhold Publishing*
CATEGORY: *Photography-Spread*
AWARD: *Merit*

281

PUBLICATION: *Progressive Architecture*
ART DIRECTOR: *Kenneth Windsor*
DESIGNER: *Kenneth Windsor*
PHOTOGRAPHER: *Oberto Gili*
PUBLISHER: *Reinhold Publishing*
CATEGORY: *Photography-Spread*
AWARD: *Merit*

282

PUBLICATION: *Progressive Architecture*
ART DIRECTOR: *Kenneth Windsor*
DESIGNER: *Kenneth Windsor*
PHOTOGRAPHER: *Arthur Meyerson Photography*
PUBLISHER: *Reinhold Publishing*
CATEGORY: *Photography-Spread*
AWARD: *Merit*

283

PUBLICATION: *Progressive Architecture*
ART DIRECTOR: *Kenneth Windsor*
DESIGNER: *Kenneth Windsor*
PHOTOGRAPHER: *Barbara Karant*
PUBLISHER: *Reinhold Publishing*
CATEGORY: *Photography-Spread*
AWARD: *Merit*

284

PUBLICATION: *Progressive Architecture*
ART DIRECTOR: *Kenneth Windsor*
DESIGNER: *Kenneth Windsor*
PUBLISHER: *Reinhold Publishing*
CATEGORY: *Design-Spread*
AWARD: *Merit*

Portfolio

Great revivals

Some furniture, like some fashion, never goes out of style. Demand for Le Corbusier's chaise longue, Marcel Breuer's Wassily chair and his ever-popular Cesca, and even Mies van der Rohe's pricey Barcelona chair seems only to increase with the passage of time. These classics are, however, only the core of a general revival of early 20th-Century furniture which has gained considerable momentum over the past several years. Shown on these pages are some of the more recent offerings, an eclectic portfolio ranging from the organic art furniture of Erik Gunnar Asplund to the rationalist work of Giuseppe Terragni.

While these nine pieces are significant in and of themselves, each also represents a broader commitment on the part of manufacturers and distributors to make available not just the odd collector's item but a whole series of works by a given designer. The Breuer couch is only the latest in a long line of Breuer pieces reproduced by Thonet over the years. ICF expects to add to its collection of furniture by Eliel Saarinen on a yearly basis, while Jack Lenor Larsen's introduction of the Riemerschmid Music Room Chair follows last year's Armchair. Atelier International has reintroduced three Asplund designs, and Furniture of the Twentieth Century carries a total of six pieces by Terragni.

Herman Miller has begun to reproduce Isamu Noguchi's 1947 organic collectable (below) as part of a whole program of reissued classics by Noguchi, George Nelson, and Charles Eames, whose last work, a posthumously manufactured leather sofa with padded arms, was also reintroduced this year. The Noguchi table, which balances a heavy plate-glass top on two identical members carved from solid wood, has been out of production only since 1973. Its return is a welcome sign of the times. (DARALICE D. BOLES) ■

Although trained as a painter, Richard Riemerschmid moved quickly into the applied arts, playing a major role in the 1907 formation of the Deutscher Werkbund. His Music Room Chair, reissued this year by Jack Lenor Larsen, was first shown at the Dresden Exhibition of 1899. Its striking diagonal cross brace, slightly curved, is an elegant, organic solution to the problem of stabilization. The chair is available in golden natural or ebonized beechwood and studded seat cushions.

196 *Progressive Architecture 9:84*

Progressive Architecture 9:84

RECORDS

Masterful funk for the mind and booty

George Clinton and company recapture the dance-floor crown

URBAN DANCE FLOOR GUERILLAS
P. FUNK ALL-STARS
Uncle Jam/CBS
★★★★

YOU SHOULDN'T-NUF BIT FISH
GEORGE CLINTON
Capitol
★★★

BY DEBBY MILLER

"Free your mind and your ass will follow" has always been George Clinton's foremost message to the world. But even while he campaigns to unlock your mind, it's clear his real goal is to shake your tail feathers. Which is why *Urban Dancefloor Guerillas* may be his most perfect record: Not only is it filled with the wonderfully hilarious wordplay of Clinton and his team, it's a whole LP of consistently great dance music.

Last year, Clinton had a huge hit, at least in the metropolises, with "Atomic Dog," whose thundering bass notes barked "Woof! Woof!" *Urban Dancefloor Guerillas*, by Clinton's P.Funk All-Stars, is more the follow-up to that infectious dance track than his new "solo" album, *You Shouldn't-Nuf Bit Fish*. In fact, it's the P.Funk record that contains "Copy Cat," a reprise of the hit that moves from woof to meow: "Yakety yak, bring in the dog, let's put out the cat." The solo record is a fine album, too, but it's no match for the un-

ROLLING STONE, MARCH 15, 1984 · 47

285

PUBLICATION: *Rolling Stone*
ART DIRECTOR: *Derek Ungless*
DESIGNER: *Elizabeth Williams*
ILLUSTRATOR: *Mark Marek*
PUBLISHER: *Straight Arrow Publishers*
CATEGORY: *Illustration-Spread*
AWARD: *Merit*

286

PUBLICATION: *Rolling Stone*
ART DIRECTOR: *Derek Ungless*
DESIGNER: *Derek Ungless*
PHOTOGRAPHER: *Laurie Kratochvil*
PUBLISHER: *Straight Arrow Publishers, Inc.*
CATEGORY: *Design-Spread*
AWARD: *Merit*

287

PUBLICATION: *Rolling Stone*
ART DIRECTOR: *Derek Ungless*
DESIGNER: *Elizabeth Williams*
PHOTOGRAPHER: *Hiro*
PUBLISHER: *Straight Arrow Publishers, Inc.*
CATEGORY: *Design-Spread*
AWARD: *Merit*

288

PUBLICATION: *Rolling Stone*
ART DIRECTOR: *Derek Ungless*
DESIGNER: *Elizabeth Williams*
PHOTOGRAPHER: *Richard Avedon*
PUBLISHER: *Straight Arrow Publishers, Inc.*
CATEGORY: *Photography*
AWARD: *Merit*

RollingStone

THE BONFIRE OF THE VANITIES

TOM WOLFE

CHAPTER I

Yo! Goldberg!

AND THEN say what? Say, 'Forget you're hungry, forget you got shot inna back by some racist cop – Charlie was here? Charlie come up to Harlem – ' "

"No, I'll *tell* you what – "

" 'Charlie come up to Harlem and – ' "

"I'll *tell* you what – "

"Say, 'Charlie come up to Harlem and gonna take care a

289

PUBLICATION: *Rolling Stone*
ART DIRECTOR: *Derek Ungless*
DESIGNER: *Derek Ungless*
ILLUSTRATOR: *Lois & Lars Hokanson*
PUBLISHER: *Straight Arrow Publishers, Inc.*
CATEGORY: *Design-Spread*
AWARD: *Merit*

"My job was not to write about John's fantasy."

Bob Woodward

"The man in 'Wired' is not the man I knew."

Judy Jacklin

The Controversy Over 'Wired'

Reporter Bob Woodward wrote the only kind of book he knew how: just the facts, ma'am. John Belushi's outraged widow, Judy Jacklin, says those facts are wrong. This is the tale of their obsessions. **By Lynn Hirschberg**

Rolling Stone, September 27, 1984

290

PUBLICATION: *Rolling Stone*
ART DIRECTOR: *Derek Ungless*
DESIGNER: *Elizabeth Williams*
PHOTOGRAPHER: *William Coupon*
PUBLISHER: *Straight Arrow Publishers, Inc.*
CATEGORY: *Photography-Spread*
AWARD: *Merit*

RECORDS

U2 tones down its guitar attack on new LP

Alliance with Eno yields flawed album

THE UNFORGETTABLE FIRE
U2
Island
★★★

BY KURT LODER

THE TITLE OF U2'S FIFTH ALBUM IS perversely suggestive. Over the course of three studio LPs and one live-in-concert item, this stormy Irish guitar band, borne aloft by its grand, anthemic roar and an earnest concern for social issues, had ascended to the verge of substantial rock stardom in this country. Unfortunately, with *The Unforgettable Fire*, U2 flickers and nearly fades, its fire banked by a misconceived production strategy and occasional interludes of soggy, songless self-indulgence. This is not a "bad" album, but neither is it the irrefutable beauty the band's fans anticipated. What happened?

Initially, U2's decision to abandon the pop-conscious ministrations of its previous producers, Steve Lillywhite and Jimmy Iovine, and to hire instead the veteran experimentalist Brian Eno and his current collaborator, Canadian producer Daniel Lanois, seemed not only interesting but also admirably consistent with the band's vaunted idealism. The four members felt artistically constricted by their chart-tested monster-guitar format; the right producer – somebody with serious art credentials – would understand their impasse, would be able to help them grow. It sounded like a brave gamble: art over gold.

But idealism is not art. As a producer – as opposed to a producer-songwriter, the role he played with Talking Heads – Eno is most valuable as a conceptual organizer and sonic strategist, a master of atmospheres. But with guitarist Dave "the Edge" Evans churning out squalls

46 : Rolling Stone, October 11, 1984

RECORDS

Rickie Lee Jones gets personal

Her new 'Magazine' is hard to read

THE MAGAZINE
RICKIE LEE JONES
Warner Bros.
★★★★

BY DON SHEWEY

RICKIE LEE JONES HAS ALWAYS been idiosyncratic. The very first song on her first album had her gossiping about friends by their nicknames, tossing around private slang and presuming that we were interested enough to care what she was talking about. Of course we were – anybody that sure of herself is pretty irresistible.

Even so, her new album is a true test of our friendship. Flipping through *The Magazine*, her most stubbornly cryptic, perversely private work so far, you can't help thinking something crucial has been left out. It's so full of personal codes and abrupt changes of subject that even her sturdiest followers would throw up their hands in exasperation if she weren't so funny, such a good singer, so damned *charming*.

Jones calls the last three numbers on the album "Rorschachs," which is some joke: the whole record is nothing but abstract word paintings, beautifully arranged and executed with help from a crew of L.A. session giants, carefully designed to avoid anything too straightforward. The songs are like poetic home movies, or images from dreams groggily sketched at dawn and left wide-open to interpretation. Whadda you think, doc?

Well, let's say the album is the story of a woman who's tormented by the expectation of true love and wonders how she ever got that way. "Gravity," with its cinematic instrumental overture, depicts three scared girls torching a newsstand by moonlight in some sort of witchy love ritual. "I could not say no to

Rolling Stone, November 8, 1984 : 63

291

PUBLICATION: *Rolling Stone*
ART DIRECTOR: *Derek Ungless*
DESIGNER: *Elizabeth Williams*
ILLUSTRATOR: *Ian Pollack*
PUBLISHER: *Straight Arrow Publishers, Inc.*
CATEGORY: *Illustration-Spread*
AWARD: *Merit*

292

PUBLICATION: *Rolling Stone*
ART DIRECTOR: *Derek Ungless*
DESIGNER: *Elizabeth Williams*
ILLUSTRATOR: *Ian Pollack*
PUBLISHER: *Straight Arrow Publishers, Inc.*
CATEGORY: *Illustration-Single Page*
AWARD: *Merit*

295

PUBLICATION: *Self Magazine*
ART DIRECTOR: *Christopher Austopchuk*
DESIGNER: *Christopher Austopchuk*
PHOTOGRAPHER: *Margaret McKenna for Chuck Baker*
PUBLISHER: *Conde Nast Publications*
CATEGORY: *Photography-Spread*
AWARD: *Merit*

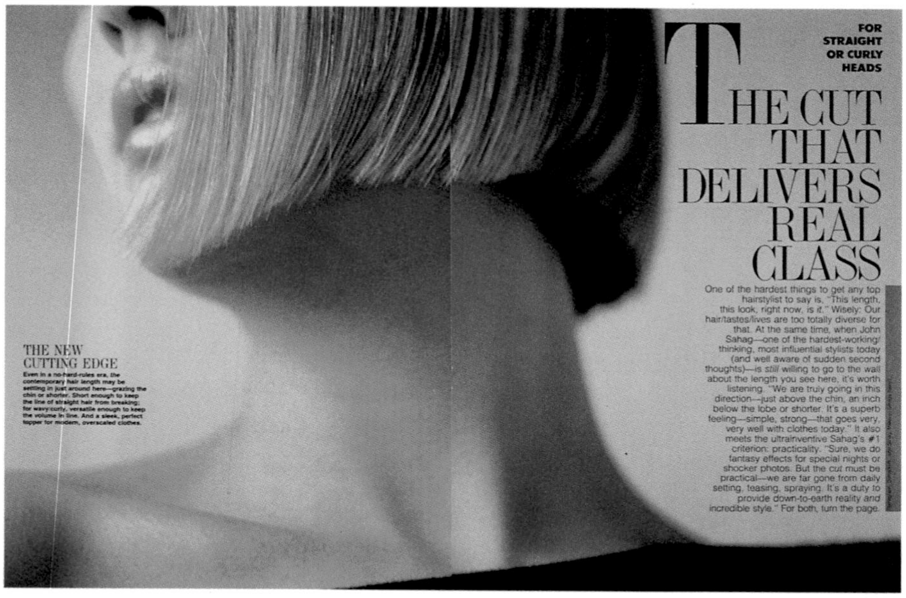

296

PUBLICATION: *Self Magazine*
ART DIRECTOR: *Christopher Austopchuk*
DESIGNER: *Christopher Austopchuk*
PHOTOGRAPHER: *Comte*
PUBLISHER: *Conde Nast Publications*
CATEGORY: *Photography-Spread*
AWARD: *Merit*

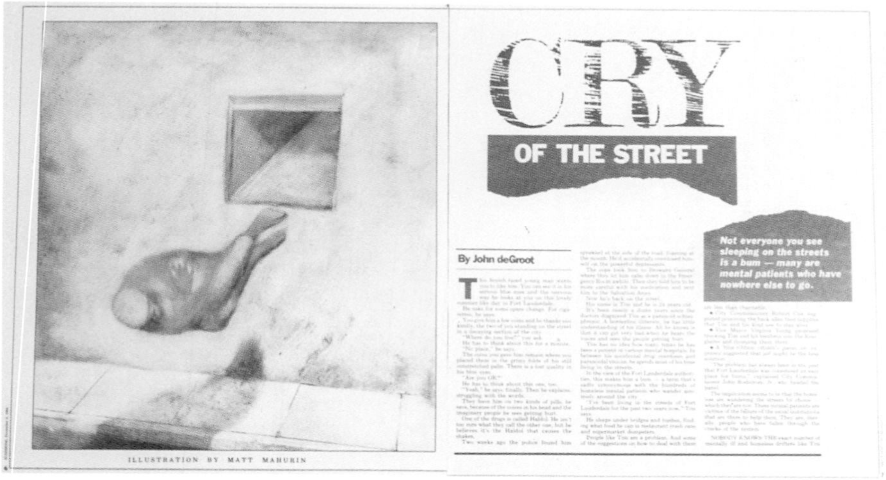

297

PUBLICATION: *Sunshine Magazine*
ART DIRECTOR: *Greg Paul*
DESIGNER: *Greg Paul*
ILLUSTRATOR: *Matt Mahurin*
PUBLISHER: *Fort Lauderdale News & Sun Sentinel*
CATEGORY: *Design-Spread*
AWARD: *Merit*

298

PUBLICATION: *Sunshine Magazine*
ART DIRECTOR: *Greg Paul*
DESIGNER: *Greg Paul*
PHOTOGRAPHER: *Steve Hill*
PUBLISHER: *Fort Lauderdale News & Sun-Sentinel*
CATEGORY: *Design-Spread*
AWARD: *Merit*

Two Faced

Putting a public face on your private feelings can make you crazy. Here's how to keep your smile and your sanity.

One of the challenges of working as a server is that your whole being gets a complete workout during every shift. It's a physical job that requires strength and endurance. And it's a mental job that taxes the brain.

But it isn't enough to take the orders, serve the drinks, bring the food, and deliver the check. You have to put personality in the work, too. You have to convince yourself and your customers that you *love* what you do. That's why being a server is one of the most emotionally demanding jobs in the world.

Cindy Cotter, an experienced waitress, knows how emotionally draining serving can be. She woke up one morning after several particularly hectic weeks at work and found herself reaching for a cigarette before she had even rolled out of bed. That's when she realized that she had been smoking more than usual because of recent pressures on the job.

"Not that I didn't enjoy my work," Cotter says. "It was just that my job was placing such an emotional strain on me. I had to constantly interact with all these people, and in order to get good tips, I had to react to each table differently," she

Article by *Carol Byrd*

Illustration by *Guire Vaka*

299

PUBLICATION: *Tables*
ART DIRECTOR: *Blair Caplinger*
ILLUSTRATOR: *Michel Guire Vaka*
CATEGORY: *Illustration-Spread*
PUBLISHER: *13•30 Corporation*
AWARD: *Merit*

Acting Up

Would you tap-dance for your tables? Some servers are saying yes as they learn that playing up to customers' wants can mean big bucks.

John stood at his station looking at the dollar in his hand from table six. He couldn't believe he'd gotten such a low tip. After all, he had politely shown the customers to their table, had promptly brought them their food, and had correctly added up the check. True, at one point they had tried to talk with him and he had just nodded a quick reply, smiled politely, and kept on working. But he felt he had given them quick, courteous service. Wasn't that enough to please them?

What John and many other servers—both experienced and new on the job—don't realize is that many customers come into your restaurant for more than just a

Illustration by
ANITA KUNZ

300

PUBLICATION: *Tables*
ART DIRECTOR: *Blair Caplinger*
DESIGNER: *Blair Caplinger*
ILLUSTRATOR: *Anita Kunz*
PUBLISHER: *13•30 Corporation*
CATEGORY: *Illustration-Spread*
AWARD: *Merit*

Little

BABY BLUE

Within hours of her birth, our otherwise perfect daughter started showing signs of serious heart trouble. Then came many months in and out of hospitals and a seemingly endless struggle to keep her alive and my family in one piece.

by Scott Nelson

Our second daughter, Carrie, was born on an August afternoon, in what appeared to be perfect condition. Throughout my wife's pregnancy, Jane and I had exercised care and good nutrition and had closely followed all the latest medical pronouncements. Waiting at the Mother Frances Hospital in Tyler for our child to be born, I watched the other prospective fathers, many of whom were teens about half my age, and thought how obviously unprepared they seemed. Mentally, I placed my family in an entirely different class, one based not on wealth (I am a college teacher) but on, well, maturity.

To my relief, Jane came through the delivery beautifully. Even during labor she remarked that the pains were not too bad, and the birth of this child seemed swift compared with that of Amy, our three-year-old. This time the mood was much more relaxed, even fun. The baby looked healthy and strong, both in the nursery and later when she was brought to her mother's room for a first feeding. We were, in short, elated. I had even been privately rooting for a girl.

As evening approached, I left Jane to get her rest and, after picking up Amy, returned to our home in Kilgore. We ate hot dogs and phoned friends with the news. Finally I put Amy to bed and plopped down in an easy chair to watch a baseball game, intending to unwind and then retire. Around eleven the phone rang. Jane's voice caught me by surprise; I had expected her to be asleep.

"The baby's starting to turn blue," she said. I could tell from her choked voice that she was frightened. "The nurses are worried, and they've called a pediatrician to come look at her. There's something wrong with her heart."

I told myself and Jane that there was no cause for alarm. "Call me back after the doctor examines her," I said confidently. Then I did a strange thing: I went to bed. It was as if pretending that everything was all right would make it that way.

Congenital heart disease is one of those curious ailments that strike newborns by what appears to be random selection, like a macabre lottery. No one knows the cause; it has to do with the genetic signals that are sent when humans are conceived, or even before. Such "blue babies" are frequently cited in history and literature (William Faulkner's

Texas Primer

THE STICKER BUR

Into each and every barefoot Texas childhood a little sticker bur must fall.

by Mimi Swartz

THE ECCENTRIC GENIUS OF TRAMMELL CROW

AND NOW HE'S CHANGED THE FACE OF AMERICA.
BY JOSEPH NOCERA

301

PUBLICATION: *Texas Monthly Magazine*
ART DIRECTOR: *Fred Woodward*
DESIGNER: *Fred Woodward*
ILLUSTRATOR: *Paola Piglia*
PUBLISHER: *Texas Monthly Inc.*
CATEGORY: *Illustration-Spread*
AWARD: *Merit*

303

PUBLICATION: *Texas Monthly Magazine*
ART DIRECTOR: *Fred Woodward*
DESIGNER: *Fred Woodward*
ILLUSTRATOR: *David Kampa*
PUBLISHER: *Texas Monthly, Inc.*
CATEGORY: *Illustration-Spread*
AWARD: *Merit*

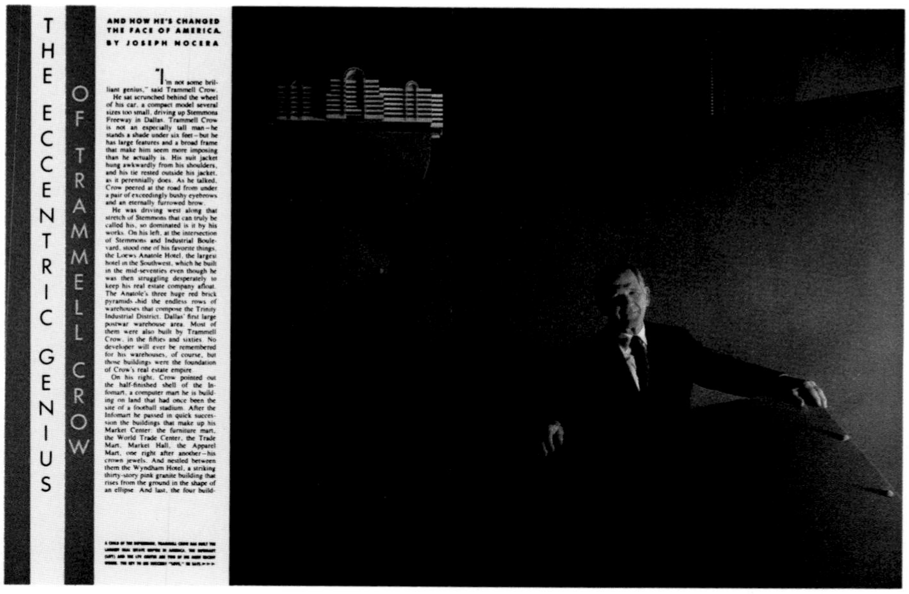

304

PUBLICATION: *Texas Monthly Magazine*
ART DIRECTOR: *Fred Woodward*
DESIGNER: *Fred Woodward*
PUBLISHER: *Texas Monthly, Inc.*
CATEGORY: *Photography-Spread*
AWARD: *Merit*

305

PUBLICATION: *Town & Country*
ART DIRECTOR: *Melissa Tardiff*
DESIGNER: *Richard Turtletaub*
PHOTOGRAPHER: *Tom Hollyman*
PUBLISHER: *Hearst Corp.*
CATEGORY: *Design-Spread*
AWARD: *Merit*

306

PUBLICATION: *Town & Country*
ART DIRECTOR: *Melissa Tardiff*
DESIGNER: *Richard Turtletaub*
PHOTOGRAPHER: *Lee Botin*
PUBLISHER: *Hearst Corp.*
CATEGORY: *Design-Spread*
AWARD: *Merit*

307

PUBLICATION: *Town & Country*
ART DIRECTOR: *Melissa Tardiff*
DESIGNER: *Richard Turtletaub*
PHOTOGRAPHER: *Jillian Levine*
PUBLISHER: *Hearst Corp.*
CATEGORY: *Design-Spread*
AWARD: *Merit*

A TRAVELER'S GUIDE TO
JAPAN
BEHIND THE MYSTIQUE

Photographed by Burt Glinn

Torii Gates at Fushimi Inari Shrine

THE ESSENCE OF JAPAN

Understanding the concepts of a culture
by Donald Richie

308

PUBLICATION: *Travel & Leisure*
ART DIRECTOR: *Adrian Taylor*
DESIGNER: *Adrian Taylor*
                  Kenneth Kleppert
PHOTOGRAPHER: *Burt Glynn, Steve Elmore*
                  George Obremski, Fred Maroon
                  Brian Blake
PUBLISHER: *American Express*
CATEGORY: *Photo-Story Presentation*
AWARD: *Merit*

An Art and a flower arrangement

The carving of house and garden

A garden of rocks and stones

A stone well with bamboo pipe

Warming up for Japan's traditional sumo wrestling

Ballet dancers, everywhere at the barre

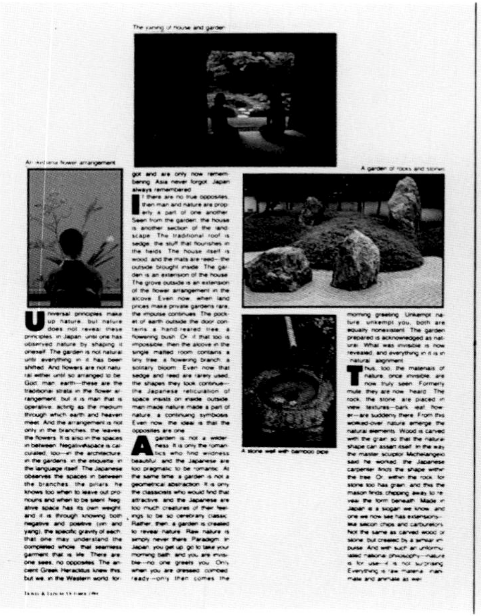

II, the area is famous for its coffeehouses, cheap but good restaurants, movie theaters and raunchy amusements. There are also huge department stores around the station, with Isetan the favorite of many foreigners. Finally, to the southeast of the station there is one of Tokyo's most beautiful gardens, **Shinjuku Gyoen,** once the estate of a leading daimyo (feudal lord) family.

Harajuku

Perhaps no other neighborhood offers such a complete view of the contrasts in Japanese life. Within 10 minutes' walk of each other you can visit the placid grounds of the Meiji Shrine, stroll the most chic street in Tokyo, and on Sunday, watch groups of young Japanese dance in the streets. Sunday is indeed the day to go, and Harajuku is worth three or four hours of your time.

Start along **Omotesando-dori,** the treelined boulevard that leads southeast from the JNR Harajuku Station. Here Japan's first affluent generation hangs out in designer clothes at restaurants serving foreign foods and at endless stylish coffee shops where the comparatively high price you pay for a cup of coffee also buys you space, for a while, in one of the world's most crowded cities. (This neighborhood's land is valued at almost $45,000 a square meter.) West of the station, **Yoyogi Park** fills up on Sunday afternoon with crowds of teenagers, decked out in get-ups from the American Fifties, who sway in carefully choreographed moves to the sounds blaring from portable cassette players. It makes an interesting scene alongside the graceful sweeps and arches of celebrated architect Kenzo Tange's temple-inspired building created for the swimming events at the Tokyo Olympics in 1964.

Those of you with memories of postwar occupation days will recognize the Harajuku area as the site of Washington Heights, Tokyo headquarters and housing for U.S. military personnel. A few of the shops that sold the best souvenirs in town to the armed forces remain today, still favorites, but with a new kind of clientele. The first stop is the **Oriental Bazaar** (5-9-13 Jingumae, Shibuya-ku, telephone 400-3933), which still sells some of the best souvenirs both old and new. The next place on the list is **Kiddy Land** (6-1-9 Jingumae, Shibuya-ku, 409-3434), as crowded with young customers as it is with the games, toys and accessories they buy.

Beyond Harajuku Station, to the northwest, you will find the sedate **Meiji Shrine,** with its *hinoki* (Japanese cypress) torii gates made from gigantic trees said to be more than 1,700 years old. Walk under the torii to explore the quiet paths, and pause to admire the inner compound shrine honoring the Emperor Meiji, who guided Japan through its great transition in the late 1800s when, almost overnight, it changed from a feudal country shut off from the world to a modern Western-oriented state.

Ginza

This is a name many visitors recognize. It is most commonly referred to as "the Ginza," denoting the main street that is home to some of Tokyo's most exclusive shops and biggest department stores, but it is really an entire neighborhood located to the east of Tokyo Station.

The name means "the place where silver is coined," and money is still the game here as giant department stores battle for customers. In the back streets (look for tiny entrance gardens graced with a touch of bamboo and water-sprinkled stones) are some of the city's most exclusive clubs, where any question concerning prices would be considered gauche. Astronomical bills are delivered by messenger to the offices of the clubs' guests for payment, with only the total amount due provided. For less extravagant tastes—and pocketbooks—there are *yatai* carts from which vendors serve everyday foods such as *oden* (a sort of stew) and *soba* (noodles) for a few

Wherever you go in Tokyo, there are vivid reminders that past and present exist together. The noted Kabuki actor Ebizo (opposite) is in full costume just before making his entrance. A Japanese street punk (below) flaunts a regalia of different style.

know this lady was no featherbrained dilettante. Lady Murasaki Shikibu, in her *Tale of Genji,* produced something of a roman à clef, her hero being Prince Genji, a paragon of all courtly manners, a calligrapher, poet, meticulous dresser and ladies' man par excellence. His entertaining exploits fill seven volumes, which bring the doings of his era astonishingly to life. Murasaki (her name means purple, the imperial color) retired for a time in Buddhist seclusion to the eighth-century Ishiyama Temple, which has, besides a famous pagoda and belfry, a building called the Hall of Genji, where Murasaki is said to have written her romantic classic.

But if Kyoto was a city of ineffable elegance, it was also a hotbed of intrigue, of blood and thunder, owing to the power struggles of the daimyos, the great feudal lords whose retainers were the samurai, the hereditary warrior class. The Emperor, revered as the descendant of the Shinto gods, came in time to be a father figure and protector of the culture rather than an administrator. The real power behind the throne was vested in the shogun, who was appointed by the Emperor from the daimyo class. History indicates that there could be plenty of skulduggery on the way to the shogunate, for the daimyos were in continual contention for the prize position.

A prime example of such struggles is the career of Hideyoshi Toyotomi, a 16th-century generalissimo (*taiko*) who wielded all the power of a shogun and unified Japan. He was no daimyo at all but a farm boy who schemed and sword-slashed his way to the top. For a riveting story along these lines, read—if you haven't already—James Clavell's *Shōgun.* This novel is based on the rise to power of the 17th-century shogun Ieyasu Tokugawa, assisted by a marooned English pilot who, in real life, was William Adams, an English mariner employed by the Dutch East India Company.

Kyoto is a place for the thoughtful traveler. The hyperkinetic sightseers who whirl from high spot to high spot will hardly get its message. Indeed, it can be a traveler's rest cure if you relax and absorb its treasures leisurely, even if you cover only a few of them. No one could possibly take in all that is offered here on one or one hundred visits. Among Kyoto's wooded hills, there are some 200 Shinto shrines and 1,500 Buddhist temples, little villages in themselves. There are walks to take among the pines and maples and cryptomeria, villas to visit, palaces to see, gardens in which to catch your breath.

This fifth-largest city in Japan sprawls, but it has an excellent system of electric trains, trolleys, buses and subways to get you anywhere you want to go, if you're game enough to try them (preferably armed with written directions from your hotel concierge). Ideally, you will have a personal guide-interpreter in a hired car or taxi; that is the most comfortable and efficient way to go. But do not spurn the guided tour, because Japan, whose inhabitants are among the most avid travelers in their own land, has made an art of the sightseeing tour.

Kyoto's own **Tourist Information Center,** or TIC (telephone 075-371-2108), located across the plaza in front of the railroad station, has a smart multilingual staff that can be of great help in telling you where and how to go. The **Japan National Tourist Organization** also has a helpful staff. It's across the railroad station

In the tree-shaded garden of the Moss Temple (above) sunlight streams through the branches, revealing hundreds of variations of the color green. In Gionmachi (opposite), one of the oldest parts of Kyoto, geishas are a common sight.

SPECIAL REPORT
THE ART OF HARNESSING STRESS

Overcoming TYPE A Mania

Are You Type A?

ALEXANDER HAIG IS, LEE IACOCCA PROBABLY IS, TOO. But then, so is 75% of America's adult population. The problem is stress, the pattern a predictable one. Type A's are strivers who don't know when to quit. They're tense and competitive in the workplace, uptight and irritable when they get home. They keep driving even after they've arrived, and as psychiatrists have been suggesting ever since Dr. Meyer Friedman coined the term in 1959, the price Type A's pay is a sharply increased risk of coronary trouble.

The symptoms are easy enough to observe. Type A's have a chronic sense of urgency; they constantly glance at their watches. They feel a strong need for power, and an accompanying fear of dependence. Impatient, determined to meet difficult deadlines they often set for themselves, they cannot relax without feeling guilty. To most activities that do not directly affect their work, they give short shrift; when they do engage in recreation they play competitive sports—and always to win, even when they play with children.

Inevitably, this behavior shows in day-to-day mannerisms: hurrying the speech of others or interrupting outright; blinking or moving eyes rapidly while speaking, clicking lips or nodding the head or sucking in air; jiggling a knee or fingers; even a periodic bulging of the eyes that shows white above and below the pupil. Type A's tend to have tense muscles, to draw in their stomachs and puff out their chests—exactly like apes trying to intimidate their rivals. Says stress expert Sam Keen, "They're in a chronic fight-or-flight reaction, and they do everything they can to stimulate that hyper-alert, aggressive state: drink coffee, eat sugar, smoke cigarettes, and sometimes snort cocaine." Even without heart attacks, Type A's incur angina, persistent coughs and neuroses, dissatisfaction and low self-esteem.

Can they hope to change? One recent study—by San Francisco Mount Zion Hospital and Medical Center together with the Stanford University School of Education in Palo Alto—considered some 800 male victims of recent heart attacks. Half the group received basic medical treatment; the other half received the same treatments but in addition to those attended 44 counseling sessions over the study's three years. Informed of typical Type A traits, the men in the latter group were then shown videotapes of their own Type A behavior; many found the tapes too painful to watch.

When the men were taught certain new ways of looking at their lives, they reported feeling happier and having more fun. That feeling, the researchers found, translated into fact: of the patients who failed to reduce their Type A traits through counseling over the course of the study, 19% had heart attacks again. Of the counseled group, only 9%, or less than half, suffered that same fate.

The Type B man, it should be noted, is not a man without stress. Most psychologists agree that all of us need a certain amount of stress to motivate us. But Type B's manage to work without agitation, to play for fun rather than competition, and to relax without guilt. They stay in touch with body time, too, more than chronological time, letting themselves daydream if they feel like it, spending a few contemplative moments lying in bed before they drift off to sleep and before they bolt upright from sleep the next day. To a hardcore Type A, all this may seem mere laziness and tomfoolery. But if living a happier and longer life is not enough reason to change, here's one more: Type B's, as casual as they may appear, tend to be more successful in their careers than their bug-eyed, breast-beating Type A counterparts. ▲

Where to Begin

Most of what the researchers advise is, in fact, homespun wisdom that might be put under the general heading of Stopping to Smell the Flowers.

A sampling:

- Take 15 minutes alone and do nothing except listen to music.
- Show interest in your children (in their schoolwork, not their grades).
- Admit to being wrong, even if you are not.
- Listen to someone talk without thinking about something else and don't say anything until he is finished.
- Let some minor error escape your criticism instead of harping on it.
- Play a game and plan to lose.
- Laugh at yourself.
- Look at yourself in the mirror at midday and again after work to see if your face shows signs of irritation or anger.
- Call or write to an old friend.
- Avoid other angry Type A's.
- Remind yourself daily that life by its very nature is unfinished.
- Engage in more tennis, jogging and recreational walking.
- Engage in yoga.
- Talk more slowly and less emphatically.
- Gesture less abruptly with your head and hands, and cut down on fidgeting and jiggling.
- Try to find humor in a situation.
- Cut back on observing or participating in highly competitive events. ▲

Vision 10 Illustration By Anders Wenngren Premier Issue 11 Vision

310

PUBLICATION: *Vision*
ART DIRECTOR: *Terry Koppel*
DESIGNER: *Drew Hodges, Terry Koppel*
ILLUSTRATOR: *Alexa Grace*
PUBLISHER: *Alexis, Parks Publishing*
CATEGORY: *Design-Spread*
AWARD: *Merit*

STORY PRESENTATIONS

TWENTIETH PUBLICATION DESIGN ANNUAL

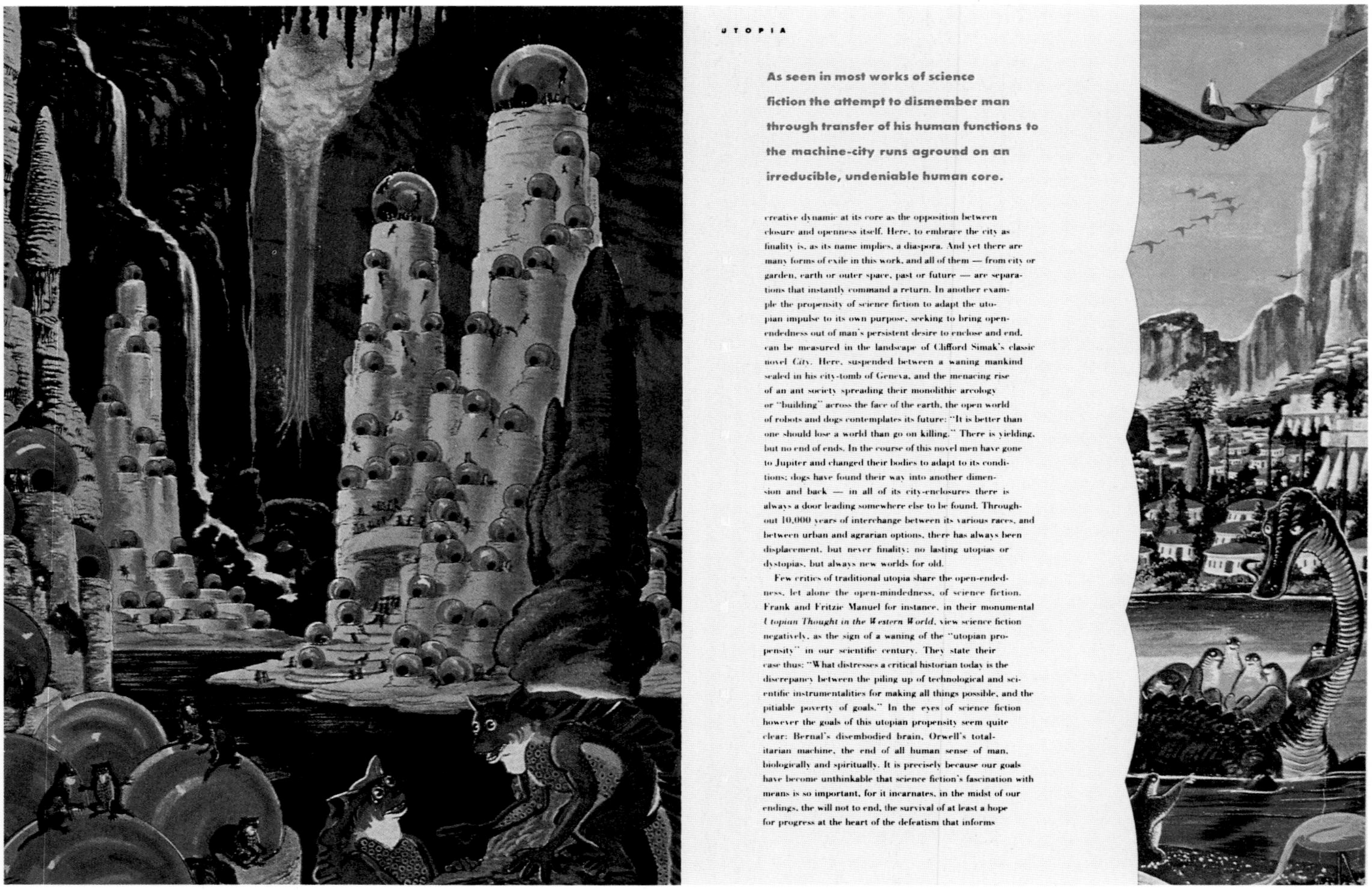

UTOPIA

As seen in most works of science fiction the attempt to dismember man through transfer of his human functions to the machine-city runs aground on an irreducible, undeniable human core.

creative dynamic at its core as the opposition between closure and openness itself. Here, to embrace the city as finality is, as its name implies, a diaspora. And yet there are many forms of exile in this work, and all of them — from city or garden, earth or outer space, past or future — are separations that instantly command a return. In another example the propensity of science fiction to adapt the utopian impulse to its own purpose, seeking to bring open-endedness out of man's persistent desire to enclose and end, can be measured in the landscape of Clifford Simak's classic novel *City*. Here, suspended between a waning mankind sealed in his city-tomb of Geneva, and the menacing rise of an ant society spreading their monolithic arcology or "building" across the face of the earth, the open world of robots and dogs contemplates its future: "It is better than one should lose a world than go on killing." There is yielding, but no end of ends. In the course of this novel men have gone to Jupiter and changed their bodies to adapt to its conditions; dogs have found their way into another dimension and back — in all of its city-enclosures there is always a door leading somewhere else to be found. Throughout 10,000 years of interchange between its various races, and between urban and agrarian options, there has always been displacement, but never finality; no lasting utopias or dystopias, but always new worlds for old.

Few critics of traditional utopia share the open-endedness, let alone the open-mindedness, of science fiction. Frank and Fritzie Manuel for instance, in their monumental *Utopian Thought in the Western World*, view science fiction negatively, as the sign of a waning of the "utopian propensity" in our scientific century. They state their case thus: "What distresses a critical historian today is the discrepancy between the piling up of technological and scientific instrumentalities for making all things possible, and the pitiable poverty of goals." In the eyes of science fiction however the goals of this utopian propensity seem quite clear: Bernal's disembodied brain, Orwell's totalitarian machine, the end of all human sense of man, biologically and spiritually. It is precisely because our goals have become unthinkable that science fiction's fascination with means is so important, for it incarnates, in the midst of our endings, the will not to end, the survival of at least a hope for progress at the heart of the defeatism that informs

311

PUBLICATION: *Arts & Architecture*
ART DIRECTOR: *Rip Georges*
DESIGNER: *Rip Georges*
CATEGORY: *Design-Story Presentation*
PUBLISHER: *Arts & Architecture, Inc.*
AWARD: *Gold*

312

PUBLICATION:	*Mother Jones Magazine*
ART DIRECTOR:	*Louise Kollenbaum*
DESIGNER:	*Dian-Aziza Ooka*
ILLUSTRATOR:	*Marshall Arisman, Matt Mahurin, Brad Holland, John Collier, Sue Coe*
PUBLISHER:	*Foundation For National Progress*
CATEGORY:	*Illustration-Story Presentation*
AWARD:	*Gold*

312

PUBLICATION: *Mother Jones Magazine*
ART DIRECTOR: *Louise Kollenbaum*
DESIGNER: *Dian-Aziza Ooka*
ILLUSTRATOR: *Marshall Arisman, Matt Mahurin, Brad Holland, John Collier, Sue Coe*
PUBLISHER: *Foundation For National Progress*
CATEGORY: *Illustration-Story Presentation*
AWARD: *Gold*

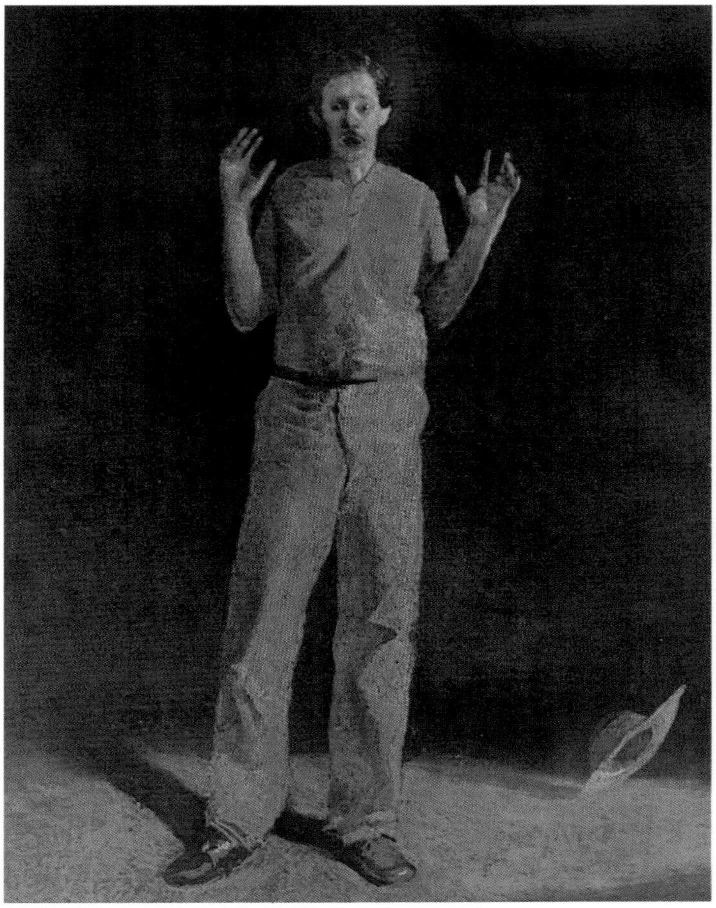

Let ThEm eat CAK
RONALD REAGAN'S
$1000 A PLATE
BASH

SPRING FASHION

PALE FIRE

BY
Wendy
Goodman

PHOTOGRAPHED
BY
Tony
McGee

Linen shift by Shamask Couture, about $500 at Moss (860 Madison Avenue, at 70th) and Saks Fifth Avenue. Model: Lara Young, of Elite Model Management.

Nineteenth-century French hand-painted screen from Rose Cumming, Inc.

MARCH 5, 1984/NEW YORK 43

313

PUBLICATION: *New York Magazine*
ART DIRECTOR: *Robert Best*
DESIGNER: *Patricia Von Brachel*
PHOTOGRAPHER: *David Walters, Tony McGee*
PUBLISHER: *Murdoch Magazines*
CATEGORY: *Design-Story Presentation*
AWARD: *Gold*

Hair: Suga, of Suga Salon. Makeup: George Newell. Flowers: Paul Bott, of Twigs.

Fashion associates: Valarie Ebner and Michael Eisenhower.

Spring. The anticipation of renewal and exhilaration. Time to get out in the air—and down to the bone. In sportswear, the offerings from American designers have never been more elegant. The silhouettes are clean and classic, the colors pale to pulsating, the accessories minimal. From the luxury of a long linen skirt to the panache of a picture hat, the feeling is easy. Eminently wearable. Pure and simple.

JOAN VASS

Metallic-embroidered silk-and-rayon dress, about $630 at Bergdorf Goodman, Henri Bendel, Saks. Austrian-crystal earrings by Jessica Rose, $120 at Artwear (409 West Broadway); antique gold chain, $2,750; thirties diamond-and-gold locket, $1,500; and antique garnet-and-gold buckle bracelet, $2,750, at James Robinson (15 East 57th Street); court pumps, $240 at Vittorio Ricci (645 Madison Avenue, near 60th); stockings by Fogal.

CALVIN KLEIN

Ankle-length linen camisole dress, $190 at Bergdorf's, Bloomingdale's, Macy's (early March), Saks (mid-March); antique crystal-and-gold seal pendant, $1,500, and gold chain, $2,750, at James Robinson.

CALVIN KLEIN

Right: hand-knitted cotton sweater, $230, and ankle-length linen skirt, $170, at Bloomingdale's and Saks; lizard belt with horn buckle, $44 at B. Altman.

Calvin Klein gave the American woman a new elegance and an understated ease. These designs—a graceful sweep of linen for evening, a belted cotton sweater for day—sum up his mood for spring.

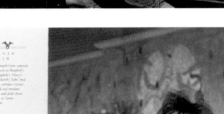

314

PUBLICATION: *Texas Monthly*
ART DIRECTOR: *Fred Woodward*
DESIGNER: *Fred Woodward*
David Kampa
ILLUSTRATOR: *Various*
PUBLISHER: *Texas Monthly, Inc.*
CATEGORY: *Illustration-Story Presentation*
AWARD: *Gold*

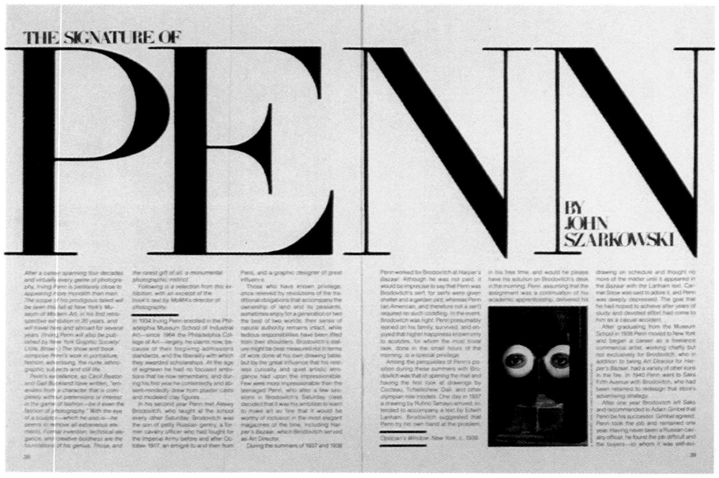

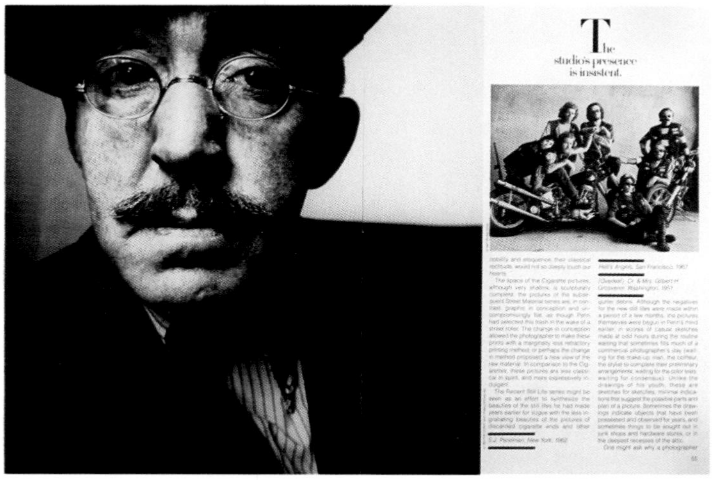

315

PUBLICATION: *American Photographer*
ART DIRECTOR: *Will Hopkins*
DESIGNER: *Will Hopkins*
PHOTOGRAPHER: *Irving Penn*
PUBLISHER: *CBS Publishing*
CATEGORY: *Design-Story Presentation*
AWARD: *Silver*

Houston Townhouses
STEPHEN FOX

316

PUBLICATION: *Arts & Architecture*
ART DIRECTOR: *Rip Georges*
PHOTOGRAPHER: *Paul Hester*
PUBLISHER: *Arts & Architecture, Inc.*
CATEGORY: *Design-Story Presentation*
AWARD: *Silver*

GEO KNOWLEDGE
Nature's Pharmacy
Over the ages, people have said that garlic heals wounds, mint relieves stomach cramps and dandelions cure gout. They're right.
Foxglove
Article by Stephen Brewer
Photos by Susan Wood

317

PUBLICATION: *Geo Magazine*
ART DIRECTOR: *Mary K. Baumann*
PHOTOGRAPHER: *Susan Wood*
PUBLISHER: *Knapp/Communications Corp*
CATEGORY: *Design-Story Presentation*
AWARD: *Silver*

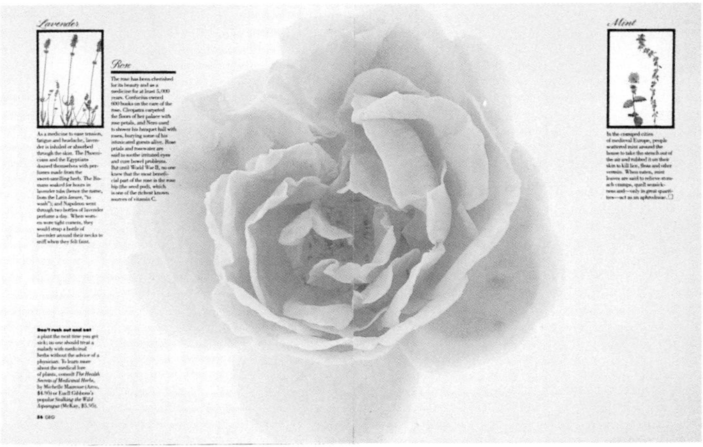
Lavender
Rose
Mint

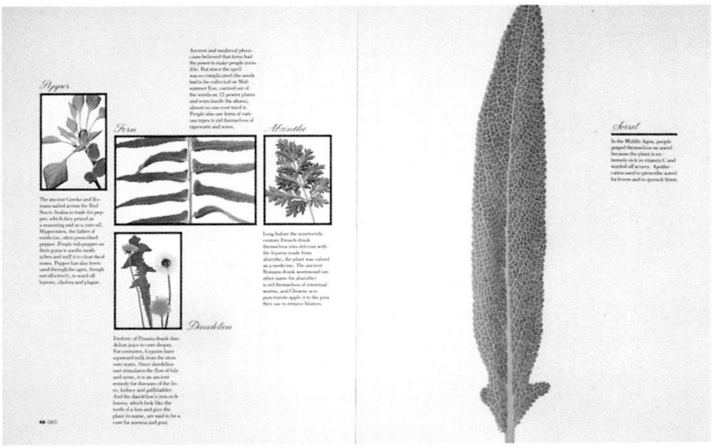
Pepper
Fern
Absinthe
Dandelion
Sorrel

GEO IN ENGLAND
CANTERBURY
TRAILS
Pilgrims—both pious and frivolous—have been treading the 116 miles from Winchester to Canterbury for 800 years.
34 GEO

318

PUBLICATION: *Geo Magazine*
ART DIRECTOR: *John Tom Cohoe*
DESIGNER: *John Tom Cohoe*
PHOTOGRAPHER: *Neal Slavin*
PUBLISHER: *Knapp Communications, Corp.*
CATEGORY: *Design-Story Presentation*
AWARD: *Silver*

Article by Erla Zwingle • Photos by Neal Slavin
If you were to awake on the Hampshire Downs during high summer to a wide expanse of sky swept clean by clouds, to swelling hillsides rich with wheat and hay and oats, to hedges blossoming with butterflies and wild flowers . . . if you were to awake to such a morning, you might announce that St. Thomas had come to you in a dream and told you to leave for Canterbury immediately.
In the great days between 1170 and 1538, thousands of pilgrims—most of whom put frivolity before piety, since a pilgrimage was the perfect and just about the only legitimate excuse for a vacation—received just such a call and did set out for Canterbury. They were drawn there by the shrine of Thomas à Becket, the archbishop who was murdered in 1170 by overzealous knights of Henry II after years of dispute over whether the church or the state had the final say. The sick and dying struggled to Canterbury hoping for a miraculous cure by touching Becket's tomb or by drinking the water from his well, which was supposedly tinctured with his blood. Kings came to make offerings, to request military victory or give thanks for same—as did Henry V for his triumph at Agincourt and Richard Coeur de Lion when he was finally freed from his Austrian prison.
Today the relics and the shrine are gone, though you can still see the pump that drew the wonder-working water attached to what is now the wall of H. V. Bacon & Sons, Leather Goods. It was a stupendous thing, the tomb, on its mar-
The Pilgrim's Way winds through starkly beautiful terrain—such as this meadow near Hollingbourne—but it afforded pilgrims little protection from the elements.
In Saxon and Norman times, Winchester was the capital of England. It was fitting, then, that its cathedral be the longest in the kingdom—526 feet.
36 GEO
GEO 37

Two charities run the 850-year-old Hospital of St. Cross outside Winchester. Travelers may still stop for a "wayfarers dole" of bread and beer.

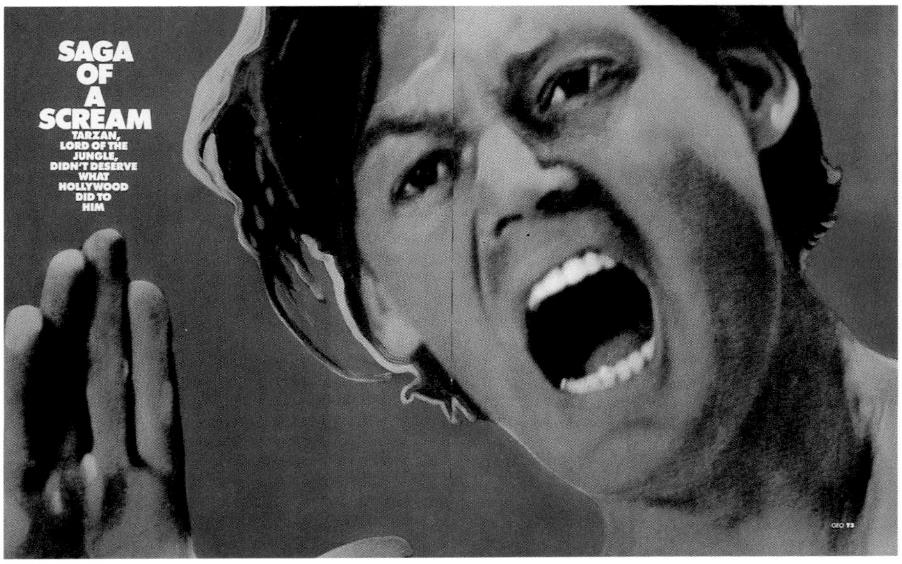

SAGA OF A SCREAM
TARZAN, LORD OF THE JUNGLE, DIDN'T DESERVE WHAT HOLLYWOOD DID TO HIM
GEO 73

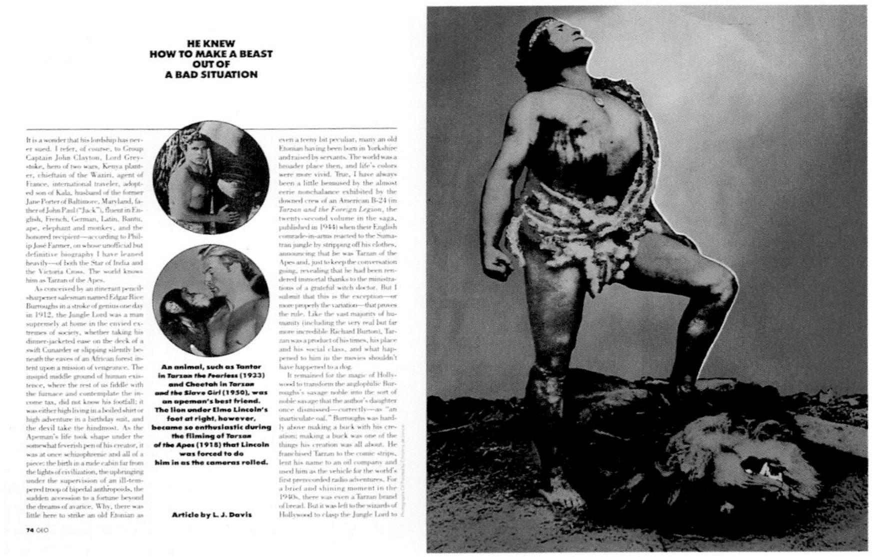

HE KNEW HOW TO MAKE A BEAST OUT OF A BAD SITUATION
An animal, such as Tantor in Tarzan the Fearless (1933) and Cheetah in Tarzan and the Slave Girl (1950), was an apeman's best friend. The lion under Elmo Lincoln's foot at right, however, became so enthusiastic during the filming of Tarzan of the Apes (1918) that Lincoln was forced to do him in as the cameras rolled.
Article by L. J. Davis
74 GEO

319

PUBLICATION: *Geo Magazine*
ART DIRECTOR: *Mary K. Baumann*
PHOTOGRAPHER: *Photos oil painted by: Christina De Lancie*
PUBLISHER: *Knapp Communications Corp.*
CATEGORY: *Design-Story Presentation*
AWARD: *Silver*

GEO REPORT
The Voice Of The Body
For centuries people have painted, adorned and altered their bodies to make striking statements about themselves.
Photos by Michael O'Neill
66 GEO

320

PUBLICATION: *Geo Magazine*
ART DIRECTOR: *Mary K. Baumann*
PHOTOGRAPHER: *Michael O'Neill*
PUBLISHER: *Knapp Communications Corp.*
CATEGORY: *Design-Story Presentation*
AWARD: *Silver*

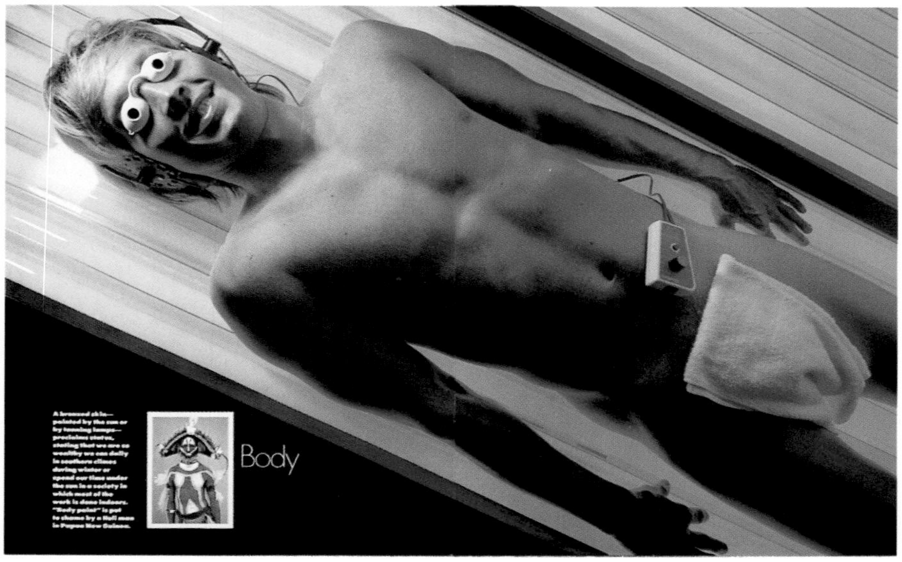

321

PUBLICATION: *House & Garden*
ART DIRECTOR: *Lloyd Ziff*
DESIGNER: *Karen Lee Grant*
PHOTOGRAPHER: *Francis Halard*
PUBLISHER: *Conde Nast Publications*
CATEGORY: *Design-Story Presentation*
AWARD: *Silver*

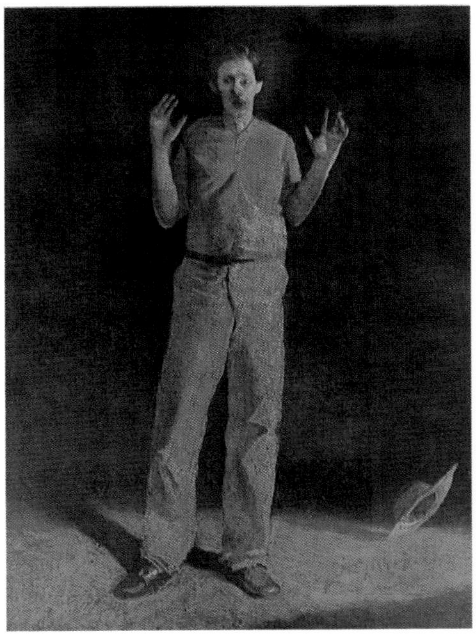

322

PUBLICATION:	*Mother Jones Magazine*
ART DIRECTOR:	*Louise Kollenbaum*
DESIGNER:	*Dian-Aziza Ooka*
ILLUSTRATOR:	*Marshall Arisman, Matt Mahurin, Brad Holland, John Collier, Sue Coe, Gary Panter, Milton Glaser*
PUBLISHER:	*Foundation For National Progress*
CATEGORY:	*Design-Story Presentation*
AWARD:	*Silver*

LIFE/STYLE

The Fight to Conquer Fear

Phobias afflict millions of Americans—but new therapies are providing help.

After the door to her small apartment closed behind her in 1949, Marjorie Goff went out three times in 30 years: to visit her family, for an operation and to get a dying friend some ice cream. She would still be there but for a social worker who got her back on the streets.

Fear of heights—more typically a fear of edges—often begins with an experience like that of Jerilyn Ross, who once "felt this magnet pulling me to the edge" of a mountainside-restaurant balcony. She was later unable to go above the 10th floor in any building.

LIFE/STYLE

Driving in little vehicles across wide freeways, some phobics feel like babies crawling down the hall who can be scooped up in an instant and tossed in the air unless, like Mike Javor, a Los Angeles insurance-company executive, they hold on tightly to the roof of the car.

One young truck driver was consumed with the fear that he would stop in the middle of the Chesapeake Bay Bridge and jump off. He had his wife handcuff him to the steering wheel. Police have set up an escort service to drive people across in their own cars.

Giving Fear a Proper Name

324

PUBLICATION: *Newsweek*
ART DIRECTOR: *Robert Priest*
ILLUSTRATOR: *Brad Holland*
PUBLISHER: *Newsweek, Inc.*
CATEGORY: *Illustration-Story Presentation*
AWARD: *Silver*

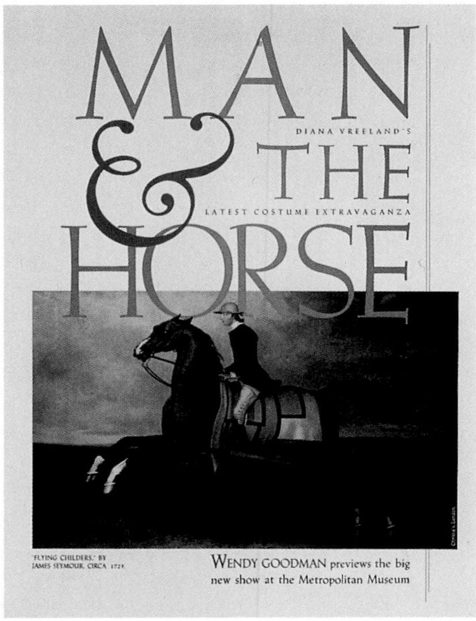

325

PUBLICATION: *New York Magazine*
ART DIRECTOR: *Robert Best*
DESIGNER: *Patricia Von Brachel, David Walters*
PHOTOGRAPHER: *Lynton Gardiner*
PUBLISHER: *Murdoch Magazines*
CATEGORY: *Design-Story Presentation*
AWARD: *Silver*

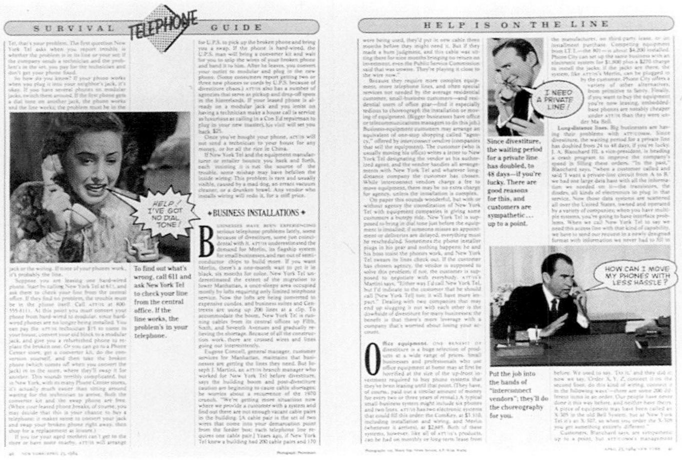

326

PUBLICATION: *New York Magazine*
ART DIRECTOR: *Robert Best*
DESIGNER: *Jordan Schaaps*
PHOTOGRAPHER: *Tohru Nakamura, Bill Kobasz*
PUBLISHER: *Murdoch Magazines*
CATEGORY: *Design-Story Presentation*
AWARD: *Silver*

327

PUBLICATION: *New York Magazine*
ART DIRECTOR: *Robert Best*
DESIGNER: *Patricia von Brachel*
PHOTOGRAPHER: *Tony McGee*
PUBLISHER: *Murdoch Magazines*
CATEGORY: *Design-Story Presentation*
AWARD: *Silver*

328

PUBLICATION: *New York Times Magazine*
ART DIRECTOR: *Ken Kendrick*
DESIGNER: *Ken Kendrick*
PHOTOGRAPHER: *Chuck Baker*
PUBLISHER: *The New York Times*
CATEGORY: *Design-Story Presentation*
AWARD: *Silver*

329

PUBLICATION: *New York Times Magazine*
ART DIRECTOR: *Ken Kendrick*
DESIGNER: *Diana LaGuardia*
PHOTOGRAPHER: *Various*
PUBLISHER: *The New York Times*
CATEGORY: *Design-Story Presentation*
AWARD: *Silver*

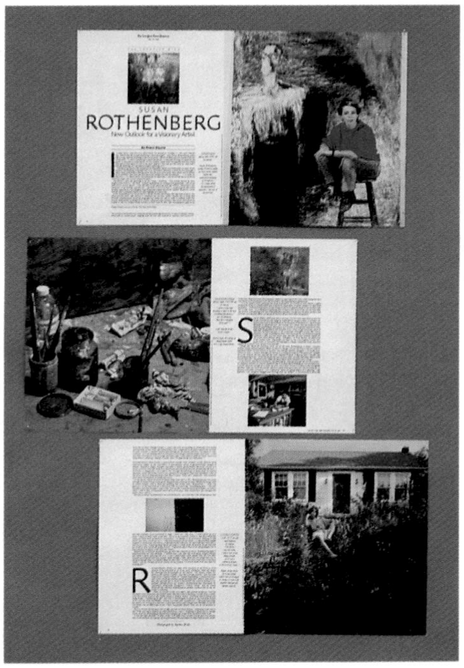

330

PUBLICATION: *New York Times Magazine*
ART DIRECTOR: *Ken Kendrick*
DESIGNER: *Diana LaGuardia*
PHOTOGRAPHER: *Barbara Walz*
PUBLISHER: *The New York Times*
CATEGORY: *Design-Story Presentation*
AWARD: *Silver*

331

PUBLICATION: *New York Times Magazine*
ART DIRECTOR: *Lucy Sisman*
DESIGNER: *Lucy Sisman*
ILLUSTRATOR: *Andrea Blanch*
PHOTOGRAPHER: *Deborah Turbeville*
PUBLISHER: *The New York Times*
CATEGORY: *Design-Story Presentation*
AWARD: *Silver*

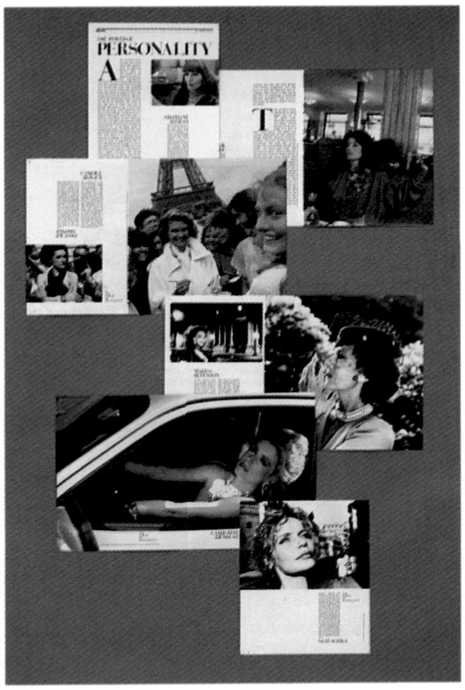

332

PUBLICATION: *New York Times Magazine*
ART DIRECTOR: *Ken Kendrick*
DESIGNER: *Ken Kendrick*
PHOTOGRAPHER: *Helmut Newton*
PUBLISHER: *The New York Times*
CATEGORY: *Design-Story Presentation*
AWARD: *Silver*

IN THE WINGS

Ballet is beautiful, onstage and off.

Ben Stevenson, the artistic director of the Houston Ballet, calls ballet a sweat factory. That's all right with me—let me stand backstage and watch as the months of rehearsals and the frenetic last-minute preparations finally produce a professional, thoughtful performance. Stevenson makes his dancers work hard, and their sweat has paid off. The Houston Ballet and its school are a regional success story—a rarity in American dance. During Stevenson's seven years with the company, it has earned a local following and a national reputation. The school has become a high-caliber enterprise, teaching an elegant, if conservative, house style. And the principals are some of the finest dancers in the country.

During the 1982-83 season

BY WL TAITTE

PHOTOGRAPHY BY GEOFF WINNINGHAM

132 TEXAS MONTHLY/MARCH 1984

333

PUBLICATION: *Texas Monthly Magazine*
ART DIRECTOR: *Fred Woodward, David Kampa*
DESIGNER: *Fred Woodward, David Kampa*
ILLUSTRATOR: *Geoff Winningham*
PUBLISHER: *Texas Monthly Inc.*
CATEGORY: *Design-Story Presentation*
AWARD: *Silver*

DRAW THE COWBOY

Test your art skills! No tracing allowed!

I remember seeing this drawing for the first time in the back of a Batman comic book when I was six. It was an ad for one of those art correspondence schools. I couldn't read all the promises it made, but that didn't matter. I had to draw that cowboy. My mother drew it too. Later, we entered hers—in my name. After a few very long weeks the reply came. I was too young for the school, it said, but the drawing showed real talent. And even though it was my mom's talent, not mine, I kept on drawing.

I guess almost every kid who thought he could draw did this; it was an introduction to both the commercial and the competitive sides of art. We've asked twenty of the finest illustrators around to draw that same cowboy. We're pretty excited about the results, but then, for most of these artists, it wasn't their first time.

-Fred Woodward

334

PUBLICATION: *Texas Monthly Magazine*
ART DIRECTOR: *Fred Woodward*
DESIGNER: *Fred Woodward, David Kampa*
PUBLISHER: *Texas Monthly, Inc.*
CATEGORY: *Design-Story Presentation*
AWARD: *Silver*

TOWN & COUNTRY

Carnival in Venice

Being presented to Venice like an ambassador of old, European beauty Frauke Quast skims beneath the Rialto Bridge on *La Veneziana*, a gilded eight-oared *bissona*, one of Venice's great ceremonial gondolas. Before her, the three-thousand-year-old phantasmagoria of *carnevale*. Through dalliance, humor and tests of virtue, Frauke—only child of a famous German architect and his wife, an interior designer—will learn that, truly, *A carnevale ogni scherzo vale*: At carnival, anything goes.

Photographs by Norman Parkinson/Produced by Nancy Tuck Gardiner

335

PUBLICATION: *Town & Country*
ART DIRECTOR: *Melissa Tardiff*
DESIGNER: *Mary Rosen*
PHOTOGRAPHER: *Norman Parkinson*
PUBLISHER: *Hearst Corp.*
CATEGORY: *Photo-Story Presentation*
AWARD: *Silver*

WESTERN ART

KOW BOI HADZ!
by Elwood H. Smith
AUGUST 1984/TEXAS MONTHLY 143

WESTERN ART
BUFFALO GAL
by Dave Calver
JUNE 1984/TEXAS MONTHLY 149

336

PUBLICATION: *Texas Monthly Magazine*
ART DIRECTOR: *Fred Woodward, David Kampa*
DESIGNER: *Fred Woodward, David Kampa*
ILLUSTRATOR: *Alexa Grace, Gary Kelley, Tom Woodruff, Elwood Smith, Dave Calver*
PUBLISHER: *Texas Monthly, Inc.*
CATEGORY: *Illustration-Story Presentation*
AWARD: *Silver*

WESTERN ART

PIERRE WAS NEW IN TOWN AND HAD NEVER
REALLY CAUGHT ANYTHING BEFORE

by Alexa Grace

WESTERN ART

DRUGSTORE COWBOY

by Gary Kelley

WESTERN ART

SERVICE ROAD

by Thomas Woodruff

337

PUBLICATION: *American Photographer*
ART DIRECTOR: *Will Hopkins*
DESIGNER: *Will Hopkins*
PUBLISHER: *CBS Publications*
CATEGORY: *Design-Story Presentation*
AWARD: *Merit*

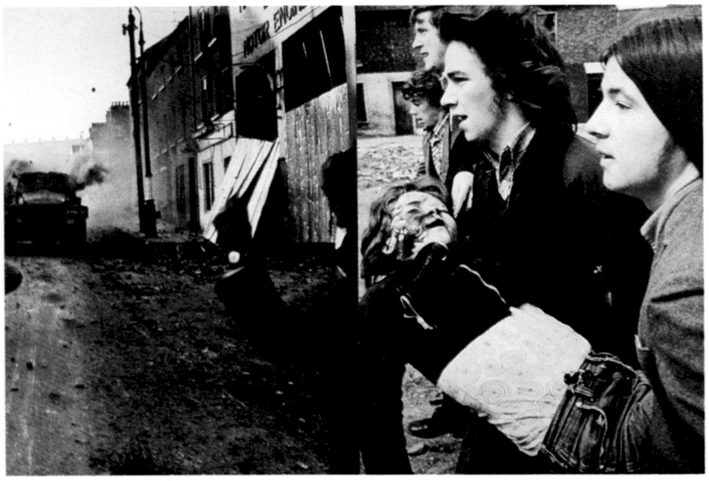

338

PUBLICATION: *American Photographer*
ART DIRECTOR: *Will Hopkins*
DESIGNER: *Will Hopkins*
PHOTOGRAPHER: *Gilless Peress*
PUBLISHER: *CBS Publications*
CATEGORY: *Design-Story Presentation*
AWARD: *Merit*

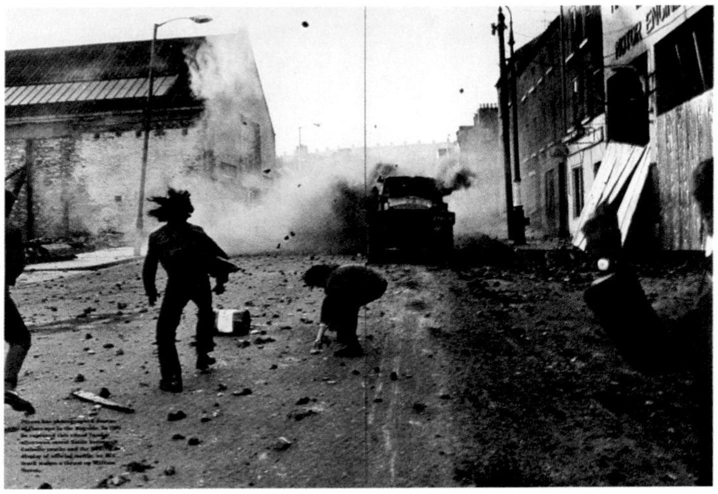

Distant Views

From its earliest stirrings landscape photography has had to wrestle with the idea of the presence of man, if only as a technical device to give the viewer a sense of scale. When nineteenth-century photographers first ventured outdoors to make pictures, they were heavily influenced by romantic landscape painting, in which any evidence of man was reduced to tiny specks in large compositions. Some eventually freed themselves from this convention. Photographers such as Carleton Watkins and Timothy O'Sullivan established a tradition of pure landscape, one unadulterated by the hand of man. That school survives today, most prominently in the work of the late Ansel Adams and his peers.

But old traditions die hard. Take the case of New Zealand photographer John Crawford. He makes a good living doing annual reports for oil companies and other heavy-industrial clients on the subcontinent. But when he has time to himself he makes personal landscape pictures that are "highly graphic, cleaner and less cluttered than the industrial sites I normally work in."

Crawford is in partnership with two other photographers, and they frequently show each other their personal work. Crawford was looking at his partner's landscapes one day when, in the spirit of friendly competition, he wisecracked, "Nice picture, but what you need in there is a nude." The comment soon became a refrain around the office whenever the photographers showed their landscapes until one day when Crawford decided to turn his one-liner into reality. The nineteenth-century conceit of the hand of man in the landscape metamorphosed into the body of a naked woman in the least likely locales. It also illustrated a twentieth-century conundrum: Is it possible to make an intelligent photograph without resorting to sex? On that issue John Crawford took the high moral ground.

Fortunately, Crawford has a friend who has a helicopter and a wife who is willing to strip down for the sake of high altitude art. They encountered a few problems. Carina Crawford had no qualms about posing nude at the end of an airport runway one time, but husband John became a little anxious when he heard over the chopper's headphones that 20 men had gathered behind a pair of high-power binoculars in the control tower. Then there was the outraged farmer who almost ran them off his property at gunpoint when he heard the photographer planned to put a naked woman in his cattle pen. "Somehow he had gotten the idea that I wanted to put his wife in my photograph," Crawford says.

As for the old argument over whether landscape photography should bear evidence of man (or woman), John Crawford wisely avoids it. He solves the problem wryly by taking a distant view. —Gonzo Niepce

On the issue of nudes in the landscape, John Crawford takes the high moral ground.

339

PUBLICATION: *American Photographer*
ART DIRECTOR: *Will Hopkins*
DESIGNER: *Will Hopkins*
PHOTOGRAPHER: *John Crauford*
PUBLISHER: *CBS Publications*
CATEGORY: *Design-Story Presentation*
AWARD: *Merit*

340

PUBLICATION: *American Photographer*
ART DIRECTOR: *Will Hopkins*
DESIGNER: *Will Hopkins*
PHOTOGRAPHER: *Annie Leibovitz*
PUBLISHER: *CBS Publications*
CATEGORY: *Design-Story Presentation*
AWARD: *Merit*

AMERICAN PHOTOGRAPHER
April, 1984

CUBA POP. 286

An Ancient Scribe for Modern Times

Jim Richardson's remarkable mission as a documentary photographer in a small Kansas town.

There is a very human tendency when talking about photographs to define and consign them to categories. We at *American Photographer* do it when we construe the medium's five constituencies to be fashion, fine art, commercial, historical and photojournalistic photography. Similarly, when looking at the pictures that appear on the next 24 pages—a lengthy selection from Denver *Post* photographer Jim Richardson's obsessive documentation of the little (pop. 286) town of Cuba, Kansas—the urge is to call the work photojournalism. Yet there is something not quite right about saying that, something about the pictures that doesn't fit the popular notions of press photography.

As individual images, Richardson's pictures are not particularly stunning or dramatic. They don't capture the searing "decisive moments" of Cartier-Bresson or possess the disarming symbolism of the work of Eugene Smith. Nor as a body of work can they be compared to the memorable *Life* magazine photo stories of a generation ago. Unlike those classic photo essays, Richardson's coverage has no discernible beginning, middle or end. But then, neither does the town of Cuba or the others like it Richardson has photographed. So rather than go about the dubious task of trying to define that which defies definition—as photojournalists are usually required to do—Richardson has enlarged his tableau, perhaps beyond reason, to record as much as the eye will see.

On the street, hanging out, watching the daily events of life go by, is Jim Richardson's job.

Like the ancient village scribe, he has made it his business to record the births and deaths, the plantings and harvests and feasts and festivals of this tiny town. And it is that *being there*, that keeping of the chronicle season to season, year after year, that is his greatest achievement, and one which has challenged talented, committed photographers since the days of Atget.

Because of the limitations of the magazine format, we cannot publish a truly comprehensive sampling of this now voluminous work in progress which has already consumed nine years of Richardson's life and amounts to more than 15,000 photographs. That alone would require a book, and Richardson hopes to publish one in about three years. Instead, we have threaded together images that capture more the spirit than the scope of Richardson's effort. The texts are Richardson's own and were adapted from the audio portion of a slide show he produced a year and a half ago about small-town life on the plains. To complete the story, writer John Harris traveled to Cuba, and on page 112 reports on the past, present and future of Richardson's remarkable mission.

—David Markus

39

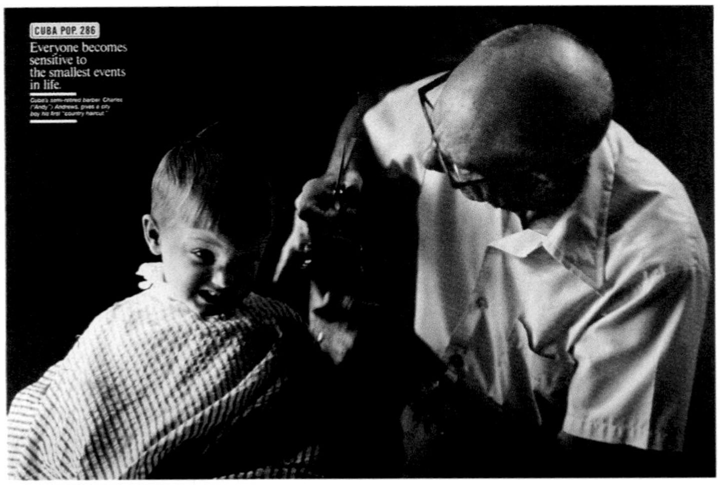

341

PUBLICATION: *American Photographer*
ART DIRECTOR: *Will Hopkins*
DESIGNER: *Will Hopkins*
PHOTOGRAPHER: *Jim Richardson*
PUBLISHER: *CBS Publications*
CATEGORY: *Design-Story Presentation*
AWARD: *Merit*

CUBA POP. 286
You find happiness and joy in *how* people do things, not *what* they do.

War Toys
The terrible technology of destruction raised to the level of pure aesthetics. Photo essay by Co Rentmeester. Text by Owen Edwards.

342

PUBLICATION: *American Photographer*
ART DIRECTOR: *Will Hopkins*
DESIGNER: *Will Hopkins*
PHOTOGRAPHER: *Co Rentmeester*
PUBLISHER: *CBS Publications*
CATEGORY: *Design-Story Presentation*
AWARD: *Merit*

343

PUBLICATION: *American Photographer*
ART DIRECTOR: *Will Hopkins*
DESIGNER: *Will Hopkins*
PHOTOGRAPHER: *Lois Greenfield*
PUBLISHER: *CBS Publications*
CATEGORY: *Design-Story Presentation*
AWARD: *Merit*

Urge to the Edge

On assignment from the *Village Voice* two years ago, Lois Greenfield photographed David Parsons, a young member of the Paul Taylor dance company and one of the Voice's ten best dancers of that year. In her studio, the photographer asked Parsons neither to re-create any of his roles in Taylor dances nor to pose for a conventional dancer's portrait. Instead, she put on some pop music and he began to jump and "hit shapes" for the camera. Parsons flew and landed for hours, and when the photo session was over Greenfield had her picture. But she and Parsons both felt they wanted to work some more.

When they got together a few months later, Parsons brought along Daniel Ezralow, a friend and another Paul Taylor dancer. For Greenfield, the dancers fed each other ideas and trimmed their flights to the 2¼-inch frame of her borrowed Hasselblad. All three of them relished the privacy of the studio session. "We felt free to take risks," Greenfield says. "There was no fear of failure. They

Lois Greenfield and an innovative pair of dancers improvise at 1/500th of a second.

72

73

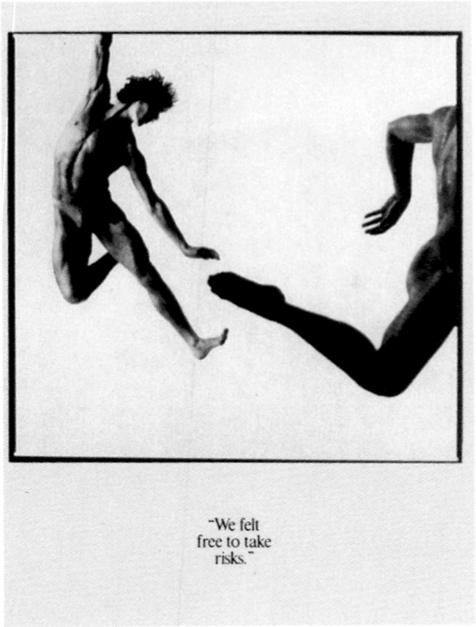

"We felt free to take risks."

They make a fraction of a second into a dance.

could give me anything I wanted."

Since then, the trio has met six times more, usually on Saturdays, for about five hours at a stretch. "We all have some idea of what we are going to do," Parsons says, "and let it go from there. We try to be as free as we can." The amounts of energy spent are awesome; the invention is tireless. "The more we do, the more pops up," says Ezralow. They have danced singly and together, dressed and half-dressed, upside-down, in clouds and with a baby for a prop. Sometimes they use Greenfield's gray cyclorama set, with a linoleum dancing floor, but more often they work on the standard 12-foot-wide seamless white paper (lit with a pair of 2400-watt-second strobes and two more as side lights), the everyday fashion photography set. When Parsons dropped by Greenfield's studio during a shoot for a lingerie line (see opening page), he slipped out of his clothes behind the model and, without a word, took off.

The work has had its effect on each

74

75

345

PUBLICATION: *Architectural Record*
ART DIRECTOR: *Alex Stillano*
DESIGNER: *Anna Schlesinger*
PHOTOGRAPHER: *Michael George*
PUBLISHER: *McGraw-Hill*
CATEGORY: *Design-Story Presentation*
AWARD: *Merit*

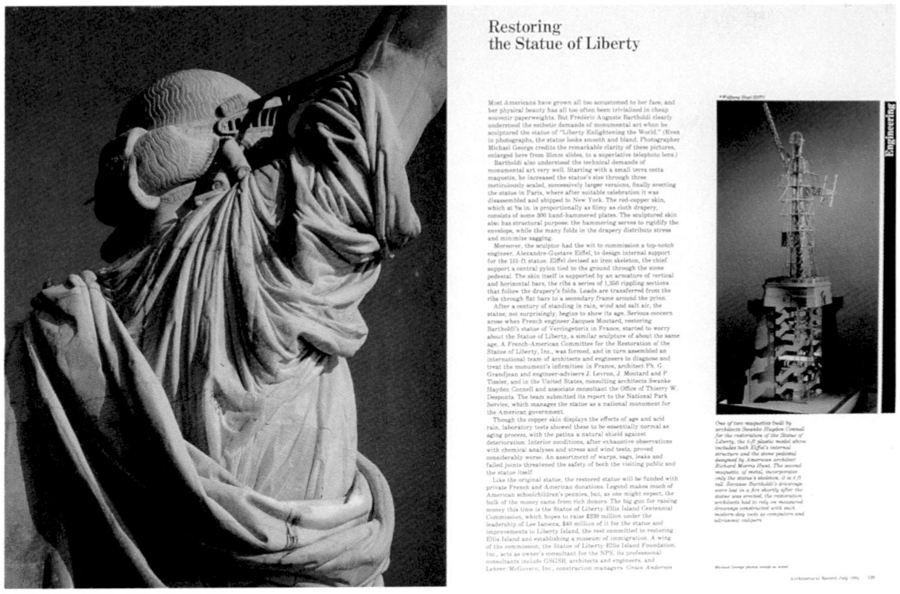

Restoring the Statue of Liberty

Most Americans have grown all too accustomed to her face, and her physical beauty has all too often been trivialized in cheap souvenir paperweights. But Frédéric Auguste Bartholdi clearly understood the esthetic demands of monumental art when he sculptured the statue of "Liberty Enlightening the World." (Even in photographs, the statue looks smooth and bland. Photographer Michael George credits the remarkable clarity of these pictures, enlarged here from 35mm slides, to a superlative telephoto lens.)

Bartholdi also understood the technical demands of monumental art very well. Starting with a small terra cotta *maquette*, he increased the statue's size through three meticulously scaled, successively larger versions, finally erecting the statue in Paris, where after suitable celebration it was disassembled and shipped to New York. The red-copper skin, which at 3/32 in. is proportionally as filmy as cloth drapery, consists of some 300 hand-hammered plates. The sculptured skin also has structural purpose: the hammering serves to rigidify the envelope, while the many folds in the drapery distribute stress and minimize sagging.

Moreover, the sculptor had the wit to commission a top-notch engineer, Alexandre-Gustave Eiffel, to design internal support for the 151-ft statue. Eiffel devised an iron skeleton, the chief support a central pylon tied to the ground through the stone pedestal. The skin itself is supported by an armature of vertical and horizontal bars, the ribs a series of 1,350 rippling sections that follow the drapery's folds. Loads are transferred from the ribs through flat bars to a secondary frame around the pylon.

After a century of standing in rain, wind and salt air, the statue, not surprisingly, begins to show its age. Serious concern arose when French engineer Jacques Moutard, restoring Bartholdi's statue of Vercingetorix in France, started to worry about the Statue of Liberty, a similar sculpture of about the same age. A French-American Committee for the Restoration of the Statue of Liberty, Inc., was formed, and in turn assembled an international team of architects and engineers to diagnose and treat the monument's infirmities: in France, architect Ph. G. Grandjean and engineer-advisers J. Levron, J. Moutard and P. Tissier, and in the United States, consulting architects Swanke Hayden Connell and associate consultant the Office of Thierry W. Despont. The team submitted its report to the National Park Service, which manages the statue as a national monument for the American government.

Though the copper skin displays the effects of age and acid rain, laboratory tests showed these to be essentially normal as aging process, with the patina a natural shield against deterioration. Interior conditions, after exhaustive observations with chemical analyses and stress and wind tests, proved considerably worse. An assortment of warps, sags, leaks and failed joints threatened the safety of both the visiting public and the statue itself.

Like the original statue, the restored statue will be funded with private French and American donations. Legend makes much of American schoolchildren's pennies, but, as one might expect, the bulk of the money came from rich donors. The big gun for raising money this time is the Statue of Liberty-Ellis Island Centennial Commission, which hopes to raise $230 million under the leadership of Lee Iacocca, $40 million of it for the statue and improvements to Liberty Island, the rest committed to restoring Ellis Island and establishing a museum of immigration. A wing of the commission, the Statue of Liberty-Ellis Island Foundation, Inc., acts as owner's consultant for the NPS; its professional consultants include GSGSB, architects and engineers, and Lehrer/McGovern, Inc., construction managers. *Grace Anderson*

Engineering

One of two maquettes built by architects Swanke Hayden Connell for the restoration of the Statue of Liberty, the 5-ft plastic model above includes both Eiffel's internal structure and the stone pedestal designed by American architect Richard Morris Hunt. The second maquette, of metal, incorporates only the statue's skeleton; it is 6 ft tall. Because Bartholdi's drawings were lost in a fire shortly after the statue was erected, the restoration architects had to rely on measured drawings constructed with such modern-day tools as computers and ultrasonic calipers.

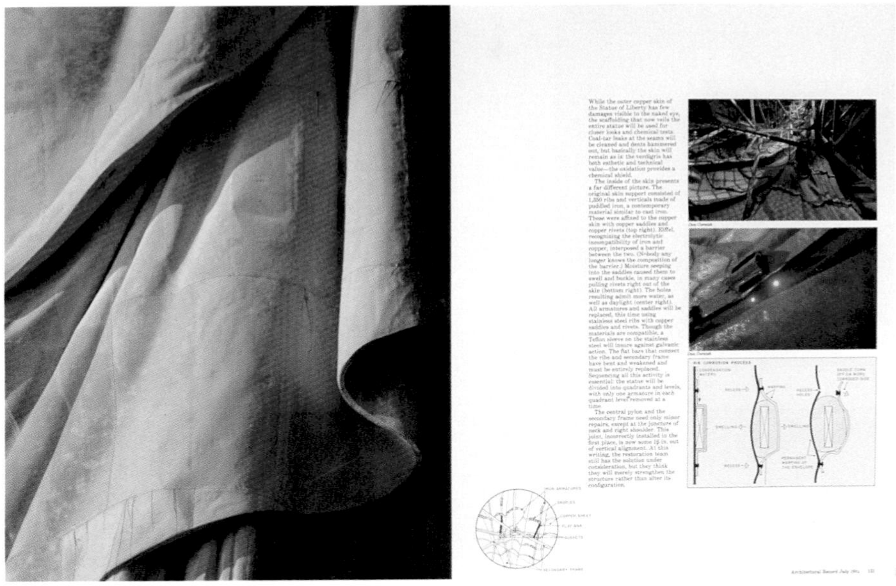

While the outer copper skin of the Statue of Liberty has few damages visible to the naked eye, the scaffolding that now veils the entire statue will be used for closer looks and chemical tests. Coal-tar leaks at the seams will be cleaned and dents hammered out, but basically the skin will remain as is: the verdigris has both esthetic and technical value—the oxidation provides a chemical shield.

The inside of the skin presents a far different picture. The original skin support consisted of 1,350 ribs and verticals made of puddled iron, a contemporary material similar to cast iron. These were affixed to the copper skin with copper saddles and copper rivets (top right). Eiffel, recognizing the electrolytic incompatibility of iron and copper, interposed a barrier between the two. (Nobody any longer knows the composition of the barrier.) Moisture seeping into the saddles caused them to swell and buckle, in many cases pulling rivets right out of the skin (bottom right). The holes resulting admit more water, as well as daylight (center right). All armatures and saddles will be replaced, this time using stainless steel ribs with copper saddles and rivets. Though the materials are compatible, a Teflon sleeve on the stainless steel will insure against galvanic action. The flat bars that connect the ribs and secondary frame have bent and weakened and must be entirely replaced. Sequencing all this activity is essential: the statue will be divided into quadrants and levels, with only one armature in each quadrant level removed at a time.

The central pylon and the secondary frame need only minor repairs, except at the juncture of neck and right shoulder. This joint, incorrectly installed in the first place, is now some 18 in. out of vertical alignment. At this writing, the restoration team still has the solution under consideration, but they think they will merely strengthen the structure rather than alter its configuration.

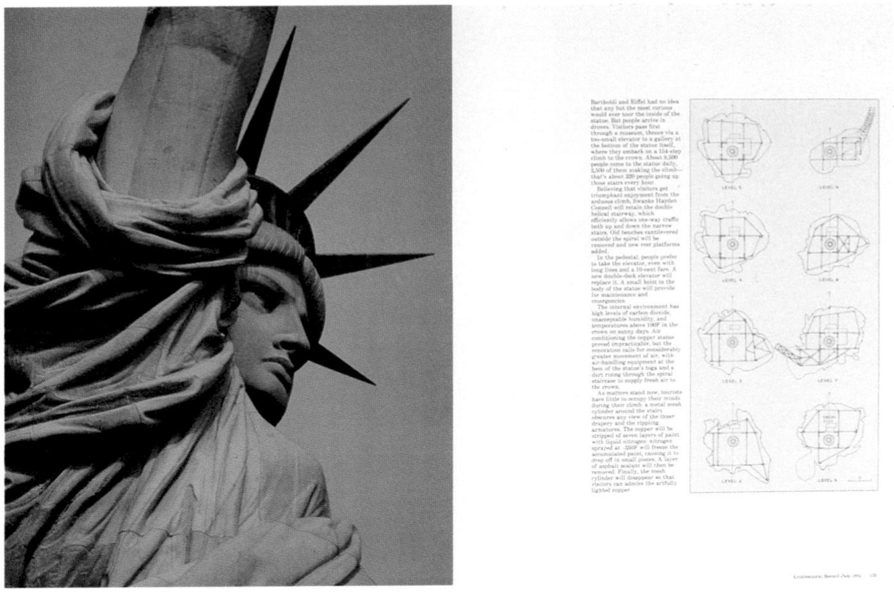

Bartholdi and Eiffel had no idea that any but the most curious would ever tour the inside of the statue. But people arrive in droves. Visitors pass first through a museum, thence via a too-small elevator to a gallery at the bottom of the statue itself, where they embark on a 154-step climb to the crown. About 8,500 people come to the statue daily, 2,500 of them making the climb—that's about 220 people going up those stairs every hour.

Believing that visitors get triumphant enjoyment from the arduous climb, Swanke Hayden Connell will retain the double helical stairway, which efficiently allows one-way traffic both up and down the narrow stairs. Old benches cantilevered outside the spiral will be removed and new rest platforms added.

In the pedestal, people prefer to take the elevator, even with long lines and a 10-cent fare. A new double-deck elevator will replace it. A small hoist in the body of the statue will provide for maintenance and emergencies.

The internal environment has high levels of carbon dioxide, unacceptable humidity, and temperatures above 100F in the crown on sunny days. Air conditioning the copper statue proved impracticable, but the renovation calls for considerably greater movement of air, with air-handling equipment at the hem of the statue's toga and a duct rising through the spiral staircase to supply fresh air to the crown.

As matters stand now, tourists have little to occupy their minds during their climb: a metal mesh cylinder around the stairs obscures any view of the inner drapery and the rippling armatures. The copper will be stripped of seven layers of paint with liquid nitrogen: nitrogen sprayed at -320F will freeze the accumulated paint, causing it to drop off in small pieces. A layer of asphalt sealant will then be removed. Finally, the mesh cylinder will disappear so that visitors can admire the artfully lighted copper.

346

PUBLICATION: *Architectural Record*
ART DIRECTOR: *Alex Stillano*
DESIGNER: *Alberto Bucchianri*
PHOTOGRAPHER: *Ezra Stoller/ESTO*
PUBLISHER: *McGraw-Hill*
CATEGORY: *Design-Story Presentation*
AWARD: *Merit*

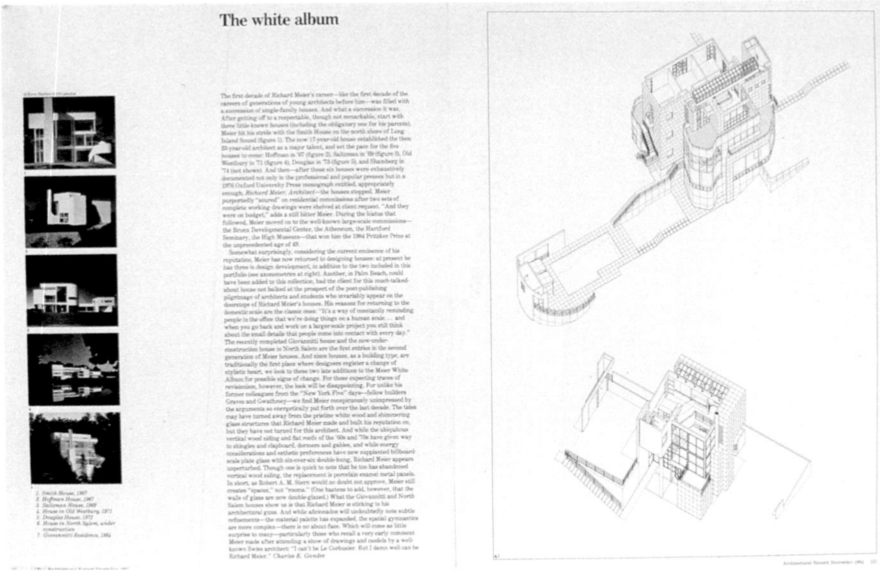

The white album

The first decade of Richard Meier's career—like the first decade of the careers of generations of young architects before him—was filled with a succession of single-family houses. And what a succession it was. After getting off to a respectable, though not remarkable, start with three little-known houses (including the obligatory one for his parents), Meier hit his stride with the Smith House on the north shore of Long Island Sound (figure 1). The now 17-year-old house established the then 33-year-old architect as a major talent, and set the pace for the five houses to come: Hoffman in '67 (figure 2), Saltzman in '69 (figure 3), Old Westbury in '71 (figure 4), Douglas in '73 (figure 5), and Shamberg in '74 (not shown). And then—after these six houses were exhaustively documented not only in the professional and popular presses but in a 1976 Oxford University Press monograph entitled, appropriately enough, *Richard Meier, Architect*—the houses stopped. Meier purportedly "soured" on residential commissions after two sets of complete working drawings were shelved at client request. "And they were on budget," adds a still bitter Meier. During the hiatus that followed, Meier moved on to the well-known large-scale commissions—the Bronx Developmental Center, the Atheneum, the Hartford Seminary, the High Museum—that won him the 1984 Pritzker Prize at the unprecedented age of 49.

Somewhat surprisingly, considering the current eminence of his reputation, Meier has now returned to designing houses: at present he has three in design development, in addition to the two included in this portfolio (see axonometrics at right). Another, in Palm Beach, could have been added to this collection, had the client for this much-talked-about house not balked at the prospect of the post-publishing pilgrimage of architects and students who invariably appear on the doorsteps of Richard Meier's houses. His reasons for returning to the domestic scale are the classic ones: "It's a way of constantly reminding people in the office that we're doing things on a human scale. . . and when you go back and work on a larger-scale project you still think about the small details that people come into contact with every day." The recently completed Giovannitti house and the now-under-construction house in North Salem are the first entries in the second generation of Meier houses. And since houses, as a building type, are traditionally the first place where designers register a change of stylistic heart, we look to these two late additions to the Meier White Album for possible signs of change. For those expecting traces of revisionism, however, the look will be disappointing. For unlike his former colleagues from the "New York Five" days—fellow builders Graves and Gwathmey—we find Meier conspicuously unimpressed by the arguments so energetically put forth over the last decade. The tides may have turned away from the pristine white wood and shimmering glass structures that Richard Meier made and built his reputation on, but they have not turned for this architect. And while the ubiquitous vertical wood siding and flat roofs of the '60s and '70s have given way to shingles and clapboard, dormers and gables, and while energy considerations and esthetic preferences have now supplanted billboard-scale plate glass with six-over-six double-hung, Richard Meier appears unperturbed. Though one is quick to note that he too has abandoned vertical wood siding, the replacement is porcelain enamel metal panels. In short, as Robert A. M. Stern would no doubt not approve, Meier still creates "spaces," not "rooms." (One hastens to add, however, that the walls of glass are now double-glazed.) What the Giovannitti and North Salem houses show us is that Richard Meier is sticking to his architectural guns. And while aficionados will undoubtedly note subtle refinements—the material palette has expanded, the spatial gymnastics are more complex—there is no about face. Which will come as little surprise to many—particularly those who recall a very early comment Meier made after attending a show of drawings and models by a well-known Swiss architect: "I can't be Le Corbusier. But I damn well can be Richard Meier." *Charles K. Gandee*

1. Smith House, 1967
2. Hoffman House, 1967
3. Saltzman House, 1969
4. House in Old Westbury, 1971
5. Douglas House, 1973
6. House in North Salem, under construction
7. Giovannitti Residence, 1984

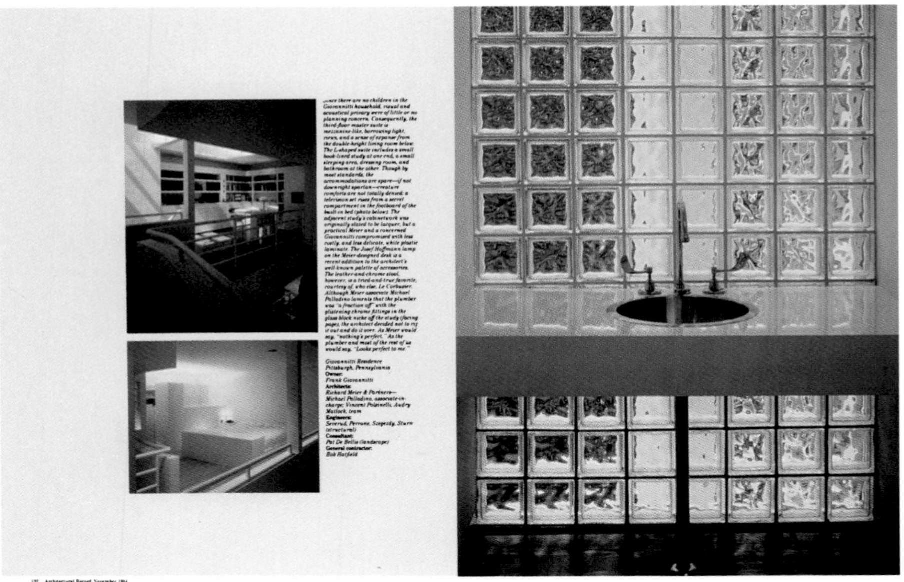

. . . since there are no children in the Giovannitti household, visual and acoustical privacy were of little or no planning concern. Consequently, the third-floor master suite is mezzanine-like, borrowing light, views, and a sense of expanse from the double-height living room below. The L-shaped suite includes a small book-lined study at one end, a small sleeping area, dressing room, and bathroom at the other. Though by most standards, the accommodations are spare—if not downright spartan—creature comforts are not totally denied: a television set rises from a secret compartment in the footboard of the built-in bed (photo below). The adjacent study's cabinetwork was originally slated to be lacquer, but a practical Meier and a concerned Giovannitti compromised with less costly, and less delicate, white plastic laminate. The Josef Hoffmann lamp on the Meier-designed desk is a recent addition to the architect's well-known palette of accessories. The leather-and-chrome stool, however, is a tried-and-true favorite, courtesy of, who else, Le Corbusier. Although Meier associate Michael Palladino laments that the plumber was "a fraction off" with the glistening chrome fittings in the glass block niche off the study (facing page), the architect decided not to rip it out and do it over. As Meier would say, "nothing's perfect." As the plumber and most of the rest of us would say, "Looks perfect to me."

Giovannitti Residence
Pittsburgh, Pennsylvania
Owner:
Frank Giovannitti
Architects:
Richard Meier & Partners—Michael Palladino, associate-in-charge; Vincent Polsinelli, Audry Matlock, team
Engineers:
Severud, Perrone, Szegezdy, Sturm (structural)
Consultant:
Pat De Bellis (landscape)
General contractor:
Bob Hatfield

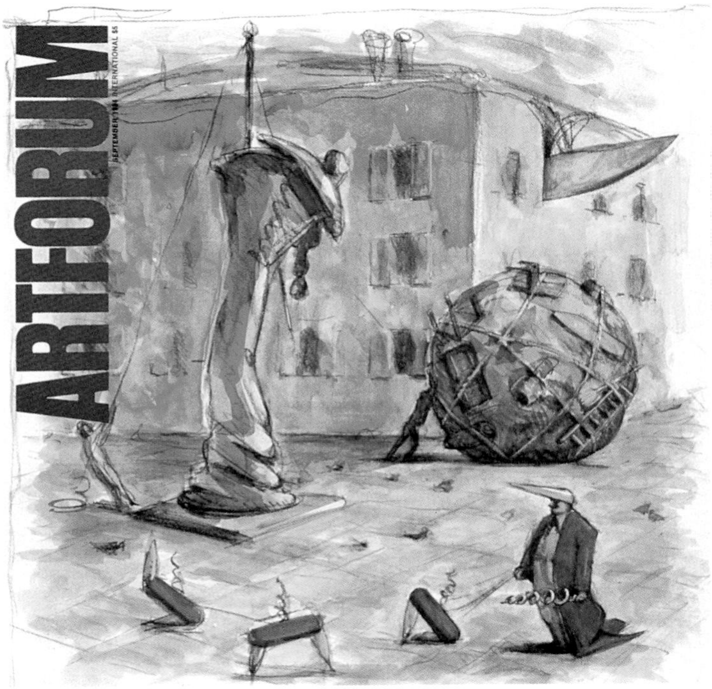

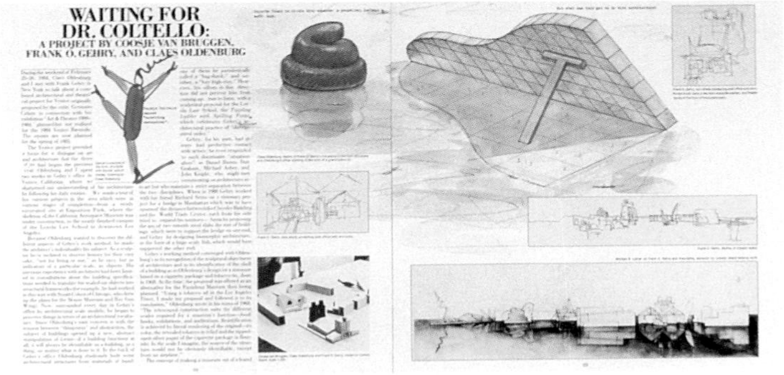

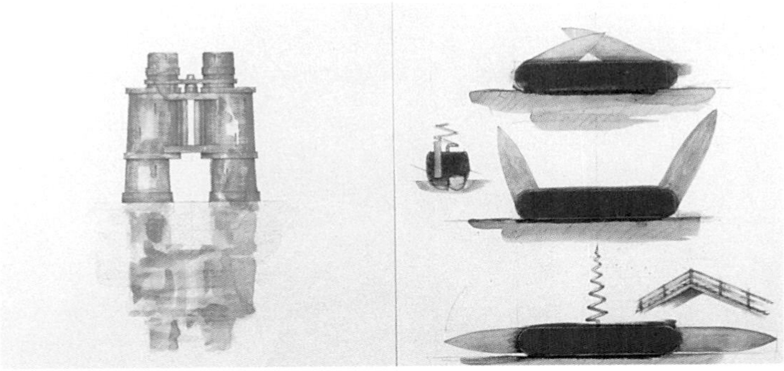

347

PUBLICATION: *Artforum*
ART DIRECTOR: *Roger Gorman*
DESIGNER: *Frances Reinfeld*
ILLUSTRATOR: *Claes Oldenberg*
Frank O'Gehry
PUBLISHER: *Reiner Design Consultants, Inc.*
CATEGORY: *Design-Story Presentation*
AWARD: *Merit*

354

PUBLICATION: *Chicago*
ART DIRECTOR: *Robert J. Post*
DESIGNER: *Robert J. Post*
PHOTOGRAPHER: *Dennis Manarchy*
PUBLISHER: *WFMT, Inc.*
CATEGORY: *Photo-Story Presentation*
AWARD: *Merit*

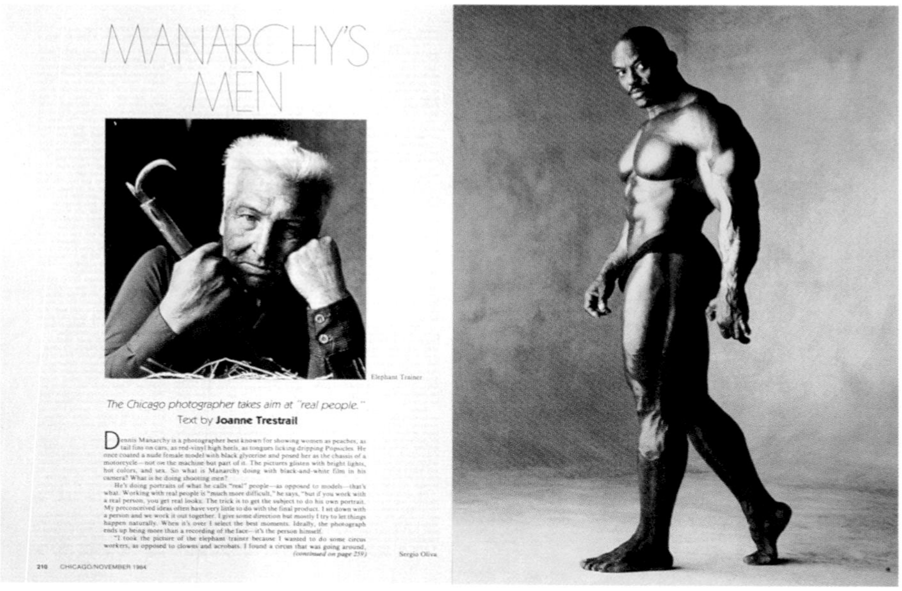

MANARCHY'S MEN

Elephant Trainer

The Chicago photographer takes aim at "real people."

Text by **Joanne Trestrail**

Dennis Manarchy is a photographer best known for showing women as peaches, as tail fins on cars, as red-vinyl high heels, as tongues licking dripping Popsicles. He once coated a nude female model with black glycerine and posed her as the chassis of a motorcycle—not on the machine but part of it. The pictures glisten with bright lights, hot colors, and sex. So what is Manarchy doing with black-and-white film in his camera? What is he doing shooting men?

He's doing portraits of what he calls "real" people—as opposed to models—that's what. Working with real people is "much more difficult," he says, "but if you work with a real person, you get real looks. The trick is to get the subject to do his own portrait. My preconceived ideas often have very little to do with the final product. I sit down with a person and we work it out together. I give some direction but mostly I try to let things happen naturally. When it's over I select the best moments. Ideally, the photograph ends up being more than a recording of the face—it's the person himself.

"I took the picture of the elephant trainer because I wanted to do some circus workers, as opposed to clowns and acrobats. I found a circus that was going around,

(continued on page 259)

Sergio Oliva

210 CHICAGO/NOVEMBER 1984

Amateur Boxer #1

Amateur Boxer #2

214 CHICAGO/NOVEMBER 1984

CHICAGO/NOVEMBER 1984 215

BY ANITA SHREVE
PHOTOGRAPHS BY ALEN MACWEENEY

H·E·X STONE

OPALS HAVE A SHIMMERING BEAUTY—
AND POSSESS,
SOME SAY, OMINOUS POWERS

Take no chances with a grain of salt, or defy it. What Saul would not fail the right of this cross set with emeralds, diamonds, and an Australian black opal. Fred Leighton Ltd.

Witches' familiar or cozy companion? It depends on where the finds her. Of her necklace there's no doubt. Made by Tiffany, 1902–15, it contains a cherry-tone-cut black opal, sapphires, garnets, and other black opals.

60

It's nice that she's come in out of the rain, but why doesn't she rate her wedlock and go into something dry, besides her carved opal lion bracelet of eighteen-karat gold and diamonds, with diamonds, emeralds, rubies, and sapphires? David Webb.

than go into her inlaws, rather than with museum-quality large stones. "When an opal gets very, very expensive, I worry. It's too vulnerable a stone," she says. "I'm always holding my breath when it's in my possession. I'm immensely relieved when we've finished setting an opal for someone and can give it back." She tells her customers never to drop an opal on the street; display it in a sardle setting; or set out all day in the sun with an opal bracelet.

Cummings travels twice a year to Hong Kong to oversee the cutting of her boulders, which are about the size of the average telephone. Their country of origin, though, is Australia, the world's chief source of opals, the town of Coober Pedy, in the

Australian outback, produces more than 80 percent of the total opal mined today.

Opal mining in Coober Pedy is a tough business. In the dry, deserted outback, an opal gouger digs a 15- to 120-foot shaft, looking for an opal seam, which is usually only a few centimeters in thickness. He is lucky if he finds such a seam, unlucky if he unwittingly destroys a fortune by shattering the precious stone that has formed in a cavity. In Coober Pedy, prospectors build their homes right into the ground next to rich veins and hope to put for a fridge on a vacation by chiseling opal from crannies in their walls. Housewives, high on opal fever, spend their after-

WHEN SHE WAS HAPPY, THE OPAL FLICKERED GAILY. WHEN SHE WAS FURIOUS, IT TURNED AN ANGRY RED.

noons "noodling"—sifting through abandoned mine dumps for opal chips. Some opals can fetch as much as $100,000, so a miner find may allow a prospector to retire for life.

The best opals continue to grow in value, and if bought at the right time and at the right price are as good an investment as any other gem of high quality. It is wise, however, say jewelers, to investigate the provenance of any investment-grade opal to determine whether it has been out of the ground long enough to have stabilized without crazing. Hong Kong is the major cutting and buying center for opals, doubtless because of the popularity of the stone in the East, particularly in Japan.

But it is an adornment, not investment, that those imprisoned

rainbows are most loved. They exude a feeling of life and warmth. "Opals catch and reflect the color of the eyes," says Angela Cummings. "They light up a woman's face."

An opal unlucky? A few years ago, a friend of mine was given an opal engagement ring and began to suffer, she says, pangs of foreboding. Worse, she inadvertently scheduled her wedding for a Friday the thirteenth. Sure enough, the couple broke up, and the wedding was cancelled. Bad luck?

Oh was it? Now happily married to someone else, my friend has laced numerous stories over the years extolling tears concerning the turbulent romantic career of her ex-fiancé. Today she says, "That wasn't bad luck, it was good luck." She still has the ring. □

Opposite: When yawning, cover your mouth to keep out evil spirits and show off your Australian boulder-opal ring set with pavé diamonds. James Robinson Inc. Above: Need thirteen be unlucky? Surely not thirteen bewitching opals—Hungarian whites, Australian blacks, an African green, a Mexican fire. From Manning Opal Co. and a private collection.

JANUARY 1989   61

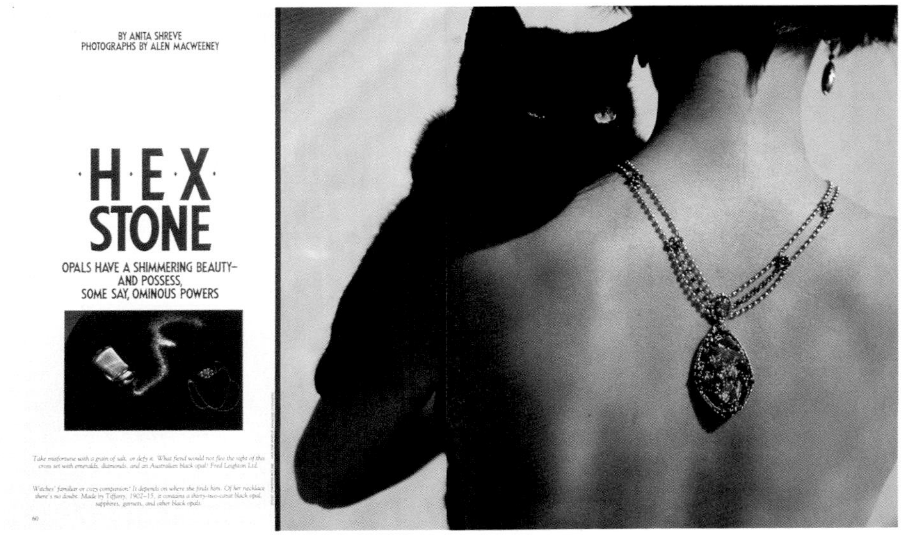

355

PUBLICATION: *Connoisseur*
ART DIRECTOR: *Carla Barr*
DESIGNER: *Carla Barr*
PHOTOGRAPHER: *Alan Macweeney*
PUBLISHER: *Hearst Corporation*
CATEGORY: *Design-Story Presentation*
AWARD: *Merit*

BY JOAN OGDEN FRESEMAN
PHOTOGRAPHS BY SANDI FELLMAN
NEO BATIK
BRINGING NEW LIFE TO AN OLD FABRIC

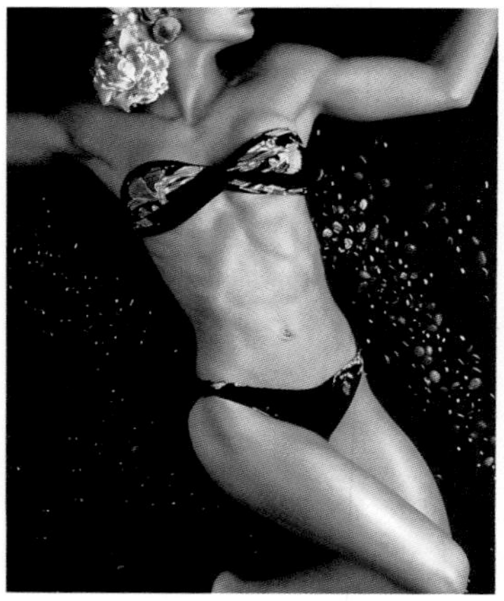

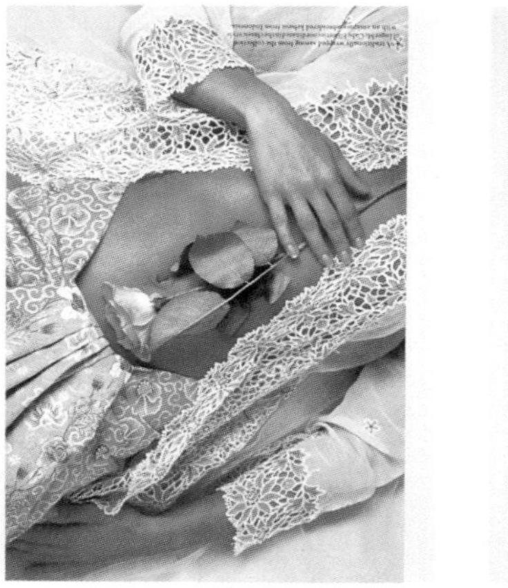

BATIK OR NOT BATIK

356

PUBLICATION: *Connoisseur Magazine*
ART DIRECTOR: *Carla Barr*
DESIGNER: *Carla Barr*
PHOTOGRAPHER: *Sandi Felman*
PUBLISHER: *Hearst Corporation*
CATEGORY: *Design-Story Presentation*
AWARD: *Merit*

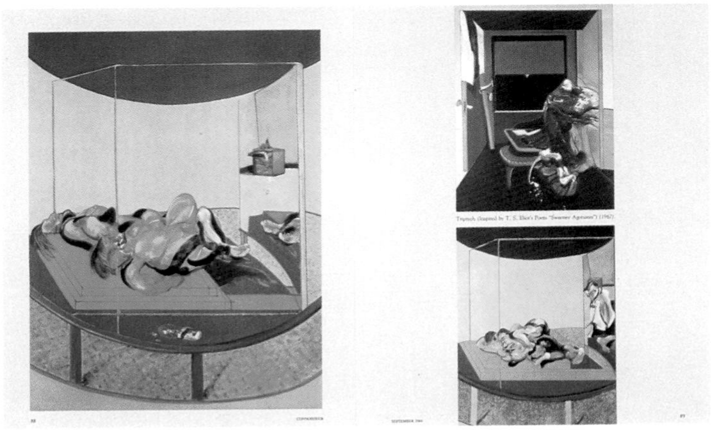

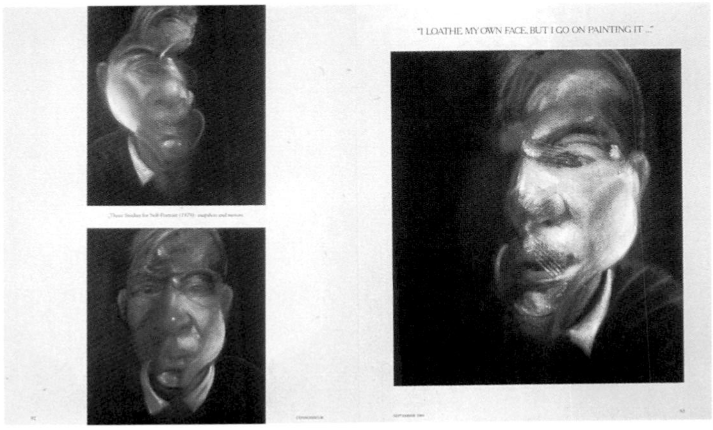

357

PUBLICATION: *Connoisseur*
ART DIRECTOR: *Carla Barr*
DESIGNER: *Carla Barr*
PHOTOGRAPHER: *Hans Namuth*
PUBLISHER: *Hearst Corporation*
CATEGORY: *Design-Story Presentation*
AWARD: *Merit*

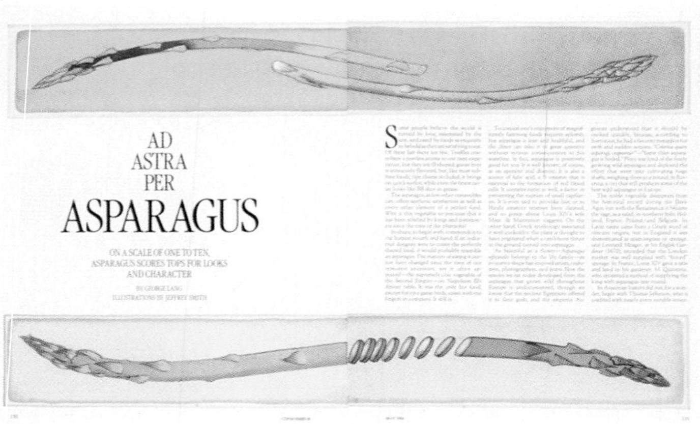

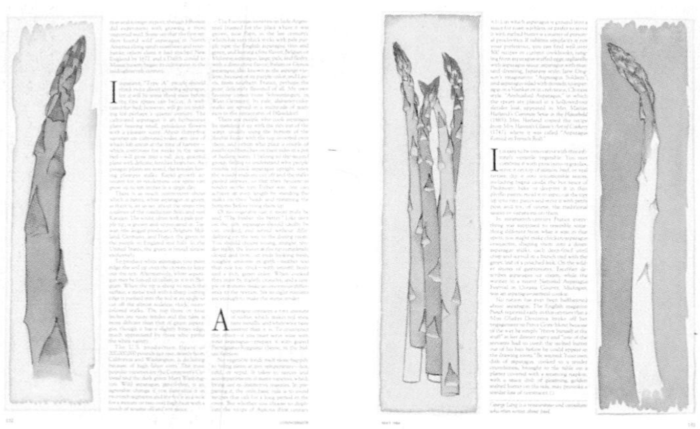

358

PUBLICATION: *Connoisseur*
ART DIRECTOR: *Carla Barr*
DESIGNER: *Carla Barr/Stephanie Phelan*
ILLUSTRATOR: *Jeffrey Smith*
PUBLISHER: *Hearst Publications*
CATEGORY: *Design-Story Presentation*
AWARD: *Merit*

359

PUBLICATION: *Connoisseur Magazine*
ART DIRECTOR: *Carla Barr*
DESIGNER: *Carla Barr*
PHOTOGRAPHER: *Alan Macweeney*
PUBLISHER: *Hearst Publications*
CATEGORY: *Design-Story Presentation*
AWARD: *Merit*

BLACK HAS BEEN
WORN BY THE REBELLIOUS
EVER SINCE HAMLET.

In a Little Black Dress all things are possible. Three immediate
possibilities appear here, ankle deep. Left, Geoffrey Beene's
wool jersey with black satin sleeves; center, his chemise with
wool jersey top and satin skirt; right, his mock corselet of wool
jersey and satin. Jewelry is by Sydie Lansing.

ELEGANCE

ARNOLD SCAASI IS AMERICA'S ANSWER TO PARIS'S TOP COUTURIERS

BY LISA SCHWARZBAUM   PHOTOGRAPHS BY ALEN MACWEENEY
PRODUCED BY KATHLEEN R. HEARST

Arnold Scaasi, America's reigning made-to-order couturier, works through the subdued reception room of his Fifth Avenue salon dropping up-dates like social kisses. There is no mistaking the air of royalty about the couture-client. In sweeping around fifty Manicured, coifed, blonded, and elegantly tailored, Scaasi is the example of a sophisticated, to discriminating woman with the time—and the bank account—for his luxurious clothes.

As rare but real spotlights, few of whom that Scaasi flavors on his happier, whichever it aristocrats in. A seamstress materializes from a back workroom to do her last progress on a new design that is

The fashion sittings and magic were full prose, right, and all Scaasi fashions on the following pages were photographed it the Kitz Bar Store Club City-Astor Show House Decorator's New York. Jewelry, Harry Winston. Rooms by Cornelius Bartholay.

Rhinestone leaves outline an orange and purple organza strapless dress, filmy black organza stole. Jewelry, David Webb. Room by Stanley Jay Friedman.

Bright brocade dance over black organza dress and jacket, below left, red organza dress aflame with rhinestone trim, right. Jewelry, David Webb. Room by Sandra Nunnerley.

HOW A DRESS BY ARNOLD SCAASI IS MADE — METICULOUSLY

From the design sketch, above left, a muslin is made and fitted to a client's mannequin, center and right; underpinnings, below left, the dress within the dress, but only line but also shape the garment, above right, the fabric is then cut, basted into shape, and attached to the shell, below left; at right, yards and yards of marvelous custom-made Scaasi lace.

360

PUBLICATION: *Connoisseur*
ART DIRECTOR: *Carla Barr*
DESIGNER: *Carla Barr*
PHOTOGRAPHER: *Alan Macweeney*
PUBLISHER: *Hearst Publications*
CATEGORY: *Design-Story Presentation*
AWARD: *Merit*

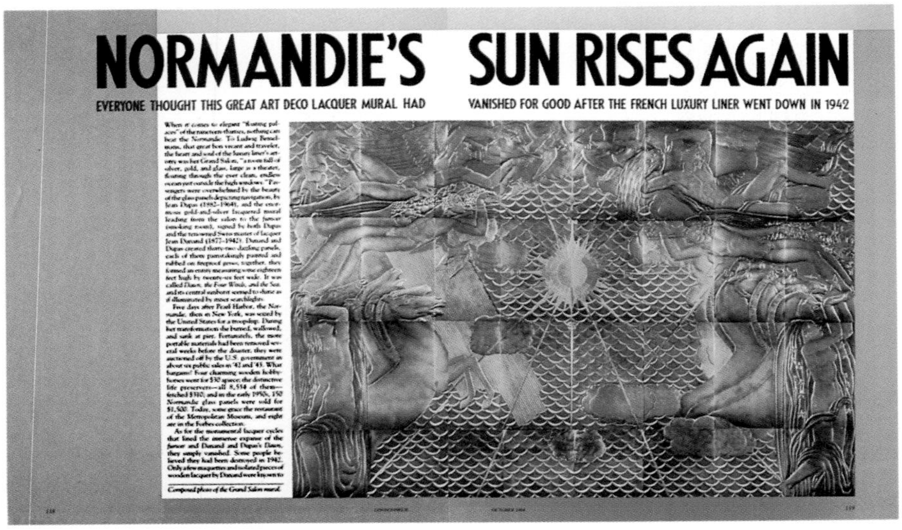

NORMANDIE'S SUN RISES AGAIN

EVERYONE THOUGHT THIS GREAT ART DECO LACQUER MURAL HAD VANISHED FOR GOOD AFTER THE FRENCH LUXURY LINER WENT DOWN IN 1942

Composed photo of the Grand Salon mural.

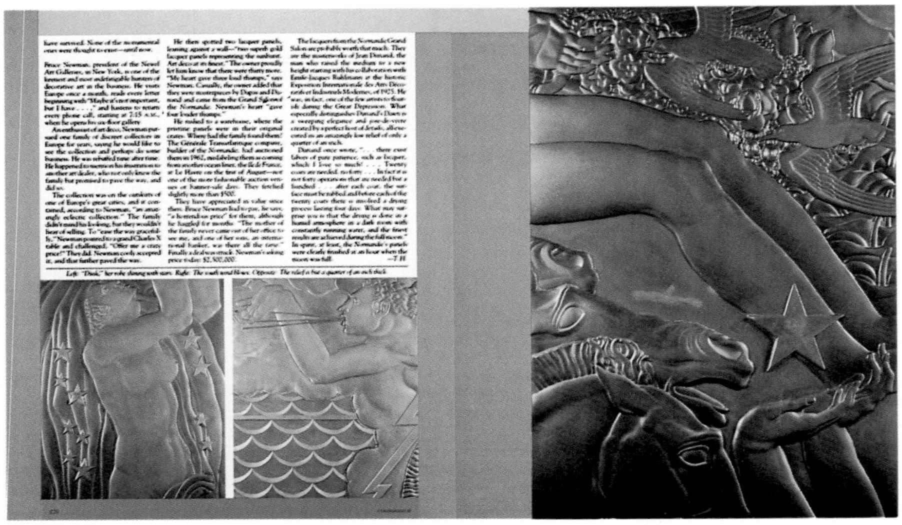

361

PUBLICATION: *Connoisseur*
ART DIRECTOR: *Carla Barr*
DESIGNER: *Carla Barr*
PUBLISHER: *Hearst Publications*
CATEGORY: *Design-Story Presentation*
AWARD: *Merit*

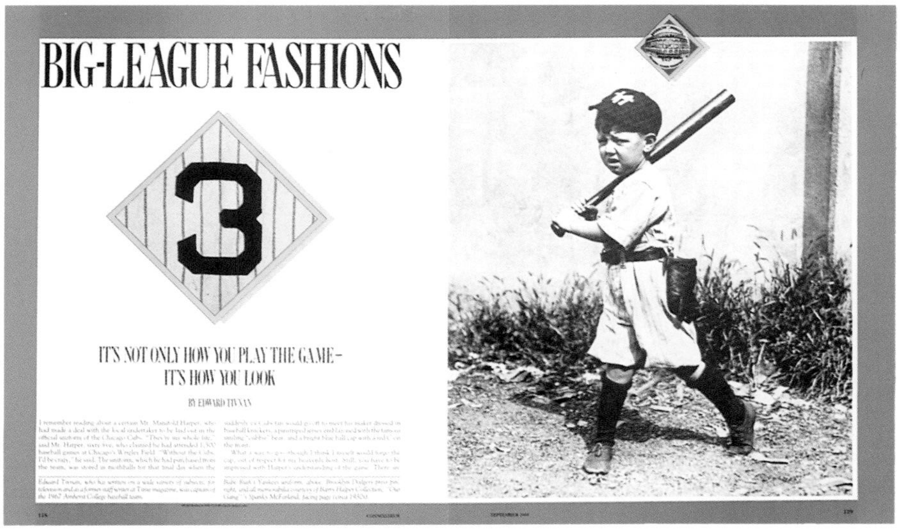
BIG-LEAGUE FASHIONS
IT'S NOT ONLY HOW YOU PLAY THE GAME – IT'S HOW YOU LOOK
BY EDWARD TIVNAN

362

PUBLICATION: *Connoisseur*
ART DIRECTOR: *Carla Barr*
DESIGNER: *Stephanie Phelan*
PHOTOGRAPHER: *Various*
PUBLISHER: *Hearst Publications*
CATEGORY: *Design-Story Presentation*
AWARD: *Merit*

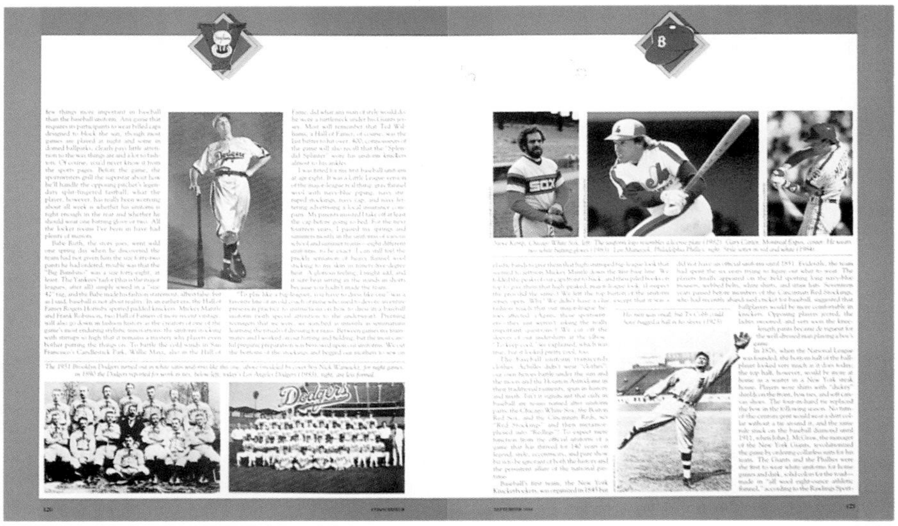

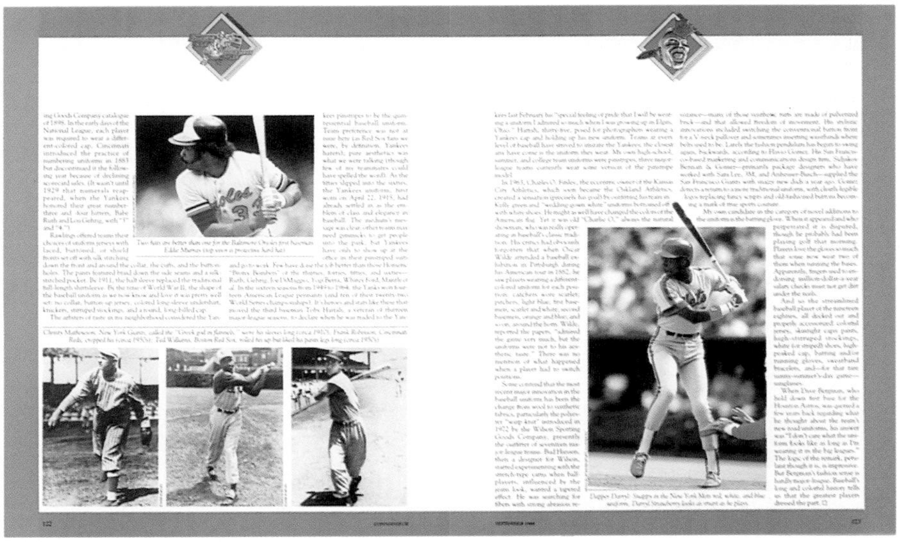

"WELCOME TO
PERUVIAN CUISINE"
HOW THE BEST FOOD IN LIMA CAME TO CHICAGO

AN ORCHESTRATION OF TASTES

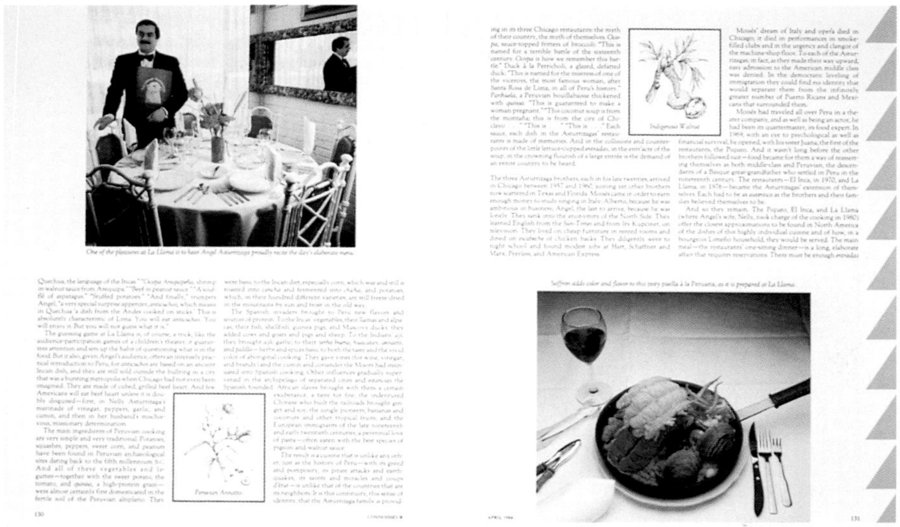

363

PUBLICATION: *Connoisseur*
ART DIRECTOR: *Carla Barr*
DESIGNER: *Stephanie Phelan*
PHOTOGRAPHER: *Marc Hauser*
PUBLISHER: *Hearst Publications*
CATEGORY: *Design-Story Presentation*
AWARD: *Merit*

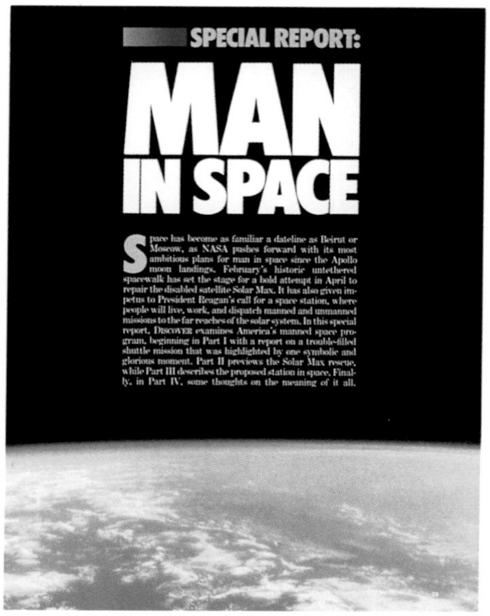

SPECIAL REPORT:

MAN IN SPACE

Space has become as familiar a dateline as Beirut or Moscow, as NASA pushes forward with its most ambitious plans for man in space since the Apollo moon landings. February's historic untethered spacewalk has set the stage for a bold attempt in April to repair the disabled satellite Solar Max. It has also given impetus to President Reagan's call for a space station, where people will live, work, and dispatch manned and unmanned missions to the far reaches of the solar system. In this special report, DISCOVER examines America's manned space program, beginning in Part I with a report on a trouble-filled shuttle mission that was highlighted by one symbolic and glorious moment. Part II previews the Solar Max rescue, while Part III describes the proposed station in space. Finally, in Part IV, some thoughts on the meaning of it all.

365

PUBLICATION: *Discover*
ART DIRECTOR: *Eric Seidman*
DESIGNER: *Theodore Kalomirakis*
PHOTOGRAPHER: *NASA*
PUBLISHER: *Time, Inc.*
CATEGORY: *Design-Story Presentation*
AWARD: *Merit*

PART I: THE MISSION

IN THE ARMCHAIR OF THE GODS

The first solo voyages by untethered astronauts and a misty Florida landing redeem a frustrating shuttle flight

In a giant leap for American spacefarers, Bruce McCandless (above) and Robert Stewart (below) flew untethered from the shuttle in NASA's new jetpacks

BY DENNIS OVERBYE

Sunlight, creeping around the blue limb of the earth 175 miles below, began to wash over the hull of the space shuttle *Challenger* as Bruce McCandless, in the shadows of the cargo bay, asked permission to abandon ship. "I'm going to head on out of the bay," he crackled, "with your permission." With his left hand he pulled up on a small handle on the armrest of his square white backpack, which looked for all the world like a bulky, legless chair. A burst of compressed nitrogen gas shot from tiny thrusters, and McCandless rose head first out of the shuttle, his dangling legs silhouetted against the bright cloud tops of the earth. As he cleared the bay, the astronaut twisted another knob on his right armrest and flipped to face the shuttle. Then he backed cautiously off into the void, dwarfed by the blackness around him as he receded. "This is neat," he reported. Then, looking down, he exclaimed, "Looks like Florida—it is Florida! It's the Cape!" Sailing over the clouds at 17,000 miles per hour, McCandless had become a human spaceship.

The image of that moment will linger as long as humans fly and dream of challenging the stars. Powered by Buck Rogers backpacks, known as manned maneuvering units (MMUs), McCandless and fellow astronaut Robert Stewart became the first human beings to venture from their spacecraft without a lifeline. Their untethered flights, their ability to navigate freely, away from the shuttle, cleared the way for a host of new activities in space. Among them: the first space rescue—the scheduled capture and repair in April of the disabled Solar Max astronomical satellite (see page 20)—and the assembly of an American space station by the early 1990s. Said McCandless, "We've opened a new frontier."

For much of *Challenger's* eight-day flight in February, it hardly seemed that way. Two $75 million communications satellites were lost in space; the shuttle's robot arm developed a bad wrist; a $450,000 balloon exploded in space; the shuttle toilet clogged again; and on its long-awaited, first-ever landing at the Kennedy Space Center in Florida, the shuttle smacked into a bird.

NASA had been determined to get the first flight of 1984 off the ground on time and successfully, especially after President Reagan, only a week before lift-off, announced his support for the agency's long sought space station. And *Challenger* did roar aloft on time on February 3. Heading the five-man crew on his second shuttle flight was Vance Brand, 52. Assisting him were pilot Robert "Hoot" Gibson, 37, and mission specialists McCandless, 46, Stewart, 41, and Ron McNair, 33.

The first order of business was to launch the communications satellites: Westar VI, owned by Western Union, and Palapa B2, belonging to the Indonesian government. To do their job of relaying data and communications, such satellites have to be in geosynchronous orbit, 22,300 miles above the Equator, where their orbital motion just matches the earth's rotation and they hover over the same area of the globe. After being sprung from the payload bay, the nearly identical satellites were to be carried into high orbit by bulbous little booster rockets known as PAMs (payload assist modules). The same combination had worked well five times on previous shuttle flights. On the first

McCandless in space: "Are you going to want the windows washed while I'm out here?"

14 PHOTOGRAPHS BY NASA DISCOVER / APRIL 1984

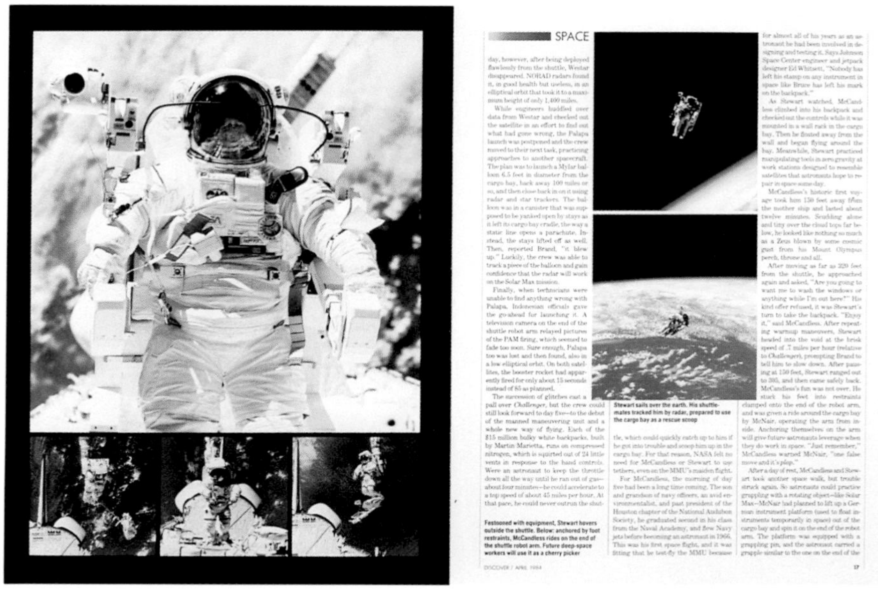

SPACE

day, however, after being deployed flawlessly from the shuttle, Westar disappeared. NORAD radars found it, in good health but useless, in an elliptical orbit that took it to a maximum height of only 1,400 miles.

While engineers huddled over data from Westar and checked out the satellite in an effort to find out what had gone wrong, the Palapa launch was postponed and the crew moved to their next task, practicing approaches to another spacecraft. The plan was to launch a Mylar balloon 6.5 feet in diameter from the cargo bay, back away 100 miles or so, and then close back in on it using radar and star trackers. The balloon was in a canister that was supposed to be yanked open by stays as it left its cargo bay cradle, the way a static line opens a parachute. Instead, the stays lifted off as well. Then, reported Brand, "it blew up." Luckily, the crew was able to track a piece of the balloon and gain confidence that the radar will work on the Solar Max mission.

Finally, when technicians were unable to find anything wrong with Palapa, Indonesian officials gave the go-ahead for launching it. A television camera on the end of the shuttle robot arm relayed pictures of the PAM firing, which seemed to fade too soon. Sure enough, Palapa too was lost and then found, also in a low elliptical orbit. On both satellites, the booster rocket had apparently fired for only about 15 seconds instead of 85 as planned.

The succession of glitches cast a pall over *Challenger*, but the crew could still look forward to day five—to the debut of the manned maneuvering unit and a whole new way of flying. Each of the $15 million bulky white backpacks, built by Martin Marietta, runs on compressed nitrogen, which is squirted out of 24 little vents in response to the hand controls. Were an astronaut to keep the throttle down all the way until he ran out of gas—about four minutes—he could accelerate to a top speed of about 45 miles per hour. At that pace, he could never outrun the shuttle, which could quickly catch up to him if he got into trouble and scoop him up in the cargo bay. For that reason, NASA felt no need for McCandless or Stewart to use tethers, even on the MMU's maiden flight.

For McCandless, the morning of day five had been a long time coming. The son and grandson of navy officers, an avid environmentalist, and past president of the Houston chapter of the National Audubon Society, he graduated second in his class from the Naval Academy, and flew Navy jets before becoming an astronaut in 1966. This was his first space flight, and it was fitting that he test-fly the MMU because for almost all of his years as an astronaut he had been involved in designing and testing it. Says Johnson Space Center engineer and jetpack designer Ed Whitsett, "Nobody has left his stamp on any instrument in space like Bruce has left his mark on the backpack."

As Stewart watched, McCandless climbed into his backpack and checked out the controls while it was mounted in a wall rack in the cargo bay. Then he floated away from the wall and began flying around the bay. Meanwhile, Stewart practiced manipulating tools in zero gravity at work stations designed to resemble satellites that astronauts hope to repair in space some day.

McCandless's historic first voyage took him 150 feet away from the mother ship and lasted about twelve minutes. Scudding alone and tiny over the cloud tops far below, he looked like nothing so much as a Zeus blown by some cosmic gust from his Mount Olympus perch, throne and all.

After moving as far as 320 feet from the shuttle, he approached again and asked, "Are you going to want me to wash the windows or anything while I'm out here?" His kind offer refused, it was Stewart's turn to take the backpack. "Enjoy it," said McCandless. After repeating warmup maneuvers, Stewart headed into the void at the brisk speed of .7 miles per hour (relative to *Challenger*), prompting Brand to tell him to slow down. After passing at 150 feet, Stewart ranged out to 305, and then came safely back. McCandless's fun was not over. He stuck his feet into restraints clamped onto the end of the robot arm, and was given a ride around the cargo bay by McNair, operating the arm from inside. Anchoring themselves on the arm will give future astronauts leverage when they do work in space. "Just remember," McCandless warned McNair, "one false move and it's *plop*."

After a day of rest, McCandless and Stewart took another space walk, but trouble struck again. So astronauts could practice grappling with a rotating object—like Solar Max—McNair had planned to lift up a German instrument platform (used to float instruments temporarily in space) out of the cargo bay and spin it on the end of the robot arm. The platform was equipped with a grappling pin, and the astronaut carried a grapple similar to the one on the end of the

Stewart sails over the earth. His shuttlemates tracked him by radar, prepared to use the cargo bay as a rescue scoop

Festooned with equipment, Stewart hovers outside the shuttle. Below: anchored by foot restraints, McCandless rides on the end of the shuttle robot arm. Future deep-space workers will use it as a cherry picker

DISCOVER / APRIL 1984 17

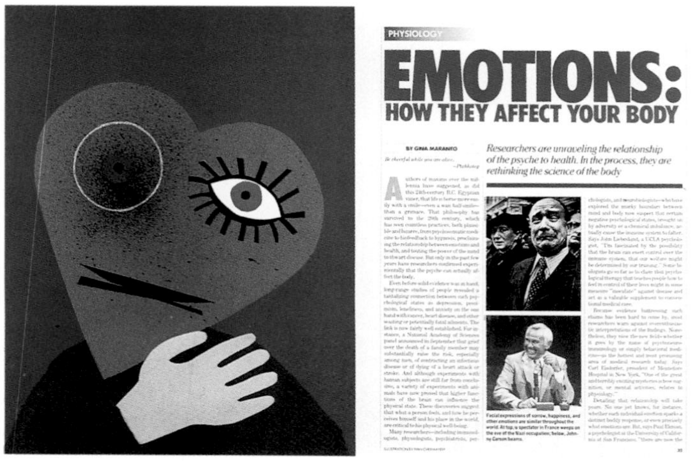
PHYSIOLOGY
EMOTIONS:
HOW THEY AFFECT YOUR BODY
Researchers are unraveling the relationship of the psyche to health. In the process, they are rethinking the science of the body

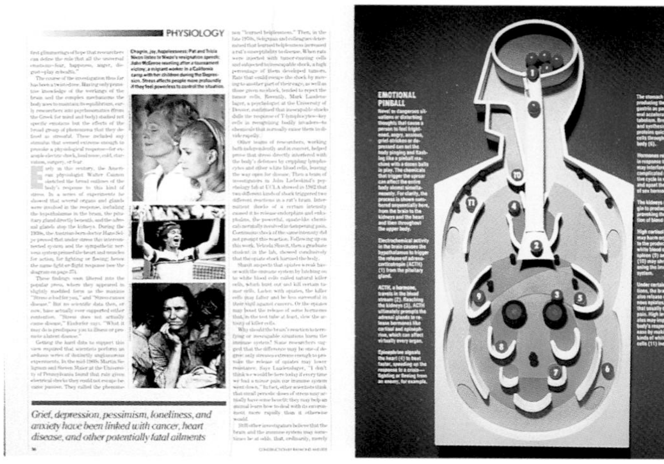
PHYSIOLOGY
Grief, depression, pessimism, loneliness, and anxiety have been linked with cancer, heart disease, and other potentially fatal ailments
EMOTIONAL PINBALL

366

PUBLICATION: *Discover Magazine*
ART DIRECTOR: *Eric Seidman*
DESIGNER: *John Thomsen*
ILLUSTRATOR: *Ivan Chermayeff*
Raymond Ameijide
PUBLISHER: *Time, Inc.*
CATEGORY: *Design-Story Presentation*
AWARD: *Merit*

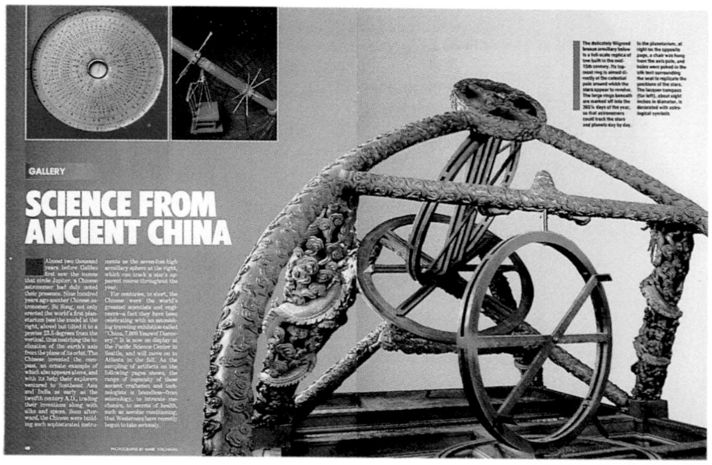
GALLERY
SCIENCE FROM ANCIENT CHINA

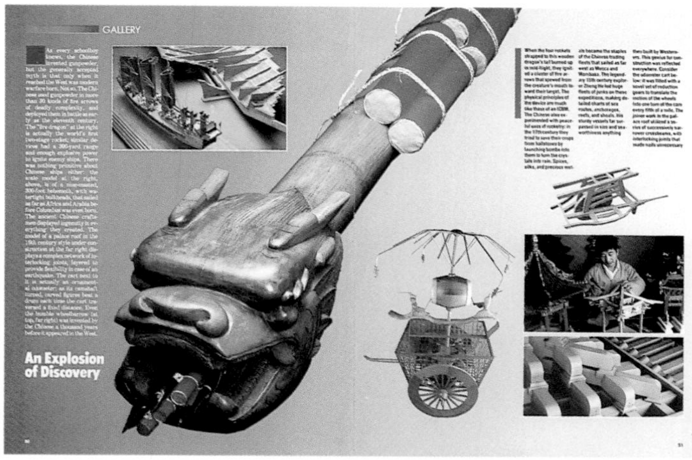
GALLERY
An Explosion of Discovery

367

PUBLICATION: *Discover*
ART DIRECTOR: *Eric Seidman*
DESIGNER: *Sandra DiPasqua*
PHOTOGRAPHER: *Mark Tuschman*
PUBLISHER: *Time, Inc.*
CATEGORY: *Design-Story Presentation*
AWARD: *Merit*

THE EYE

CATARACTS: BEHIND THE CLOUDED LENS

The causes are known. So is a surgical remedy. Now researchers are closing in on new ways to head off this common scourge of old age

BY JOHN LANGONE

LIGHTING THE WAY

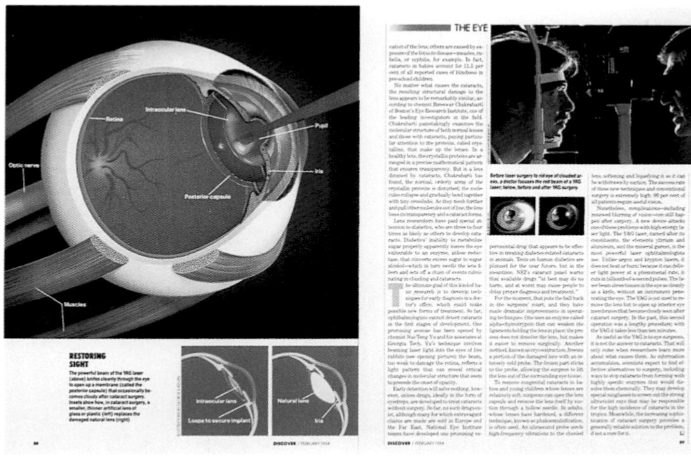
THE EYE

RESTORING SIGHT

368

PUBLICATION: *Discover*
ART DIRECTOR: *Eric Seidman*
DESIGNER: *Robert M. Daniels*
ILLUSTRATOR: *George V. Kelvin*
PUBLISHER: *Time, Inc.*
CATEGORY: *Design-Story Presentation*
AWARD: *Merit*

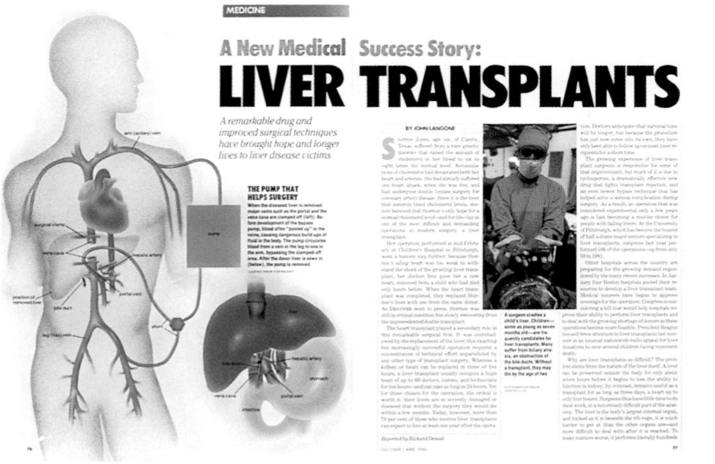
MEDICINE

A New Medical Success Story:

LIVER TRANSPLANTS

A remarkable drug and improved surgical techniques have brought hope and longer lives to liver disease victims

BY JOHN LANGONE

THE PUMP THAT HELPS SURGERY

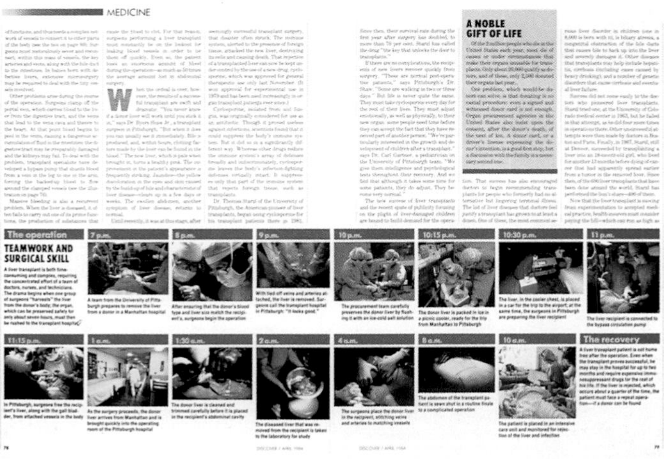
MEDICINE

A NOBLE GIFT OF LIFE

The operation

TEAMWORK AND SURGICAL SKILL

The recovery

369

PUBLICATION: *Discover*
ART DIRECTOR: *Eric Seidman*
DESIGNER: *Theodore Kalomirakis*
ILLUSTRATOR: *Kirk Moldoff*
PHOTOGRAPHER: *Ergun Cagatay*
PUBLISHER: *Time, Inc.*
CATEGORY: *Design-Story Presentation*
AWARD: *Merit*

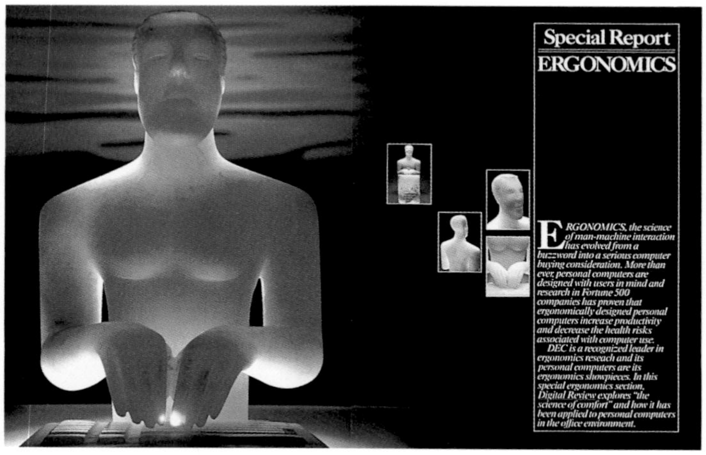

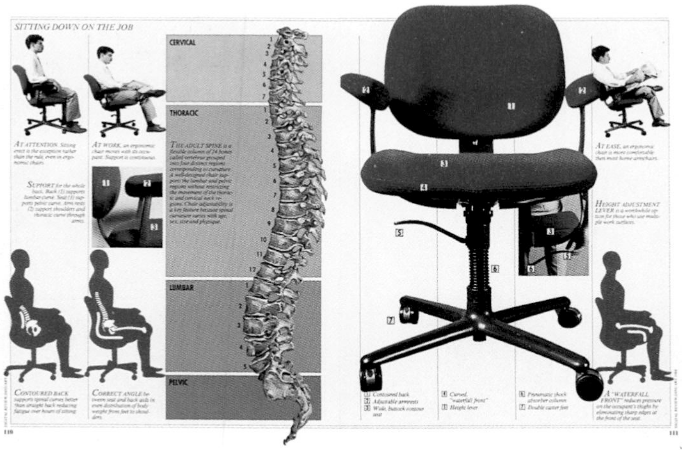

370

PUBLICATION: *Digital Review*
ART DIRECTOR: *Bill Jensen*
DESIGNER: *Bill Jensen*
PHOTOGRAPHER: *Seth Joel, A.A. Murphy, Robert Lorenz*
PUBLISHER: *Ziff-Davis*
CATEGORY: *Story Presentation*
AWARD: *Merit*

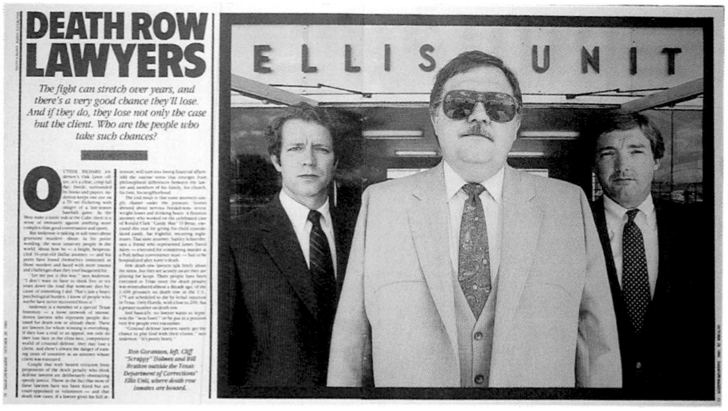

371

PUBLICATION: *Dallas Life Magazine*
ART DIRECTOR: *Ginny Pitre*
DESIGNER: *Ginny Pitre*
PHOTOGRAPHER: *Randy Grothe*
PUBLISHER: *The Dallas Morning News*
CATEGORY: *Design-Story Presentation*
AWARD: *Merit*

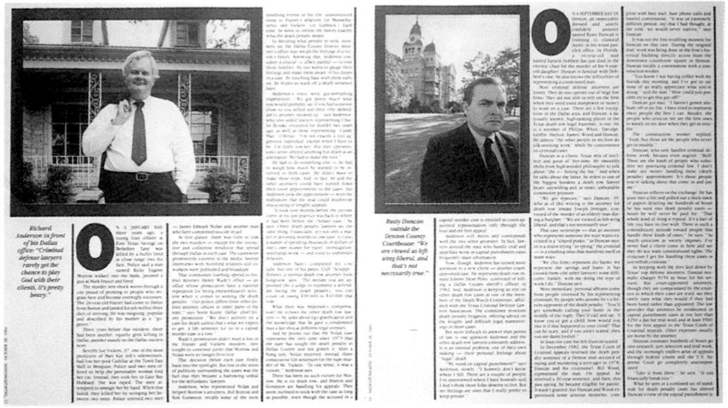
Richard Anderson in front of his Dallas office: "Criminal defense lawyers rarely get the chance to play God with their clients. It's pretty heavy."
Rusty Duncan outside the Denton County Courthouse: "We are viewed as left-wing liberal, and that's not necessarily true."

FASHION GUITAR
FLAG
Surprisingly Formal
by Vincent Boucher

372

PUBLICATION: *Esquire*
ART DIRECTOR: *April Silver*
DESIGNER: *Charles A. Brucaliere*
PHOTOGRAPHER: *Max Vadukul*
PUBLISHER: *Esquire Associates*
CATEGORY: *Photo-Story Presentation*
AWARD: *Merit*

SPY
CLICK
BIRD

ROCKMOUTH
BOTTLE

373

PUBLICATION: *Esquire*
ART DIRECTOR: *April Silver*
DESIGNER: *April Silver*
PHOTOGRAPHER: *Bill King*
PUBLISHER: *Esquire Associates*
CATEGORY: *Photo-Story Presentation*
AWARD: *Merit*

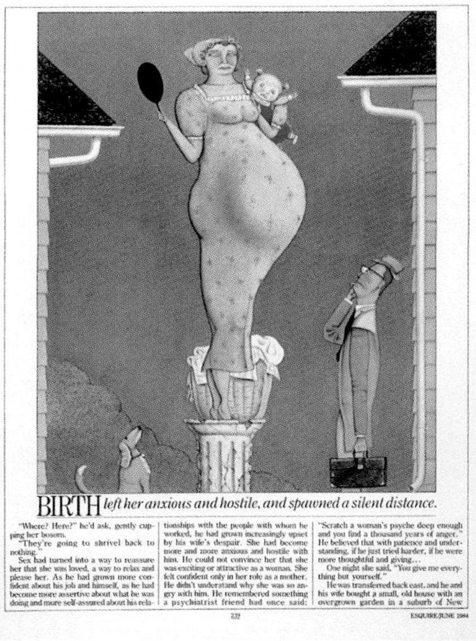

374

PUBLICATION: *Esquire*
ART DIRECTOR: *April Silver*
DESIGNER: *Judy Goldstein*
ILLUSTRATOR: *Blair Drawson*
PUBLISHER: *Esquire Associates*
CATEGORY: *Illustration-Story Presentation*
AWARD: *Merit*

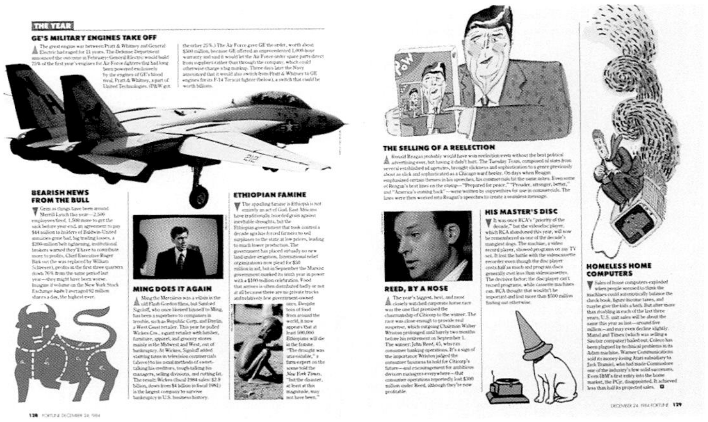

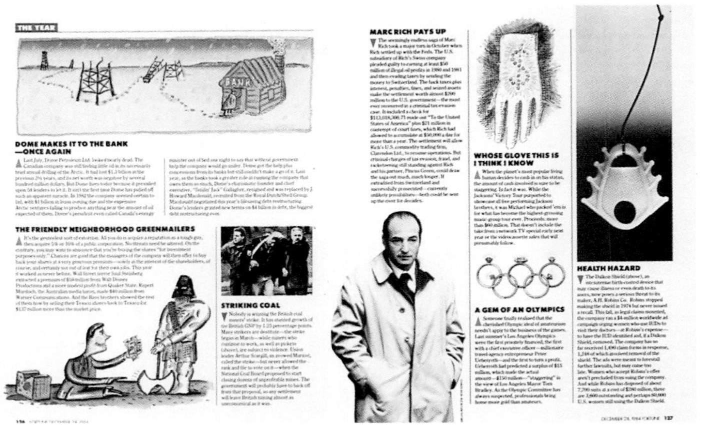

375

PUBLICATION: *Fortune Magazine*
ART DIRECTOR: *Margery Peters*
DESIGNER: *Josh Gosfield*
ILLUSTRATOR: *Marc Rosenthal*
PHOTOGRAPHER: *William Coupon*
Derek Bayes
PUBLISHER: *Fortune Magazine*
CATEGORY: *Design-Story Presentation*
AWARD: *Merit*

SELLING

BUDGET FROM $2,000 TO $4,000 for your next dinner party if you want bemedaled Pierre Bitterer to cook it. This includes eight courses of classic French fare, but neither wines nor transportation for Bitterer, his waiters, and his attaché case full of herbs. Bitterer, 59, who also runs a restaurant in Santa Rosa, California, spends 65% of his time cooking out. His longest trip was to the Philippines in 1969 to prepare a dinner party for eight for President Marcos. His service is titled appropriately: Chez Vous.

FOR $3,000 A DAY ONE CAN RENT Electra, a 96-footer, complete with captain and crew. Built in the 1930s with a leather and mahogany interior equipped with a fireplace, she sails from Newport Beach, California. Owner: Executive Aviation Services, which specializes in chartering jets, but keeps Electra floating profitably through word-of-mouth advertising. Aboard is CPA Charles Wiese of Los Angeles with guests. Wiese reserves the boat every April 16 to celebrate the end of his busy season.

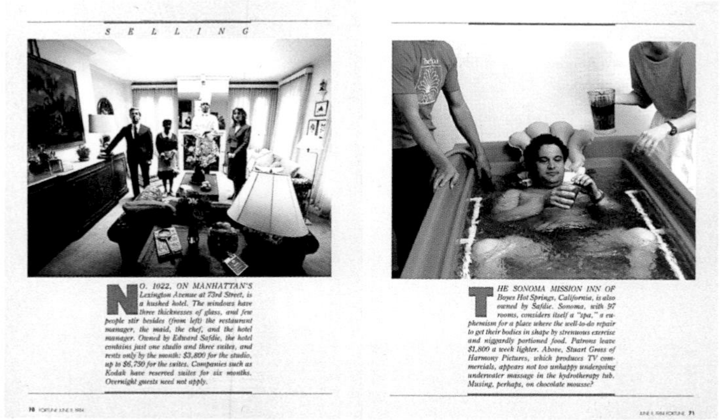

SELLING

NO. 1022, ON MANHATTAN'S Lexington Avenue at 73rd Street, is a hushed hotel. The windows have three thicknesses of glass, and few people stir besides (from left) the restaurant manager, the maid, the chef, and the hotel manager. Owned by Edward Safdie, the hotel contains just one studio and three suites, and rents only by the month: $3,800 for the studio, up to $6,750 for the suites. Companies such as Kodak have reserved suites for six months. Overnight guests need not apply.

THE SONOMA MISSION INN OF Boyes Hot Springs, California, is also owned by Safdie. Sonoma, with 97 rooms, considers itself a "spa," a euphemism for a place where the well-to-do repair to get their bodies in shape by strenuous exercise and niggardly portioned food. Patrons leave $1,800 a week lighter. Above, Stuart Gross of Harmony Pictures, which produces TV commercials, appears not too unhappy undergoing underwater massage in the hydrotherapy tub. Musing, perhaps, on chocolate mousse?

376

PUBLICATION: *Fortune Magazine*
ART DIRECTOR: *Margery Peters*
DESIGNER: *Josh Gosfield*
PHOTOGRAPHER: *Elliott Erwitt/Magnum*
PUBLISHER: *Fortune Magazine*
CATEGORY: *Design-Story Presentation*
AWARD: *Merit*

377

PUBLICATION: *Fortune Magazine*
ART DIRECTOR: *Margery Peters*
DESIGNER: *Barbara Smyth*
PHOTOGRAPHER: *Michele Singer*
PUBLISHER: *Fortune Magazine*
CATEGORY: *Design-Story Presentation*
AWARD: *Merit*

378

PUBLICATION: *Fortune Magazine*
ART DIRECTOR: *Margery Peters*
DESIGNER: *Josh Gosfield*
PHOTOGRAPHER: *Paul Chesley*
PUBLISHER: *Fortune Magazine*
CATEGORY: *Design-Story Presentation*
AWARD: *Merit*

379

PUBLICATION: *Fortune Magazine*
ART DIRECTOR: *Margery Peters*
DESIGNER: *Josh Gosfield*
PHOTOGRAPHER: *Mark Hanauer*
PUBLISHER: *Fortune Magazine*
CATEGORY: *Design-Story Presentation*
AWARD: *Merit*

380

PUBLICATION: *Geo Magazine*
ART DIRECTOR: *John Tom Cohoe*
DESIGNER: *Frank Tagariello*
ILLUSTRATOR: *Nelle Davis*
PHOTOGRAPHER: *Len Jenshel*
PUBLISHER: *Knapp Communications*
CATEGORY: *Design-Story Presentation*
AWARD: *Merit*

SINCE THE RENAISSANCE, ITALIAN ARISTOCRATS HAVE CULTIVATED SECRET GARDENS BEHIND LOFTY WALLS AND HEDGES. THEY ARE

PRIVATE EDENS

Even the worldly need privacy. So when the wealthy Italian nobles of the sixteenth century left their fortified cities and began to build lavish villas across the countryside, their architects devised the *giardino segreto* (the "secret garden"), a small garden hidden within a larger one.

They were places where the wealthy could "pick flowers and fruit, listen to the birds singing and [take] their honest enjoyment," according to an inscription in the secret garden at Villa di Papa Giulio in Rome. The secret garden was a place to be alone, to rendezvous with a lover, to entertain special guests (in the sixteenth century, Cardinal Alessandro Farnese once welcomed Pope Gregory XIII to his secret garden with a procession of white-clad maidens clashing cymbals and bearing olive branches). Many of Italy's secret gardens are now open to the public. On these pages are five of the finest.

The ivy-covered wall of a theater that the emperor Domitian built in Castel Gandolfo in the first century A.D. encloses the pope's secret garden.

Article by Thomas Christopher • Photos by Len Jenshel

38 GEO · GEO 39

VILLA FARNESE

Cardinal Alessandro Farnese spent much of his fortune on the lavish villa and gardens he began to build in the Umbrian countryside in 1547. A visiting priest once rebuked the worldly and arrogant cardinal for his extravagance and asked him if he shouldn't share his wealth with the poor of the district. "I have let them have it all little by little," Farnese replied, "but I made them earn it by the sweat of their brows."

Farnese's architect—the brilliant Giacomo da Vignola, who completed St. Peter's after the death of Michelangelo—included in his design a secret garden at the top of a wooded slope. Vignola filled the garden with statues that mimicked the antics of Farnese and his dissolute guests. A grinning shepherd pours wine from a skin; an angel with a snake coiled around its torso caresses a woman's cheek; a voluptuous matron squeezes her own breasts. Queen Christina of Sweden, a devout Catholic convert, was so taken aback by the pagan spirit of the place that she exclaimed, "I dare not speak the name of Jesus lest I break the spell."

In 1647 the defrocked cardinal Camillo Pamphili and his young bride spent a passionate summer in the garden. Young Pamphili had fallen in love and renounced his post, telling his uncle, Pope Innocent X, that as much as he admired the virtue of chastity, he could not practice it without a wife. This secret garden, where nobility once so disported itself, is now the summer retreat of Italian presidents.

A forest of chestnuts at Villa Farnese (above) opens, surprisingly, to the formal secret garden and summer pavilion (right).

62 GEO · GEO 63

A clipped hedge of dwarf boxwood in the secret garden at Villa Papale forms the pattern of Pope Pius XI's coat of arms.

VILLA PAPALE

Romans will always hate Maffeo Barberini, a self-important, power-hungry nobleman who became Pope Urban VIII in 1623. Soon after he attained the papacy, Barberini stole ancient bronzes from the Pantheon to make cannons. It was a villainous act, and the outraged citizenry took to the streets with a chant that is sometimes heard even today: "What the barbarians didn't do, the Barberini did."

Castel Gandolfo, a village in the Alban Hills some 15 miles southeast of Rome, fared better in Barberini's hands. No doubt infatuated with Castel Gandolfo's imperial connections (the emperor Domitian had ruled the Roman Empire from here), Barberini rebuilt an ancient villa in the town and hired his nephew to landscape the grounds in grand style. Popes have been spending their summers at Villa Papale in Castel Gandolfo ever since.

In 1933 Pope Pius XI commissioned noted landscape architect Emilio Bonomelli to redesign the gardens. Bonomelli provided his patron with sweeping vistas, broad allées of distinctively shaped oaks and umbrella pines, expansive terraces carpeted with flower beds and a small secret garden that is enclosed by the wall of an ancient Roman theater. The only noise in the "Garden of the Magnolia"—so called because a 30-foot-tall magnolia tree grows at its center—is the splash of fountains and the crunch of acorns underfoot. It is as peaceful a place as a pope could ever find.

VILLA GAMBERAIA

Villa Gamberaia took its name from one or the other of two former residents—the Gamberetti family, prosperous stonecutters who lived here during the fifteenth and sixteenth centuries, or the *gamberi* ("crayfish") that once abounded on this estate in the hills above Florence.

Villa Gamberaia has passed through the hands of several aristocratic owners over the centuries. The Capponi family, one of whose members, Piero, faced down the king of France when he appeared at the gates of Florence in 1494, lived here during the eighteenth century. Princess Ghyka, whose sister was Queen Natalia of Serbia, refurbished the villa at the end of the nineteenth century. And Marcello Marchi, who lives here now, rebuilt the villa and the gardens after they were devastated by Allied bombs during World War II.

With their azalea beds and long bowling green, the gardens at Villa Gamberaia seem more typical of Kent than of the Tuscan countryside. But the pleasant views they afford of olive groves, vineyards and the domes of Florence are definitely Italian. "An Italianized Englishman would be the devil himself," says the old Tuscan proverb. The closest the devil comes to making an appearance at Villa Gamberaia is in the small secret garden hidden in a stand of 250-year-old cypresses. He takes the form of a diabolic-looking old faun who brandishes a trident and presides over a very pleasant rustic fountain.

Past residents of Villa Gamberaia used the small, circular secret garden (right) as a theater; the massive fountain (below) was the stage.

60 GEO · GEO 61

AT HOME IN HARDY'S ENGLAND

The bucolic county of Dorset was the model for Thomas Hardy's Wessex. Visitors there today share the footpaths with characters from his novels.

People like hurdle-maker Bill Poore (left) are the characters, and villages like Cerne Abbas the settings, of Hardy novels.

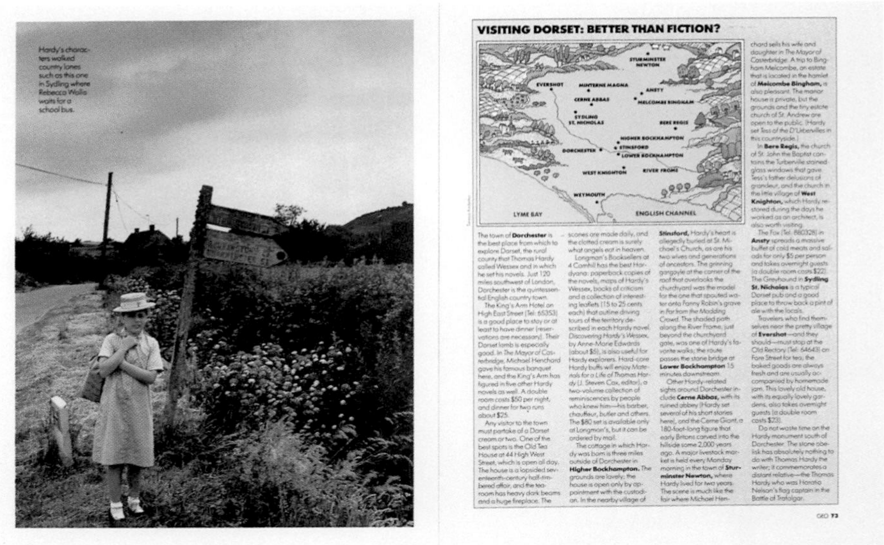

381

PUBLICATION: *Geo Magazine*
ART DIRECTOR: *John Tom Cohoe*
DESIGNER: *John Tom Cohoe*
ILLUSTRATOR: *Teresa Anderko*
PHOTOGRAPHER: *Kenneth Griffiths*
PUBLISHER: *Knapp Communications*
CATEGORY: *Design-Story Presentation*
AWARD: *Merit*

Hardy's characters walked country lanes such as this one in Sydling where Rebecca Wallis waits for a school bus.

VISITING DORSET: BETTER THAN FICTION?

Americans (also, strangely, the Japanese) have an incurable — and to the natives inexplicable — weakness for Thomas Hardy.

A Badger House

The River Frome (top left) runs through several Hardy novels; Waterston Manor was Bathsheba's house in Far from the Madding Crowd; E. G. White's horse knows the way home from the pub.

GARDEN
GAMES
It's easy enough to enter one of
Britain's famous mazes. Getting out? That's another story.
GEO 65

HOW TO SOLVE A MAZE

Hampton Court Maze

Chevening Maze

perimeter hedge · central island · minor islands

The maze at Hampton Court has been frustrating people for the past 300 years, but the solution is quite simple. Since the maze consists of only one very long, continuous hedge, all you need to do is keep your hand on the hedge to either your right or left. Eventually you'll come to the center. In the nineteenth century, the third earl of Stanhope came up with a new twist when he built his maze at Chevening Park: he placed the goal within a separate hedge inside the maze. To solve this type of maze, follow one hedge until the goal, which usually has a tree or a statue in it, is separated from you by a single hedge. Transfer your allegiance to that hedge and follow it to the goal.

Solutions:

The 1887 stone maze in Alkborough Church is based on the maze at right.

coins, on Roman pillars at Pompeii, in Scandinavian stone carvings dating to the Bronze Age and on a rock face near Tintagel, a remote area of Cornwall that was supposedly the stomping grounds of King Arthur.

Centuries ago, the Romans or some other ancient people cut mazes of the same design into the foggy downs of England by removing strips of grass between pathways to reveal the clay soil. Of the hundreds of these turf mazes known to have existed in Britain at one time or another, only eight have survived. They pose no puzzle—there are no dead ends, no wrong turns. You simply follow the path to reach the center. But while walking the path, you feel something propelling you forward; your movements take on an age-old rhythm.

Countryfolk used turf mazes for revels and games. Men raced toward their ladies at the center or laid down wagers in gallons of ale for running the maze. Supposedly, a man could run from the Breamore turf maze to Gallows Hill and back—well over a mile—in the same amount of time it took another man to run through the maze.

The labyrinth was adapted to Christian purposes during the thirteenth century, when French craftsmen emphasized the cross at its nucleus and laid mazes into the floors of Chartres and other Gothic cathedrals. Mazes also adorn the floors of many British churches, including Ely Cathedral (see photo on page 66). Penitents followed the intricate patterns on their knees, and since the mazes were said to represent the tortuous pilgrimage to the Holy Land, they came to be known as the Paths to Jerusalem.

A cross cuts through the center of Julian's Bower maze in Alkborough.

In 1950, Canon Harry Cheales of Wyck Rissington, a picturesque village in the Cotswolds, had a dream in which a tall man told him to build a maze. Cheales knew nothing of such matters, but he painstakingly planted the hedges in the garden of the rectory. The first portion of the maze represented life on earth, then came death (a tunnel of hedges) and the Garden of Eden. Heaven lay at the center.

"The wrong turnings were the sins we commit and the mistakes we make," says Cheales. "And the secret of solving the maze was to always make a right turn. It's a good motto in life: Always keep to the right." Several years ago, a man of a more secular bent than Cheales had the maze bulldozed—a common fate for mazes.

Today, though, mazes are making something of a comeback. Adrian Fisher and Randoll Coate of Minotaur Designs in London have created 12 mazes within the past 8 years. In Liverpool, they've built a Beatles maze

70 GEO · GEO 71

The Victorians built about 100 mazes, including this one at Glendurgan.

382

PUBLICATION: *Geo Magazine*
ART DIRECTOR: *John Tom Cohoe*
DESIGNER: *John Tom Cohoe*
ILLUSTRATOR: *John West*
PHOTOGRAPHER: *Kenneth Griffiths*
PUBLISHER: *Knapp Communications*
CATEGORY: *Design-Story Presentation*
AWARD: *Merit*

383

PUBLICATION: *Geo Magazine*
ART DIRECTOR: *Mary K. Baumann*
PHOTOGRAPHER: *Chris Callis*
PUBLISHER: *Knapp Communications*
AWARD: *Merit*

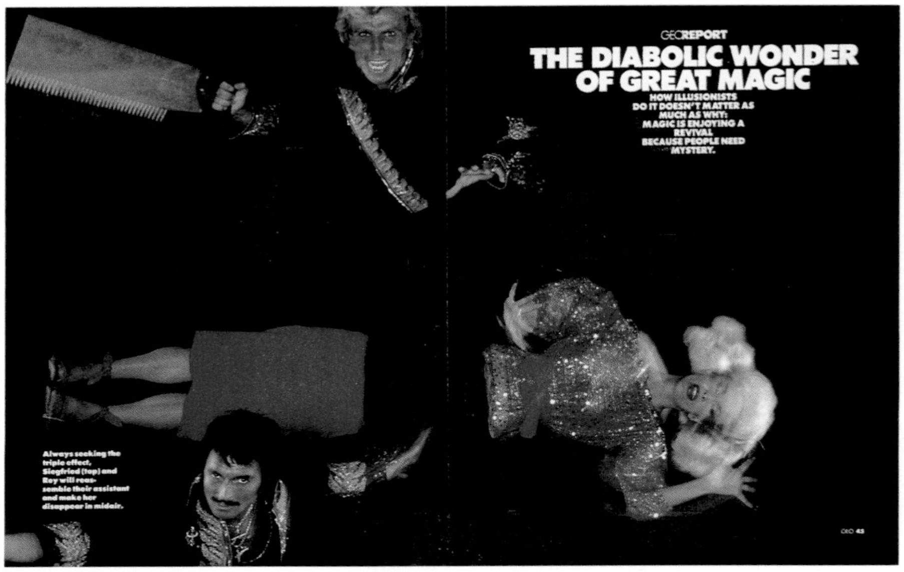
GEOREPORT

THE DIABOLIC WONDER OF GREAT MAGIC

HOW ILLUSIONISTS DO IT DOESN'T MATTER AS MUCH AS WHY: MAGIC IS ENJOYING A REVIVAL BECAUSE PEOPLE NEED MYSTERY.

Always seeking the triple effect, Siegfried (top) and Roy will reassemble their assistant and make her disappear in midair.

GEO 43

Caught midway between now-you-see-it and now-you-don't, a white tiger roars, then exits, center stage.

THE AUDIENCE HELPS TO CREATE A MYSTERIOUS, SOMETIMES DEMONIC OTHER WORLD.

(they earn about $5 million a year, more than any other magic act in history), Siegfried and Roy are to magic—as Tom Snyder once introduced them—what Frank Sinatra is to music. Over the past 13 years, working almost exclusively in Las Vegas, they have created their own legend as the superstars of magic. Says Richard Robinson, "They are the leading exponents of the 'new' magic, which means they rely more on props and technical wizardry than on suggestion or atmosphere. But they are quite simply better at it than anyone else. They have style, they're fast and they know how to generate excitement, which is really the secret of their success."

Like the great magicians of the past, Siegfried and Roy operate on a grand scale, but they also have a gimmick. They have developed the use of wild animals in their act to such an extent that it has become their trademark. Although in principle there is no difference between vanishing a coin and an elephant, they think of themselves as illusionists who manipulate the minds of the audience rather than as conjurors performing tricks by sleight of hand. Indeed, their grand-scale illusions and dramatic style of presentation have a larger-than-life quality that exerts a powerful, almost sinister, fascination. At the same time, it satisfies the demand of a high-production Las Vegas show for spectacle and razzmatazz.

Performing year round to packed houses in their own showroom at the Frontier Hotel, Siegfried and Roy have amazed and mystified more than 1 million people since *Beyond Belief* first opened in the fall of 1981. A magic spectacular with lavish sets and costumes, a song-and-dance troupe, full orchestra, supporting acts and the obligatory seminude show girls, *Beyond Belief* can be a dazzling new experience for anyone who is seeing large-scale illusion for the first time.

Yet most of the magic in the show has been around for a long, long time. As Siegfried and Roy are the first to point out, there has been nothing really new in magic for the past 60 years. While accounts of deception practiced as entertainment go back to the Egyptians (some of the classic illusions, such as the Indian basket trick, are ancient beyond trace), magic, in the broadest sense, has probably always been with us. And ever since the first priest or shaman used trickery to keep his job—cultivating an aura of mystery to win the confidence of the tribe in his supernatural powers—so have magicians.

Modern magic, dominated by large-scale illusion, owes its development to the technological revolution of the eighteenth and nineteenth centuries. Magicians like Robert-Houdin, a French watchmaker, and John Nevil Maskelyne, who had a genius for inventing automata, were the first to use mechanical devices to create elaborate stage effects. During the great period of magic, from the 1880s to the 1930s, when the master magicians—the Herrmanns, Kellar, Houdini and Thurston—toured the world, the five basic categories of large-scale illusion were established: appearance, disappearance, levitation, transformation and the divided woman. Although the variations on each theme are limitless (in his show with partner Jane Wymore, Robinson plays the divided man), no new category of illusion has been added to the list since P. T. Selbit first sawed a woman in half on a London stage in 1920.

When *The Magic Show* opened on Broadway more than a (*Continued on page 100*)

Far right: Siegfried levitates Roy above Fremont Street in Las Vegas. When they mix space-age effects with age-old stunts, the result is magic.

52 GEO

HOUSTON
HOME & GARDEN

THE SPIRIT OF CHRISTMAS PAST

A family's period New England home lends extra richness to their old-fashioned Christmas.

BY JOETTA MOULDEN
PHOTOGRAPHY BY DAVID J. LUND

DECEMBER 1984 HOUSTON HOME & GARDEN 117

HOUSTON
HOME & GARDEN

BLACK-AND-WHITE MAGIC

A stark, minimalist backdrop reverberates with startling, often whimsical, counterpoints of art deco.

BY FLORENCE OLSEN
PHOTOGRAPHY BY FRAN BRENNAN

Richard Maier had long been intrigued by the 1927 Tudor-style home. "It stood on such a proud corner on such a proud street," he says of the enormous brick structure. That proud neighborhood is one of Houston's oldest and most graceful, a quiet haven where gnarled oaks form canopies over grassy esplanades. It is the kind of neighborhood, Maier knew from eight years as a realtor, where homes rarely come on the market. And when one does go up for sale, the owner

NOVEMBER 1984 HOUSTON HOME & GARDEN 105

384

PUBLICATION: *Houston Home & Garden*
ART DIRECTOR: *Michaele Cox O'Dwyer*
DESIGNER: *Michaele Cox O'Dwyer*
PHOTOGRAPHER: *David J. Lund*
PUBLISHER: *City Home Publications*
CATEGORY: *Design-Story Presentation*
AWARD: *Merit*

385

PUBLICATION: *Houston Home & Garden*
ART DIRECTOR: *Michaele Cox O'Dwyer*
DESIGNER: *Michaele Cox O'Dwyer*
PHOTOGRAPHER: *Fran Brennan*
PUBLISHER: *City Home Publications*
CATEGORY: *Design-Story Presentation*
AWARD: *Merit*

The living room is freshly contemporary by day and as glamorous as mink at night.

386

PUBLICATION: *House & Garden*
ART DIRECTOR: *Lloyd Ziff*
DESIGNER: *Lloyd Ziff*
PHOTOGRAPHER: *Robert Mapplethorpe*
PUBLISHER: *Conde Nast Publications*
CATEGORY: *Design-Story Presentation*
AWARD: *Merit*

387

PUBLICATION: *House & Garden*
ART DIRECTOR: *Lloyd Ziff*
DESIGNER: *Lloyd Ziff*
PHOTOGRAPHER: *Marina Schinz*
PUBLISHER: *Conde Nast Publications*
CATEGORY: *Design-Story Presentation*
AWARD: *Merit*

388

PUBLICATION: *House & Garden*
ART DIRECTOR: *Lloyd Ziff*
DESIGNER: *Karen Lee Grant*
PHOTOGRAPHER: *Mick Hales*
PUBLISHER: *Conde Nast Publications*
CATEGORY: *Design-Story Presentation*
AWARD: *Merit*

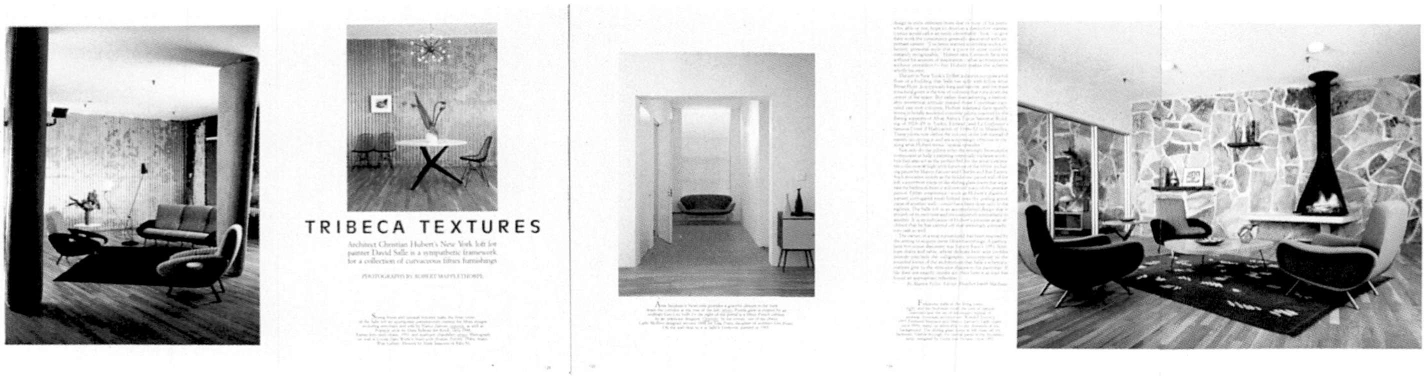

399

PUBLICATION: *House & Garden*
ART DIRECTOR: *Lloyd Ziff*
DESIGNER: *Karen Lee Grant*
PHOTOGRAPHER: *Jaques Dirand*
PUBLISHER: *Conde Nast Publications*
CATEGORY: *Design-Story Presentation*
AWARD: *Merit*

400

PUBLICATION: *House & Garden*
ART DIRECTOR: *Lloyd Ziff*
DESIGNER: *Lloyd Ziff*
PHOTOGRAPHER: *Jaques Henri Lartigue*
PUBLISHER: *Conde Nast Publications*
CATEGORY: *Design-Story Presentation*
AWARD: *Merit*

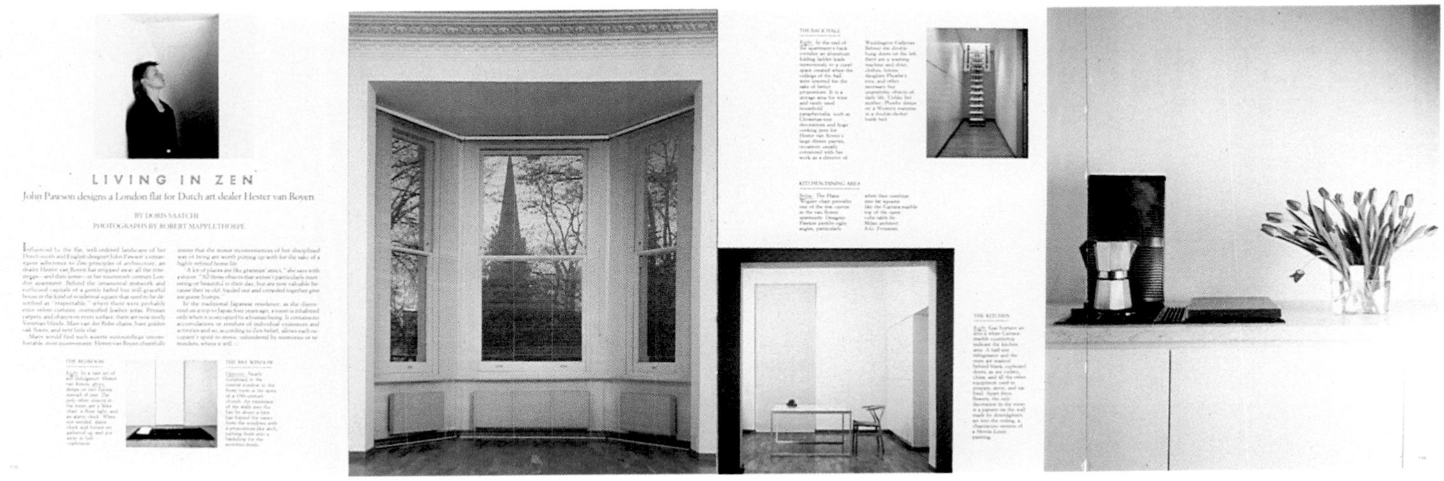

401

PUBLICATION: *House & Garden*
ART DIRECTOR: *Lloyd Ziff*
DESIGNER: *Lloyd Ziff*
PHOTOGRAPHER: *Robert Mapplethorpe*
PUBLISHER: *Conde Nast Publications*
CATEGORY: *Design-Story Presentation*
AWARD: *Merit*

402

PUBLICATION: *House & Garden*
ART DIRECTOR: *Lloyd Ziff*
DESIGNER: *Lloyd Ziff*
PHOTOGRAPHER: *Tim Street-Porter*
PUBLISHER: *Conde Nast Publications*
CATEGORY: *Design-Story Presentation*
AWARD: *Merit*

403

PUBLICATION: *Inc. Magazine*
ART DIRECTOR: *Lynn Staley*
DESIGNER: *Lynn Staley, Cyndee Mulligan*
ILLUSTRATOR: *Gene Grief*
PUBLISHER: *Inc. Publishing Corp.*
CATEGORY: *Illustration-Story Presentation*
AWARD: *Merit*

404

PUBLICATION: *M Magazine*
ART DIRECTOR: *Owen Hartley*
DESIGNER: *Owen Hartley*
PUBLISHER: *Fairchild Publications*
CATEGORY: *Design-Story Presentation*
AWARD: *Merit*

"I CAN'T WEAR THAT COLOR"
OH YES, YOU CAN!
Forget what you've heard from your mother, best friend or color consultant about which colors to wear and which to avoid. Color is the key word in fashion now; why should you miss out on any of it? What it takes to break the color rules: the daring to mix colors you love with some that you've shunned; makeup to play off against colors you think you can't wear; trust in your own good judgment and taste when putting outfits together. You can wear any color you want—and look dazzling, too!

Each of my palettes includes some colors that make me ill

405

PUBLICATION: *McCall's Magazine*
ART DIRECTOR: *Modesto Torre, Mary Lynn Blasutta*
DESIGNER: *Mary Lynn Blasutta*
PHOTOGRAPHER: *Steven Anderson*
PUBLISHER: *McCall's Publishing Company*
CATEGORY: *Design-Story Presentation*
AWARD: *Merit*

EXTRAVAGANCE
The High Cost of Making It in Hollywood
In the Tinseltown money game, the object is to squander your income as visibly as you can.
by Marlys Harris

"Beatrice."
Repairing a septum perforated by cocaine abuse can run $6,000.
High tax-free income
SCUDDER
1-800-453-3305
Stars long to be victimized. Why else do they act so dumb?
Sequel Chatter Arts
Inventors Body Jocks
Crime Medics Couples
Up Front Bio Coping
Spirit Lookout Style
People

406

PUBLICATION: *Money Magazine*
ART DIRECTOR: *Ellen Blissman*
ILLUSTRATOR: *Arnold Roth*
PUBLISHER: *Time, Inc.*
CATEGORY: *Illustration-Story Presentation*
AWARD: *Merit*

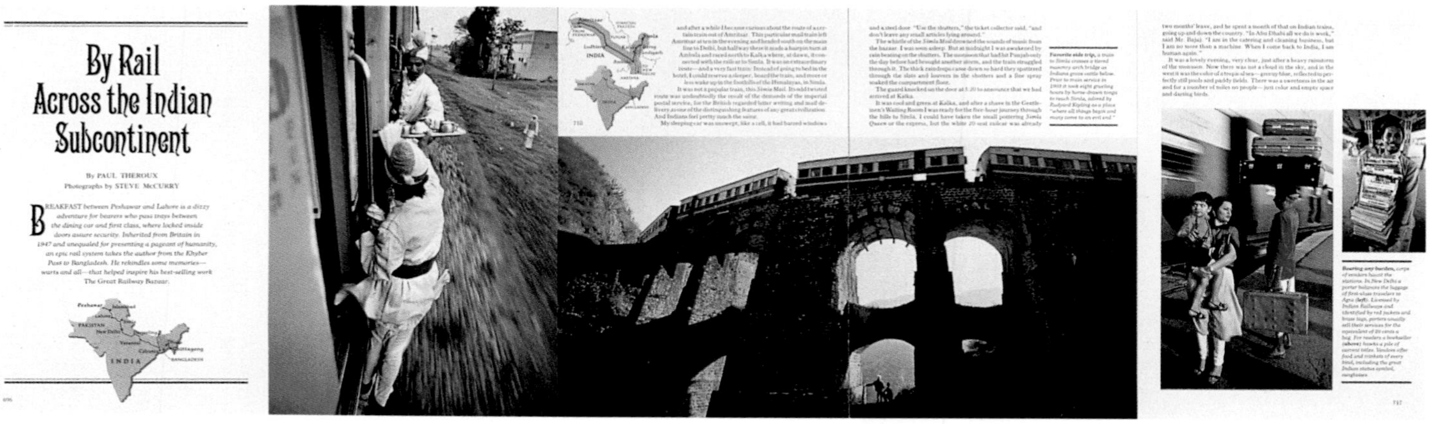

By Rail Across the Indian Subcontinent
By PAUL THEROUX
Photographs by STEVE McCURRY
BREAKFAST between Peshawar and Lahore is a dizzy adventure for bearers who pass trays between the dining car and first class, where locked inside doors assure security. Inherited from Britain in 1947 and unequaled for presenting a pageant of humanity, an epic rail system takes the author from the Khyber Pass to Bangladesh. He rekindles some memories—warts and all—that helped inspire his best-selling work The Great Railway Bazaar.
INDIA

407

PUBLICATION: *National Geographic*
PHOTOGRAPHER: *Steve McCurry*
PUBLISHER: *National Geographic Society*
CATEGORY: *Design-Story Presentation*
AWARD: *Merit*

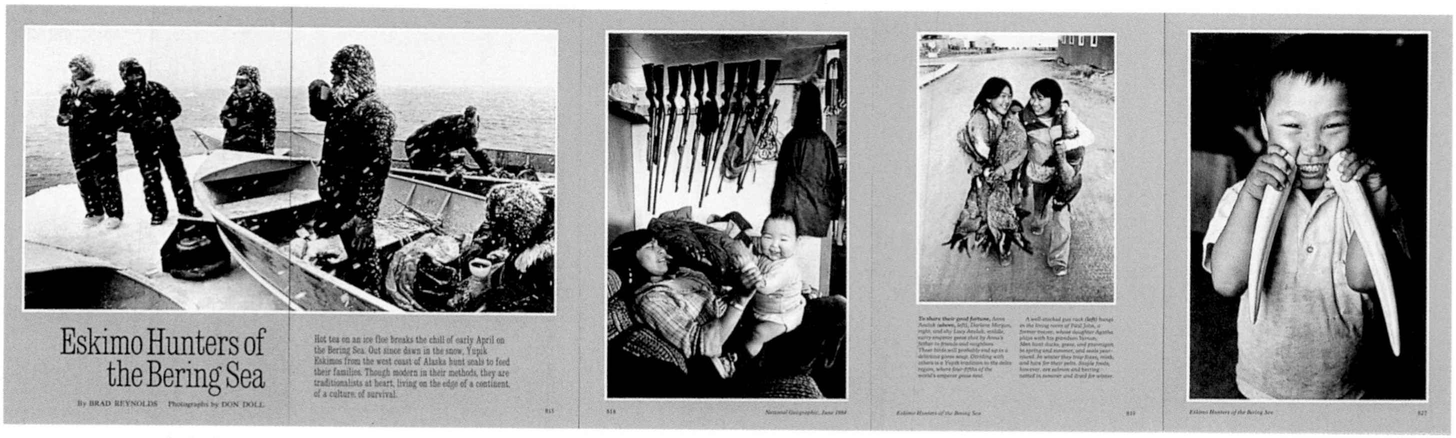

Eskimo Hunters of the Bering Sea
By BRAD REYNOLDS Photographs by DON DOLL
Hot tea on an ice floe breaks the chill of early April on the Bering Sea. Out since dawn in the snow, Yupik Eskimos from the west coast of Alaska hunt seals to feed their families. Though modern in their methods, they are traditionalists at heart, living on the edge of a continent, of a culture, of survival.

408

PUBLICATION: *National Geographic*
ART DIRECTOR: *Ed Kim*
PUBLISHER: *National Geographic Society*
CATEGORY: *Design-Story Presentation*
AWARD: *Merit*

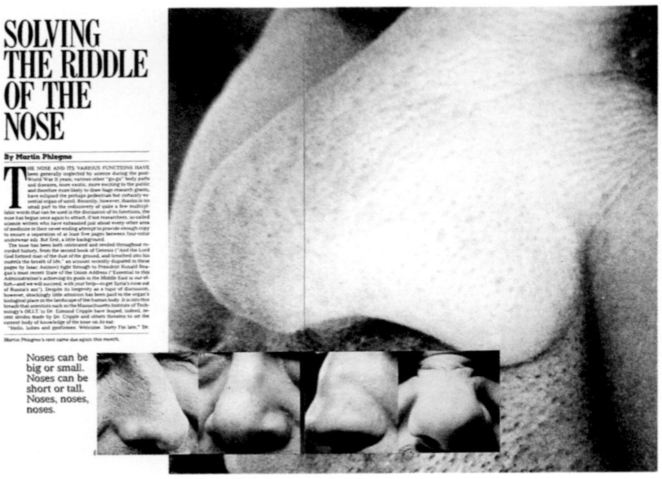
SOLVING THE RIDDLE OF THE NOSE
By Martin Phlegme
Noses can be big or small. Noses can be short or tall. Noses, noses, noses.

Parvenu
It's very new, very rich, and very, very you.
From ARRIVISTE
Off-Colored Language
By William Sapphire
Exterminating the Ethiopes
Calvin Klein

JANUARY 16, 1984
$1.75
TIME
GIRLS, GIRLS! America Loves 'Em!
THE PRESIDENT'S BRAIN IS MISSING
Is Ronald Reagan Dead?
...And Will He Run In '84?

Nation
Where's the Rest of Him?
A nation mourns the napping Ronald Reagan

409

PUBLICATION: *National Lampoon*
ART DIRECTOR: *Michael Grossman*
DESIGNER: *Michael O. Delevante, Marianne Gaffney, Timothy McCarthy, Tracy Glick*
ILLUSTRATOR: *Agin, Alexa Grace, Howard Lewis, Bob Rakita, Gary Rudell, Phillip Schever, Peter Thorpe, Michael Witte*
PHOTOGRAPHER: *Ronald G. Harris, Hero Ihara, Dan Nelken, Eric Richmond, Michael Watson, etc.*
PUBLISHER: *Mid-America Web Press*
CATEGORY: *Design-Story Presentation*
AWARD: *Merit*

410

PUBLICATION: *National Lampoon*
ART DIRECTOR: *Michael Grossman*
DESIGNER: *Marianne Gaffney, Michael O. Delevante, Tracy Glick*
ILLUSTRATOR: *Michael DiBiase, Mark Marek, Phillip Schever*
PHOTOGRAPHER: *John Farten, Lee Frank JMD, Ronald G. Harris, Bernard Vidal, Michael Watson, etc.*
PUBLISHER: *Mid-America Web Press*
CATEGORY: *Design-Story Presentation*
AWARD: *Merit*

SEASCAPES:
HARRY DEZITTER'S PANORAMIC VISION

411

PUBLICATION: *Nautical Quarterly*
ART DIRECTOR: *Marilyn Rose*
DESIGNER: *Marilyn Rose*
PHOTOGRAPHER: *Harry Dezitter*
PUBLISHER: *Nautical Quarterly*
CATEGORY: *Design-Story Presentation*
AWARD: *Merit*

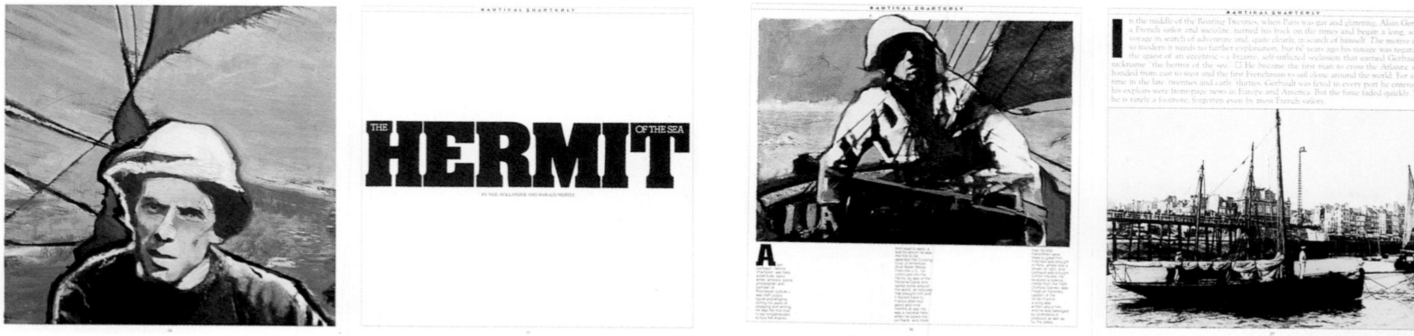
THE HERMIT OF THE SEA

412

PUBLICATION: *Nautical Quarterly*
ART DIRECTOR: *Marilyn Rose*
DESIGNER: *Marilyn Rose*
ILLUSTRATOR: *Carol Wald*
PUBLISHER: *Nautical Quarterly*
CATEGORY: *Design-Story Presentation*
AWARD: *Merit*

413

PUBLICATION: *Nautical Quarterly*
ART DIRECTOR: *Marilyn Rose*
DESIGNER: *Marilyn Rose*
ILLUSTRATOR: *Norma Jay*
PUBLISHER: *Nautical Quarterly*
CATEGORY: *Design-Story Presentation*
AWARD: *Merit*

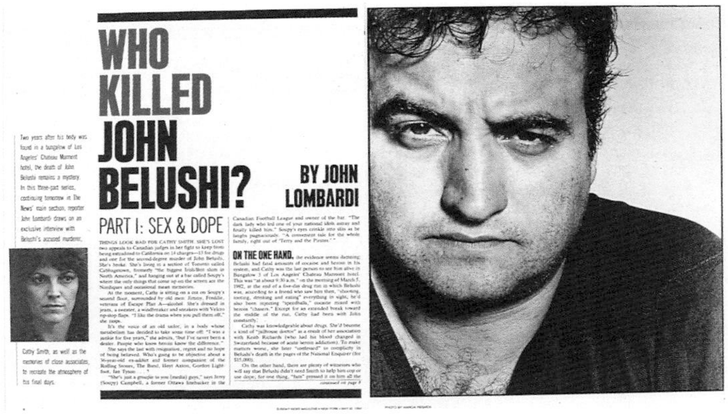

414

PUBLICATION: *Daily News Magazine*
ART DIRECTOR: *Janet Froelich, Thomas R. Ruis*
PHOTOGRAPHER: *Marcia Resnick*
PUBLISHER: *New York News, Inc.*
CATEGORY: *Design-Story Presentation*
AWARD: *Merit*

415

PUBLICATION: *Daily News Magazine*
ART DIRECTOR: *Janet Froelich*
Thomas P. Ruis
PHOTOGRAPHER: *Ken Korotkin*
PUBLISHER: *New York News, Inc.*
CATEGORY: *Design-Story Presentation*
AWARD: *Merit*

OLD HABITS
Heroin addicts who have made it to retirement.
By Eric Nadler
'Nobody knew these people were out there. How the hell did they survive?'

416

PUBLICATION: *Daily News Magazine*
ART DIRECTOR: *Janet Froelich*
Thomas P. Ruis
PHOTOGRAPHER: *Tom Arma*
PUBLISHER: *New York News, Inc.*
CATEGORY: *Design-Story Presentation*
AWARD: *Merit*

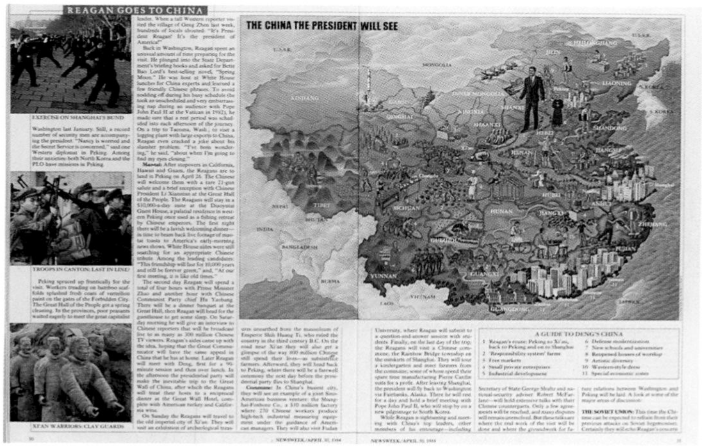

418

PUBLICATION: *Newsweek*
ART DIRECTOR: *Robert Priest*
ILLUSTRATOR: *Kinuko Craft*
PUBLISHER: *Newsweek, Inc.*
CATEGORY: *Design-Story Presentation*
AWARD: *Merit*

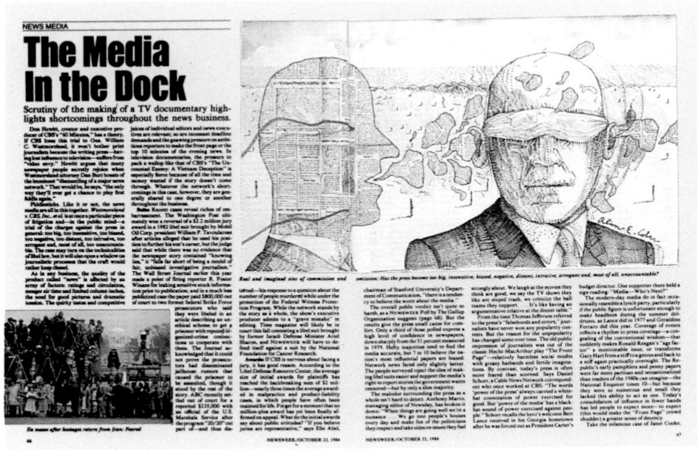

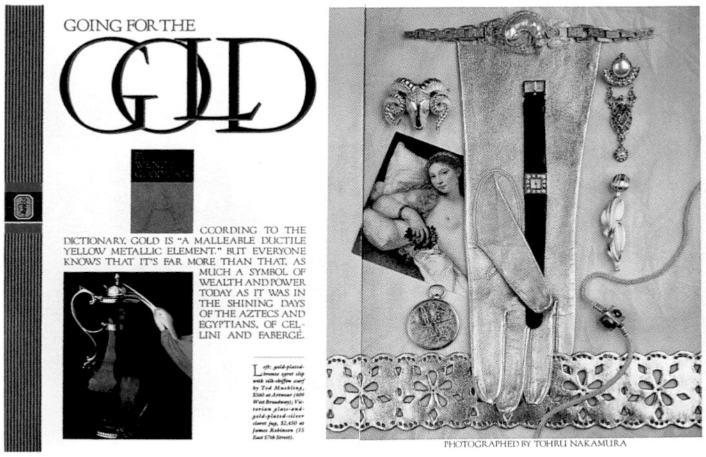

419

PUBLICATION: *Newsweek*
ART DIRECTOR: *Robert Priest*
ILLUSTRATOR: *Alan E. Cobler*
PUBLISHER: *Newsweek, Inc.*
CATEGORY: *Illustration-Story Presentation*
AWARD: *Merit*

420

PUBLICATION: *New York Magazine*
ART DIRECTOR: *Robert Best*
PHOTOGRAPHER: *Tohru Nakamura*
PUBLISHER: *Murdoch Magazines*
CATEGORY: *Design-Story Presentation*
AWARD: *Merit*

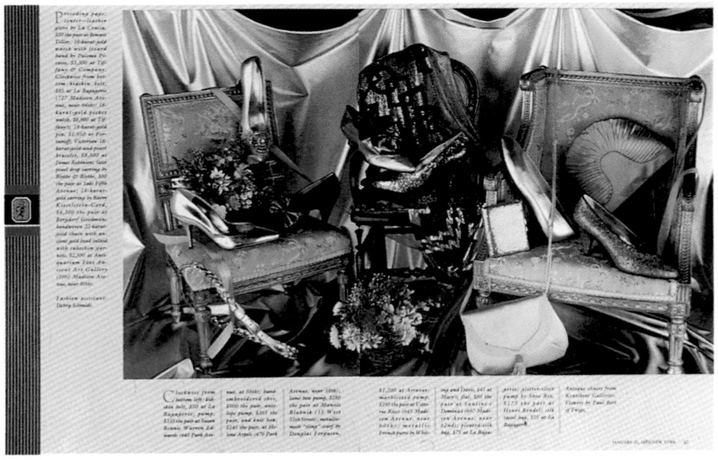

MoMA UNVEILS ITS TREASURES
DEPARTMENTS

THE HOUSE THAT ART BUILT
BY CARTER WISEMAN

421

PUBLICATION: *New York Magazine*
ART DIRECTOR: *Robert Best*
DESIGNER: *Patricia Von Brachel*
PHOTOGRAPHER: *Adam Bartos*
PUBLISHER: *Murdoch Magazines*
CATEGORY: *Design-Story Presentation*
AWARD: *Merit*

MoMA UNVEILS ITS TREASURES
The Museum of Modern Art is the finest institution of its kind in the world. Since January, it has been closed for the final stages of a massive renovation and expansion begun over a decade ago. It reopens this week, making the best bigger and even better.
BY KAY LARSON
New York
PHOTOGRAPHED BY ADAM BARTOS

THE FOUR SEASONS AT 25
THE SHIMMERING POOL ROOM IS A PLACE FOR SEDUCTION ROMANTIC AND CORPORATE
BY GAEL GREENE
ILLUSTRATED BY JAMES McMULLAN

422

PUBLICATION: *New York Magazine*
DESIGNER: *Robert Best*
ILLUSTRATOR: *James McMullan*
PUBLISHER: *Murdoch Magazines*
CATEGORY: *Design-Story Presentation*
AWARD: *Merit*

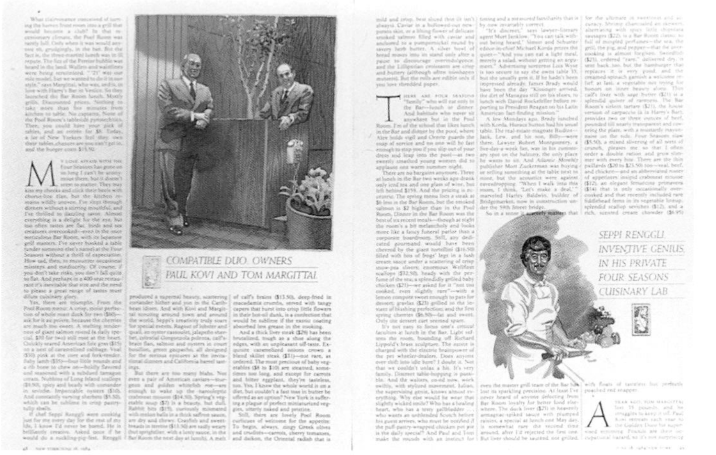
COMPATIBLE DUO: OWNERS
PAUL KOVI AND TOM MARGITTAI
SEPPI RENGGLI
INVENTIVE GENIUS
IN HIS PRIVATE
FOUR SEASONS
CUISINARY LAB

HIP-HOPPING
THE CLUB BEAT
BY AMY VIRSHUP
The Environment Clubs

423

PUBLICATION: *New York Magazine*
ART DIRECTOR: *Robert Best*
DESIGNER: *Patricia Von Brachel*
ILLUSTRATOR: *Karen Barbour*
PUBLISHER: *Murdoch Magazines*
CATEGORY: *Illustration-Story Presentation*
AWARD: *Merit*

The East Village

The Dance Clubs
ILLUSTRATED BY KAREN BARBOUR

SIMPLY DELICIOUS
Holiday Entertaining
BY BARBARA COSTIKYAN
Now is the season when New Yorkers get seriously social. People are determined to dress up, tables are festive, food is bountiful, and the hostess asks "What do I serve?"—because winter's the time for culinary bravura. There are always vogues in food, but in cold weather we think about traditional fare. So, for this "Holiday Entertaining" issue, we have chosen the comfort foods of winter—those classic one-pot dishes like cassoulet and pot-au-feu, fricassee and ragout. They are rich yet simple, most may be cooked beforehand, and all are the masterpieces of many generations. We asked seven well-known cooks—Barbara Kafka, Paul Prudhomme, Madeleine Kamman, George Lang, Paula Wolfert, James Beard, and Lee Bailey—to prepare their favorite one-pot recipes and show us how they serve them to friends. There are always pleasures and surprises when they cook, and each produced a very personal kind of dish, either updating a time-honored recipe or remembering a meal from childhood. The result: pages of warmth and hospitality—and wonderful, welcoming food.
PHOTOGRAPHED BY BRIAN HAGIWARA

PAULA WOLFERT
POSH PISTACHE

424

PUBLICATION: *New York Magazine*
ART DIRECTOR: *Robert Best*
DESIGNER: *Patricia Von Brachel*
David Walters
PHOTOGRAPHER: *Brian Hagiwari*
PUBLISHER: *Murdoch Magazines*
CATEGORY: *Design-Story Presentation*
AWARD: *Merit*

Born Too Late?
Expect Too Much?
Then You May Be...
FOREVER SINGLE
By Patricia Morrisroe

SELECT, DON'T SETTLE: "The women I get involved with," says one man, "are intellectually stimulating but unstable, or stable but boring. But I'm not willing to compromise my dreams."

425

PUBLICATION: *New York Magazine*
ART DIRECTOR: *Robert Best*
DESIGNER: *Patricia Von Brachel*
Don Morris
ILLUSTRATOR: *Patty Dryden*
Brad Holland
PUBLISHER: *Murdoch Magazines*
CATEGORY: *Illustration-Story Presentation*
AWARD: *Merit*

LIFE ENDS AT 40: A woman, 38, says she doesn't stand a chance. "I've gone out with 55-year-old guys who tell me I'm too old."

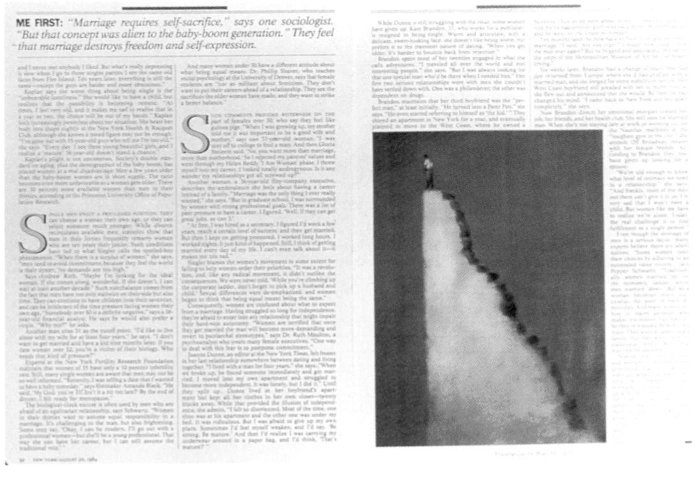

ME FIRST: "Marriage requires self-sacrifice," says one sociologist. "But that concept was alien to the baby-boom generation." They feel that marriage destroys freedom and self-expression.

426

PUBLICATION: *New York Magazine*
ART DIRECTOR: *Robert Best*
ILLUSTRATOR: *Alan Cober*
PUBLISHER: *Murdoch Magazines*
CATEGORY: *Illustration-Story Presentation*
AWARD: *Merit*

427

PUBLICATION: *New York Magazine*
ART DIRECTOR: *Robert Best*
DESIGNER: *Patricia Von Brachel*
Karen Mullarkey
PHOTOGRAPHER: *Tony McGee*
PUBLISHER: *Murdoch Magazines*
CATEGORY: *Photography-Story Presentation*
AWARD: *Merit*

SHORT SKIRTS,
STRONG SUITS

PUT TOGETHER—
WITH PANACHE

THE IMPACT OF
SATIN ON TWEED

ROUGHING IT
The use of sunscreens should be encouraged at an early age.

429

PUBLICATION: *The New York Times Magazine*
ART DIRECTOR: *Ken Kendrick*
DESIGNER: *Ken Kendrick*
PHOTOGRAPHER: *Bruce Weber*
PUBLISHER: *The New York Times*
CATEGORY: *Photography-Story Presentation*
AWARD: *Merit*

THE POWER OF
PERSONALITY
VERUSCHKA

430

PUBLICATION: *The New York Times Magazine*
ART DIRECTOR: *Ken Kendrick*
DESIGNER: *Diana LaGuardia*
PHOTOGRAPHER: *Ethan Hoffman*
PUBLISHER: *The New York Times*
CATEGORY: *Photography-Story Presentation*
AWARD: *Merit*

SUSAN
ROTHENBERG
New Outlook for a Visionary Artist

431

PUBLICATION: *The New York Times Magazine*
ART DIRECTOR: *Ken Kendrick*
DESIGNER: *Diana LaGuardia*
PHOTOGRAPHER: *Barbara Walz*
PUBLISHER: *The New York Times*
CATEGORY: *Photography-Story Presentation*
AWARD: *Merit*

ALL THAT GLITTERS

The new fashions that are lavishly embroidered and beaded have ancestors in other eras and cultures.

BY PAULA DEITZ

432

PUBLICATION: *The New York Times Magazine*
ART DIRECTOR: *Lucy Sisman*
DESIGNER: *Lucy Sisman*
PHOTOGRAPHER: *Andrea Blanch*
PUBLISHER: *The New York Times*
CATEGORY: *Design-Story Presentation*
AWARD: *Merit*

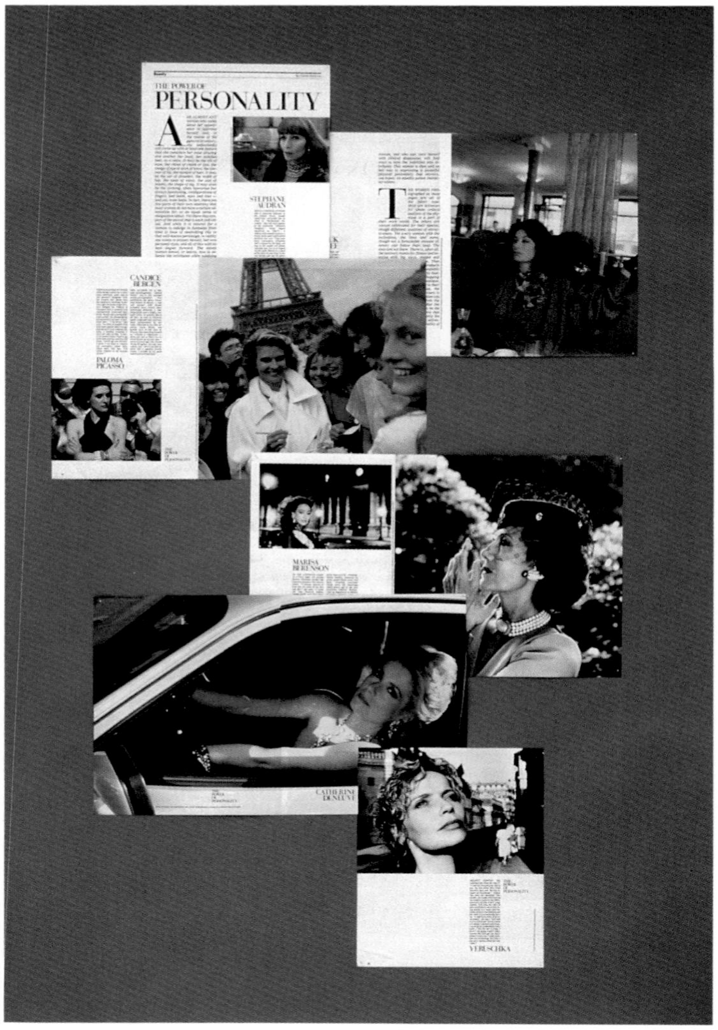

434

PUBLICATION: *The New York Times Magazine*
ART DIRECTOR: *Ken Kendrick*
DESIGNER: *Ken Kendrick*
PHOTOGRAPHER: *Helmut Newton*
PUBLISHER: *The New York Times*
CATEGORY: *Photography-Story Presentation*
AWARD: *Merit*

Noted With Pleasure

The Politics of Music

While counterpoint might be seen as a dialectical principle in Western music, or even a melodic and harmonic line of argument, Edward W. Said, author of "Orientalism," goes quite a bit further in his essay in "Glenn Gould and His Friends," a collection edited by John McGreevy (Quill).

To master counterpoint is therefore in a way almost to play God, as Adrian Leverkühn, the hero of Thomas Mann's "Doctor Faustus," understands. Counterpoint is the total ordering of sound, the complete management of time, the minute subdivision of musical space, and absolute absorption for the intellect. Running through the history of Western music, from Palestrina and Bach to the dodecaphonic rigors of Schoenberg, Berg, and Webern, is a contrapuntal mania for inclusiveness, and it is a powerful allusion to this that informs Mann's Hitlerian version of a pact with the devil in "Faustus," a novel about a polyphonic German artist whose aesthetic fate encapsulates his nation's overreaching folly. Gould's contrapuntal performances come as close as I can imagine to delivering an inkling of what *might* be at stake in the composition and performance of counterpoint, minus perhaps any grossly political import. Not the least of this achievement, however, is that he never recoils from the comic possibility that high counterpoint may only be a parody, pure form aspiring to the role of world-historical wisdom.

A Kiss for the Poor Entrepreneur

In "The Spirit of Enterprise," (Simon & Schuster), the intellectual maverick George Gilder paints a romantic, almost a religious portrait of the entrepreneur.

It is the entrepreneurs who know the rules of the world and the laws of God. Thus they sustain the world. In their careers, there is little of optimizing calculation, nothing of delicate balance of markets. They overthrow establishments rather than establish equilibria. They are the heroes of economic life. To them this book is devoted, in the hope that the entitled children around the world may come to see and follow their example and earn their redemption and their happiness, reconciled with the world of work and risk on the perpetual frontier of human life.

Bite Your Tongue

According to Judith S. Neaman and Carole G. Silver, anxiety influences our diction, causing us to substitute innocuous words for those that make us nervous. In "Kind Words: A Thesaurus of Euphemisms," (McGraw-Hill) they point out that our circumlocutions vary according to class and social climate.

While the aristocracy served as an inventive and even radical force in making language, the middle class was conservative, eschewing direct reference to sex, the Lord, death and the excretory functions — in fact, to nearly everything but money. James I of England, whose coronation ceremony of 1603 was dramatically interrupted by a group of petitioners from the rising Dissenters of the middle class, in 1623 signed an act levying a fine of 12d. on any blaspheming. Thus, he became the first English monarch to decree a fine against swearing. This event signaled the start of a reign of middle-class attitudes that would exercise strong restraints against not only religious but also political invective. The seventeenth century was to prove a hothouse of governmental and political, even more then sexual, euphemism.

Poetry That Works for a Living

In the last few decades, many poets have been turning away from academic subjects toward ordinary life. An apt example of poetry taking to the streets is the Angolan Antonio Jacinto's "Poem of Alienation" in "The Penguin Book of Modern African Poetry," edited by Gerald Moore and Ulli Beier. These are the fourth and sixth stanzas.

My poem runs through the streets
with a putrid cloth pad on its head
offering itself
offering
"mackerel, sardine, sprats
fine fish, fine fi-i-i-sh"

My poem goes into the cafés
"lott'ry draw-a tomorra lott'ry draw-a tomorra"
and the draw of my poem
wheel as it wheels
whirl as it whirls
never changes
"lott'ry draw-a tomorra
lott'ry draw-a tomorra"

To Rest in Soft Peace

The tired but gratified feeling of the literary traveler at the end of the day is nicely caught by Patrick Leigh Fermor, who was 18 years old when, in 1933, he walked from Rotterdam to Hungary. In "A Time of Gifts" (Penguin), he describes his arrival at a Heidelberg inn, where his landlady greets him with a line from Goethe.

It was dark by the time I climbed the main street and soon softly-lit panes of colored glass, under the hanging sign of a Red Ox, were beckoning me indoors. With freezing cheeks and hair caked with snow, I clumped into an entrancing haven of oak beams and carving and alcoves and changing floor levels. A jungle of impedimenta encrusted the interior — mugs and bottles and glasses and antlers — the innocent accumulation of years, not stage props of forced conviviality — and the whole place glowed with a universal patina.

This was the moment I longed for every day. Settling at a heavy inn-table, thawing and tingling, with wine, bread and cheese handy and my papers, books and diary all laid out; writing up the day's doings, hunting for words in the dictionary, drawing, struggling with verses, or merely subsiding in a vacuous and contented trance while the snow thawed off my boots. An elderly woman came downstairs and settled by the stove with her sewing. Spotting my stick and rucksack and the puddle of melting snow, she said, with a smile, "Wer reitet so spät durch Nacht und Wind?" My German, now fifteen days old, was just up to this: "Who rides so late through night and wind?" □

47

435

PUBLICATION: *The New York Times- Book Review*
ART DIRECTOR: *Steve Heller*
DESIGNER: *Brian Callanan*
ILLUSTRATOR: *Brian Callanan*
PUBLISHER: *The New York Times*
CATEGORY: *Tabloid/Newsprint*
Story Presentation
AWARD: *Merit*

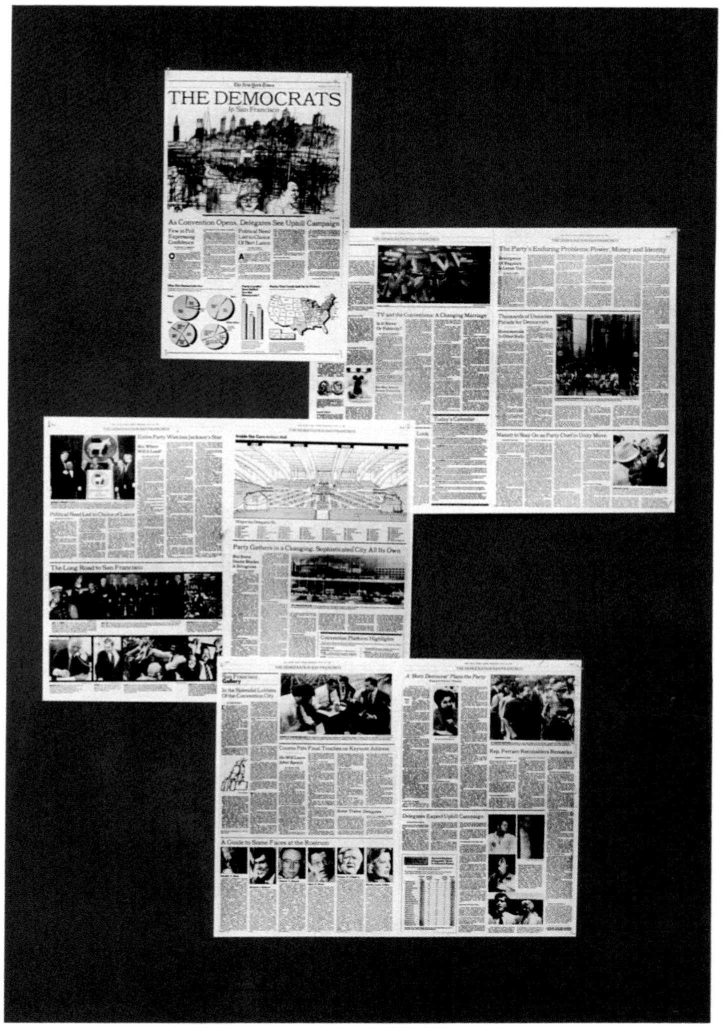

436

PUBLICATION: *The New York Times*
ART DIRECTOR: *Jerelle Kraus*
PUBLISHER: *The New York Times*
CATEGORY: *Tabloid/Newsprint Design-Story Presentation*
AWARD: *Merit*

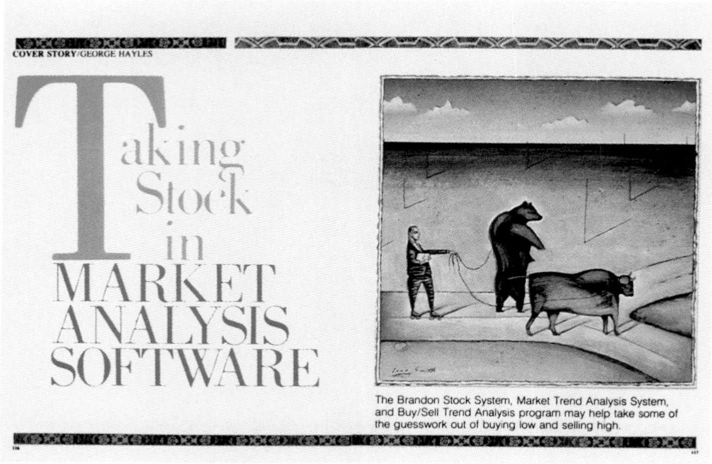

437

PUBLICATION: *PC Magazine*
ART DIRECTOR: *Mitch Shostak, Mary Zisk*
Creative Director, Peter Blank
DESIGNER: *Gerard Kunkel, Louise White, Roz Migdal*
ILLUSTRATOR: *Lane Smith, Mark Penberthy, Andrew Shachat, Akio Matsuyoshi*
PUBLISHER: *Ziff-Davis*
CATEGORY: *Illustration-Story Presentation*
AWARD: *Merit*

438

PUBLICATION: *PC Magazine*
ART DIRECTOR: *Mitch Shostak, Mary Zisk, Creative Director, Peter Blank*
ILLUSTRATOR: *Robert Goldstrom*
PUBLISHER: *Ziff-Davis*
CATEGORY: *Illustration-Story Presentation*
AWARD: *Merit*

439

PUBLICATION: *PC Magazine*
ART DIRECTOR: *Mitch Shostak, Mary Zisk, Creative Director, Peter Blank*
DESIGNER: *Marjorie Crane, Louise White*
ILLUSTRATOR: *Mark Penberthy*
PUBLISHER: *Ziff-Davis*
CATEGORY: *Illustration-Story Presentation*
AWARD: *Merit*

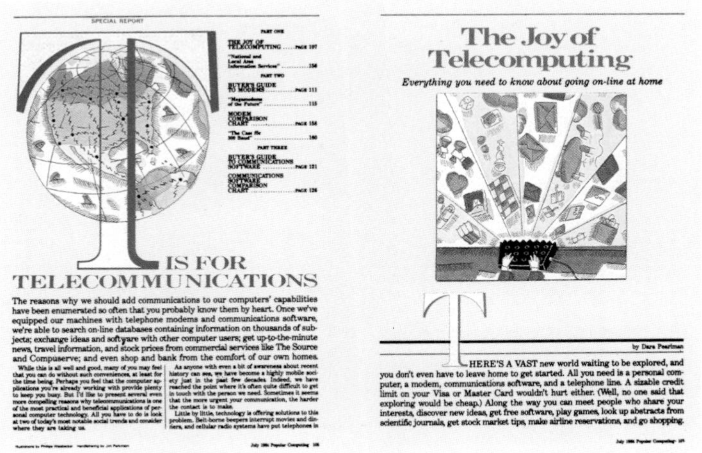

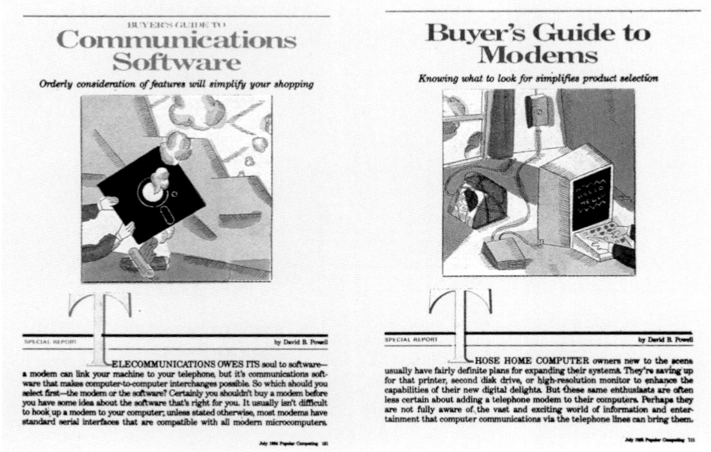

440

PUBLICATION: *Popular Computing*
ART DIRECTOR: *Erik Murphy*
DESIGNER: *Lettering-*
Jim Parkinson
ILLUSTRATOR: *Phillipe Weisbecker*
PUBLISHER: *McGraw-Hill*
CATEGORY: *Design-Story Presentation*
AWARD: *Merit*

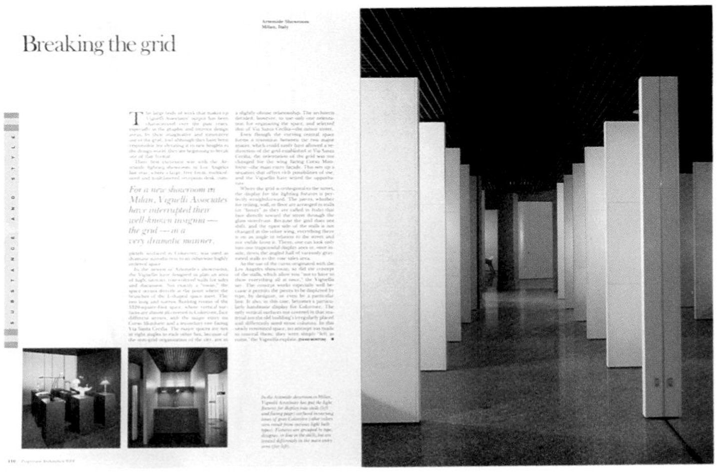

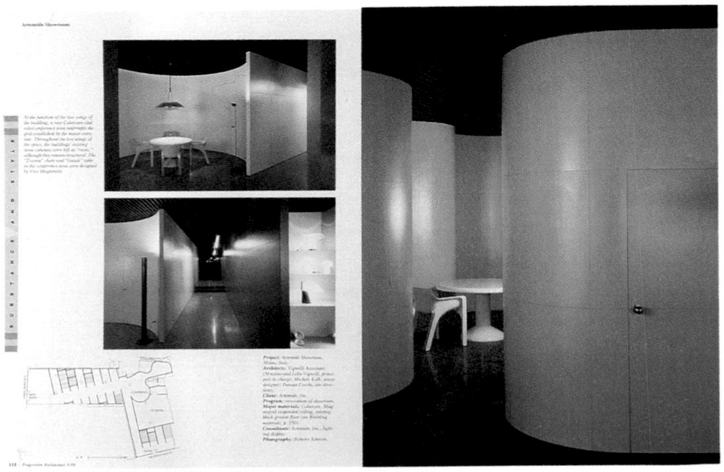

441

PUBLICATION: *Progressive Architecture*
ART DIRECTOR: *Kenneth Windsor*
DESIGNER: *Kenneth Windsor*
PHOTOGRAPHER: *Robert Schezen*
PUBLISHER: *Reinhold Publishing*
CATEGORY: *Design-Story Presentation*
AWARD: *Merit*

443

PUBLICATION: *Progressive Architecture*
ART DIRECTOR: *Kenneth Windsor*
DESIGNER: *Kenneth Windsor*
PHOTOGRAPHER: *Richard Bryant*
PUBLISHER: *Reinhold Publishing*
CATEGORY: *Design-Story Presentation*
AWARD: *Merit*

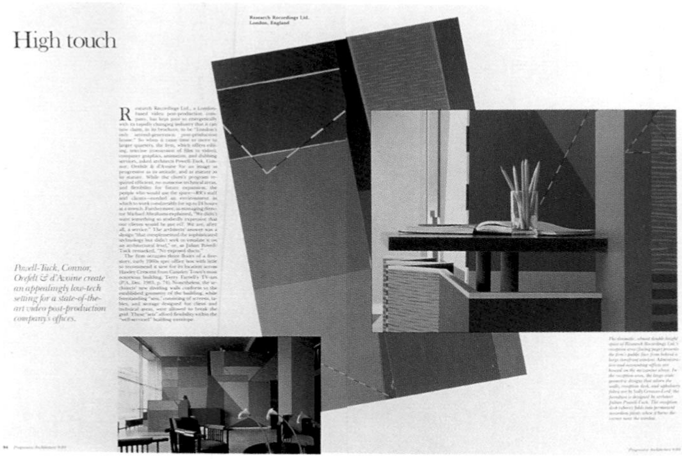
Research Recordings Ltd.
London, England

High touch

Powell-Tuck, Connor, Orefelt & d'Avoine create an appealingly low-tech setting for a state-of-the-art video post-production company's offices.

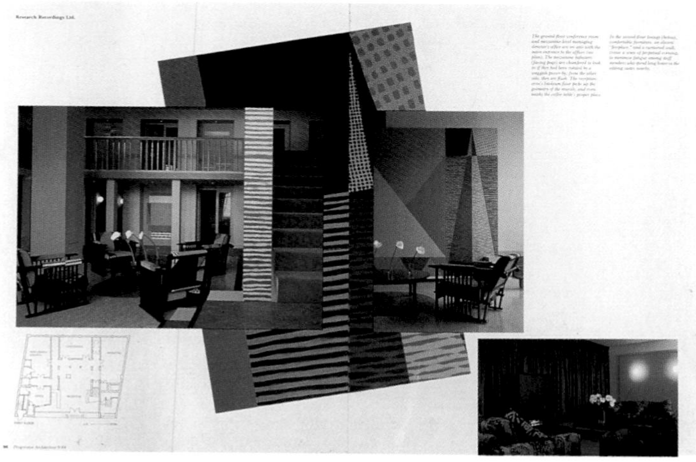
Research Recordings Ltd.

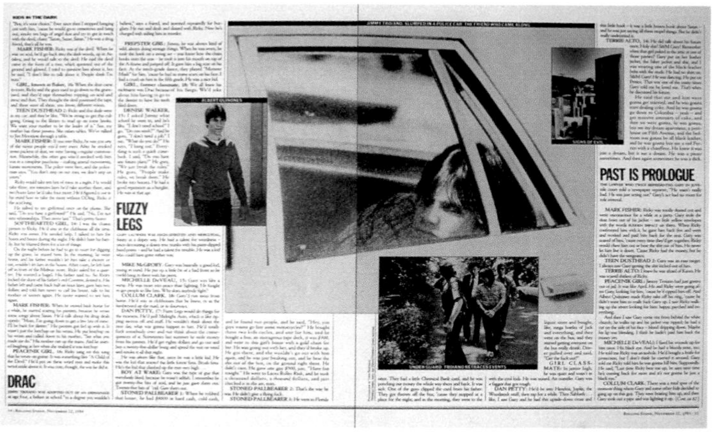

444

PUBLICATION: *Rolling Stone*
ART DIRECTOR: *Derek Ungless*
DESIGNER: *Elizabeth Williams*
PHOTOGRAPHER: *Laurie Kratochvil*
PUBLISHER: *Straight Arrow Publishers, Inc.*
CATEGORY: *Design-Story Presentation*
AWARD: *Merit*

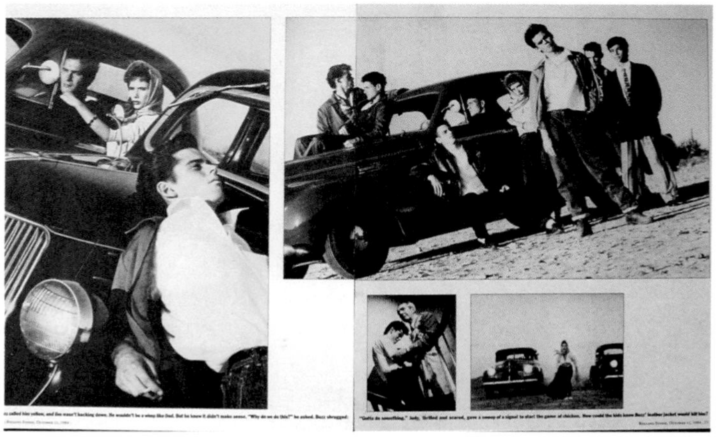

445

PUBLICATION: *Rolling Stone*
ART DIRECTOR: *Derek Ungless*
DESIGNER: *Elizabeth Williams*
PHOTOGRAPHER: *Herb Ritts*
Laurie Kratochvil
PUBLISHER: *Straight Arrow Publishers, Inc.*
CATEGORY: *Photography-Story Presentation*
AWARD: *Merit*

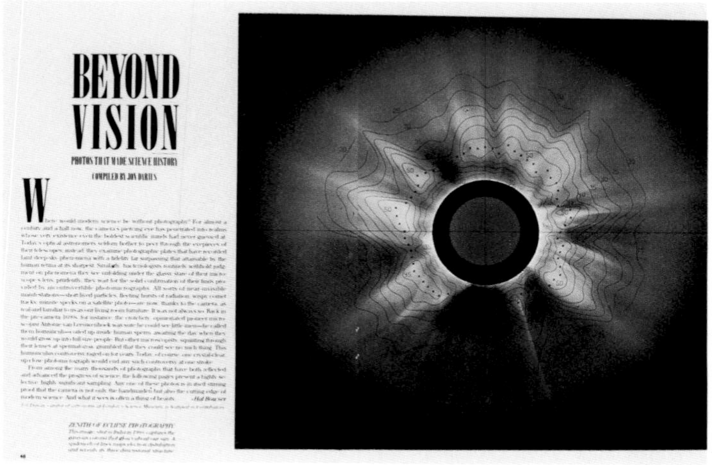

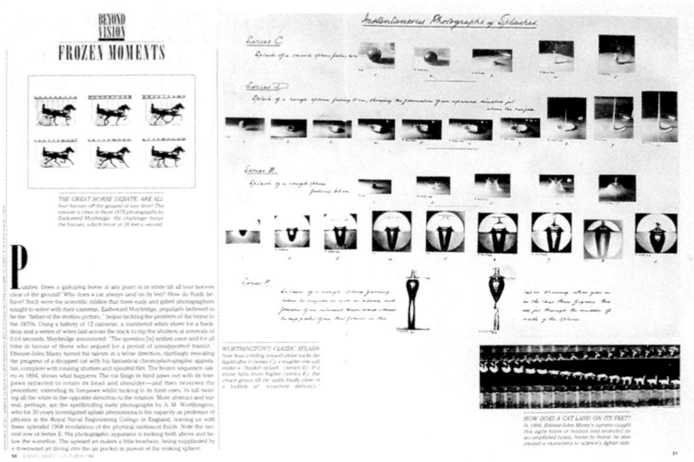

447

PUBLICATION: *Science Digest*
ART DIRECTOR: *Michael Valenti*
DESIGNER: *Michael Valenti*
PHOTOGRAPHER: *Various*
PUBLISHER: *Hearst Corporation*
CATEGORY: *Design-Story Presentation*
AWARD: *Merit*

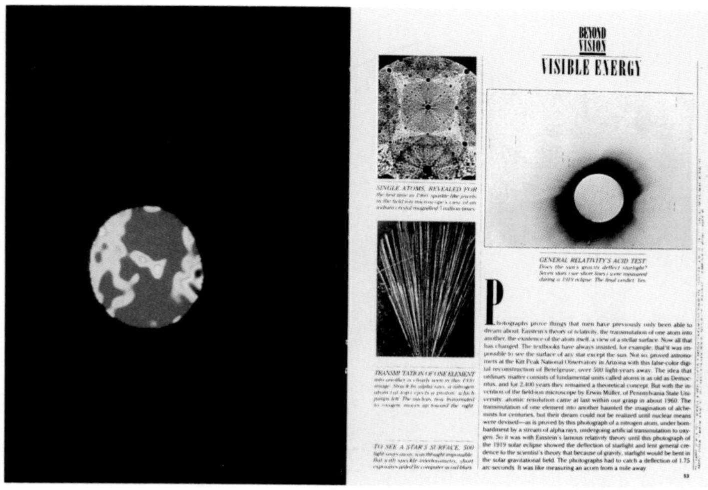

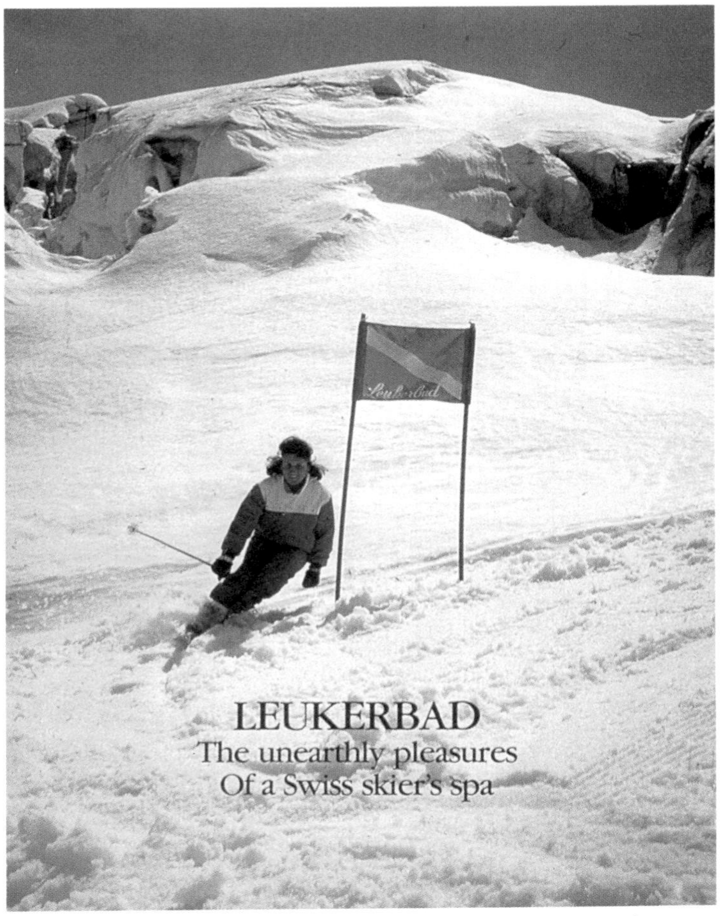
LEUKERBAD
The unearthly pleasures
Of a Swiss skier's spa

At 8800 feet, a skier at
Mount Torrenthorn's summit
jumps above the clouds

From the Gemmi Pass,
Leukerbad's baths and
Torrenthorn's challenging
trails beckon the visitor
to enjoy

448

PUBLICATION: *Snow*
ART DIRECTOR: *Linda Stillman*
DESIGNER: *Linda Stillman*
PHOTOGRAPHER: *Alexander Tsiaras*
PUBLISHER: *Snow Publications, Inc.*
CATEGORY: *Photography-Story Presentation*
AWARD: *Merit*

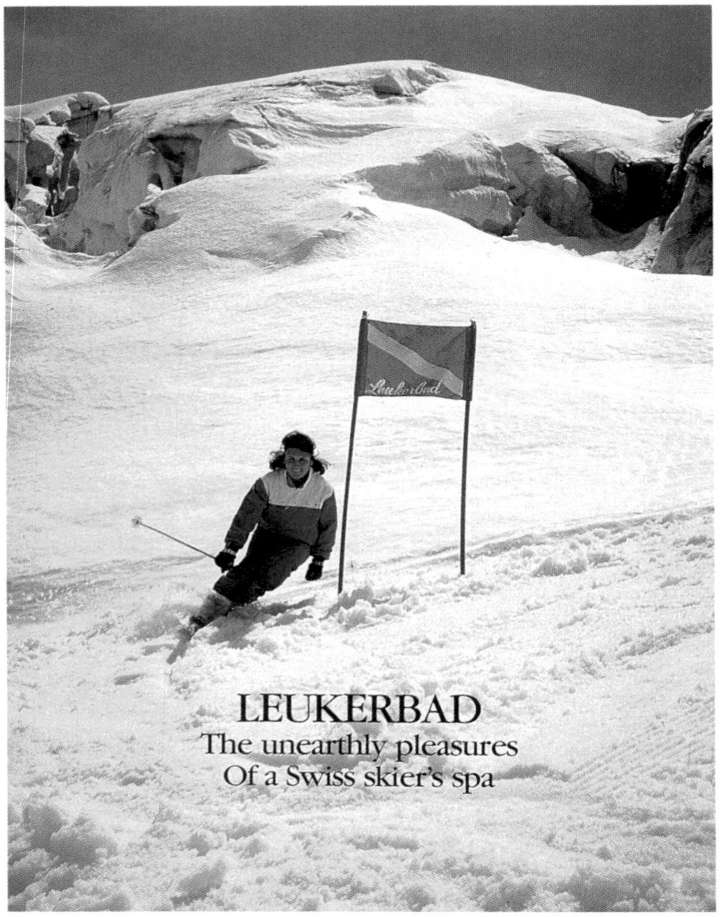
LEUKERBAD
The unearthly pleasures
Of a Swiss skier's spa

Insatiable skiers take to Torrenthorn's illuminated run, or test their mettle on the cross country trail of Gemmi's Glacial Lake

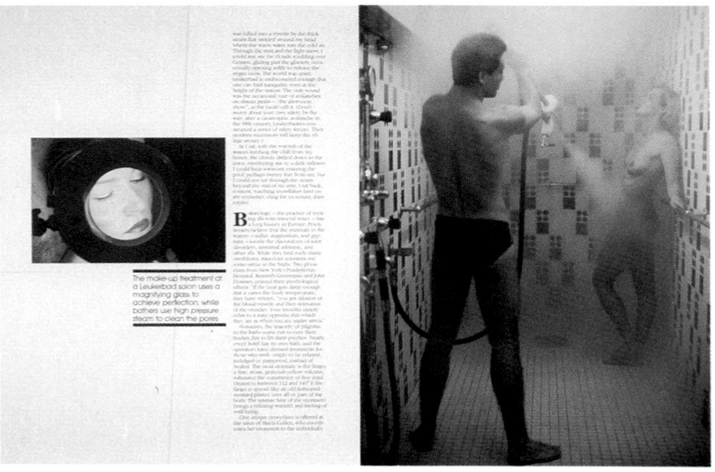
The make-up treatment at a Leukerbad salon uses a magnifying glass to achieve perfection, while bathers use high pressure steam to clean the pores

449

PUBLICATION: *Snow*
ART DIRECTOR: *Linda Stillman*
DESIGNER: *Linda Stillman*
PHOTOGRAPHER: *Alexander Tsiaras*
PUBLISHER: *Snow Publications, Inc.*
CATEGORY: *Design-Story Presentation*
AWARD: *Merit*

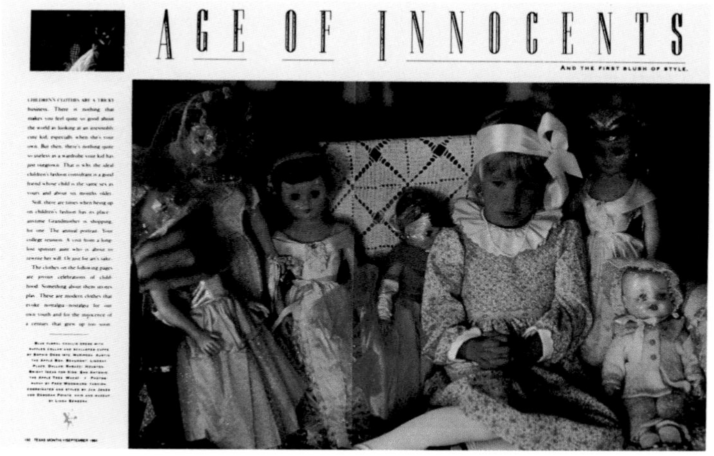
AGE OF INNOCENTS
AND THE FIRST BLUSH OF STYLE.

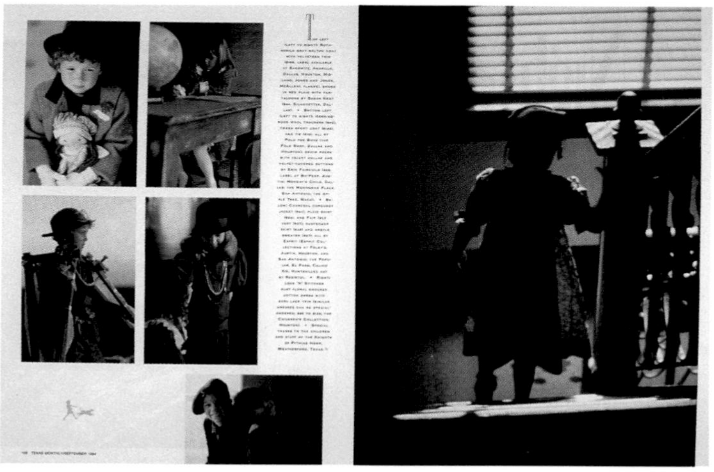

450

PUBLICATION: *Texas Monthly Magazine*
ART DIRECTOR: *Fred Woodward*
DESIGNER: *Fred Woodward*
PHOTOGRAPHER: *Fred Woodward*
PUBLISHER: *Texas Monthly, Inc.*
CATEGORY: *Photography-Story Presentation*
AWARD: *Merit*

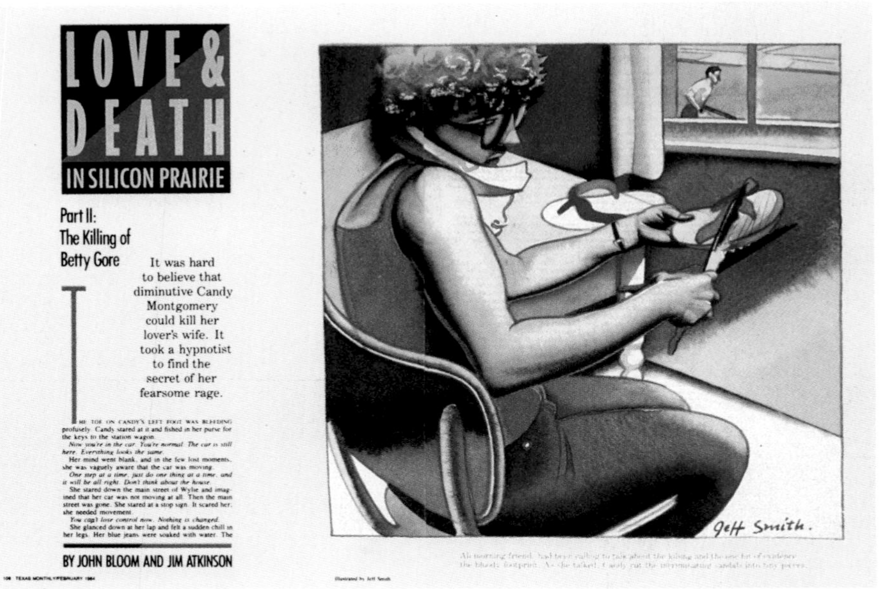
LOVE & DEATH
IN SILICON PRAIRIE
Part II:
The Killing of
Betty Gore
It was hard to believe that diminutive Candy Montgomery could kill her lover's wife. It took a hypnotist to find the secret of her fearsome rage.
BY JOHN BLOOM AND JIM ATKINSON
Jeff Smith.

"In a deep trance Candy admitted, 'I hate her. She's messed up my whole life.' 'What's happening in the utility room?' the doctor asked. 'I won't let her hit me again. I don't want him. She can't do this to me.'"

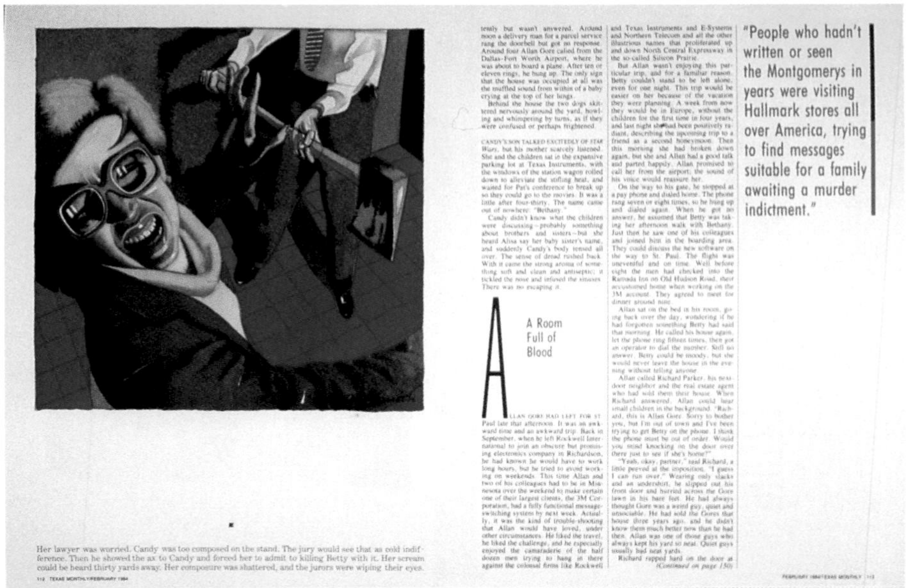
A Room Full of Blood
"People who hadn't written or seen the Montgomerys in years were visiting Hallmark stores all over America, trying to find messages suitable for a family awaiting a murder indictment."

451

PUBLICATION: *Texas Monthly Magazine*
ART DIRECTOR: *Fred Woodward*
DESIGNER: *Fred Woodward*
ILLUSTRATOR: *Jeff Smith*
PUBLISHER: *Texas Monthly, Inc.*
CATEGORY: *Illustration-Story Presentation*
AWARD: *Merit*

452

PUBLICATION: *Texas Monthly Magazine*
ART DIRECTOR: *Fred Woodward*
DESIGNER: *Fred Woodward*
ILLUSTRATOR: *Kent Barker*
PUBLISHER: *Texas Monthly, Inc.*
CATEGORY: *Photography-Story Presentation*
AWARD: *Merit*

HOWDY, SON. I'M THE LAW IN THIS COUNTY

TEXAS SHERIFFS IN ALL THEIR GLORY

BY DICK J. REAVIS

PHOTOGRAPHY BY KENT BARKER

Nobody stands as tall as rural sheriffs in Texas. In their communities, they personify the frontier tradition, they stand guard over male values, and despite the fact that nearly everyone would like to be sheriff—and upstarts are always trying—they usually outpoll all other candidates for office. County judges, their rivals for courthouse control, may be more highly regarded in church houses and news offices, but at beer joints, football games, and civic barbecues, the leading celebrity is the sheriff. Everybody wants to shake the sheriff's hand.

Today sheriffs can seem an embattled breed, as each day's paper brings news of yet another lawman under investigation or even under indictment. (In the last six years, six sheriffs have been convicted of crimes.) But it would be unfair to paint all of them as somehow crooked; many of the state's 254 county sheriffs still command respect, including the fourteen men pictured on the cover and these pages. These are seasoned hands, seniors among sheriffs; most have been wearing a badge for more than thirty years. They are men who remember the era before the 1966 Miranda warning, the days when, they say, no lawman apologized for the star on his chest, when sheriffs spoke of themselves not as "peace officers" but simply as "the law."

In their heyday, sheriffs were like elected royalty. In ceremonial, albeit Western costume, they presided over rodeo openings, headed posses in parades, and judged cattle at county fairs; some still do. But our frontier traditions are fading under the heat of commercial development, and today most sheriffs are clearing traffic for parades, not leading them. Parade saddles and silver-tipped boots are becoming scepters of the past.

The work of a sheriff varies with the natural and legal terrain. Sheriff George Whatley of Marion County made his mark by sniffing out stills in the East Texas woods. Dalton Hogg of Terrell County established his reputation by tracking out of the desert the Mexican desperado who had shot and very nearly killed Hogg's predecessor as sheriff. Across the state, family disputes are what takes the most of a lawman's time. "A man and his wife will get to battling, fussing, and they will just continue on through it, but they want

Raymond Weatherby

CRANE COUNTY

"I won't hire a deputy who isn't married. In a little town, where everybody knows everything, if you've got a single boy working for you, every little thing he does you're going to get called on. Why fool with getting calls on it when he can get married?"

150 TEXAS MONTHLY/NOVEMBER 1984

NOVEMBER 1984/TEXAS MONTHLY 151

Rufe Jordan

GRAY COUNTY

"I don't suspect that I've fired a pistol in ten or twelve years, not even just in practice sessions."

156 TEXAS MONTHLY/NOVEMBER 1984

NOVEMBER 1984/TEXAS MONTHLY 157

Brantley Barker

SAN SABA COUNTY

"What makes me feel so good is to go to a family fuss, and they was ready to separate and divide up all the furniture, and I talk to them awhile. They'd go back together, and then I get a letter from them telling me how they appreciated me sitting there talking to them that night."

Wayne Hitt

SAN PATRICIO COUNTY

"I can look a man in the eyes, and sometimes his eyes will tell me things his mouth won't tell me. I'm no psychoanalyst or anything, but I'm a pretty good judge of people."

Lester Gunn

"I get threats, I'd say, once or twice a month. I've had them call me and tell me they're going to kill me. I say, 'Well, why don't you come face to face with me? I'd be glad to meet you. I'll get up tonight and come meet you, if you want me to.' But they generally hang up, you know."

H. F. Fenton

COLEMAN COUNTY

"If [a suspect] walks up here and calls you a son of a bitch and you haul off and hit him in the mouth, then he'll file on you for his civil rights, then sue you in federal court. Back when law was law, well, you could knock his damn head off, go put him in jail, and file on him for calling you a son of a bitch. But I still don't let none of them call me a son of a bitch. I'll knock their damn heads off and let them go get a lawyer, that's what I'll do."

154 TEXAS MONTHLY/NOVEMBER 1984

NOVEMBER 1984/TEXAS MONTHLY 155

Dan Saunders

MARTIN COUNTY

"This is a dry county, very dry. We don't have any bootleggers here, and all the beer drinkers carry posthole diggers in the backs of their cars. They don't throw the beer cans out, they bury them."

somebody to come out and listen," says Sheriff Stuart Huffman of Cleburne. "When it's all said and done, they'll patch it up and live together another day or two."

The sheriffs on these pages are as alike as heads of grain. They were farm boys, mainly, and veterans of World War II, a couple of them heroes of the Army's 36th Division. All but two of them have dragged a cotton sack through Indian summer fields. They are all Anglo and Protestant in an age when Texas has a dozen Hispanic sheriffs. Several will retire at the end of this year, and when they do, their successors will be younger men raised with a new and more hesitant approach to law enforcement.

These men made themselves fathers to young men on the road to trouble, and nothing pleases them more than seeing a few youngsters heed their advice. "I always felt that if you help a kid, then you've done a lot more than if you help an old thing fifty or sixty years old," says H. F. Fenton, 62, of Coleman County. If they had to sum up their work in one phrase, it would be "to help people." In their optimistic moods, they are indistinguishable from scoutmasters.

Their philosophies are strikingly similar. Each says the same sorts of things about life and work. Always remember, they say, that every man is a human being, regardless of his crime. Always look a man in the eye. Don't be afraid to use your fists or even your firearms. Don't make any threats that you won't carry out. In other words, be sure you're right, then go ahead.

To a man, these sheriffs are advocates of capital punishment and long prison terms. They oppose handgun control because they believe what the bumper stickers say: if guns are outlawed, only outlaws will have guns. Yet if there is any difference in the attitudes these men have toward their jobs, it is best shown in a pistol count. Almost half of them don't carry a weapon, and most of them will retire without ever having fired a shot at anyone.

There's another thing these men have in common, something that you should note and remember, something more important than pistols, parade saddles, or even the statistics on crime. Look at these pictures—these sheriffs really do wear white hats.

Walter Fellers

[illegible]

Kenneth Kelley

"I don't carry a pistol, because I found out that I could run faster without one."

Dalton Hogg

TERRELL COUNTY

"I believe that for any good officer, you can give his wife about 75 per cent of the credit."

George Whatley

MARION COUNTY

"Everybody is guilty, as far as I'm concerned, when I go to arrest him."

Stuart Huffman

JOHNSON COUNTY

"I'm a firm believer in the old hanging tree."

453

PUBLICATION: *Town & Country*
ART DIRECTOR: *Melissa Tardiff*
DESIGNER: *Richard Turtletaub*
PHOTOGRAPHER: *Slim Aarons*
PUBLISHER: *Hearst Corporation*
CATEGORY: *Design-Story Presentation*
AWARD: *Merit*

454

PUBLICATION: *Town & Country*
ART DIRECTOR: *Melissa Tardiff*
DESIGNER: *Melissa Tardiff*
PHOTOGRAPHER: *Skrebneski*
PUBLISHER: *Hearst Corporation*
CATEGORY: *Photography-Story Presentation*
AWARD: *Merit*

455

PUBLICATION: *Town & Country*
ART DIRECTOR: *Melissa Tardiff*
DESIGNER: *Melissa Tardiff*
PHOTOGRAPHER: *Skrebneski*
PUBLISHER: *Hearst Corporation*
CATEGORY: *Photography-Story Presentation*
AWARD: *Merit*

456

PUBLICATION: *Town & Country*
ART DIRECTOR: *Melissa Tardiff*
DESIGNER: *Melissa Tardiff*
PHOTOGRAPHER: *Silano*
PUBLISHER: *Hearst Corporation*
CATEGORY: *Photography-Story Presentation*
AWARD: *Merit*

457

PUBLICATION: *Town & Country*
ART DIRECTOR: *Melissa Tardiff*
DESIGNER: *Melissa Tardiff*
PHOTOGRAPHER: *Skrebneski*
PUBLISHER: *Hearst Corporation*
CATEGORY: *Photography-Story Presentation*
AWARD: *Merit*

458

PUBLICATION: *Town & Country*
ART DIRECTOR: *Melissa Tardiff*
DESIGNER: *Melissa Tardiff*
PHOTOGRAPHER: *Silano*
PUBLISHER: *Hearst Corporation*
CATEGORY: *Photography-Story Presentation*
AWARD: *Merit*

459

PUBLICATION: *Travel & Leisure*
ART DIRECTOR: *Adrian Taylor*
DESIGNER: *Adrian Taylor*
Kenneth Kleppert
PHOTOGRAPHER: *John Bulmer*
PUBLISHER: *American Express*
CATEGORY: *Design-Story Presentation*
AWARD: *Merit*

The low rise unity of Vienna's Old City is lifted by the spires of St. Stephen's Cathedral (above left) and it is cushioned by the soft greenery of its many surrounding parks (above right). The grand entryway of the Kunsthistorisches (opposite) heralds the myriad treasures at the top of the stairs.

Vienna is an echo, an insistent melody that floats almost out of hearing even as you stand amidst its mellow splendors. In an age devoid of grace and nuance, with high rises obliterating the open sky, with last week's restaurant consigned to the history books, with the affluent guerrilla look the dernier cri in urban chic, Vienna is the great European rediscovery.

Its place on the world stage has been reduced to a bit part but think how often an actor underplaying a small role remains etched in your memory long after the star has faded. Vienna with its gently tenacious hold on the imperial past and its present full of welcome formality of dress and behavior, has just that insinuating charm.

I know that some claim Vienna is now just a smug small town, a record played at the wrong speed, but I found it brimming over with the pleasures of any major capital—great art and harmony of architecture, monumental squares and intriguing side streets, music to light every night. And cafés. Those fabled cafés—part shrine, part gathering place—where sober men devouring newspapers sit side by side with ladies carrying their minuscule dogs. They all have, it seems, an enviable infinity of time to linger over pastries and gossip.

Cafés in other cities are pleasant adjuncts to the life that rushes by; in Vienna they are the center of life. They are what keep the metabolism of the city at a civilized pace—although pace seems too active a word. For visitors used to a headlong pitch, Vienna is like a week in an old world spa. It is the loveliest least frenetic big city in the world.

In the last few decades, though, Vienna has been mecca mainly for music lovers, who find a feast, not just in the quality of performances but in the knowledgeable audiences and in the ornate auditoriums that are as much theater as what goes on behind the proscenium. The city has not been on most travelers' itineraries. Vienna seems set apart, away from the main stream. It is where Western Europe comes to a screeching halt before the Iron Curtain. Once a crossroads of empire that stretched from the Netherlands and Spain to Sardinia and Hungary, Vienna is no longer on the way to anywhere, except perhaps to Budapest and Prague. But I have been hearing the word "Vienna" on the lips of more and more sophisticated travelers.

In the meantime, before everyone else arrives, what a delightful interlude in which to visit. Vienna is a city that lives its own quiet life, has impeccable manners for visitors and a grace

Vienna's version of Art Nouveau is encountered everywhere as a joyous surprise—from this delicate subway entrance (above) to the light-filled Church am Steinhof (right).

steps from the hotel past the State Opera House and the fabled Hotel Sacher, along the Karntnerstrasse, an immaculate and stylish sweep of pedestrian mall. The cafés were brimming over with people, but the shops were closed on Saturday afternoon. So I had to just gaze into the windows of Lobmeyr, whose crystal has adorned chandeliers as far away as New York's Metropolitan Opera House; of Augarten, displaying delicate and mannerly porcelain, and of W.F. Admuller, with its trim and pricey knits.

So, except for the purchase of an ice cream cone, piety won out over commerce, and I entered the Gothic vastness of St. Stephen's Cathedral. It may not be the most beautiful church in Christendom—I found it more outsize than ethereal—but it resonates with the beginning of Hapsburg rule in the 13th century, when Vienna was still a backwater. It also provides an overview of architecture, with a Romanesque portal, Gothic interior and a Baroque altarpiece (the Renaissance passed Vienna by). Then too, St. Stephen's is a symbol of Austria's reverence for its own history: the Cathedral was quickly restored after near total destruction in World War II.

Down every lane and byway leading from St. Stephen's and the Kärntnerstrasse are more traces of ancient Vienna—exquisite medieval houses and St. Rupert's Church, which echoes with the 11th century. Strolling is the best way to wrap yourself in the subtle beauty of Vienna. Everywhere I looked, I saw plaques proclaiming that Mozart or Schubert or Beethoven slept here. The stones in the secret courtyards still ring with their music. But you can also hear today's voices. The old Archbishop's Palace shares quarters with a rather racy lingerie shop. Near the university is Alte Schmiede, a medieval blacksmith shop that is now a restaurant and hangout for students. Boutiques and bookshops are tucked away in venerable buildings.

As the afternoon wore on, so did I. I knew in my heart that the only way to survive was to take part in some more legend—this time culinary. I settled in at the Hotel Sacher Café to watch the world go by the Opera House, as I sighed over a slice of Sacher torte *mit schlag*, that chocolate-on-chocolate cake with a cloud of whipped cream to lighten it. The coffee arrived in a tiny pot on one of the 11 million tiny trays in Vienna. Coffee, tea or chocolate is served, even in the lowliest of cafés, with ceremony, almost reverence. This was my first important lesson in how time can gently flow by in a capital city.

The next morning, I took a city bus tour for a few hours of orientation. I saw the Danube (not the imposing presence I had hoped for), and I got to Schönbrunn Palace, which is most people's dream of Baroque. We waltzed after our guide through about 25 (or was it 45?) of its 1,441 rooms. The palace was built, although that seems like an inadequate word, by the celebrated architect J.B. Fisher von Erlach under the order of Emperor Josef I and finished by 1713. The royal presence most strongly

Old world civility and grace reign in Vienna's cafés. The Hotel Sacher (above) envelops guests in scarlet splendor, and the Imperial Café (right) casts a warmly mellow glow.

that has not given way to expedience. And it is almost totally free of the tourist trash—T-shirts and key rings—that has washed up on the beaches of tourism on the farthest reaches of the planet.

In Vienna, you see with unparalleled clarity the last great gesture of empire. It is the mid 19th century vision of Emperor Franz Josef who, blind to the near future of crumbling monarchies, tore down the Roman walls encircling the Old City and made a lasting statement about the present. The stone battlements gave way to the Ring, that broad boulevard lined with noble mansions and princely palaces built in a frenzy of ornament.

Frederic Morton, in his beguiling book *A Nervous Splendor* describes just one year, 1888-1889, in this remarkable reign. It was a time in which the blazing talents of men such as composers Gustav Mahler, Johann Strauss and Johannes Brahms, playwright Arthur Schnitzler and artist Gustav Klimt, pioneers Sigmund Freud and Theodor Herzl all coexisted. "Names," as Morton says, "destined to be trumpet blasts." It was also the year Sarah Bernhardt came to play at the Theater an der Wien. Crown Prince Rudolph—who saw the wave of the future as his father and most of Austria remained rooted in the past—shot himself at Mayerling. And it was the year Adolf Hitler was born.

These are not just cold facts confined to encyclopedias or tucked away in the dark recesses of some museum. They are vivid and full of illumination in the Vienna of today. The trumpet blasts may be a bit muted, but then we are the aftereffects of the last century. It is just the mellowed memory that comes to us through time.

Oh, there are contemporary touches. I even saw some break dancing, but in this setting, it seemed more mannered than the music of Johann Strauss that still fills the parks and concert halls. A Volksoper production of *Die Fledermaus*, an extravagance of acres of silk ball gowns and a stageful of more people than D.W. Griffith would have cast, was not an exercise in nostalgia the night I heard it. It was the Viennese equivalent of MTV. The audience, about half locals who hummed and conducted silently in their seats, experienced it as if for the first time. The man next to me, as wide as he was tall, nibbled on the fingers of his matching wife in high romantic ecstasy as the rather overage Rosalinda misbehaved saucily on stage.

The golden days of Vienna are right now. And you can relive them, just as I did for a week this past summer. The best way to begin is by checking into a hotel within the Ring. I chose the Bristol, which seems the soul of *Alte Wien*, or Old Vienna (I could have sworn a trio of violinists accompanied me to my room.) You can sink into its turn of century elegance as you would into an overstuffed brocade armchair.

On my first afternoon there, torn between the splits of Champagne in my minibar and the call of the music, chaise longue, I chose an even more attractive alternative: a walk. Just a few

Saluting the Statue of Liberty

And remembering Ellis Island

AMERICA'S GREATEST MUSEUM

THE MET

With dazzling new wings and age-old treasures, it's bigger and better than ever

PHOTOGRAPHED BY ARNOLD NEWMAN

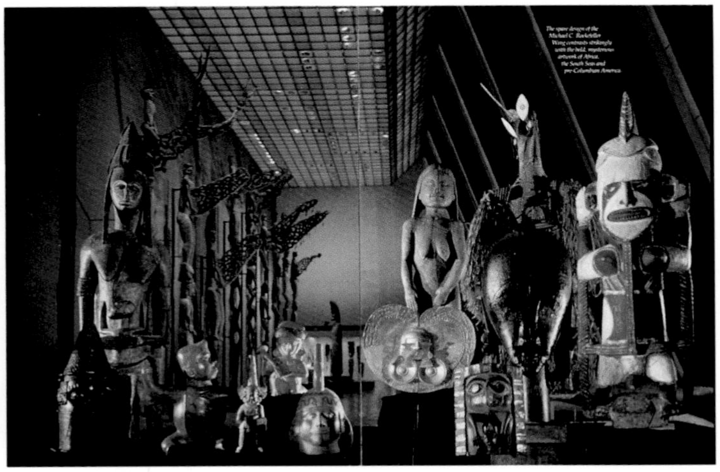

460

PUBLICATION: *Travel & Leisure*
ART DIRECTOR: *Adrian Taylor*
DESIGNER: *Adrian Taylor*
PHOTOGRAPHER: *Jay Maisel, Peter Kaplan, Amos Schliak & others*
PUBLISHER: *American Express*
CATEGORY: *Design-Story Presentation*
AWARD: *Merit*

461

PUBLICATION: *Travel & Leisure*
ART DIRECTOR: *Adrian Taylor*
DESIGNER: *Adrian Taylor*
PHOTOGRAPHER: *Arnold Newman*
PUBLISHER: *American Express*
CATEGORY: *Design-Story Presentation*
AWARD: *Merit*

New American Wing

CONTEMPORARY ARTISTS AT THE MET

VERMONT'S SNOWY STOWE
Winter pleasures of a New England town
by Andrew Nemethy
Photographed by John Lewis Stage

TEN ACRES LODGE

462

PUBLICATION: *Travel & Leisure*
ART DIRECTOR: *Adrian Taylor*
DESIGNER: *Kenneth Kleppert*
Adrian Taylor
PHOTOGRAPHER: *John Lewis Stage*
PUBLISHER: *American Express*
CATEGORY: *Design-Story Presentation*
AWARD: *Merit*

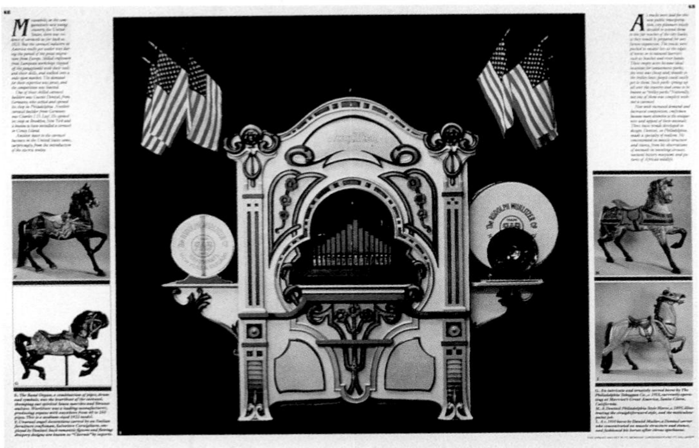

463

PUBLICATION: *Upper & Lower Case*
ART DIRECTOR: *B. Martin Pedersen*
DESIGNER: *B. Martin Pedersen*
PHOTOGRAPHER: *Reprint Carousel Animal Zypher Press*
PUBLISHER: *International Typeface Corporation*
CATEGORY: *Design-Story Presentation*
AWARD: *Merit*

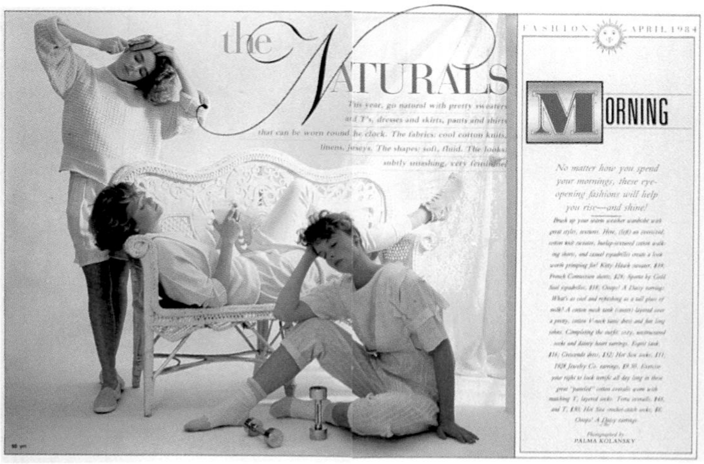

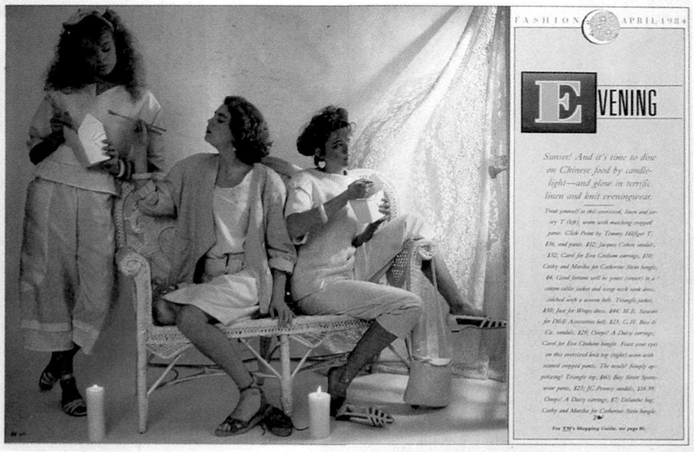

464

PUBLICATION: *Young Miss Magazine*
ART DIRECTOR: *Renna Franco*
DESIGNER: *Nancy Campbell, Renna Franco*
ILLUSTRATOR: *Philip Anderson*
PHOTOGRAPHER: *Palma Kolansky*
PUBLISHER: *Gruner & Jahr USA*
AWARD: *Merit*

SINGLE SPECIAL ISSUES

TWENTIETH
PUBLICATION
DESIGN
ANNUAL

The Boston Globe

ETHIOPIA
Famine and flight

'The great dying has begun. The more people who stay here, the more people who will die.'

Refugees, above, fleeing to food relief camps in Sudan, move down a dried-out riverbed in Tigray Province, Ethiopia.

This special section is an account of suffering people as seen by Globe staff reporter Colin Nickerson and Globe staff photographer Stan Grossfeld, who returned to Boston Friday from a two-week journey into rebel-held Tigray Province in Ethiopia.

ETHIOPIA
Famine and flight

A guerrilla from the Tigray People's Liberation Front crosses the cracked surface of the dried-out Gash River in Tigray Province.

Stan Grossfeld and Colin Nickerson in Ethiopia
Photo by Gary Fairman

Design: Lucy Bartholomay

The Boston Globe

465

PUBLICATION: *The Boston Globe*
ART DIRECTOR: *Lucy Bartholomay*
DESIGNER: *Lucy Bartholomay*
ILLUSTRATOR: *Deborah Perugi-MAP*
PHOTOGRAPHER: *Stan Grossfeld*
PUBLISHER: *Globe Newspaper Co.*
CATEGORY: *Single/Special Issue*
AWARD: *Gold*

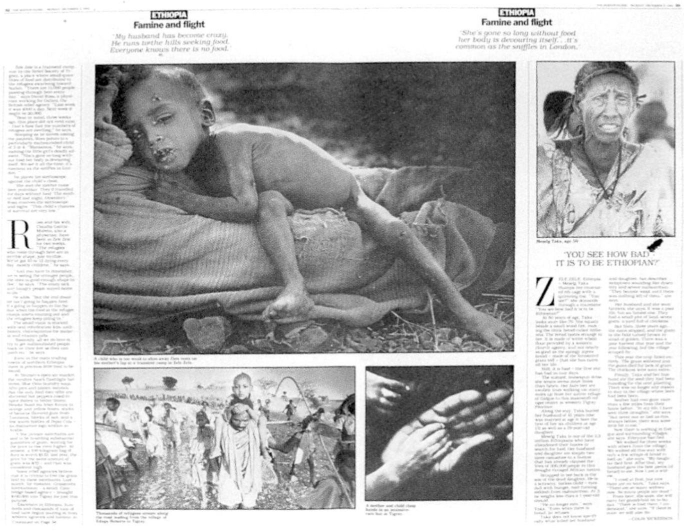

ETHIOPIA

Famine and flight

'My husband has become crazy. He runs tothe hills seeking food. Everyone knows there is no food.'

ETHIOPIA

Famine and flight

'She's gone so long without food her body is devouring itself. . .It's common as the sniffles in London.'

"YOU SEE HOW BAD IT IS TO BE ETHIOPIAN?"

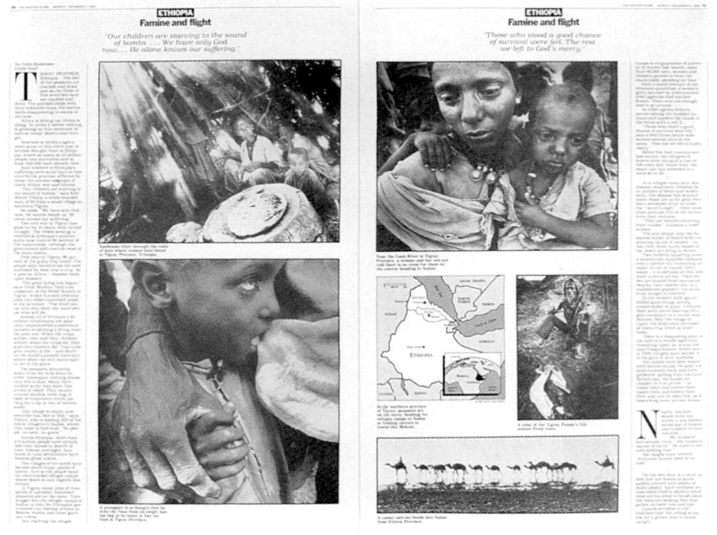

ETHIOPIA

Famine and flight

"Our children are starving to the sound of bombs . . . We have only God now. . . He alone knows our suffering."

ETHIOPIA

Famine and flight

'Those who stood a good chance of survival were fed. The rest we left to God's mercy.'

CONTENTS

THE CITY
Glorious traditions, political realities 4

THE PEOPLE
Boston's vital link: the neighborhoods 14

THE GROWTH
$3 billion in projects changing the cityscape 22

THE CHOICE
Learn from the past or fail in the future 34

The Boston Globe

A plan for Boston

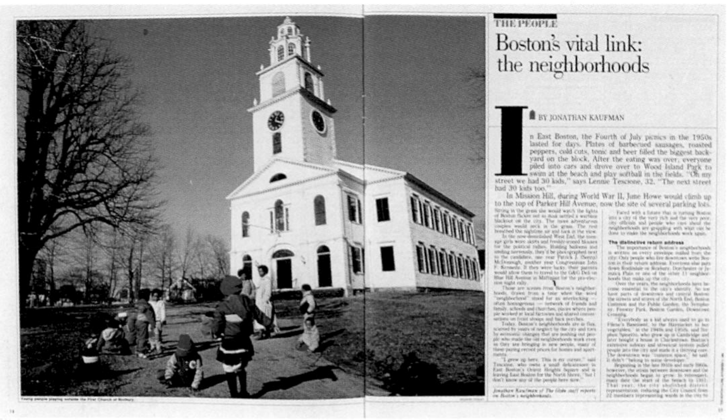
THE PEOPLE

Boston's vital link: the neighborhoods

BY JONATHAN KAUFMAN

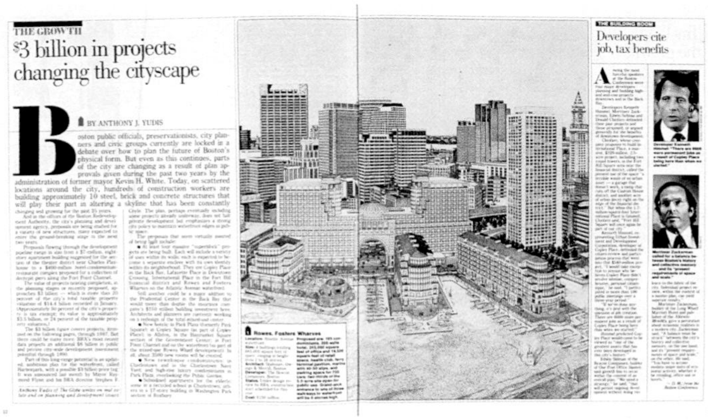
THE GROWTH

$3 billion in projects changing the cityscape

BY ANTHONY J. YUDIS

Developers cite job, tax benefits

466

PUBLICATION: *The Boston Globe*
ART DIRECTOR: *Lucy Bartholomay*
DESIGNER: *Lucy Bartholomay*
PUBLISHER: *Globe Newspaper Co.*
CATEGORY: *Tabloid/News Single/Special Issue*
AWARD: *Silver*

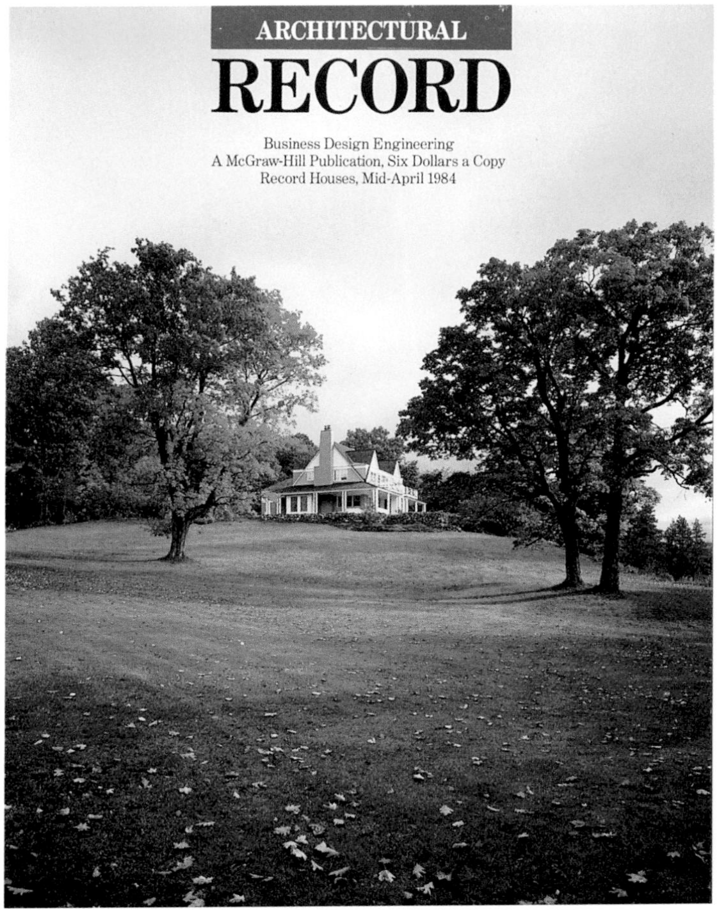

467

PUBLICATION: *Architectural Record*
ART DIRECTOR: *Massimo Vignelli*
DESIGNER: *Anna-Egger-Schlesinger*
PUBLISHER: *McGraw-Hill*
CATEGORY: *Single/Special Issue Design*
AWARD: *Merit*

468

PUBLICATION: *Architectural Record*
ART DIRECTOR: *Alex Stillano*
DESIGNER: *Alberto Bucchianeri*
PUBLISHER: *McGraw-Hill*
CATEGORY: *Single/Special Issue Design*
AWARD: *Merit*

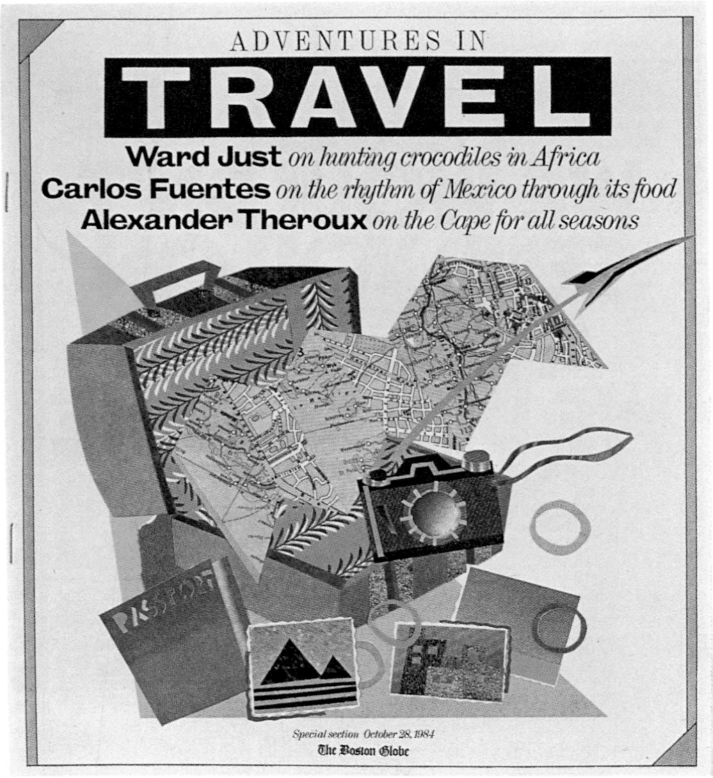
ADVENTURES IN
TRAVEL
Ward Just on hunting crocodiles in Africa
Carlos Fuentes on the rhythm of Mexico through its food
Alexander Theroux on the Cape for all seasons
Special section October 28, 1984
The Boston Globe

Hunting Crocodiles · In Africa, things are often not what they seem.
By Ward Just

By Carlos Fuentes
RHYTHMS of Mexico
The plaza and the restaurant

Dwindling days, widening vistas
Off season on the Cape
By Alexander Theroux

469

PUBLICATION: *The Boston Globe Magazine*
ART DIRECTOR: *Ronn Campisi*
DESIGNER: *Ronn Campisi*
PUBLISHER: *Globe Newspaper Co.*
CATEGORY: *Special Issue*
AWARD: *Merit*

470

PUBLICATION: *Esquire Magazine*
ART DIRECTOR: *April Silver*
DESIGNER: *April Silver*
PUBLISHER: *Esquire Associates*
CATEGORY: *Special Issue*
AWARD: *Merit*

471

PUBLICATION: *Esquire Magazine*
ART DIRECTOR: *April Silver*
DESIGNER: *April Silver*
PUBLISHER: *Esquire Associates*
CATEGORY: *Single/Special Issue Design*
AWARD: *Merit*

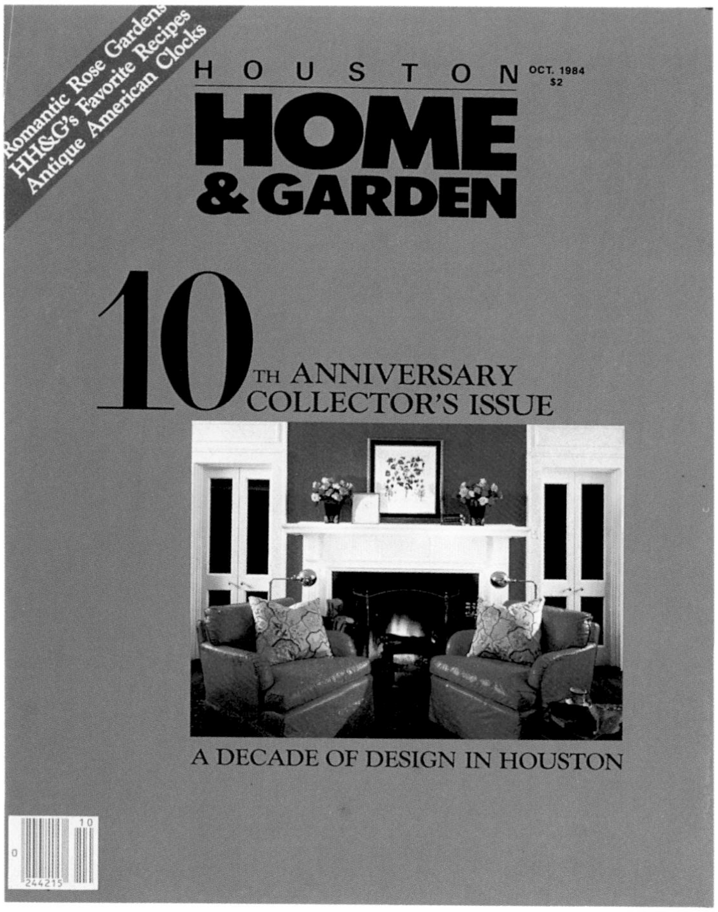

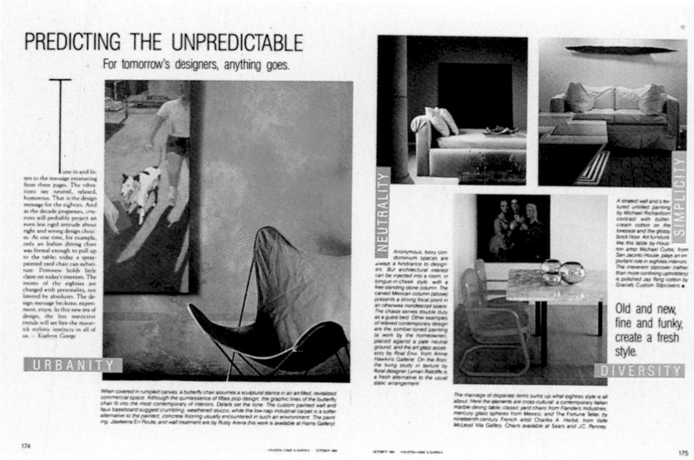

472

PUBLICATION: *Houston Home & Garden*
ART DIRECTOR: *Michael Cox O'Dwyer*
PHOTOGRAPHER: *Fran Brennan, David Lund, Ardon Brown*
PUBLISHER: *City Home Publications*
CATEGORY: *Special Issue*
AWARD: *Merit*

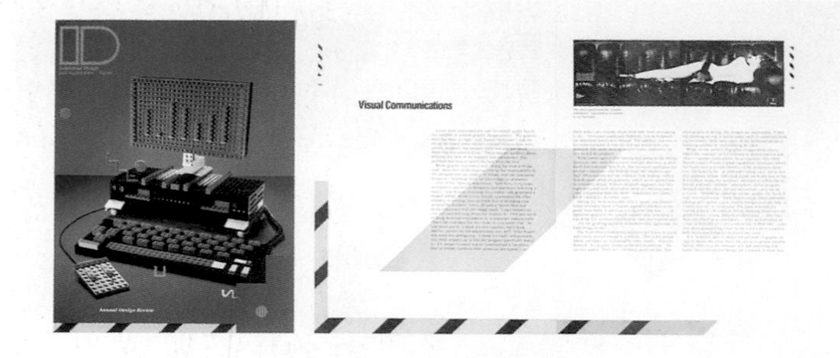

473

PUBLICATION: *Industrial Design Magazine*
ART DIRECTOR: *Karen Krieger*
DESIGNER: *Annlee Polos*
PHOTOGRAPHER: *Tom Wedell, Andrew Gordon*
PUBLISHER: *Design Publications, Inc.*
CATEGORY: *Single/Special Issue*
AWARD: *Merit*

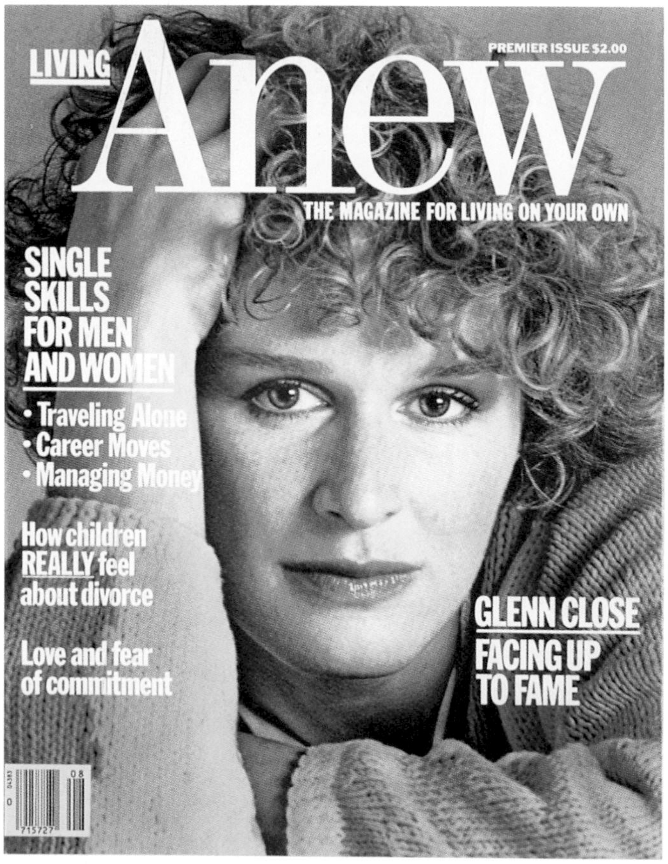

474

PUBLICATION: *Living Anew*
ART DIRECTOR: *Terry Kopel*
DESIGNER: *Terry Kopel*
PUBLISHER: *Mantel, Koppel & Scher*
CATEGORY: *Single/Special Issue*
AWARD: *Merit*

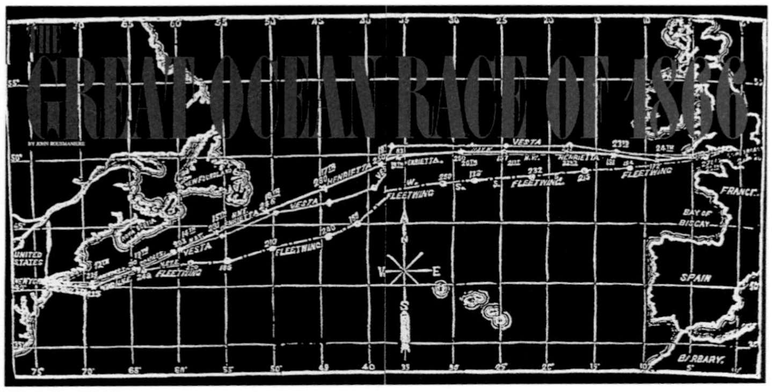

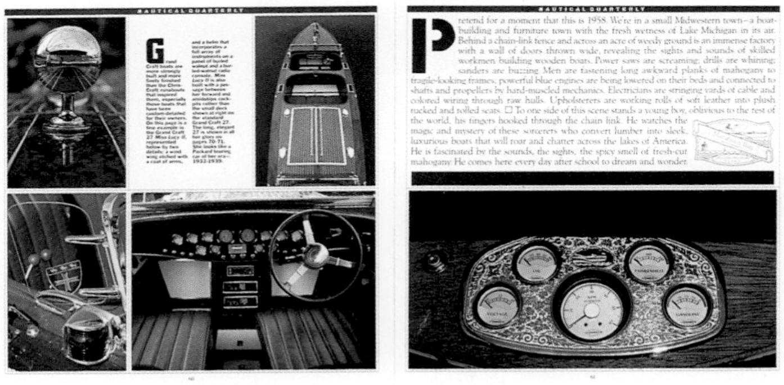

475

PUBLICATION: *Nautical Quarterly*
ART DIRECTOR: *Marilyn Rose*
DESIGNER: *Marilyn Rose*
PUBLISHER: *Nautical Quarterly*
CATEGORY: *Special Issue Design*
AWARD: *Merit*

476

PUBLICATION: *New York Magazine*
ART DIRECTOR: *Robert Best*
DESIGNER: *Patricia Von Brachel*
David Walters
PUBLISHER: *Murdoch Magazines*
CATEGORY: *Special Issue Design*
AWARD: *Merit*

477

PUBLICATION: *New York Magazine*
ART DIRECTOR: *Robert Best*
DESIGNER: *Patricia Von Brachel, Don Morris*
PUBLISHER: *Murdoch Magazines*
CATEGORY: *Single/Special Issue*
AWARD: *Merit*

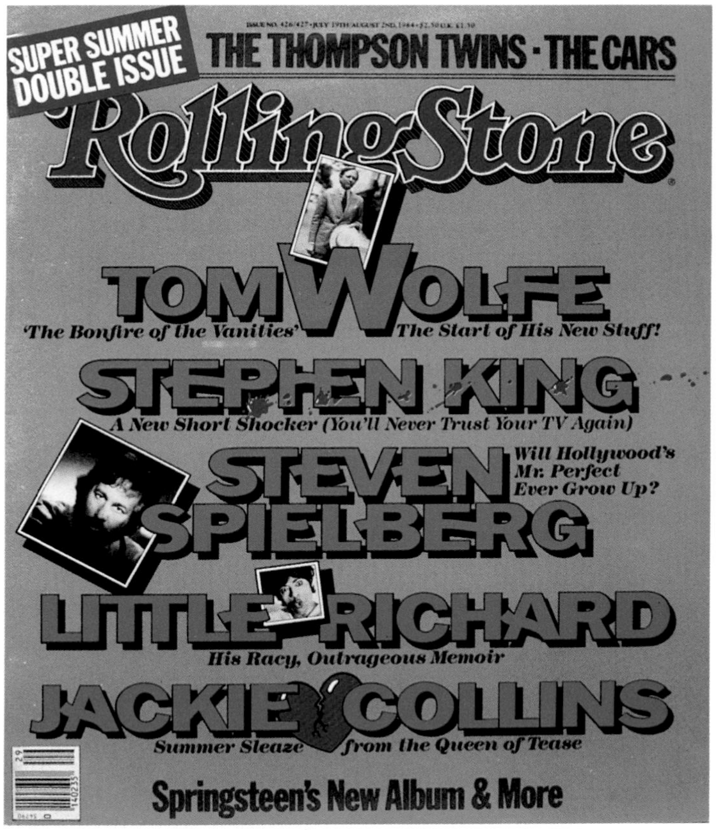

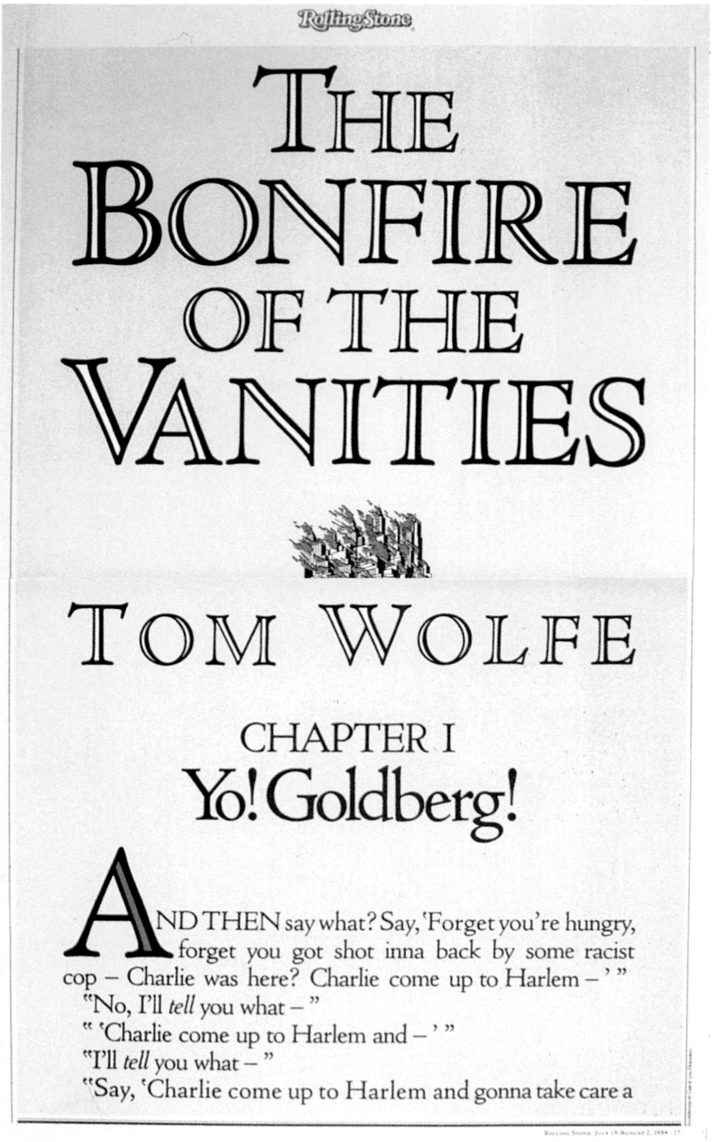

Rolling Stone

THE BONFIRE OF THE VANITIES

TOM WOLFE

CHAPTER I
Yo! Goldberg!

AND THEN say what? Say, 'Forget you're hungry, forget you got shot inna back by some racist cop – Charlie was here? Charlie come up to Harlem – ' "
"No, I'll *tell* you what – "
" 'Charlie come up to Harlem and – ' "
"I'll *tell* you what – "
"Say, 'Charlie come up to Harlem and gonna take care a

481

PUBLICATION: *Rolling Stone*
ART DIRECTOR: *Derek Ungless*
DESIGNER: *Derek Ungless*
PHOTOGRAPHER: *William Coupon*
PUBLISHER: *Straight Arrow Publishers, Inc.*
CATEGORY: *Single/Special Issue*
AWARD: *Merit*

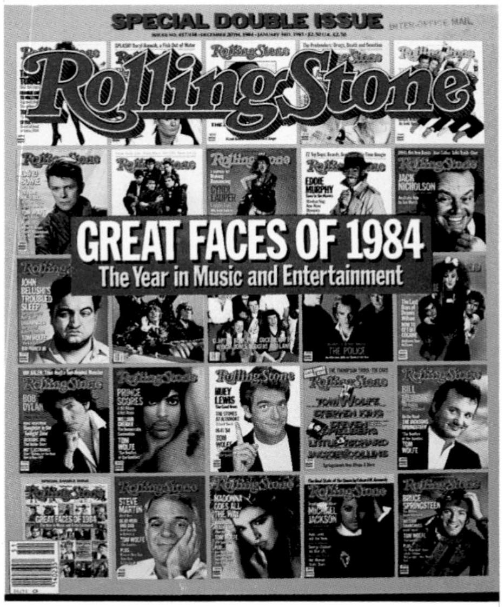
SPECIAL DOUBLE ISSUE
Rolling Stone
GREAT FACES OF 1984
The Year in Music and Entertainment

ILLUSTRATED BY PETER DE SEVE
THE BONFIRE OF THE VANITIES
TOM WOLFE
With the latest chapter, we also present the story thus far
ROLLING STONE YEARBOOK 1984

PHOTOGRAPHED BY E. J. CAMP
Billy Idol
In one article, he said, 'I can be an "idol" just by calling myself one – that's how flimsy it all is.' If he's that full of crap, fine. Maybe in ten years he'll wind up in a suit and be a stockbroker.
— Fabian
ROLLING STONE YEARBOOK 1984

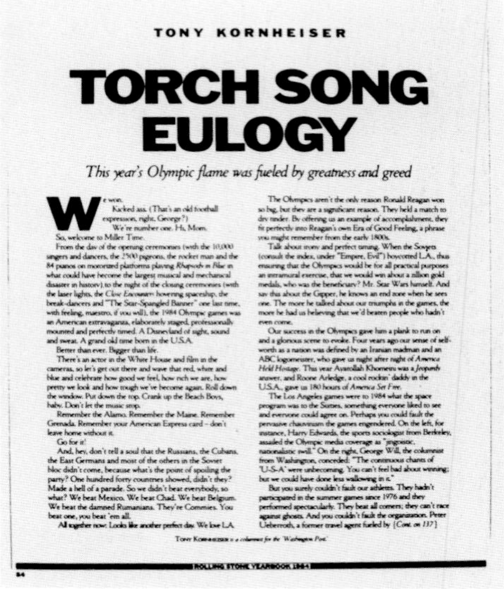
TONY KORNHEISER
TORCH SONG EULOGY
This year's Olympic flame was fueled by greatness and greed
ROLLING STONE YEARBOOK 1984

KURT LODER
1984 Record Guide
A look at the year's noteworthy albums
Illustrated by Ian Pollock
ROLLING STONE YEARBOOK 1984

482

PUBLICATION: *Rolling Stone*
ART DIRECTOR: *Derek Ungless*
DESIGNER: *Tracy Glick*
PHOTOGRAPHER: *Laurie Kratochvil*
PUBLISHER: *Straight Arrow Publishers, Inc.*
CATEGORY: *Special Issue*
AWARD: *Merit*

483

PUBLICATION: *Time Magazine*
ART DIRECTOR: *Rudy Hoglund*
DESIGNER: *Tom Bentkowski*
PUBLISHER: *Time, Inc.*
CATEGORY: *Special Issue*
AWARD: *Merit*

It's A Global Affair

They come, bearing skills, to the appointed arena. And every Olympic athlete brings along another possession as well: a heritage conditioned by distinctive language, customs and geography. This haze of individuality is burned off by the heat of competition: swimmers, runners, jumpers, gymnasts, all of them, doing what they do best, can come to seem alike. That homogeneity defines, in large measure, the Olympic ideal. But the flame feeds on man's diversities as well as similarities. In this portfolio of photographs, TIME portrays some of the men and women who will be competing in Los Angeles. To see them in the places where they have grown is to recognize both a universal quest for excellence and the sustaining powers of home.

It would take stony faces indeed not to smile at the exuberance of Mary Decker. Her joy as competing seems irresistibly contagious. Says the top U.S. women's middle-distance runner: "I live to run." Some of Decker's zeal may stem from her childhood, the feuding and eventual divorce of her parents. "If you come out of things like that in the right frame of

mind, you're just more competitive." Such resolve exacts a toll. Her relentless training has led to a series of injuries, including one that kept her out of the 1976 Olympics. Then came her two dramatic victories last summer at the world championships in Helsinki, making Decker, who will run only the 3,000 meters in Los Angeles, the favorite for Olympic gold.

Photographs for TIME by Neil Leifer

United States Mary Decker

Why We Play These Games

As Los Angeles raises its Olympic banners and 2 billion viewers sit back to cheer, athletes from 140 nations of the world prepare to meet a human need

Eight thousand banners, did you say? Covering 120 miles of Los Angeles? Hanging from 300 different types of lampposts? O.K. Some of the brackets for the banners had to be different too: a real headache. Certainly not, you wouldn't want to use just any colors. Had to be magenta, vermilion, chrome yellow, violet, aqua "Festive Federalism," the designers call it. (What does that mean? Oh, sorry. Please go on. You were talking about construction: 3,500 construction workers at 67 different sites, including Olympic Villages, places for the Games, training facilities, parking lots. That is, if the cars can get there. Gridlock city, eh? No! Fifty-two miles of chain-link fence? Well, you can't be too careful. By all means, read the grocery list for the athletes. Pork, 63,300 lbs.; beef, 206,555 lbs.; 70,000 dozen eggs. (You do deliver?) You say that if someone laid those eggs end to end they'd stretch for 25 miles? One pooped chicken. That's a joke, son. No harm, no foul.

But where is the center of this thing? No, not the $525 million budget or the anticipated inflation of $3.3 billion into the local economy or the 269,000 dozen cookies. One million saw trees planted by a conservation group? Good for them. Nothing like a tree. The question is why. Why, as the magenta was going up at the Los Angeles Coliseum, were 7,800 athletes from 140 nations loading their gear and kissing Mother goodbye? Numbers? Here's a number. On July 28, 2 billion people of the great trembling bipolar world will lay down their washing and watch these Games. Why?

Looking mighty Establishment in his white open-collar shirt and navy-blue suit, John Carlos sits at a table in the headquarters of the Los Angeles Olympic Organizing Committee, where he now works. Behind one shoulder the American flag, behind the other the Olympic flag. But for a bum ankle, he says, he could still tear up the track. The last time we saw John Carlos was 1968 on a podium in Mexico City, standing in the grainy evening light rigid as an exclamation point. The black-

power salute, an antique of the '60s. He is speaking of something else.

"I was a fair-to-exciting swimmer. I guess I put as much energy into swimming at that age [ten] as I ever did into track and field. I wanted to swim the English Channel. I told my father: I want to know something about this English Channel. Why are these people swimming it? How does one swim with, you know, the sharks? How do swimmers go to the bathroom? What happens in the night? And then I learned about the Olympic Games. And I said: Oh, wow. I'd like to do that.

"Then I started to ask more questions about swimming. And my father pulled me aside, and he said: Look. Swimming is a bad way to go. You have to be in the water at least six, seven hours a day. He said: Where would you train? You can't train in the Harlem River: you lose seven or eight guys a year drowning, which is true. And he said you can't go to the ocean. The water's too rough. He said you can't go to the public pool: everybody's trying to cool off. Everything he said made sense. So I started to walk off like with my lip stuck out. And he tapped me on the shoulder and he said: Look, man, the heaviest hasn't come yet. They have private clubs, but you can't join any of them. And I said: Why? Because we can't afford it? He said no. Because you're colored: they won't let you in. So I walked off in a kind of mystic mood, dejected but not dejected. My old man looked at me and asked: Well, what you going to do? You gonna quit? Just look around and find something else.

Where is the center of this thing? A man who learned how fast his legs could move because as a boy he outran cops in Harlem, who worked out in corduroy shoes on the F.D.R. Drive because his father was a cobbler and cordovans last? Does one watch the Olympics to see a spectacle of individuals? A festival of nerve? Perhaps something collective as well. Something America bursts into song at the torch relay, and 7 million tickets go on sale.

But they said the boycott would kill the Games. Evidently not. No boycott has done real damage, not the

U.S. boycott in 1980 or that of the Africans in 1976 or of some Arab states in 1956 in response to the crisis over Suez. As for this year of Soviet revenge, not only are more nations than ever sending delegations, but people are saying that the Games may be better off without an East-West brawl. Quieter countries will get a chance to strut.

But they said commercialism would kill the Games. Hardly. In a world where weapons are sold like hot cakes, who really worries about getting and spending at a sports event? To the contrary, the commercialism feels right, at least it does for the U.S. Competition in the Games, competition around them. Ever see an amateur capitalist?

So Botswana, a land so arid that its currency is called rain, proudly sends a yachtsman to represent the nation. And Israel cheers 30 athletes and promises 1,000 tourists, though the country has yet to win a single medal. This will be Communist China's first major presence in the Olympics, they are bringing a contingent of 353. Egypt and Italy will be sending the largest delegations they have ever sent. Singapore wouldn't miss it, except for boycotting in 1980, that country has participated in every Olympics since 1948.

Even war does not get in the way. Lebanon sends (fittingly) a team of skeet and trapshooters. (On the TV news recently, the shooters complained—that: they were not getting enough practice.) The Irelands unite North and South for a moment to create a single team. Astonishingly, the Koreas considered doing the same. They matter, these Games: to Belgium's cyclists, Argentina's single sculler, Holland's swimmers, the boxers from the Seychelles, India's field hockey team is out to prove something against Pakistan. Kenya's long-distance runners have things to prove to themselves. Cheers for the Chadians. Hail to the Swazis. Where else would these people come together so eagerly? Not the U.N.

In this the center, then? An international Woodstock? "The Olympic flame is the only hope for brotherhood, understanding and dialogue," says Juan Antonio

Samaranch, president of the International Olympic Committee. What else would he say? "The Olympics are the only times in the history of the world when so many nations come together in one spot in an association of friendship," says Charles Palmer, president of the British Olympic Association. Vested interest. According to Kurthan Fisek, a professor of public management from the University of Ankara: "No single institution in the entire history of mankind has been able to equate itself with world peace as effectively and consistently." Let's not get carried away.

Yes, not all of this is cant. Michael Jordan of the U.S. team pretends not to see the basket, then lunges toward it, as if stumbling on the court. Suddenly he leaps, glides, hangs in the air. The ball is cradled in the palm of his hand at the side of his head. Still flying, he flicks his wrist forward, as if waving hello, and the ball sets off on a flight of its own. When the hoop is scored, Jordan is airborne still. Why are we pleased?

Heroes must be part of the answer. There are those like Jordan, Mary Decker, Carl Lewis who enter the Olympics with greatness already thrust upon them, one will test their performances against their reputations. Better still, sudden heroes always seem to emerge and establish themselves, often in sports one has dismissed as boring or has paid no attention to before. Olga Korbut and Nadia Comaneci created gymnastics for most Americans, not because Americans never heard of gymnastics, but because they had not seen the sport performed by virtuosos. A subtle surprise of the Olympics is how individuals can transform the events in which they participate. Boxing enrages and disgusts you. Then Sugar Ray Leonard skips into the ring, and the sport is God and country.

Much of the appeal of the Olympics centers on individual heroes, yet heroism in the Games is lightweight: it bears none of the mythic armor of professional sports. With professional athletes, allegories develop with the records. Mantle was pain.

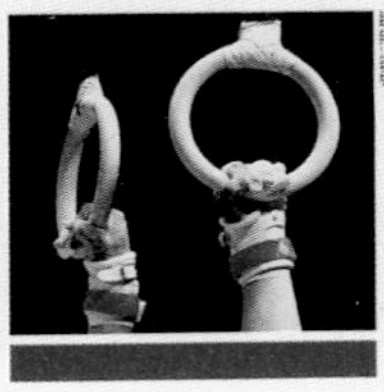

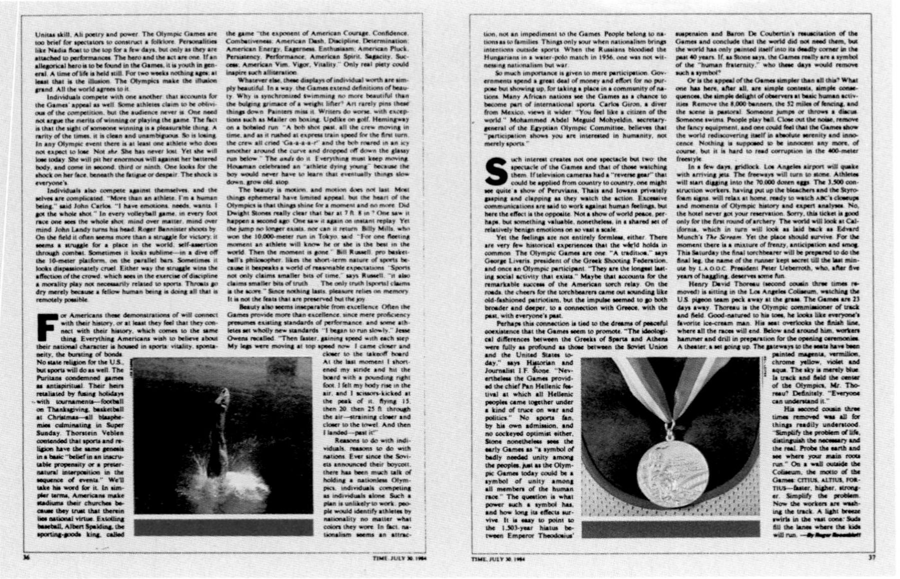

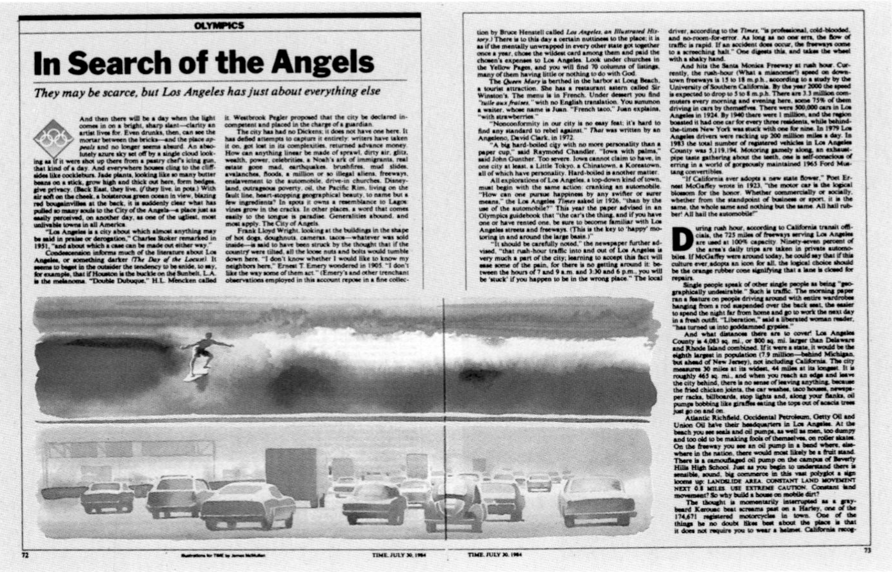

OLYMPICS
In Search of the Angels
They may be scarce, but Los Angeles has just about everything else

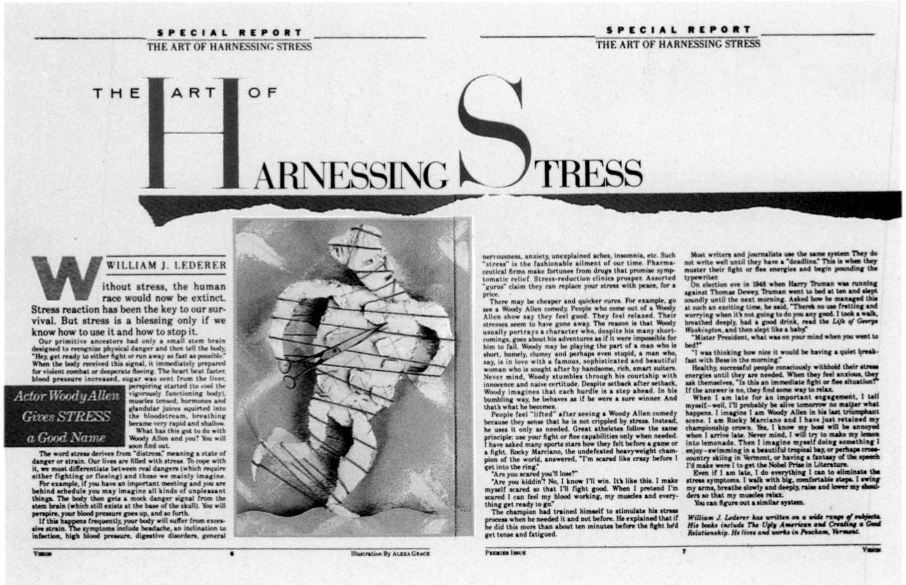

SPECIAL REPORT
THE ART OF HARNESSING STRESS
THE ART OF HARNESSING STRESS
WILLIAM J. LEDERER
Without stress, the human race would now be extinct. Stress reaction has been the key to our survival. But stress is a blessing only if we know how to use it and how to stop it.
Actor Woody Allen Gives STRESS a Good Name

484

PUBLICATION: *Vision*
ART DIRECTOR: *Terry Kopel*
DESIGNER: *Drew Hodges*
Terry Koppel
PUBLISHER: *Alexis, Parks Publishing*
CATEGORY: *Special Issue*
AWARD: *Merit*

ENTIRE ISSUES

TWENTIETH
PUBLICATION
DESIGN
ANNUAL

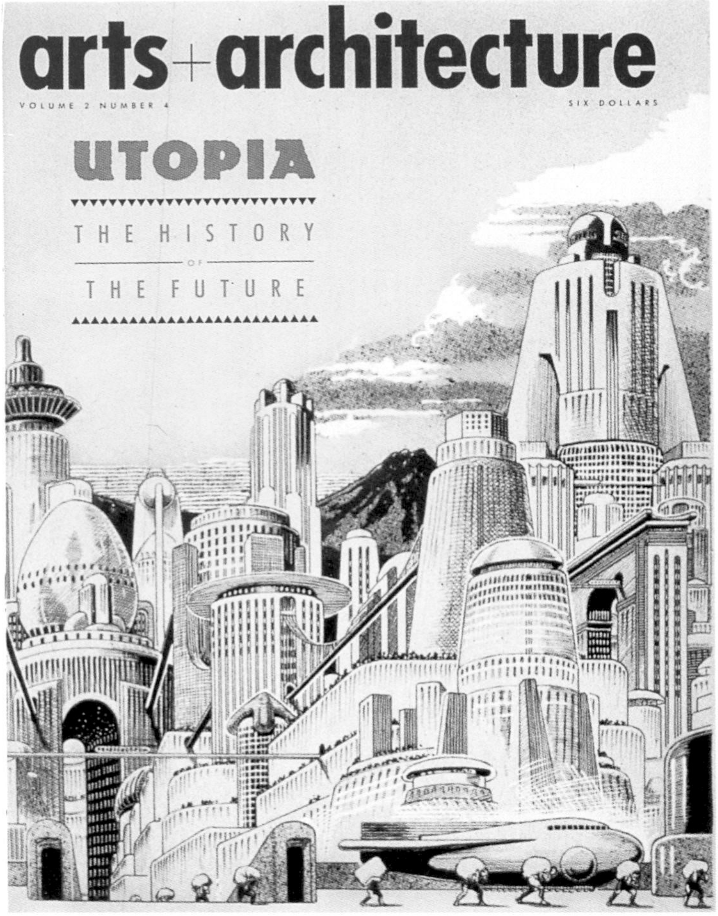

485

PUBLICATION: *Arts & Architecture*
ART DIRECTOR: *Rip Georges*
PUBLISHER: *Arts and Architecture Incorporated*
CATEGORY: *Design-Entire Publication*
AWARD: *Gold*

486

PUBLICATION: *AT &T Magazine*
ART DIRECTOR: *Peter Deutsch*
DESIGNER: *Mark Ulrich*
ILLUSTRATOR: *Various*
PHOTOGRAPHER: *Various*
PUBLISHER: *Anthony Russell, Inc.*
CATEGORY: *Design-Entire Publication*
AWARD: *Silver*

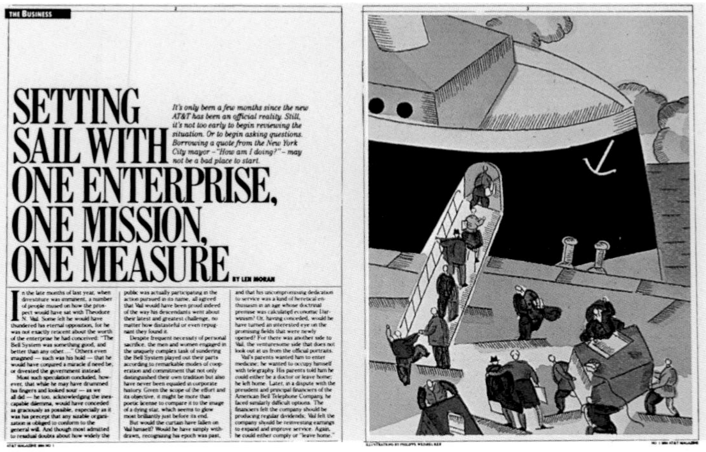

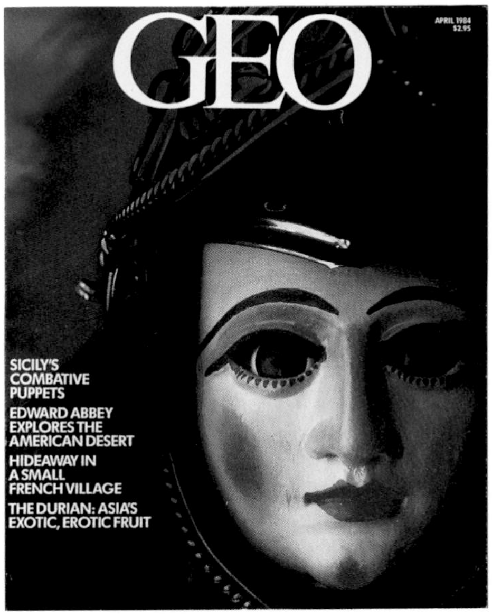

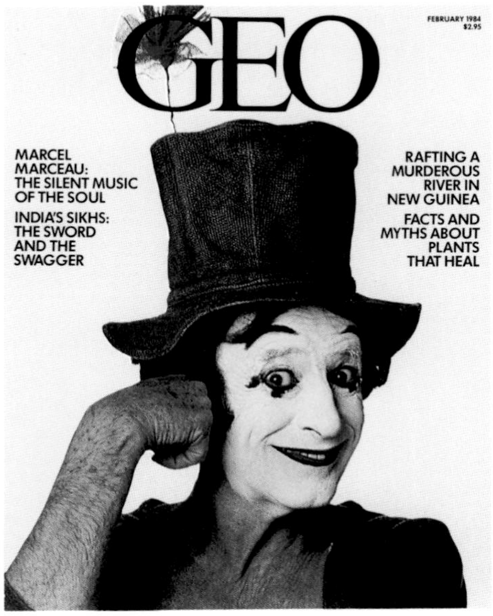

487

PUBLICATION: *Geo Magazine*
ART DIRECTOR: *Mary K. Baumann*
PUBLISHER: *Knapp Communications Corp.*
CATEGORY: *Design-Entire Publication*
AWARD: *Silver*

488

PUBLICATION: *House & Garden*
ART DIRECTOR: *Lloyd Ziff*
DESIGNER: *Lloyd Ziff*
Karen Lee Grant
PUBLISHER: *The Conde Nast Publications, Inc.*
CATEGORY: *Design-Entire Publication*
AWARD: *Silver*

489

PUBLICATION: *Progressive Architecture*
ART DIRECTOR: *Kenneth Windsor*
DESIGNER: *Kenneth Windsor*
CATEGORY: *Design-Entire Publication*
AWARD: *Merit*

REDESIGNS

TWENTIETH
PUBLICATION
DESIGN
ANNUAL

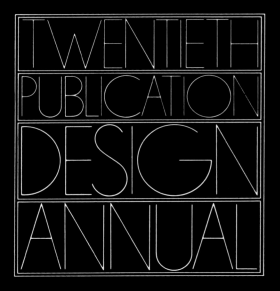

490

PUBLICATION: *Discover Magazine*
ART DIRECTOR: *Eric Seidman*
DESIGNER: *Eric Seidman*
Theodore Kalomirakis
PUBLISHER: *Time, Inc.*
CATEGORY: *Redesign Before/After Issue*
AWARD: *Silver*

ANNUAL REPORTS

TWENTIETH
PUBLICATION
DESIGN
ANNUAL

Letter to Shareholders
been and is a hard school, and they have learned their lessons well, emerging better prepared than ever before to meet whatever the future may bring.
We have remained faithful to one fixed and immutable commitment: *our total dedication to quality in all goods and services that carry our brands.* We regard our relationship with the consumer as a franchise that will endure only so long as we meet her needs on a continuing basis.
We are dedicated to maintaining the strength of our balance sheet, now greater than at any other time in our history. We have kept debt at controllable levels.
We have consistently avoided short-term tactics that might give temporary satisfaction, emphasizing instead long-term measures that will eventually elevate the company to higher and more solid ground.
We are keenly aware that the vast majority of the world's people do not have access to our products. We regard this not as a shortcoming so much as a challenge and a source of tremendous potential. We have already broken ground in Africa with Zimbabwe's Olivine Industries, the country's leading food processor. Vigorous searches are under way for opportunities in other Third World locations, notably in Africa and Southeast Asia.
This is the kind of thinking that engages us as we contemplate what the decades ahead may bring to Heinz. We expect that those who sign this letter in the year 2004 will be able to report that the company has grown vastly larger and more profitable, serving a greater variety of markets with a greater variety of goods than it is possible to predict today.
For the immediate future, we expect that fiscal 1985 will bring a continuation of the conspicuous success we have enjoyed for so many years. In saying so, we salute the vital role played by our shareholders and employees in that success. Finally, we are mindful of the contribution made by the millions of consumers whose demands have constantly challenged us and whose enthusiastic acceptance of what we offer has made us as strong as we are.
Henry J. Heinz II
Chairman of the Board
Anthony J. F. O'Reilly
President and Chief Executive Officer

Dale Chihuly
"We discovered the technique for our cylinders in the summer of 1974 at Pilchuck, our farm north of Seattle, and I remember how thrilled we were to find we could lay out a drawing with bits of glass which, when we came down on it with molten glass, would fuse and mold together as it was blown out. I began a series of cylinders to further explore the idea of drawing into glass. I go back to the series now and then because the process is still unpredictable and continues to stimulate me.
"I saw some Northwest Coast Indian blankets in the Tacoma Historical Society and thought I would try blowing some very thin basketlike forms which would appear crumpling and collapsing under their own weight. I didn't want them symmetrical. It was quite a discovery to see what I could do with just air, fire and gravity using hardly any tools. In the summer of 1977, I made about 100 baskets, all the same color (tabak), and they were shown on a steel table at the Seattle Art Museum.
"At one point, I went to Murano to study. Strange, I and others are still carrying on the Venetian tradition. They're losing it over there because of modern technology. There doesn't seem to be the desire for handmade glasses when glasses made by machines are available at less cost. People would rather drive a Porsche, which is made by machine, than a more expensive Rolls Royce, which is primarily made by hand.
"We start blowing at 4 a.m. and work straight through with no breaks. The blowing just seems to go better on the early schedule. It's quieter and the shop is cooler and the glass is at its best in the morning. I don't know why. And we have more privacy. We then stop for a big lunch — lots of Italian style. This has a pull on my social life. Maybe that's why I never got married.
The last few years I've been a kind of nomad, working with my traveling team in many different universities and shops around the United States and in Europe.
"When I'm not traveling for my work, I'm often traveling for pleasure. Every year or two, I visit some unusual archipelago of islands — most recently the Orkneys and the Scilly Islands off Great Britain and the coast of Brittany. I love islands. I'm fascinated by the fact that, being isolated, they develop uniquely."

491

PUBLICATION: *H. J. Heinz Co. 1984*
ART DIRECTOR: *Bennett Robinson*
DESIGNER: *Bennett Robinson*
Paula Zograhpos
PHOTOGRAPHER: *Bill Hayward, Ronn & Peggy Barnett*
PUBLISHER: *Corporate Graphics, Inc.*
CATEGORY: *Annual Report*
AWARD: *Silver*

493

PUBLICATION: *Shell Oil Company*
ART DIRECTOR: *Len Fury*
DESIGNER: *Len Fury*
PHOTOGRAPHER: *Steve Kromguard*
PUBLISHER: *Corporate Annual Reports, Inc.*
CATEGORY: *Annual Report*
AWARD: *Merit*

INDEX

TWENTIETH
PUBLICATION
DESIGN
ANNUAL

Art Directors

Designers

Illustrators

Photographers

Publishers

ADVERTISEMENTS

TWENTIETH
PUBLICATION
DESIGN
ANNUAL

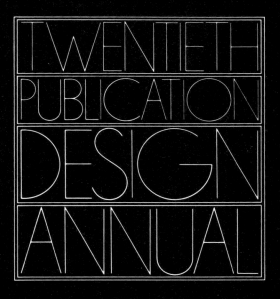

GRAYBAR
THE
MENDOLA
DESIGN STUDIO

A M E R I C A N

Limited Edition Commemorative Print from Nestea
© Nestle Foods Corporation, 1985

Client: Nestle's Corporation
Artist: Chuck Hamrick

Mendola Design Studio • 420 Lexington Avenue • Suite 2911 • New York, N.Y. 10170 • (212) 986-5680

Client: Mobil

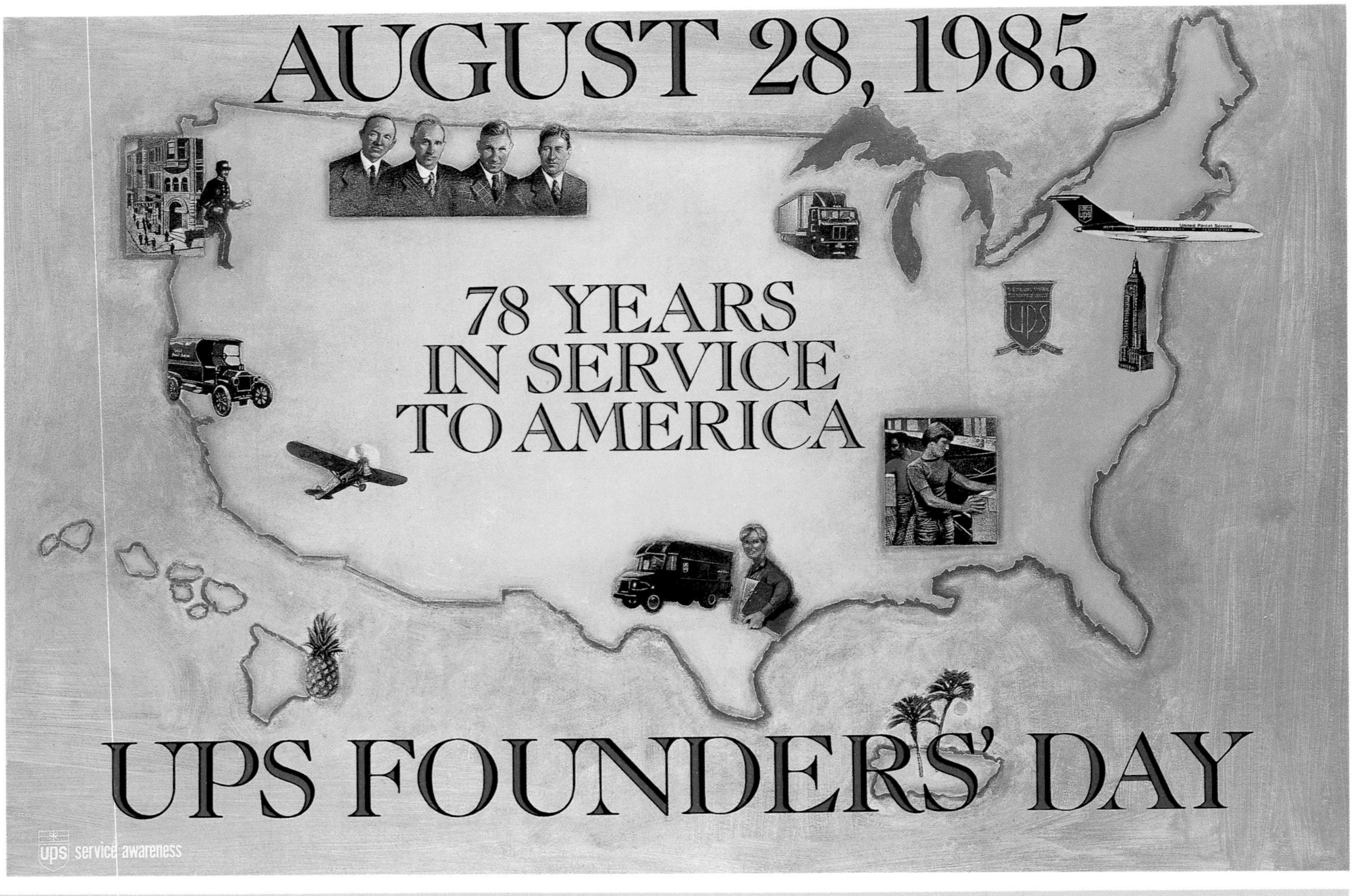

Client: U.P.S.
Artist: Greg Rudd

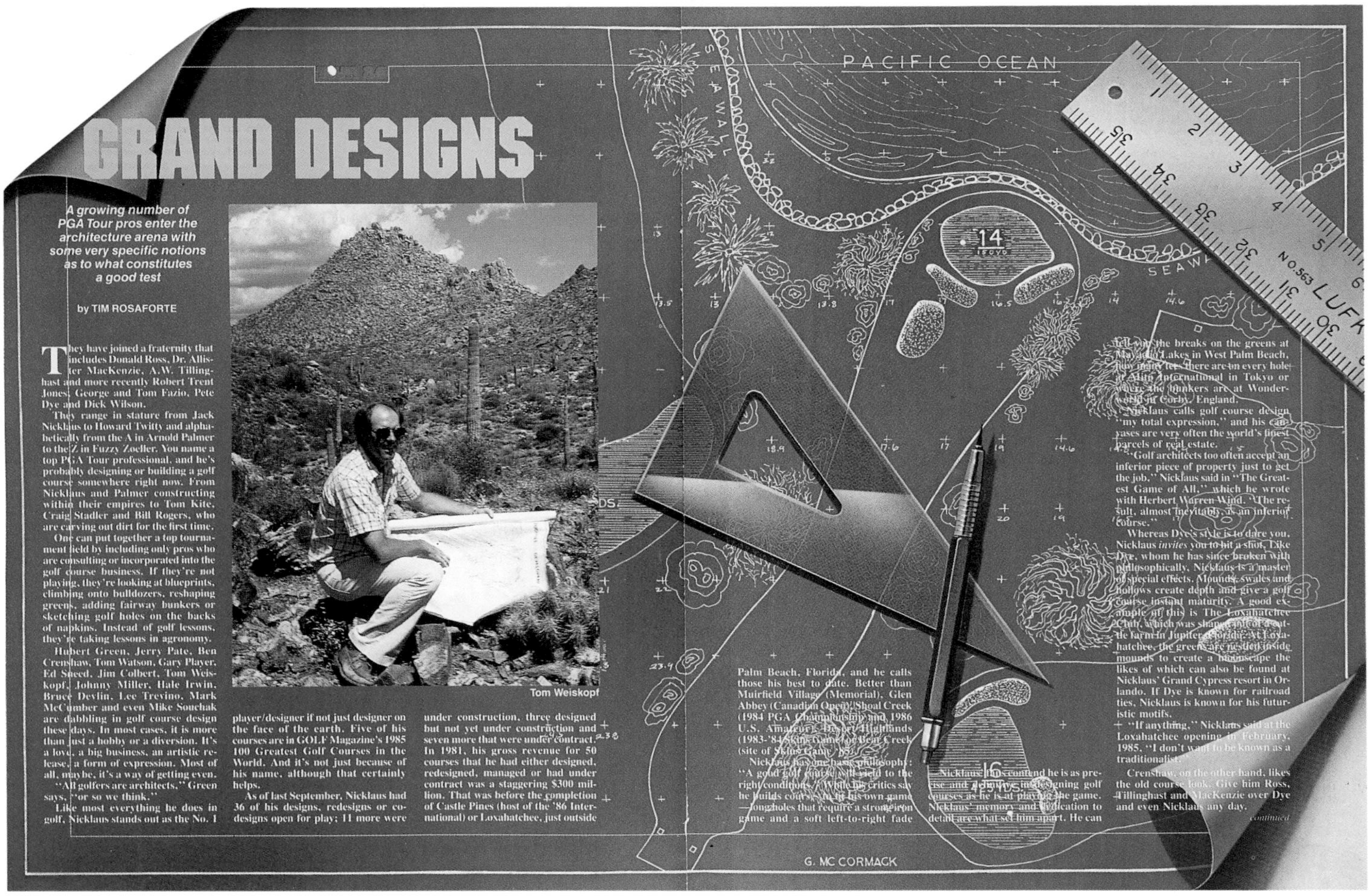

GRAND DESIGNS

A growing number of PGA Tour pros enter the architecture arena with some very specific notions as to what constitutes a good test

by TIM ROSAFORTE

They have joined a fraternity that includes Donald Ross, Dr. Allister MacKenzie, A.W. Tillinghast and more recently Robert Trent Jones, George and Tom Fazio, Pete Dye and Dick Wilson.

They range in stature from Jack Nicklaus to Howard Twitty and alphabetically from the A in Arnold Palmer to the Z in Fuzzy Zoeller. You name a top PGA Tour professional, and he's probably designing or building a golf course somewhere right now. From Nicklaus and Palmer constructing within their empires to Tom Kite, Craig Stadler and Bill Rogers, who are carving out dirt for the first time.

One can put together a top tournament field by including only pros who are consulting or incorporated into the golf course business. If they're not playing, they're looking at blueprints, climbing onto bulldozers, reshaping greens, adding fairway bunkers or sketching golf holes on the backs of napkins. Instead of golf lessons, they're taking lessons in agronomy.

Hubert Green, Jerry Pate, Ben Crenshaw, Tom Watson, Gary Player, Ed Sneed, Jim Colbert, Tom Weiskopf, Johnny Miller, Hale Irwin, Bruce Devlin, Lee Trevino, Mark McCumber and even Mike Souchak are dabbling in golf course design these days. In most cases, it is more than just a hobby or a diversion. It's a love, a big business, an artistic release, a form of expression. Most of all, maybe, it's a way of getting even.

"All golfers are architects," Green says, "or so we think."

Like most everything he does in golf, Nicklaus stands out as the No. 1 player/designer if not just designer on the face of the earth. Five of his courses are in GOLF Magazine's 1985 100 Greatest Golf Courses in the World. And it's not just because of his name, although that certainly helps.

As of last September, Nicklaus had 36 of his designs, redesigns or co-designs open for play; 11 more were under construction, three designed but not yet under construction and seven more that were under contract. In 1981, his gross revenue for 50 courses that he had either designed, redesigned, managed or had under contract was a staggering $300 million. That was before the completion of Castle Pines (host of the '86 International) or Loxahatchee, just outside Palm Beach, Florida, and he calls those his best to date. Better than Muirfield Village (Memorial), Glen Abbey (Canadian Open), Shoal Creek (1984 PGA Championship and 1986 U.S. Amateur), Desert Highlands (1983-'84 Skins Game) or Bear Creek (site of Skins Game '85).

Nicklaus has one basic philosophy: "A good golf course will yield to the right conditions." While his critics say he builds courses to fit his own game—long holes that require a strong iron game and a soft left-to-right fade—Nicklaus' fans contend he is as precise and definitive in designing golf courses as he is at playing the game. Nicklaus' memory and dedication to detail are what set him apart. He can tell you the breaks on the greens at Mayacoo Lakes in West Palm Beach, how many tees there are on every hole at Aiito International in Tokyo or where the bunkers are at Wonderworld in Corby, England.

Nicklaus calls golf course design "my total expression," and his canvases are very often the world's finest parcels of real estate.

"Golf architects too often accept an inferior piece of property just to get the job," Nicklaus said in "The Greatest Game of All," which he wrote with Herbert Warren Wind. "The result, almost inevitably, is an inferior course."

Whereas Dye's style is to dare you, Nicklaus *invites* you to hit a shot. Like Dye, whom he has since broken with philosophically, Nicklaus is a master of special effects. Mounds, swales and hollows create depth and give a golf course instant maturity. A good example of this is The Loxahatchee Club, which was shaped out of a cattle farm in Jupiter, Florida. At Loxahatchee, the greens are nestled inside mounds to create a moonscape the likes of which can also be found at Nicklaus' Grand Cypress resort in Orlando. If Dye is known for railroad ties, Nicklaus is known for his futuristic motifs.

"If anything," Nicklaus said at the Loxahatchee opening in February, 1985, "I don't want to be known as a traditionalist."

Crenshaw, on the other hand, likes the old course look. Give him Ross, Tillinghast and MacKenzie over Dye and even Nicklaus any day.

continued

Client: Tour Magazine
Artist: Geoff McCormick

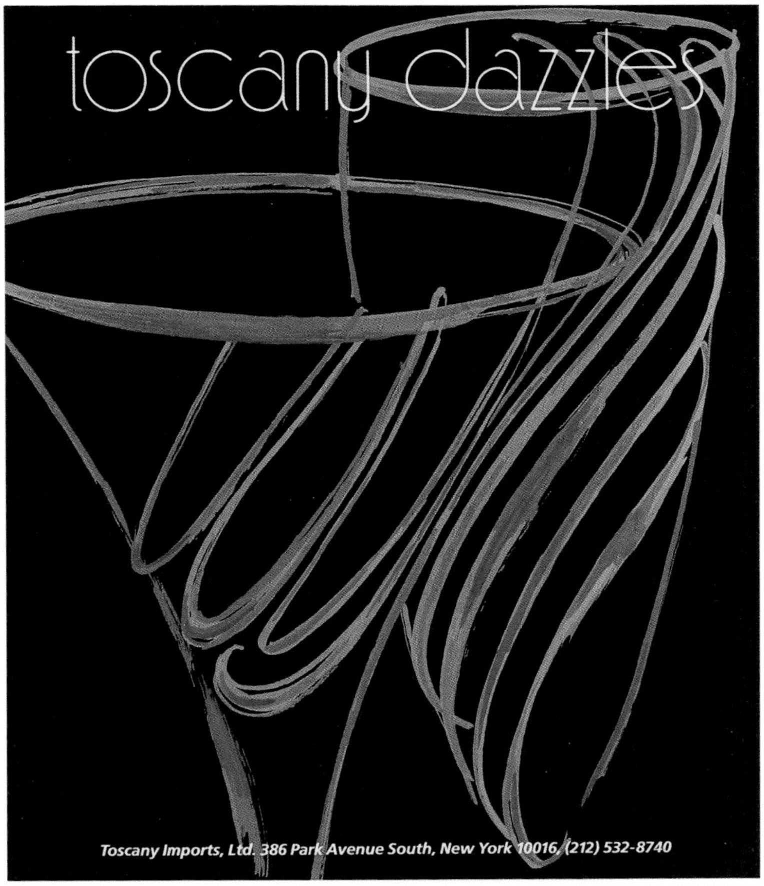

Client: Sonet Agency
(Toscany Ad Campaign)

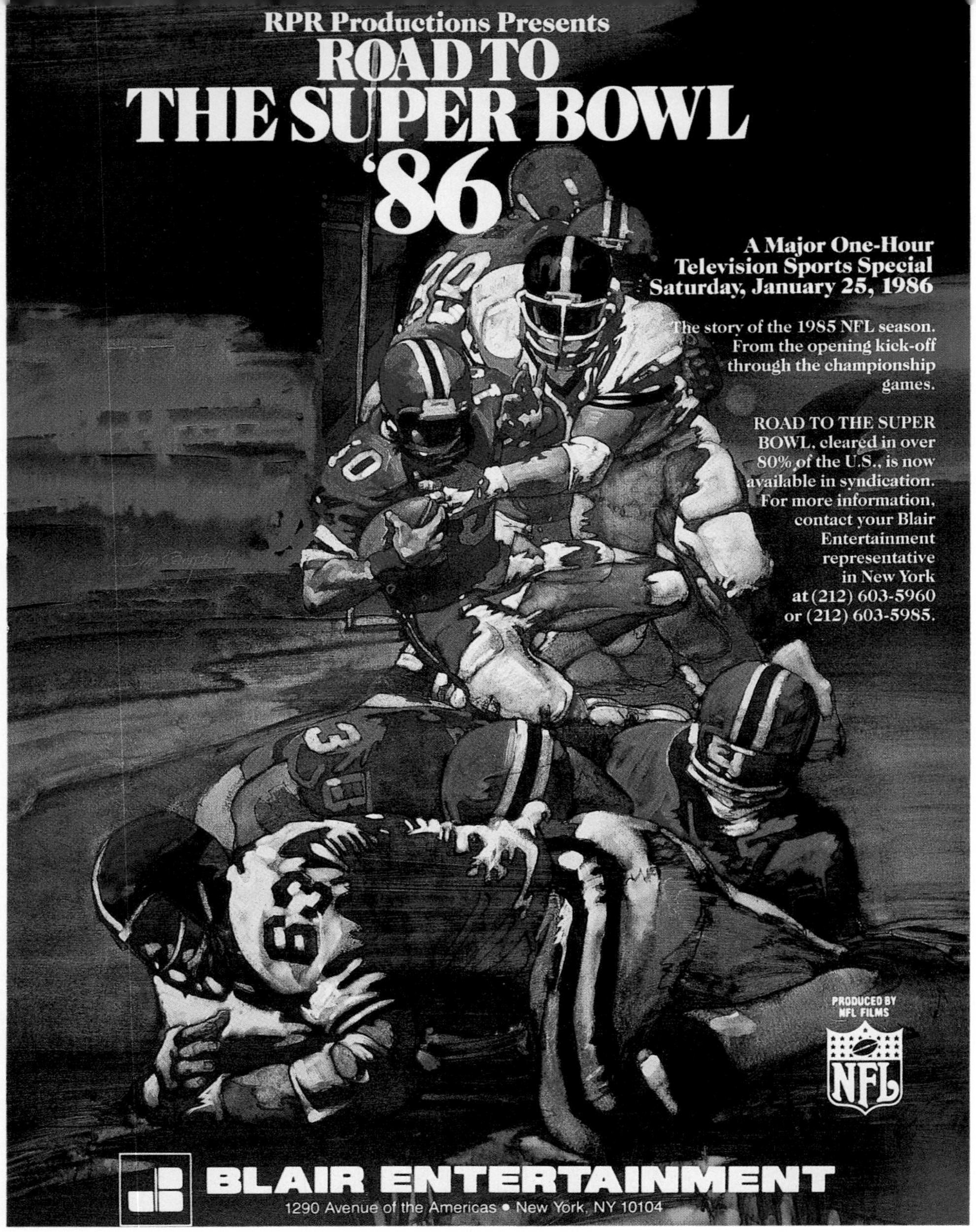

Client: Blair Entertainment
Artist: Jim Cambell

Client: Blair Entertainment
Artist: Norman Gorbaty

Tom Newsom

John Eggert

Hector Garrido

Mendola Ltd. • 420 Lexington Avenue • Suite 2911 • New York, N.Y. 10170 • (212) 986-5680

Rosanne Kaloustian

Romas

Allen Welkis

Mendola Artists

Michael Smollin

Ben Wohlberg

Ann Meisel

Mendola Ltd. • 420 Lexington Avenue • Suite 2911 • New York, N.Y. 10170 • (212) 986-5680

TWO NEW BOOKS THAT SHOULD BE IN EVERY ARTIST'S LIBRARY

Essential reference sources for graphics professionals. One of these volumes offers important business and legal guides, the other presents outstanding examples of dynamic new illustration. There is much to be learned from each of these important books.

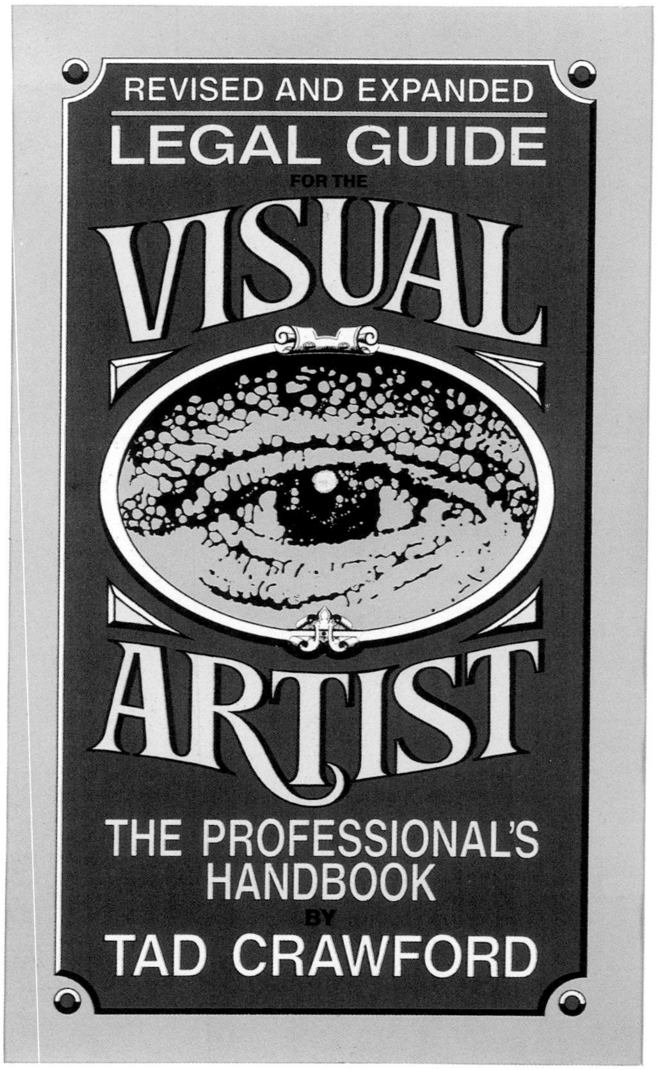

THE NEW ILLUSTRATION
From the Exhibition held at the Society of Illustrators. A look at the tradition-breaking show that stirred up controversy and applause. The energy explodes from these artists of the post-Viet Nam, post-industrial generation as they run the gamut from high-tech elegance to simple looniness. See the work of Mick Haggerty, Lou Beach and 88 others in full color. 160 pages. 9½x9½.
ISBN 0-942604-06-7 **$24.95**

LEGAL GUIDE FOR THE VISUAL ARTIST, Revised Edition
by Tad Crawford
An indispensable text on the visual artist's legal problems. Covers copyright, contracts, censorship, moral rights, sales of art and reproduction rights, publishing contracts, taxation, hobby losses, estate planning and taxation, collecting, and grants. Model contracts included. 256 pages. 7x12.
ISBN 0-942604-08-3 **$16.95**

MADISON SQUARE PRESS

10 EAST 23rd STREET, NEW YORK, NY 10010

MORE TOP ANNUALS

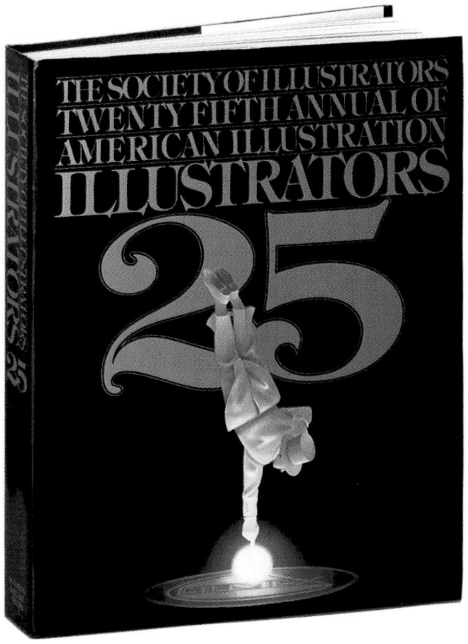

ILLUSTRATORS 25
THE 25th ANNUAL OF AMERICAN ILLUSTRATION
PUBLISHED FOR THE SOCIETY OF ILLUSTRATORS

Edited by Art Weithas   Designed by Robert Anthony

Illustrators 25 is the first issue to be printed entirely in full color!

This magnificent book marks the Silver Anniversary of the Society of Illustrators Annuals. Considered the most outstanding publication of its kind, this series has shown the finest contemporary illustration for the past quarter of a century.

Within the pages of this 440 page volume are over 400 illustrations in the Editorial, Advertising, Book and Institutional categories.

ISBN 0-942604-02-4

List $49.95   **MSP Price $41.95**

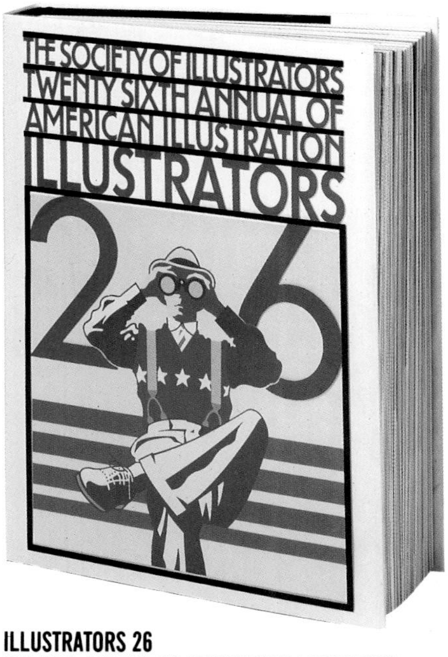

ILLUSTRATORS 26
THE 26th ANNUAL OF AMERICAN ILLUSTRATION
PUBLISHED FOR THE SOCIETY OF ILLUSTRATORS

Edited by Art Weithas   Designed by Robert Anthony

This lavish, full-color volume is the oldest and most prestigious illustration annual on the market. It is an exceptional source of creative ideas and an excellent reference for all who need to see the work of new talents and the new work of old talents. Four panels of notable jurors selected the 551 illustrations in the four categories—Advertising, Editorial, Book and Institutional—from more than 7,500 entries submitted.

A section in front of the book is devoted to the Society of Illustrators Hall of Fame, Hamilton King Award and New Acquisitions of the Society's Permanent Collection. The back section contains information and pictures of the Society's many activities and exhibitions.

ISBN 0-942604-05-9

$49.95

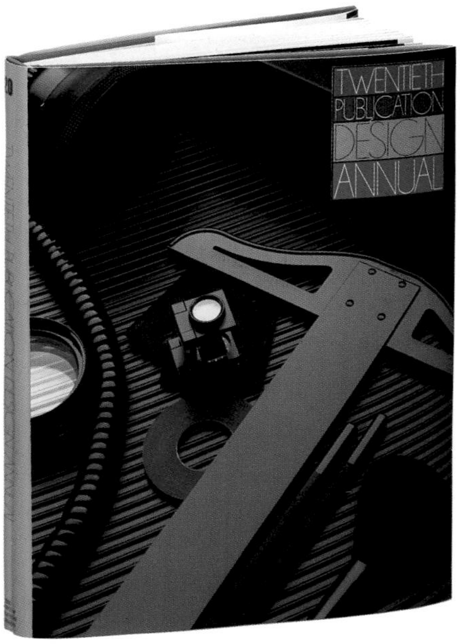

THE SOCIETY OF PUBLICATION DESIGNERS
TWENTIETH PUBLICATION DESIGN ANNUAL

This volume, handsomely designed by B. Martin Pedersen, contains the most outstanding designs of the year from publications in all areas: consumer, trade and corporate magazines, newspapers, annual reports, house organs.

the design solutions represented in this book will serve as an inspiration for everyone in the industry.

244 pages. 9x12

ISBN 0-942604-10-5

$39.95

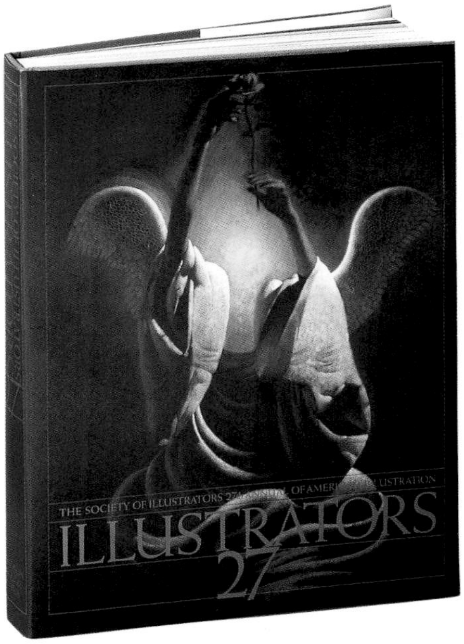

ILLUSTRATORS 27
THE 27th ANNUAL OF AMERICAN ILLUSTRATION
PUBLISHED FOR THE SOCIETY OF ILLUSTRATORS

Edited by Arpi Ermoyan   Designed by Robert Anthony

Illustrators 27 is the largest annual in the history of the Society of Illustrators. Lavishly reproduced in full color, this 440 page volume is brimming with 668 of the best illustrations of the year.

The contents of this massive book will serve as a lasting record of the best in a highly competitive area of the graphic arts and an Indispensable tool for art buyers as well as an inspiration for illustrators and students worldwide.

ISBN 0-942604-09-1

$49.95

ILLUSTRATION HISTORY AT LOW PRICES

200 YEARS OF AMERICAN ILLUSTRATION

A comprehensive record of American illustration based on the Society of Illustrators' bicentennial exhibition at the New-York Historical Society. Approximately 900 illustrations, from Paul Revere's engraving to contemporary work, by over 500 artists.

A must for the serious collector. Indispensable for schools and libraries.
436 pages. 10½x12
ISBN 0-394-41474-8 List $39.95 **MSP price $25.95**

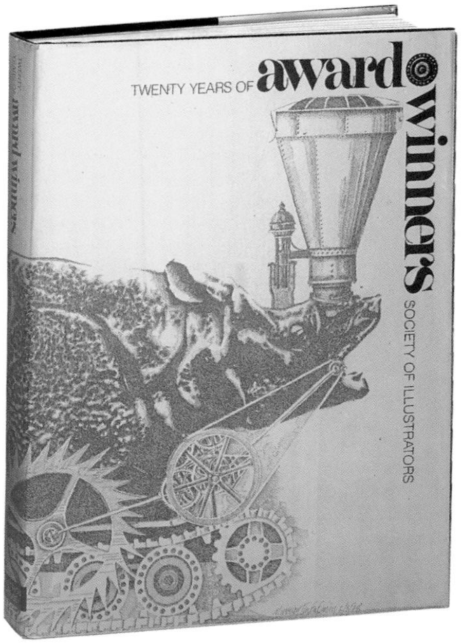

TWENTY YEARS OF AWARD WINNERS

Of the more than 500 illustrations which appear in the Society of Illustrators Exhibition each year, a select number are awarded the Gold or Silver Medal. This book presents the award winning art work from the first two decades of the Society of Illustrators Annual Exhibitions.

Professionals and students alike will be inspired by this collection of art by the top illustrators in the country.
Over 325 pages. 9x12
ISBN 0-8038-7224-0 List $65.00 **MSP price $39.00**

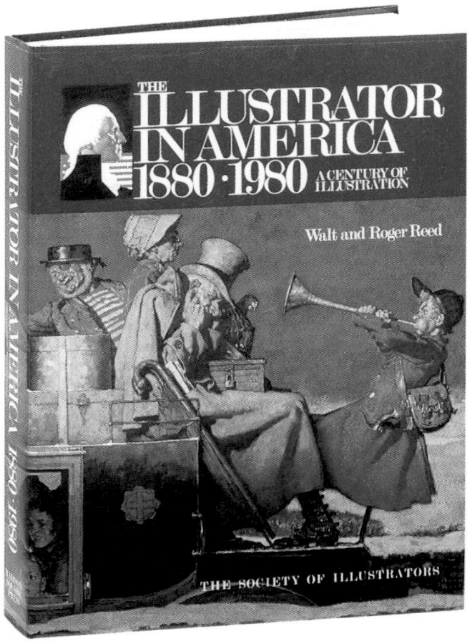

THE ILLUSTRATOR IN AMERICA 1880-1980
by Walt and Roger Reed

A complete pictorial and biographical history, decade by decade, of the prominent illustrators from 1880-1980. Over 700 images by 460 artists.

This is a unique portrait of American life and society seen through the eyes of the greatest illustrators of that period. A must for the serious student and collector and a valuable reference for everyone in the profession.
352 pages. 9x12
ISBN 0-94260403-2 List $48.50 **MSP price $38.50**

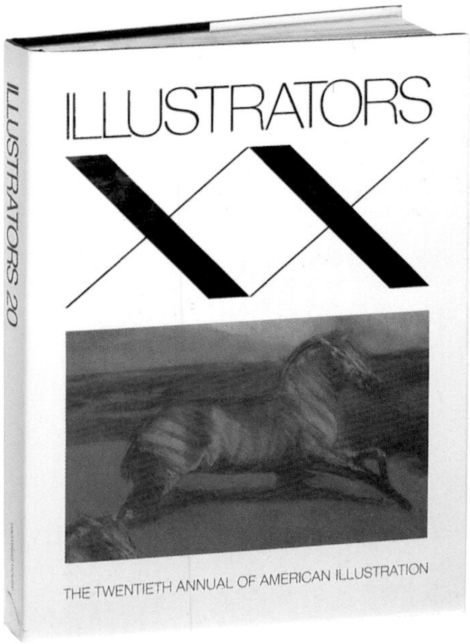

ILLUSTRATORS 20
THE 20th ANNUAL OF AMERICAN ILLUSTRATION
PUBLISHED FOR THE SOCIETY OF ILLUSTRATORS

Edited by Gerald McConnell Designed by Robert Hallock

Since 1959 the Society of Illustrators has held an Annual National Exhibition of the most outstanding work done each year in the major areas of illustration. Out of thousands of entries submitted, about 500 are selected for exhibition, then compiled into a handsome volume.

This Illustrators 20 edition contains the juried selections and award winners in the Advertising, Editorial, Book, Institutional, Film and Television categories.

A unique record of the social mores and attitudes of the times, this is history seen through the eyes of artists, the most acute observers of all.
ISBN 8038-3420-9 List $29.50 **MSP price $17.95**

GREAT DISCOUNTS ON THE BEST ANNUALS IN THE BUSINESS

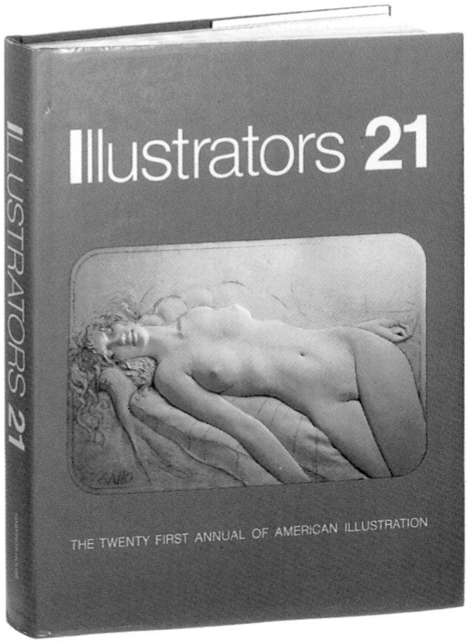

ILLUSTRATORS 21
THE 21st ANNUAL OF AMERICAN ILLUSTRATION
PUBLISHED FOR THE SOCIETY OF ILLUSTRATORS

Edited by Gerald McConnell   Designed by Robert Hallock

Thirty-eight eminent professionals in the graphics industry distilled more than 5,000 entires submitted to the Society of Illustrators Annual Exhibition down to the 586 examples shown in this volume. Covering a wide range of techniques and styles, this book offers a multitude of inspirational ideas for students and educators as well as established professionals.

Included are the illustrations selected as the best in Advertising, Editorial, Book, Institutional and TV/Film categories.

ISBN 8038-3427-6   List $35.00   **MSP price $17.95**

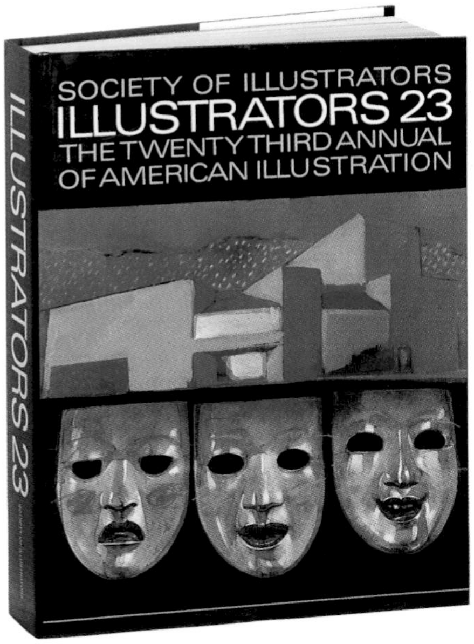

ILLUSTRATORS 23
THE 23rd ANNUAL OF AMERICAN ILLUSTRATION
PUBLISHED FOR THE SOCIETY OF ILLUSTRATORS

Edited by Howard Munce   Designed by Robert Hallock

The skilled and imaginative work of the 337 diverse individuals reproduced in this volume is a silent compliment to the countless talented people—art directors, editors and writers—who worked with them in the commercial chain of command. Included are 591 superb examples of paintings, drawings and dimensional art that appeared in the Society of Illustrators 23rd Annual Exhibition.

In addition to the Advertising, Editorial, Book, Institutional and TV categories is a bonus supplement of 48 illustrations in the Foreign category.

ISBN 8038-3435-7   List $39.95   **MSP price $21.95**

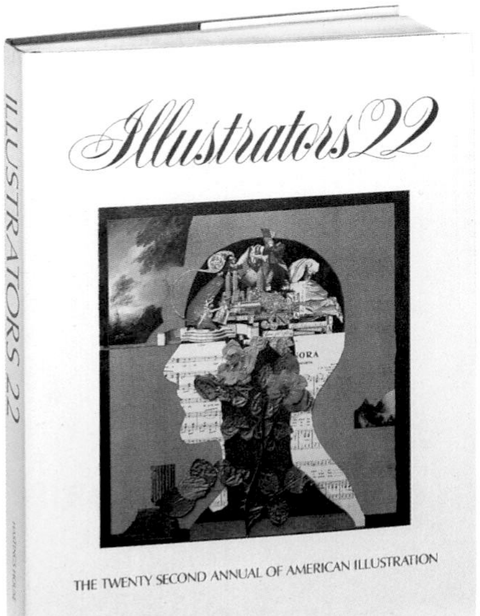

ILLUSTRATORS 22
THE 22nd ANNUAL OF AMERICAN ILLUSTRATION
PUBLISHED FOR THE SOCIETY OF ILLUSTRATORS

Edited by Forbes Linkhorn   Designed by Robert Hallock

Within the pages of this 22nd Annual is a comprehensive collection of exciting talent. These volumes have become standard reference sources for art directors, creative directors and all buyers of illustration.

Included are all the juried selections and award winners from the Society of Illustrators 22nd Annual National Exhibition. Of added interest are capsule biographies and examples of the work of Hall of Fame award winners Howard Chandler Christy, James Montgomery Flagg and Saul Tepper.

ISBN 8038-3433-0   List $37.50   **MSP price $17.95**

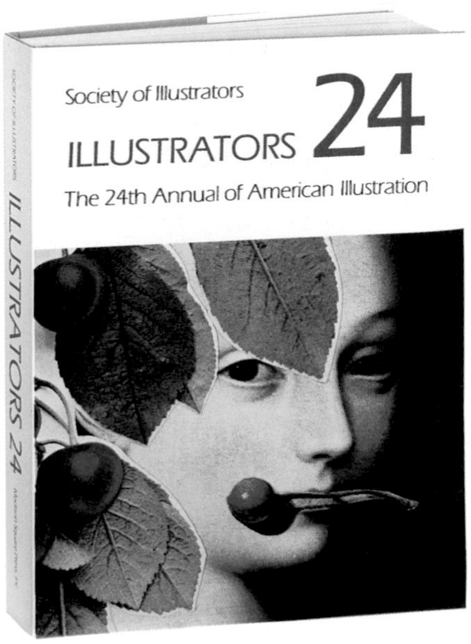

ILLUSTRATORS 24
THE 24th ANNUAL OF AMERICAN ILLUSTRATION
PUBLISHED FOR THE SOCIETY OF ILLUSTRATORS

Edited by Art Weithas   Designed by Robert Hallock

Four distinguished panels of jurors selected these 501 examples of American illustration from thousands of entries of both published and unpublished work: 113 in the Editorial category, 138 in Book, 149 in Advertising and 101 in the Institutional category. Over 160 illustrations are reproduced in full color.

An interesting supplement of the Society of Illustrators' activities, including its Museum of American Illustration, Permanent Collection, Hall of Fame, Annual Scholarship Competition, Exhibitions, Art Auction, and Evening workshops, appears in this volume.

ISBN 0-942604-00-8   List $39.95   **MSP price $21.95**

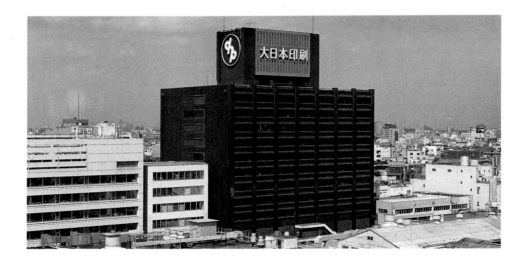

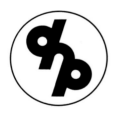